P9-CDU-648

In the Trenches with Microsoft® Office Project 2007

ELAINE J. MARMEL

PUBLISHED BY
Microsoft Press
A Division of Microsoft Corporation
One Microsoft Way
Redmond, Washington 98052-6399

Copyright © 2009 by Elaine Marmel

All rights reserved. No part of the contents of this book may be reproduced or transmitted in any form or by any means without the written permission of the publisher.

Library of Congress Control Number: 2008940529

Printed and bound in the United States of America.

1 2 3 4 5 6 7 8 9 QWT 4 3 2 1 0 9

Distributed in Canada by H.B. Fenn and Company Ltd.

A CIP catalogue record for this book is available from the British Library.

Microsoft Press books are available through booksellers and distributors worldwide. For further information about international editions, contact your local Microsoft Corporation office or contact Microsoft Press International directly at fax (425) 936-7329. Visit our Web site at www.microsoft.com/mspress. Send comments to mspinput@microsoft.com.

Microsoft, Microsoft Press, Excel, SQL Server, Visual Basic, Visual Studio, Windows, and Windows Vista are either registered trademarks or trademarks of the Microsoft group of companies. Other product and company names mentioned herein may be the trademarks of their respective owners.

The example companies, organizations, products, domain names, e-mail addresses, logos, people, places, and events depicted herein are fictitious. No association with any real company, organization, product, domain name, e-mail address, logo, person, place, or event is intended or should be inferred.

This book expresses the author's views and opinions. The information contained in this book is provided without any express, statutory, or implied warranties. Neither the authors, Microsoft Corporation, nor its resellers, or distributors will be held liable for any damages caused or alleged to be caused either directly or indirectly by this book.

Acquisitions Editor: Juliana Aldous Atkinson
Developmental Editor: Sandra Haynes
Project Editor: Victoria Thulman
Editorial Production: Online Training Solutions, Inc.
Technical Reviewer: Jim Peters; Technical Review services provided by Content Master, a member of CM Group, Ltd.
Cover: Tom Draper Design

Body Part No. X15-28132

Acknowledgments

BOOKS ABOUT MICROSOFT OFFICE PROJECT so readily demonstrate the "team" concept. As with all books, this one is the combined effort of several people. Juliana Aldous, thank you for giving me the opportunity to write this book. Jim Peters, thanks (again) for keeping me technically accurate. Terence Maikels, thanks for making sure that I'm understandable. Sandra Haynes, Kathy Krause, and Victoria Thulman, thank you for making the process so easy for me. And thank you to the graphics artists, layout specialists, and other folks with whom I don't have direct contact (Jean Trenary, Lisa Van Every, Jenny Moss Benson, and Jaime Odell, to name just a few)—I really appreciate that you make me look good.

—Elaine Marmel

About the Author

Elaine Marmel is President of Marmel Enterprises, LLC, an organization that specializes in technical writing and software training. Elaine has an MBA from Cornell University and has worked on projects to build financial management systems for New York City and Washington, D.C. This prior experience provided the foundation for Marmel Enterprises, LLC, to help small businesses manage the project of implementing a computerized accounting system.

Elaine left her native Chicago for the warmer climes of Arizona (by way of Cincinnati, Ohio; Jerusalem, Israel; Ithaca, New York; Washington, D.C.; and Tampa, Florida), where she basks in the sun with her PC, her dog Josh, and her cats Cato, Watson, and Buddy, and sings barbershop harmony with the Scottsdale Chorus, 2006 Sweet Adelines International Chorus Champions.

Elaine spends most of her time writing; she has authored and co-authored more than 50 books about Microsoft Office Project, QuickBooks, Peachtree, Quicken for Windows, Quicken for DOS, Microsoft Office Excel, Microsoft Office Word, Microsoft Office Word for Mac, Windows 98, 1-2-3 for Windows, and Lotus Notes. From 1994 to 2006, she also was the contributing editor to the monthly publications *Peachtree Extra* and *QuickBooks Extra*.

Contents

Introduction   *xiii*

Part 1   **Defining Your Project**

Chapter 1   **Scoping Out Your Project's Details**   **3**

■ Getting Started   4

Setting the Project's Goals and Defining
the Project's Scope   4

Creating a Project   5

Recording General Project Information   7

Setting the Project Calendar   9

■ Creating Tasks   14

Determining How Granular to Make Your Tasks   14

Understanding Task Types   15

Summary Tasks and Subtasks   17

The Project Summary Task   19

Reorganizing Your Project Schedule   21

A Word About Task Timing   22

Establishing the Task's Duration   22

Creating Milestones   23

Using Recurring Tasks Effectively   24

■ Identifying Resources Before You Have Resources   25

■ About Connecting with Other Projects in Your Company   26

What do you think of this book? We want to hear from you!

Microsoft is interested in hearing your feedback so we can continually improve our books and learning resources for you. To participate in a brief online survey, please visit:

microsoft.com/learning/booksurvey

Chapter 2   **How Dependencies and Constraints Affect Your Project** — **29**

■ What Are Dependencies? — 29
Choosing the Right Dependency for Your Needs — 30
Setting Dependencies — 34
What Are Lag and Lead Time? — 36
How Many Dependencies Are Too Many? — 38

■ Viewing Dependencies — 40

■ Dependency Actions That Affect Your Plan — 42
Deleting Dependencies — 43
Creating Dependencies to External Projects — 44

■ Working with Constraints — 44
Understanding the Types of Constraints — 45
How Constraints and Dependencies Affect Each Other — 46
Choosing Between Dependencies and Constraints — 47
How Do Deadline Dates Work? — 48
Setting Constraints and Deadlines — 50

■ What Causes Unexpected Start Dates? — 50

Chapter 3   **Pinning Down Your Budget** — **53**

■ Identifying the Resources You Need — 54
Matching Skill Sets to Skills Needed — 54
Don't Forget about Those Non-Human Resources — 56

■ Choosing the Right Resource Type — 58
Creating Resources in a Project — 59
Resources and Project Server — 61

■ Assigning Resources to Tasks — 63

■ Assigning Resource Costs — 65
Assigning a Cost per Use to a Resource — 66
Assigning Fixed Costs — 66
How Cost Accrual Methods Work — 68

■ How Organizational Structure Affects Resource
Availability   70

   Managing Projects from a Central Office   70

   Handling Projects As They Arise   70

   Managing Projects Within Each Functional Unit   71

   How Organizational Structures Impact
   Project Management   71

■ Understanding How Availability Affects Your Project   72

   Accounting for Availability   72

   Setting Resource Calendars   73

   Checking Availability While Assigning Resources   75

   Using Overtime Wisely   78

■ Printing Cost Reports   79

Part 2   Working Out the Kinks

Chapter 4   Finding the Information You Need   83

■ Understanding Views   83

   Picture Views   85

   Form Views   86

   Sheet Views   87

   Combination Views   88

■ Understanding Tables   91

   Adding a Field to a Table   93

   Working with the Details Portion of a Usage View   94

■ Sorting Information   96

■ Filtering to Find What You Need   98

   Using Built-in Filters   99

   Using AutoFilters   99

■ Grouping Information   100

■ Using Custom Fields   102

　Understanding Custom Fields   103

　Creating a Custom Field That Includes
　a Data Entry List   104

　Storing Information in a Custom Field   107

　Custom Fields, Formulas, and Indicators   108

Chapter 5　**Controlling an Out-of-Control Schedule**　**111**

■ Focusing on Tasks   111

■ Tasks and Timing   113

　Identifying Task Drivers   114

　How Task Types Affect Task Timing   116

　Exploring the Effort-Driven Equation   120

　When Should You Use a Task Calendar?   123

　What Are Your Task Constraints Doing
　to Your Schedule?   126

■ Scheduling from Start or Finish   128

　Understanding Scheduling   128

　What about Scheduling Backwards?   130

　Understanding What Calendar Settings Actually Do   131

■ Managing Slack   133

　Ways to Identify Slack   134

　Ways to Build in Slack   137

Chapter 6　**Solving Resource Conflicts**　**143**

■ What Causes Resource Conflicts?   143

■ Identifying Resource Conflicts   145

　The Resource Graph View   145

　The Resource Allocation View   146

　The Resource Usage View   147

■ Techniques to Resolve Conflicts   149

    Swapping Out Resources   150

    Using Overtime   153

    Adding Resources   155

    Using a Shared Resource   155

    Part-Time Assignments   156

    Staggering Work Time   159

    How Resource Leveling Really Works   167

    What If You Had More Time?   176

Chapter 7   Taming That Monster Budget   177

■ How to Use Cost Resources Effectively   177

■ Anticipating Cost Hikes Realistically   180

■ What Are Budget Resources
and When Do You Use Them?   184

    Creating Budget Resources   185

    Assigning Resources to Budget Resource Categories   186

    Establishing the Value of Budget Resources   189

    Reviewing Budget Amounts and Assigned Amounts   192

■ Tips for Trimming the Bottom Line   194

Chapter 8   Completing the Planning Phase in Project   195

■ Reviewing What You've Got   196

■ Redefining Project Scope   200

■ Identifying the Critical Path   202

■ Working with Baselines and Interim Plans   206

    Setting a Baseline or an Interim Plan   207

    Comparing Baseline and Actual Information   209

Part 3   Setting Up Your Infrastructure

Chapter 9   **Determining How to Communicate
with Your Team**   **213**

■ The Lines of Communication   213

■ How Much Information Do You Need?   215

■ The Pros and Cons of Project Server and SharePoint 216

■ How Additional Software Can Help You Communicate   219

   Using Microsoft Office Outlook   219

   Sharing Files   220

   Enhancing Reporting in Project   220

■ Anticipating Reporting Needs   221

   Using Outline Numbers and Codes in Project Plans 221

   Using WBS Codes in Project Plans   228

   Reviewing Reports   232

Chapter 10   **Establishing Guidelines for Tracking**   **239**

■ Identifying the Information to Collect   240

■ Tracking Too Often or Not Often Enough   241

■ Designating How Resources Report Activity   242

   Setting Up a Reporting Form   243

   Using Timesheet Information   243

   Using Project Server for Tracking Information   244

   Confirming the Plan for Each Reporting Period   245

   Encouraging Team Members to Report   246

■ How to Record Progress   246

   Setting the Project Status Date   247

   Reviewing Calculation Options   248

   Making Notes As You Go   251

   Estimating Percent Complete   252

   Recording Start and Finish Dates   256

Recording Actual and Remaining Durations   256

Recording Actual Work   257

Tracking the Use of Materials   261

Chapter 11   **Dealing with Management**   **263**

■ Approaching the Change Discussion   263

■ Explaining What a Network Diagram Says
About Your Project   264

Changing the Network Diagram Layout   266

Changing the Style of Network Diagram Boxes   268

Changing the Information Displayed
in Network Diagram Boxes   269

■ Reviewing Your Budget   273

Understanding Earned Value Fields   273

Evaluating Variance   275

The Difference Between the % Complete
and Physical % Complete Fields   279

■ Managing Changes to the Plan 101   281

Part 4   **Problem Solving in the Trenches**

Chapter 12   **You're Behind Schedule: Now What?**   **285**

■ Comparing Estimates with Actual Progress   285

Understanding the Tracking Gantt View   286

Adding Progress Lines to a Gantt View   288

■ How Do You Get Back on Track?   290

Sorting and Filtering   291

How Adding or Changing Resources Affects Timing   292

Reviewing Dependencies   293

Making Changes to Save Time   296

■ Deciding When to Redefine Your Project   298

Chapter 13   **Managing Cross-Project Conflicts**   **301**

■ Examining Consolidated Projects   301

Setting Up Subprojects   302

Consolidating Subprojects   303

Linking Subprojects   306

Examining the Critical Path of a Consolidated Project   309

Using Consolidation with Project Server 2007   312

■ Using a Resource Pool   314

Setting Up a Resource Pool   315

Opening a Project Connected to a Resource Pool   319

How Project Handles Assignments
from a Resource Pool   320

Updating the Resource Pool   322

How to Quit Sharing Resources   322

Index   *325*

What do you think of this book? We want to hear from you!

Microsoft is interested in hearing your feedback so we can continually improve our books and learning resources for you. To participate in a brief online survey, please visit:

microsoft.com/learning/booksurvey

Introduction

PROJECT PLANNING has been around longer than any of us can remember; one might speculate that project planning began when groups of people first started living together, making multiple resources available to do the tasks needed to live. That first project manager might have been the one who ultimately became "chief" of the group by demonstrating good management skills in "getting the job done" while best utilizing existing resources and generally making sure that everything that needed to be done got done efficiently. Project management and project managers concern themselves with scheduling, budgeting, managing resources, and tracking and reporting progress.

As we've progressed, project management has become a discipline made up of a variety of tools and techniques that have become "standards" after being proven successful at helping project managers achieve their goals. Initially, tools were manual; project managers made cost calculations using calculators and drew charts and diagrams by hand that represented the way a project would unfold.

Enter the computer age, and tools like Microsoft Office Project 2007 became available to remove much of the mundane work, leaving project managers to focus on the aspects of the project that require decision-making: "If I had more time, what could I accomplish?" "If I had more people, how much time could I save? And at what cost?" "How can I monitor how things are going?" "How can I show management where we are and what we need to do next?" And so on.

Who This Book Is For

Project is a complicated piece of software because it can do lots of things. In addition to calculating project costs and producing the pictures that describe the project, Project can provide information to help project managers answer questions that require decision-making.

As is true with any complex piece of software, learning to use Project can seem quite daunting. And just mastering the menus doesn't really mean you've learned how to use it. Project is, in many ways, a "situational" piece of software; you do certain things under certain circumstances. And the things you do are driven by the goal you want to achieve. For example, not everyone assigns resources; there are valid reasons to assign resources and not to assign resources.

This book isn't about teaching you everything there is to know about Project; there are other books out there that focus on that. Instead, this book is about fitting Project into the stuff you need to do to manage a project, and about the results Project produces based on your actions. Sure, you'll find "how-to" information in this book, but the focus will be on the results you get when you follow the steps.

This book helps you use Project in project management situations. It helps you select actions to take, given a particular set of circumstances. And it shows you the results of those actions, helping you to make the right choices for your situation. Will this book solve all of your problems? No. But in cases where it doesn't, it hopefully will help you find the answers you need to make your project a success.

What This Book Is About

This book starts by focusing on the process you use when creating a project plan and then examines reviewing that plan while still in the planning phase. The book then examines ways to manage the project while it's in progress and looks at options available to you when things don't go as planned.

Part 1, "Defining Your Project," reviews the process of creating a project plan in Project and the impact associated with the choices you make.

Chapter 1, "Scoping Out Your Project's Details," examines how to structure a project.

Chapter 2, "How Dependencies and Constraints Affect Your Project," explores the dependencies you can establish between tasks and the effects dependencies and constraints have on a project schedule.

Chapter 3, "Pinning Down Your Budget," addresses the types of resources you can assign to tasks and how the cost of resources affects the cost of your project.

Part 2, "Working Out the Kinks," helps you find the best way to look at the project plan you've developed, resolve resource conflicts, deal with the project's budget implications, and tackle scheduling issues.

Chapter 4, "Finding the Information You Need," examines tools—such as views, tables, sorting, and grouping—that you can use to find information.

Chapter 5, "Controlling an Out-of-Control Schedule," focuses on tasks and the factors that affect the timing of tasks and your schedule.

Chapter 6, "Solving Resource Conflicts," explores ways you can resolve the conflicts that inevitably arise when you assign resources to tasks.

Chapter 7, "Taming That Monster Budget," looks at ways to examine and potentially reduce costs on your project.

Chapter 8, "Completing the Planning Phase in Project," walks you through reviewing your project, examining the critical path, and setting a baseline.

Part 3, "Setting Up Your Infrastructure," helps you focus on how you're going to manage the project once it starts.

Chapter 9, "Determining How to Communicate with Your Team," explores ways that you and your team can share information, including reporting.

Chapter 10, "Establishing Guidelines for Tracking," discusses how often to track progress and describes methods you can use to track progress.

Chapter 11, "Dealing with Management," provides ideas and approaches you can use to determine whether your project is on time and within budget and to present the information to management.

Part 4, "Problem Solving in the Trenches," looks at available options when things don't work out the way you planned.

Chapter 12, "You're Behind Schedule: Now What?" reviews actions you can take to try to put your project back on schedule.

Chapter 13, "Managing Cross-Project Conflicts," explores the effects of using shared resources and consolidating projects to examine cross-project dependencies and critical paths across projects.

Now let's get started.

Getting Support

Every effort has been made to ensure the accuracy of the information contained in this book. If you do run into problems, please contact the sources below for assistance.

Support for the Book

As corrections or changes are collected, they will be added to a Microsoft Knowledge Base article.

Microsoft Press provides support for books at the following Web site:

www.microsoft.com/learning/support/books/

Support for Software

If you have questions regarding software, and not about the content of this book, consult the Microsoft Knowledge Base at:

support.microsoft.com/search/?adv=1

In the United States, Microsoft software product support issues not covered by the Microsoft Knowledge Base are addressed by Microsoft Product Support Services. Location-specific software support options are available from:

support.microsoft.com/gp/selfoverview

Questions and Comments

If you have comments, questions, or ideas regarding the book or questions that are not answered by visiting the sites above, please send them to Microsoft Press via e-mail to:

mspinput@microsoft.com

Or via postal mail to:

> Microsoft Press
> Attn: Victoria Thulman, Editor
> One Microsoft Way
> Redmond, WA 98052-6399

Please note that Microsoft software product support is not offered through the above addresses.

Defining Your Project

CHAPTER 1

Scoping Out Your Project's Details

WHENEVER YOU'RE FACED WITH A NEW PROJECT, you begin the planning phase of the project. It is during this phase that you figure out how to structure the project. You need to define the project's goal, which helps you identify the project's scope so that you don't bite off more than you can chew and so that you don't do less than management or your client expects. When you establish a project's goal and scope, you need to make sure that everyone involved in the project understands and agrees that the goal and scope you've identified are, indeed, the goal and scope of the project.

You can then begin to organize the details of the project, identifying when the project will begin and the tasks you need to include, along with figuring out the timing of the tasks. You might also identify resources, assign them to tasks, and then resolve resource overallocations. And you deal with the cost of the project.

This chapter focuses on the actions you take during the planning phase that help you get started on your project.

Getting Started

To get started on a project, you need to define the project and its boundaries. Then you can start Microsoft Office Project 2007 to create your project and establish its overall settings. Be aware that the planning phase can and usually does take a considerable amount of time. In fact, most project managers will tell you that the more time you spend planning effectively, the less likely you are to meet with surprises along the way and the more likely you are to achieve your goal in the timeframe and within the budget you estimate.

Setting the Project's Goals and Defining the Project's Scope

Setting goals for a project and defining a project's scope are two different things. Before you even start Project, you should identify the goal(s) of your project. Talk to the person who asked you to take on this project, talk to your boss, talk to other people who were involved in the discussions when the project was approved. Find out from all of these people what they think the purpose of the project is. Ask each of them, "What should my project achieve? What should change when I complete my project?" You might find that each of them has different, possibly conflicting, ideas. Before you start working, you need to resolve any conflicts and establish a cohesive set of goals for your project; otherwise, the project is doomed to fail because you won't satisfy everyone involved. Write a goal statement that outlines why you think you're doing the project and what you hope to achieve by it; then run it by all of the people you interviewed. Get them to sign off, preferably in writing, on the project's goals. And don't establish goals by outlining deliverables; save that for your scope statement.

Your scope statement should help define for you and all involved in the project what your project will and won't do. In your scope statement, you identify an estimated total cost for your project, along with a general idea of how long you expect the work on the project to last and the deliverables you expect to produce. Don't go into excessive detail here, because you'll refine the estimates once you begin the detailed planning phase of your project. But you need to provide enough information so that your project team understands the most important aspects of the project. Ask yourself questions like, "What is my project's budget?" and "Who will be affected by my project?" Identify the people who will work on or contribute to your project and the deadline date for your project. Don't forget to include criteria by which you and other stakeholders can determine whether your project is complete.

Your goal statement and your scope statement help you and your team focus your energies and therefore stay on track.

In some organizations, you also use your goal and scope statements to prepare a project charter, which typically formalizes your project. The project charter includes your project's name and written authorization to begin work and to draw on a budget, along with a list of responsibilities.

Remember, projects can last for months or years. As you work on a project, things come up that you didn't anticipate; that's the nature of working on a project. Nobody's perfect and, so far, nobody has been proven to predict the future. So until "knowing the future" becomes a reality, accept the fact that your project will grow and change in unpredictable ways. At some point, you might need to redefine the scope of your project to address these unpredictable events.

> **SEE ALSO**   You'll find more information about redefining the scope of your project in Chapter 8, "Completing the Planning Phase in Project."

Creating a Project

In Project, you can create a new project from scratch by using a blank project. Or you can create a project based on an existing project or a template that comes with Project or a template you created yourself. Using a template saves you time by establishing a series of tasks for you so that you don't have to create them yourself. But if your projects don't resemble each other, you will most likely want to work from a blank project.

STORING OFTEN-USED INFORMATION

If your organization performs the same basic type of work for each of its projects, you can easily create a project that contains all of the tasks you might need to use and save that project as a template. If your organization doesn't use Microsoft Office Project Server 2007 but you do use the same set of resources for each project, you can create a separate project that contains only resources. You can then create a new project based on your organization's template and copy and paste the resources you plan to use from the resource project into your project.

What if your organization uses Project Server? You can still create the project template for your new projects, but you don't need a project that contains resources, because Project Server uses the Enterprise Resource Pool, and you'll get your resources from there.

"If I don't use Project Server, can I store my resources in the company's project template?" Yes, you can, but if you create any consolidated projects, you're going to need a project file that contains only resources to share among the projects you consolidate. So I suggest you store resources in a separate Project file.

A new blank project appears each time you start Project, or you can click the New button on the Standard toolbar to display a new blank project (see Figure 1-1).

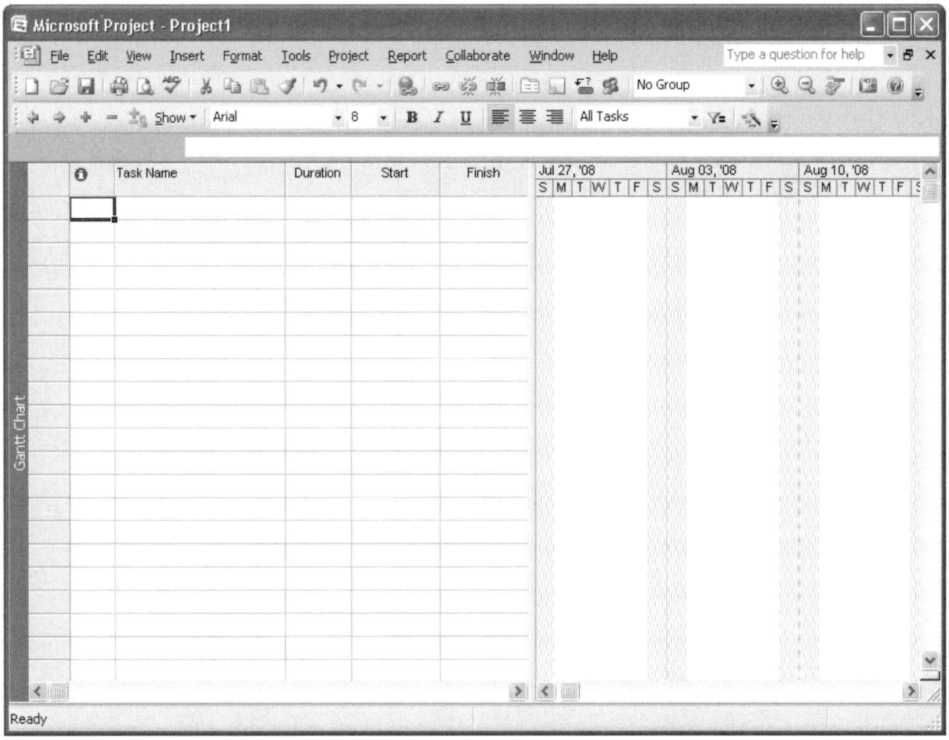

FIGURE 1-1 Project always displays a new blank project when you start the program.

To start a new project from a template, on the File menu, click New; in the Task pane that appears, click the On Computer link. Project displays the Templates dialog box; click the Project Templates tab to see the available templates that come with Project. Click the General tab to see the templates you have created.

CREATING A TEMPLATE

To create a template, set up the information you want to store in the template. Then on the File menu, click Save As. In the Save As dialog box that appears, open the Save As Type list and click Template (*.mpt). Project automatically displays the folder in which it will save the template file. In the File Name box, type a name for the template. When you click Save, Project displays the Save As Template dialog box shown here, in which you can select the type of data that you want to remove from the template.

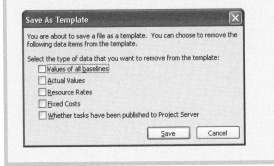

Recording General Project Information

After you start your project, you can establish some general information about your project. Most of the information affects the timing of your project. On the Project menu, click Project Information to display the Project Information dialog box (see Figure 1-2).

FIGURE 1-2 The Project Information dialog box.

TIP

This dialog box doesn't appear by default, but you can make it appear each time you start a new project, which might be a good idea. That way, you won't forget to set general project information. On the Tools menu, click Options, and on the General tab of the Options dialog box that appears, select the Prompt For Project Info For New Projects check box.

NOTE

The bottom portion of this dialog box appears if you use Project Professional; if you connect your project to Project Server, custom fields stored in Project Server also appear.

In the Project Information dialog box, you can make a number of choices for your project. Some of the choices you make determine whether other choices are available to you. For example, either the Start Date field or the Finish Date field is available, depending on the choice you make in the Schedule From field.

- **Schedule From** This field controls whether Project calculates the schedule from the start or the ending date of your project. The choice you make in this field also determines whether Project makes the Start Date or the Finish Date field available (refer to Figure 1-2).

- **Start Date** Using this field, you can set a start date for the project. Project uses this date as the start date for all tasks you create until you assign timing or dependencies to them.

- **Finish Date** Using this field, you can set a finish date for the project. Project uses this date as the finish date for all tasks you create until you assign timing or dependencies to them. If you know your project's deadline, you can enter it here and then work backward to schedule your project; this approach helps you figure out when you need to start your project to make your deadline.

- **Current Date** By default, Project displays your computer's current date setting in this field. If you adjust this date, you can, for example, generate reports that provide information on your project as of the date you select.

- **Status Date** You set the Status Date when you start recording progress on your project. Project uses the date you set in this field to make earned-value calculations and to display progress lines in your project. If you leave the status date set at NA, Project assumes that the status date should be the same as your computer's current date setting.

- **Calendar** Project comes with three overall calendars that you can assign to your project, based on the hours resources work in your organization; if none of these works for you, you can create your own calendar. We'll examine these three calendars more in the next section.

- **Priority** Project uses the Priority field—there's one available for the project and for every task in the project—to try to recalculate the schedule to resolve conflicts. The available priority values are the numbers between 1 and 1000; the higher the number, the less likely Project will opt to delay the project or task. The project's priority number comes into play when you connect projects through consolidation and then try to reschedule to resolve conflicts.

> **SEE ALSO** See Chapter 13, "Managing Cross-Project Conflicts," for more information on using priorities at the project level.

Setting the Project Calendar

The project calendar identifies the default working hours at your company. Project uses the project calendar when it calculates the schedule, eliminating non-working days from the calculations and fitting work into the appropriate hours available on any given day. So it's important to ensure that your project calendar accurately reflects your company's working time.

As I mentioned in the previous section, Project comes with three overall calendars that you can assign to your project, based on the typical hours and days resources work in your organization; if none of these works for you, you can create your own calendar. You also can identify non-working days.

The Standard calendar assumes that resources work five days each week (Monday through Friday), eight hours each day (from 8:00 A.M. to 5:00 P.M. with a break between noon, which Project shows as 12:00 PM in the calendar interface, and 1:00 P.M.).

The 24 Hour calendar assumes that you have resources working from midnight to midnight (which Project shows as 12:00 AM in the calendar interface).

The Night Shift calendar sets the following working times for resources:

- Monday: 11:00 PM to 12:00 AM.
- Tuesday through Friday: 12:00 AM to 3:00 AM, 4:00 AM to 8:00 AM, and 11:00 PM to 12:00 AM.
- Saturday: 12:00 AM to 3:00 AM and 4:00 AM to 8:00 AM.
- Sunday: No working time.

■ **REMEMBER** If you're using Project Standard, any changes you make to the calendar will work exactly as described here. If you're using Project Professional and you're storing your project in the Project Server database, you will need the Project Server administrator to establish the permissions that allow you to create and save calendars in the Project Server database.

Changing the Days and Hours Your Company Works

You can change the default working days and hours that Project uses on the Standard calendar by clicking Options on the Tools menu and then clicking the Calendar tab (see Figure 1-3). For example, if your company uses a four-day, 10-hour-per-day work week, you can set up the working week and workday hours here.

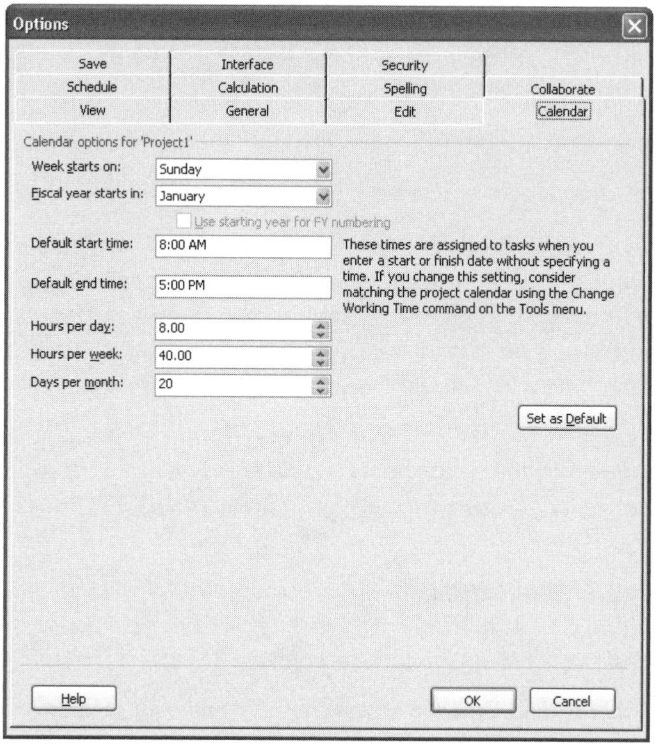

FIGURE 1-3 These options apply to all calendars used by Project.

Setting Exceptions to the Calendar

You might want to identify holidays that your company observes so that Project doesn't try to schedule resources to work on those days. You can assign any of the three calendars to your project or you can create your own calendars. For the purposes of this discussion, assume that the Standard calendar works for your company, but you want to designate company holidays as non-working days.

> **TIP** ✓ If you're more comfortable using wizards, try the Calendar Wizard, which is available in the Project Guide. On the View menu, click Turn On Project Guide. In the Project Guide pane that appears on the left side of the Project window, select the Define General Working Times link and follow the steps through the wizard.

On the Tools menu, click Change Working Time to display the Change Working Time dialog box shown in Figure 1-4. The legend at the left side of the box helps you identify the status of any given calendar day. In addition, if you click any given day, the status for that particular day appears on the right side of the calendar.

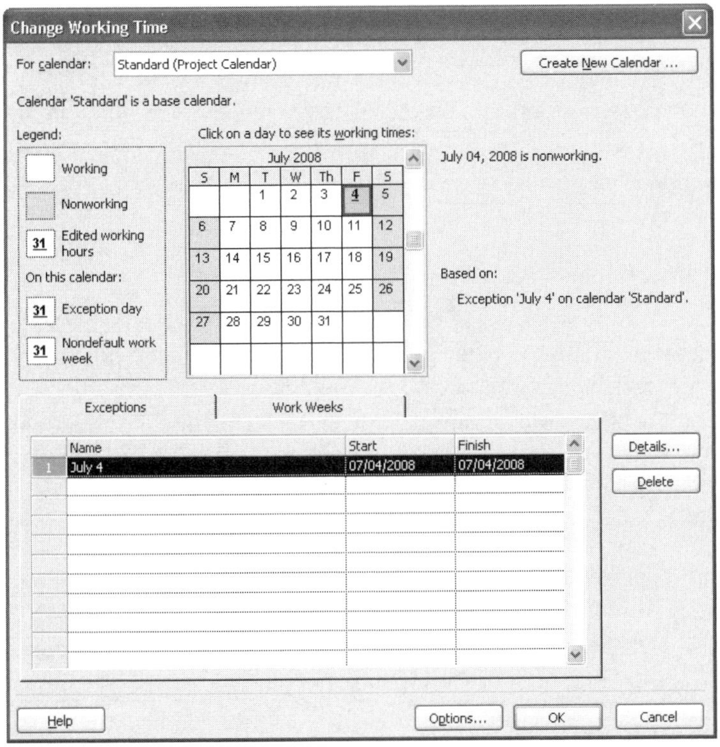

FIGURE 1-4 Use this dialog box to select or create a calendar for your project and to identify exceptions to the standard workday.

To set exceptions to the calendar for observed company holidays, follow these steps:

1. Make sure that the calendar you want to assign to your project appears in the For Calendar box.

> **TIP**
> ✓
> Although you can make changes to any of the calendars provided with Project, you might want to create a copy of the calendar and make your changes on the copy, just to make the default calendars that come with Project always available to you. When you click Create New Calendar, Project gives you the option to create a copy of the selected calendar.

2. Select the day you want to designate as a holiday. You can click the scroll bar arrows beside the calendar to display a prior or future month.

3. Click in the Name column on the Exceptions tab, type the name by which you want to identify the calendar exception, and press the Tab key.

    Project changes the appearance of the selected day to reflect the non-working time you established.

4. Click OK.

Changing the Work Week

Why would you want to modify the work week? Well, suppose that your standard work week follows the work week shown on the Calendar tab of the Options dialog box (see Figure 1-3 earlier in this chapter), but your business is closed every Monday. You can modify the work week to make all Mondays non-working days. You identify modifications to the work week on the Work Weeks tab of the Change Working Time dialog box. Click the [Default] entry and then click the Details button to display the Details dialog box for the default work week (see Figure 1-5).

Select the day you want to modify and then use the options on the right to identify the way in which you want to modify the day; for this example, I selected Set Days To Nonworking Time. Note that you can simply modify the hours of any given day. For example, you could arrange to work Wednesday mornings but not Wednesday afternoons.

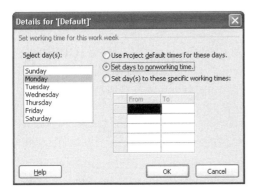

FIGURE 1-5 Use this dialog box to modify the default work week.

The Project Calendar and Scheduling

In each case, when you make changes to the calendar, Project uses the changes you identify when it calculates the schedule. Suppose, for example, that your project runs through the month of July and you have a three-day task that starts on July 2. If July 4 is a working day, the task will complete on July 4. But if you set July 4 as a non-working day, Project sets the task to finish on July 7 (see Figure 1-6).

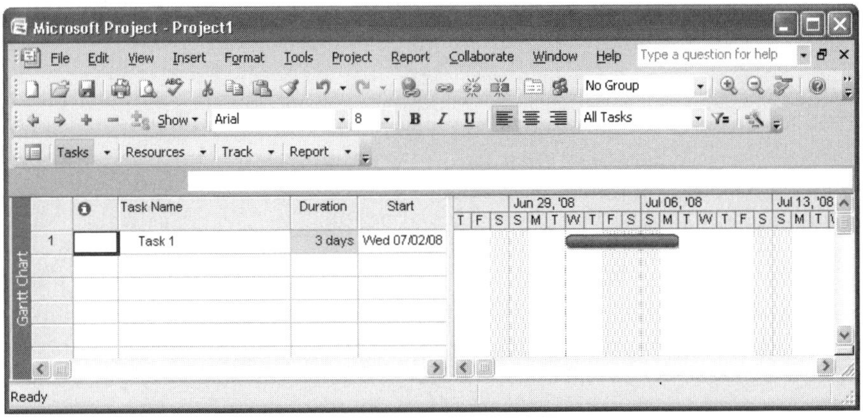

FIGURE 1-6 The shading that appears on July 4 indicates that you set that day as a non-working day, forcing a three-day task that starts on July 2 to end on July 7.

Creating Tasks

Once you establish your project's goal(s) and scope and set up the calendar that the project will use, you're ready to enter tasks. Tasks are things you need to do to complete the project. Yes, you probably started your basic propensity toward project management using a "to-do list." And you can start identifying tasks for your project in the same way—making a list of things that your team needs to do to complete the project. The initial order of things isn't important; focus on putting your ideas "on paper" or, preferably, in a Project file.

I think of this phase as "outlining" what I want to accomplish—much the same way that I produce an outline for a book. I start with the major headings, which are the chapters of my book, and then I tackle each individual chapter to identify the topics within that chapter that I want to cover. And some of those topics contain topics of their own.

Many people identify what to do in a project using a similar technique. They start by defining the major phases of a project and then define the tasks within that phase. Once again, some tasks contain subtasks of their own.

Determining How Granular to Make Your Tasks

Life is all about balance, and defining the tasks in a project is no different. Some people specify as project tasks every activity they can imagine. Others go the other direction and don't provide enough detail. So how do you find the balance?

Unfortunately, the answer here is more art than science. If you include too much informa-tion, you'll end up spending your days recording tracking information without ever really evaluating it—and you'll lose focus of the project's purpose. If you include too little, your project plan won't be useful, and the holes in your schedule might make you deliver late and exceed your budget because you won't consider the things that "might happen."

To identify phases, think about the deliverables your project must produce and key dates you need to meet along the way; that should help you begin to break your project into manageable chunks. You can then focus on each individual chunk and begin to make a list of things that you need to do within that chunk by the deliverable due date or other key date. As you consider the things you need to accomplish, you might find that listing those things in the order you need to accomplish them helps you identify other tasks. But don't get too crazy when you're listing tasks. For example, don't list tasks that your team members need to track. Instead, list the results of those tasks in your project plan and let your team members list the individual tasks that lead to the results.

TIP	You can set up *milestones* that mark the deliverable due dates and other key dates.

Understanding Task Types

You can create different types of tasks in Project. The task type you choose affects the way Project calculates the schedule. In some cases, adding resources changes the way Project handles the scheduling of a task, so it's almost impossible to talk about task types without including some discussion of resources.

- **Fixed Units Tasks** Before I explain how Project handles a fixed units task, it's important to understand what a unit is. The *units* in *fixed units* refers to assignment units, which are percentages you use to specify the amount of resource effort you want a resource to expend while working on the task. When you assign a resource to a task, you specify the number of assignment units of that resource as a percentage. In other words, if you set the assignment units for a resource to 100%, you assign the resource to work on the task full-time; if you set the assignment units to 50%, you assign the resource to work on the task half of the available time.

  When you create a fixed units task, you essentially tell Project not to make any changes to the assignment unit percentage if you change the duration of the task; that is, the resources continue to work at the assignment unit percentage you specified.

- **Fixed Duration Tasks** You use a fixed duration task to define a task that will take a specified amount of time, even if you have more than one person working on the task. Pregnancy is a fixed duration task; it takes nine months, give or take some days. If you have two pregnant women, the task of pregnancy still takes nine months for each of them.

- **Fixed Work Tasks** The duration you set for a fixed work task represents the total amount of work needed to complete the task. Suppose you create a fixed work task that is four days long; you're saying, essentially, that one person working full-time on the task can complete it in four days. If, however, you assign two resources to the task, each at an assignment unit rate of 100%, the task will take two days to complete. If you assign only one resource to the task at an assignment rate of 50%, the task will take eight days to complete. So you can conclude that, on fixed work tasks, Project assigns a percentage of effort to each resource that is sufficient to complete the task in the time allotted.

- **Effort-Driven Tasks** An effort-driven task is one that is affected by the number of resources you assign to it. By default, all fixed work tasks are effort-driven, and you can't change that behavior. If it takes one person an hour to shovel the snow after a snow storm, this fixed work, effort-driven task could be accomplished by two people in half the time, assuming they don't stop for a snowball fight or to build a snowman.

By default, Project creates fixed-unit, effort-driven tasks, and you can change a fixed-duration task to make it effort-driven also. When you change the number of resources that are assigned to a fixed-unit, effort-driven task, Project changes the duration of the task. When you change the number of resources assigned to a fixed-duration, effort-driven task, Project modifies the percentage of total work allocated to each resource working on the task. In both cases, Project doesn't modify the amount of work that's required to complete the task.

> **NOTE** The change Project calculates for any effort-driven task is strictly a mathematical calculation. For example, Project calculates that three people get work done in one-third of the time it takes one person to do the job. In real life, however, the time you save is rarely a straight, mathematical calculation. After all, people on a job talk to each other, take breaks, and so on.

So that you can compare how Project handles each task type, I've created a project containing five tasks (see Figure 1-7). Each task is four days long, originally had one resource assigned, and I've added a second resource to each task. The project contains two fixed-unit tasks, two fixed-duration tasks, and one fixed-work task. One of the fixed-unit tasks is not effort-driven, and one of the fixed-duration tasks is not effort-driven, while the other fixed-unit and fixed-duration tasks are effort-driven. Note that the fixed-work task and the fixed-unit, effort-driven task were both originally four days long, but when I added two resources to them, Project automatically recalculated the duration of the tasks, assuming that both resources would work full-time on the task.

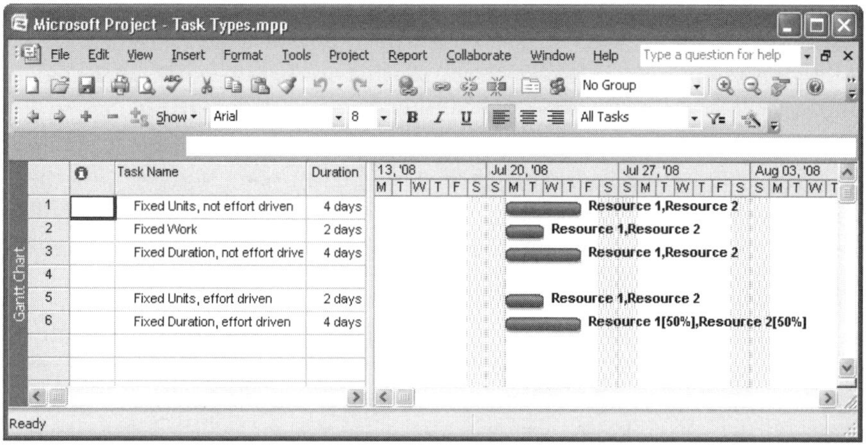

FIGURE 1-7 Compare the way Project handles the various types of tasks.

Summary Tasks and Subtasks

Earlier in this chapter, I suggested that you begin a project by listing the major phases of the project and then adding tasks to each phase. When you start entering tasks, Project assigns an estimated duration of one day to each task (the question mark indicates that the duration is estimated). Although I show durations in Figure 1-8, don't worry about task durations initially; just get that list of phases and tasks entered and do a little outline structuring. I supplied durations to show you the behavior of a summary task. Eventually, your phases will become summary tasks, and the tasks listed below each phase will become subtasks.

> **TIP** ✓ That blue highlighting that appears as you work in Project is the result of a feature called *change highlighting*. Each time you make a change, Project highlights everything in your project affected by the change; knowing the tasks affected by a change can be useful under lots of conditions. For example, knowing the tasks affected as you set up dependency links as described in Chapter 2, "How Dependencies and Constraints Affect Your Project," can be very helpful. If you don't want to view change highlighting, on the View menu, click Hide Change Highlighting. Also, each time you save your project, the highlighting disappears because Project assumes that you wanted to keep the changes you made.

You can add tasks beneath a phase by simply selecting the row immediately below the phase and pressing the Insert key on the keyboard; Project inserts a blank line, and you can then type the task name. To insert a task between two summary tasks or subtasks, click the task that should appear below the new task you intend to insert and then press the Insert key on your keyboard. Project inserts a blank row above the selected task in the table portion of the view and renumbers the rows of the tasks that fall below the new row.

> **TIP** ✓ You can delete a task by clicking the row number beside the task and pressing the Delete key on the keyboard. If you delete a summary task, you also delete all of the subtasks below that summary task.

As shown in Figure 1-8, my project contains four phases, with a varying number of tasks in each phase. I clearly identify the tasks in a particular phase by selecting them and using the Indent button on the toolbar

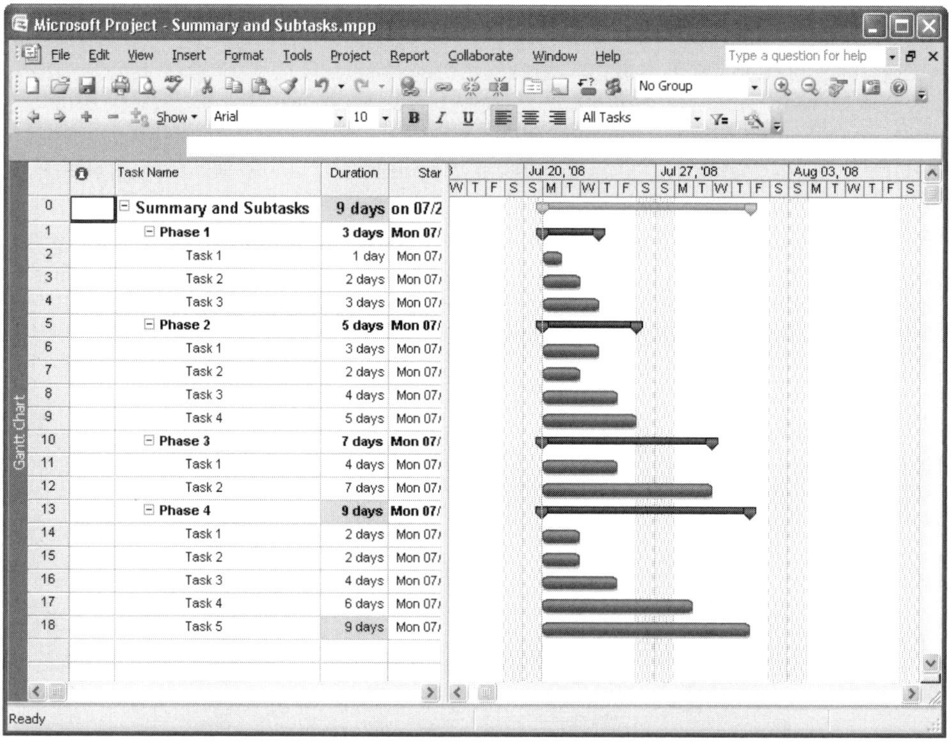

FIGURE 1-8 A project with four phases; each phase is a summary task.

When you indent a task, Project automatically turns the task above it into a *summary task*, which is a special type of task that you use to view, at a glance, the total duration and cost of the tasks indented below it, which are called either tasks or subtasks. (Project users tend to use the words *task* and *subtask* interchangeably.) The summary task is represented by boldface type in the Task Name column and a special black bar in the chart portion of the Gantt Chart view. The length of a summary task's bar will be equal to the length of the bar associated with the longest subtask below the summary task. So, for example, Phase 3's summary task bar is seven days long because Task 2 in Phase 3 is seven days long.

WARNING Although Project won't stop you, don't assign resources to a summary task and don't try to link summary tasks to other tasks. Summary tasks aren't intended to serve any purpose other than to summarize duration and cost information of the tasks indented below them. Assigning resources to a summary task can lead you to believe that cost fields don't add up and that your resources are overbooked if you happen to assign the same resource to a summary task and to one of its subtasks. Linking summary tasks can cause your Project file to develop a *circular reference* error, particularly if you link the summary task to subtasks under different summary tasks. In addition, it becomes difficult to follow the logic of your schedule if summary task links conflict with subtask links.

The Project Summary Task

You can display a summary task that represents your entire project so that you can see, at a glance, the total time and cost for your project. On the Tools menu, click Options to display the Options dialog box (see Figure 1-9). On the View page, select the Show Project Summary Task check box and click OK. Project adds the project summary task to the first row of your schedule and numbers it Row 0; the project summary task bar is light gray in color instead of black like the bars of other summary tasks (refer to Figure 1-8 earlier in this chapter).

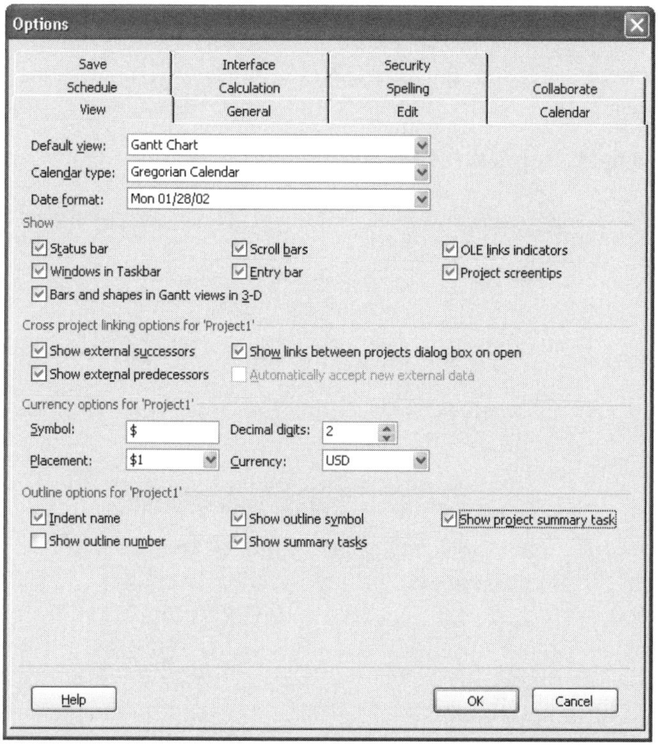

FIGURE 1-9 Use the Options dialog box to display the project summary task.

I found a very cool tip in several places on the Internet for those of you who aren't afraid to edit the registry. In Microsoft Project 2003 and earlier, the only way to display the project summary task was the way I just described. But in Project 2007, you can display the project summary task in every new project file automatically by adding a DWORD value to your registry. Follow the steps on the next page.

1. Quit Project.

2. Click the Start button and then click Run to display the Run dialog box.

3. Type **regedit** and click the OK button to display the Registry Editor window.

4. Navigate to HKEY_CURRENT_USER\Software\Microsoft\Office\12.0\MS Project\
   Options\View.

5. On the Edit menu, click New, then click DWORD Value, and finally, type **Show Project Summary**.

6. Press the Enter key on the keyboard to create a DWORD value.

7. Double-click the new Show Project Summary DWORD to display the Edit DWORD Value dialog box.

8. Type **1** in the Value Data field, as shown here.

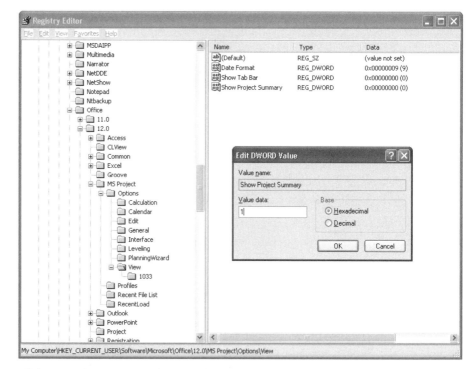

9. Click OK and close the Registry Editor window.

Once you've made this change, you should see the Project Summary Task (Row 0) automatically displayed in every new blank project whenever you start Project 2007.

Here's a list of the places where I found this tip on the Internet:

- *http://blogs.msdn.com/project/archive/2007/12/06/display-the-project-summary-task-by-default.aspx*

- *http://theprojectserverguru.spaces.live.com/Blog/cns!D74683E5EE2E06E2!341.entry*

- *http://www.projectserverexperts.com/ProjectServerFAQKnowledgeBase/DisplayProjectSummaryTask.aspx*

- *http://www.phase2.com/blog/?p=55/*

- *http://live.mscommunity.net/blogs/lugospod/archive/2008/02/26/turning-project-summary-task-on-by-default.aspx*

Reorganizing Your Project Schedule

Suppose that you realize, after you create a task, that it really doesn't belong in the phase where you created it. No problem; you can move it by using Cut and Paste or by dragging and dropping. Select the row number Project assigned to the task, and make your moves. Be aware of the following effects that moving summary tasks and subtasks can have on the schedule's outline:

- When you move a summary task, Project automatically selects its subtasks and includes them in the move. To move a summary task only (without moving any of its subtasks), you must first promote all of its subtasks so that the summary task is no longer a summary task. You can then use the Indent and Outdent buttons to readjust the positions of tasks in the outline.

- If you move a task originally positioned at a higher level of the outline to a new location just below a task with subtasks, Project demotes the task that you move.

- If you move a subtask so that it appears below a task at a higher level of the outline, Project promotes the subtask that you move.

- If you move a subtask from one phase to another and you've already set a baseline, baseline data at the summary level will no longer equal the sum of the baseline data for the tasks in both the section from which you moved the task and the section into which you moved the task.

SEE ALSO   You can display outline numbers or assign WBS codes to tasks; these numbers are independent of the row numbers Project displays and can be affected by moving tasks in the outline. See Chapter 9, "Determining How to Communicate with Your Team," for more information. For information on setting baselines, see Chapter 8.

A Word about Task Timing

It's a natural, gut reaction to want to assign a start date to each task, whether it's a summary task or a subtask. But if you do, you essentially constrain the calculations that Project does automatically when you link your tasks together by defining which tasks are dependent on other tasks. Essentially, by assigning start dates, you can accidentally end up distorting the schedule's timing. So I recommend that you *not* enter task start dates unless you have a really valid reason for that start date. I believe you'll find that, in most cases, you don't *need* to enter that start date. Instead, wait to see what start dates Project assigns when you link your tasks together.

> **SEE ALSO** For more information about dependencies, see Chapter 2. For more information about how task timing and constraints affect your schedule, see Chapter 5, "Controlling an Out-of-Control Schedule."

Establishing the Task's Duration

Assigning a duration to a task is a fairly simple, mechanical process. You simply type a value in the Duration field for the task followed by a character that represents the units in which you're specifying the duration: **d** for days, **w** for weeks, **mo** for months. You also can type **m** for minutes and **h** for hours.

Unfortunately, that doesn't tell you how to determine what the value should be. And, once again, the method is more art than science because you must estimate the value based on your experience.

Consider the types of resources you'll need to complete a task; an experienced programmer can complete a programming task faster than a new programmer. Some photocopy machines produce copies faster than others. Are the parts necessary to build a component available readily, or might there be a delay in obtaining them? And it's important to factor in the "water cooler" effect. I've never met anyone who performs at peak efficiency and productivity 100% of the time. Everybody needs a break once in awhile, and I've seen studies that show that workers really achieve complete efficiency and productivity for as little as 50% of their day and as much 75% of their day. So, when you determine that a task should take 8 person-hours, don't expect that the task will therefore be completed in one day. All of these issues should factor into your estimate.

The Project Management Institute (*www.pmi.org*) suggests that task durations range from 4 to 80 hours, as a rule of thumb, to help you keep the tasks manageable. Some managers estimate task durations by taking their "best guess" at the duration, doubling their estimate, and some even add 10% to that value. As you become more experienced, your "best guesses" will improve. If you often work on similar projects, consider reviewing other projects to see the durations you estimated and how close you were.

Remember to attempt to make your "best guess" estimates realistic; you stand to lose a great deal if they aren't. If you underestimate or overestimate how long a task will take, you won't plan for resources properly or develop appropriate methods to complete the task. Then the people involved in your project will begin to believe that all the duration estimates are unrealistic. Whether you underestimate or overestimate dramatically, resources may not be available when you need them, and team members and management alike might come to believe that delays are inevitable.

One last piece of advice: don't negotiate for time to complete a project. Do your planning homework and develop a realistic project schedule. If your schedule shows that you can complete the project in nine months and your boss wants it done in three months, don't be tempted to settle for six months. If you do and your project schedule was truly realistic, you guarantee the failure of your project. Instead of negotiating, show your boss why your schedule is realistic, given the available resources.

SEE ALSO	See Chapter 11, "Dealing with Management," for more information.

Creating Milestones

Milestones are road markers. In and of themselves, they have no duration, because they mark a point in your project that helps you evaluate progress. Although it might take you months to produce a deliverable—and producing the deliverable is a task—you might want to create a milestone for each deliverable, using the milestone as a target to mark the expected due date for the deliverable. To create a milestone, create a task and assign it a duration of 0.

TIP ✓	Unlike earlier versions of Project, Project 2007 allows tasks with zero duration. To create a task with a zero duration, double-click the task and, on the Advanced tab of the Task Information dialog box that appears, clear the Mark Task As Milestone check box.

Using Recurring Tasks Effectively

Recurring tasks can save you time when you are creating a project because they can help you avoid setting up the same task over and over again. For example, suppose that your company is bringing a new drug to market, and the government testing requirements include running a particular test weekly for six months and preparing a report of the test results. Instead of entering the same task approximately 25 times, use a recurring task. When you create a recurring task, you specify the pattern of the recurrence—monthly, weekly, daily, and so on—as well as a timeframe during which the task will occur. Project then sets up the individual recurrences of the task for you, saving you a lot of keystrokes.

To create a recurring task, select the row immediately below the phase or task where you want the recurring task to appear, and on the Insert menu, click Recurring Task. Project displays the Recurring Task Information dialog box (see Figure 1-10).

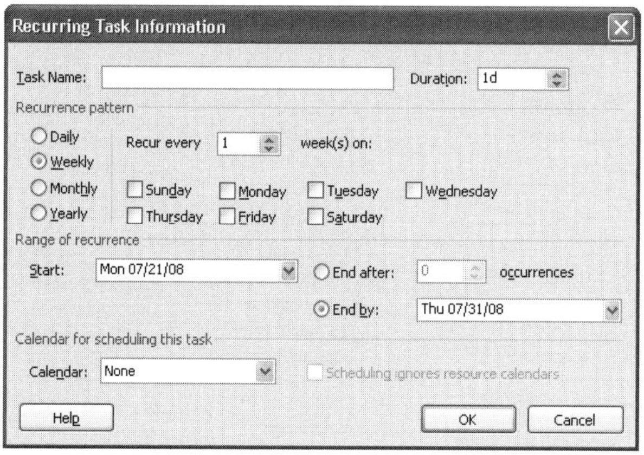

FIGURE 1-10 Supply the information for a recurring task in this dialog box.

When you click OK, Project inserts the recurring task above the task you selected and displays a pair of arrows pointing at each other in a circle in the Indicators column, which appears next to the task's row number; the icon indicates that the task is a recurring task. Project treats the recurring task as a summary task. A plus sign appears beside the task, hiding all of the subtasks you created. Click the plus sign to view the subtasks.

Identifying Resources Before You Have Resources

It's not uncommon, as you begin a project, to find that you don't know *exactly* who or what resource you need to complete a task, but that you can describe the skills or features the resource needs. In this case, you can define generic resources and use them as placeholders until the time when you need the real deal. For "people" resources (called *work resources* in Project), this approach works particularly well if your Human Resources department has job descriptions for each of the resources you might want to assign to your project.

When you define generic resources, make sure they're truly generic. Give them names, such as "Programmer" or "Lead Designer" or "Project Assistant," that describe the job they do rather than who they are. In the case of "non-human" generic resources, use names such as "Meeting Room" instead of "4th Floor Conference Room."

The generic resource feature was designed primarily for use with Project Professional and Project Server. You can create generic resources and then use the Resource Substitution Wizard to replace generic resources with actual resources stored in Project Server. Although Project Standard and Project Professional alone don't have any built-in mechanism to substitute resources, those of you who don't use Project Server might still find this use of generic resources helpful. For example, you can use generic resources when you don't care who does the work and you simply want to track the work that is completed on a project. Or you might use generic resources as you start a project and then identify for your Human Resources department that you need three engineers at a particular point in time.

You can identify a generic resource by selecting the Generic check box in the Resource Information dialog box, which is shown in Figure 1-11. You open this dialog box by displaying any resource-oriented view and double-clicking the resource that you want to make generic.

When you click OK, Project displays the icon you see in the margin beside the row number of the generic resource when you view the Resource Sheet.

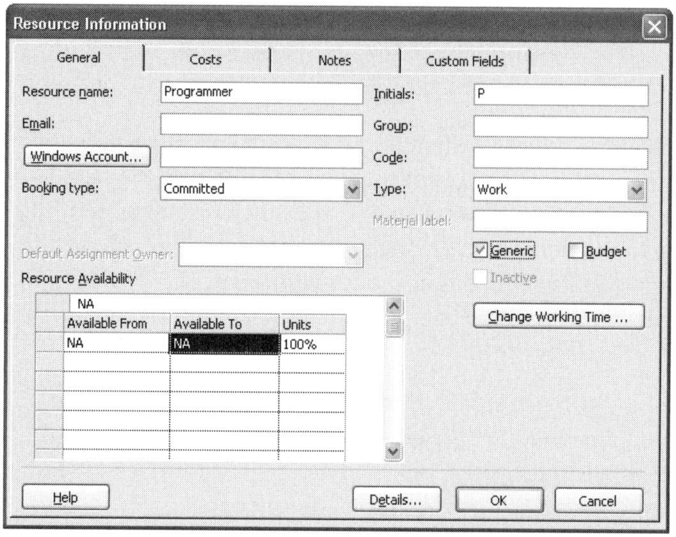

FIGURE 1-11 Select the Generic check box to designate a generic resource.

About Connecting with Other Projects in Your Company

Sometimes projects aren't isolated; they are related to other projects. In some cases, tasks of one project depend on the completion of another project or a task in another project. In other cases, projects become interrelated because they need to use the same resources, sometimes at the same time.

Project Server, in conjunction with Project Professional, provides organizations with the capability to manage many projects simultaneously and to share resources among those projects. When you use Project Server, you create projects in Project Professional and then load them into a central database—the Project Server database. The Project Server database is located on a Web server or in a server farm on your company's local area network or intranet. Team members can use a browser to connect to the database and provide updated information about task progress. Project managers can take advantage of the global resource pool available in the database to find available resources for projects. Management can view a project's Gantt chart and deal with risks and issues that arise.

Organizations that don't use Project Server but use the same resources to work on multiple projects simultaneously can take advantage of the resource pool feature in Project. You set up a project that contains nothing but the resources available in your company—this project is called the *resource pool* project. Different managers can work on various individual projects; those projects don't need to be managed by the same person. To share resources, a project manager connects an individual project to the resource pool to make resource assignments.

Whether your organization uses Project Server or simply Project, you can connect projects using consolidation. You use consolidation to help you make a large, complex project manageable. I think of consolidation as the end result; you create and save projects that are smaller, more manageable chunks of a large project, and you work with the smaller, individual projects on a daily basis. You set up the individual projects as if they truly are independent; you create task dependencies, assign resources, view the project's critical path, and track the project. When you're ready to look at the bigger picture, that's when you consolidate. Essentially, you combine the smaller pieces together into one file; that is, you *consolidate* them. And you can build links between the individual projects so that you can see the effect each project has on the other projects and on the overall schedule for the unified, complex project. In the consolidated project, you can view the critical path for the large project that takes into consideration each individual project—a reason why Project Server users might want to consolidate. You see, although Project Server views can "roll up" information, you can't see one critical path across projects in the Project Server database.

Connecting related projects is a wise step to take, but don't take it too early in the game. If you need to manage a large, complex project, start by focusing on one phase of that project and establish the tasks and dependencies. You might even save information about that phase in a single Project file, without worrying yet about other phases. This approach helps you simplify the large, complex project into manageable chunks that won't overwhelm you. While you're working on one chunk, a thought related to another chunk might pop up; just open another Project file and jot it down—then go back to work on the original chunk.

CHAPTER 2

How Dependencies and Constraints Affect Your Project

DEPENDENCIES AND CONSTRAINTS are two features in Microsoft Office Project 2007 most likely to drive the timing of your project; therefore both play a big role in the way your schedule reads. In this chapter, I'm going to explore a variety of topics concerning dependencies and constraints.

What Are Dependencies?

If you *don't* use dependencies, Project assigns to every task a start date or a finish date that matches the project's start date or finish date—the one you set up in the Project Information dialog box in the previous chapter. In such a scenario, calculating how long the project will take becomes a simple matter—the project will take as long to complete as the longest task in the project.

It's highly unlikely, though, that all of your tasks will start and run simultaneously—this isn't, after all, a horse race. So you should set dependencies to identify for Project the order in which tasks occur. Some tasks can run concurrently while other tasks run consecutively. Sometimes tasks can run concurrently, but you don't have the resources to complete the tasks concurrently, so you need to set dependencies to identify which you'll complete first. Essentially, by setting dependencies, you establish the timing logic of your project.

When you set dependencies, you *link* tasks. Don't think, "computer linking" here; we're not talking about hyperlinks. We're talking instead about connecting two tasks in a timing relationship. Terminology alert: linking two tasks is synonymous with setting dependencies.

You might be tempted to set start dates for your tasks to identify timing for your project, but if you do, you undermine Project's ability to adjust your project schedule when things change. And you *know* that conditions will change; that's the way life is. To successfully manage your project under changing conditions, you need to be able to respond to change. If you set concrete start dates for your tasks and then run into a bump in the road, you need to adjust the start date of each affected task, effectively recalculating the schedule manually. But if you use dependencies to describe the timing of your project, you need to adjust only the task that falls behind schedule or finishes early; based on the dependencies you set, Project recalculates and adjusts the rest of the schedule.

> **NOTE** Setting start date constraints and other types of constraints can also have an unforeseen impact on your schedule by artificially inflating or understating the amount of time needed to complete the project. As a general rule of thumb, avoid setting constraints. (See "Working with Constraints" later in this chapter for more information about constraints.)

Choosing the Right Dependency for Your Needs

Every dependency relationship involves two tasks; one task serves as the *predecessor task* and the other serves as the *successor task*. In most cases, the predecessor task takes place before the successor task the way that the names imply, but there will be times when the timings of the two tasks overlap.

You can set one of four types of dependency relationships for each pair of tasks: finish-to-start, start-to-start, finish-to-finish, and start-to-finish. These dependencies describe the relationships between the start and finish of the predecessor and successor tasks; the first part of each type of dependency refers to the predecessor task, and the second to the successor task. So a *finish-to-start dependency* relates the finish of the predecessor task to the start of the successor.

> **TIP** ✓ Project refers to these relationships by their initials; for example, SS refers to a start-to-start relationship.

When you link tasks, Project draws arrows—also called *link lines*—between the tasks. As you view the figures that follow, take note of the position of the link line and the direction that the arrow points between tasks. The position of the link line provides important visual clues about the type of dependency that exists between the tasks, and the arrow's direction provides important visual clues that help you identify the predecessor and successor tasks. For any type of relationship, the arrowhead points to the successor task.

Finish-to-Start Relationships

A finish-to-start relationship is the most common type of dependency link. In this relationship, the predecessor task must finish before the successor task can start. For example, you must own and possess software before you can install it on a computer. You must get your medication from the drug store before you can take it.

> **TIP** ✓ The finish-to-start relationship is the only relationship that you can create by using your mouse or the Link Tasks tool or command.

In Figure 2-1, Task 1 is the predecessor task and Task 2 is the successor task in a finish-to-start relationship. Similarly, Task 2 is the predecessor task and Task 3 is the successor task in another finish-to-start relationship. Notice that the link line starts at the finish of the predecessor task and connects to the start of the successor task.

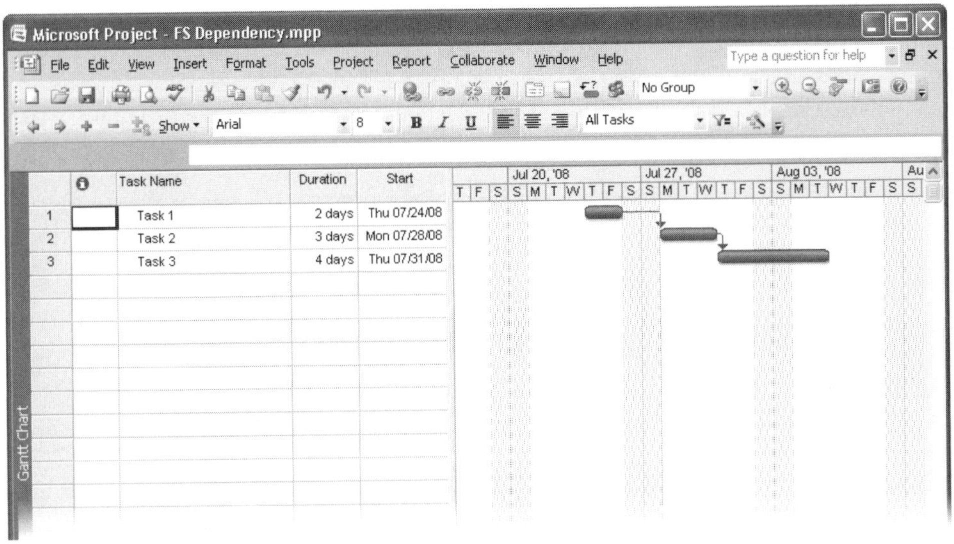

FIGURE 2-1 In the finish-to-start relationship, successor tasks can't start until predecessor tasks finish.

Start-to-Start Relationships

In a start-to-start relationship, the successor can't start until the predecessor starts. For example, suppose that you're trimming the plants in your yard. You need to start trimming plants (Task 1) before you start picking up debris (Task 2). In Figure 2-2, Task 1 is the predecessor task and Task 2 is the successor task in a start-to-start relationship. Notice that the link line starts at the beginning of the predecessor task and connects to the beginning of the successor task.

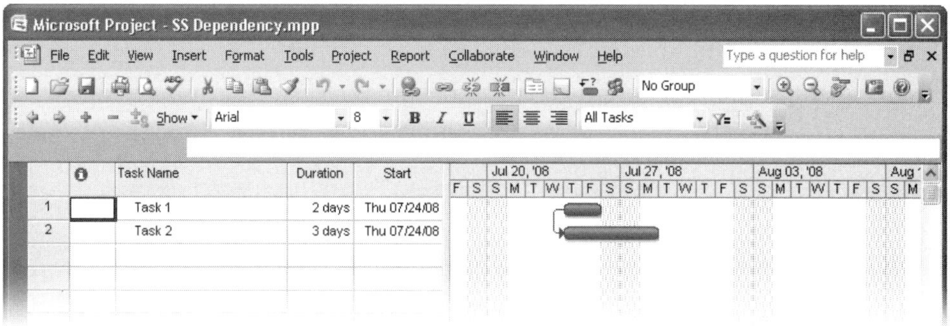

FIGURE 2-2 In the start-to-start relationship, the successor task can't start until the predecessor task starts.

Finish-to-Finish Relationships

In the finish-to-finish dependency, the successor task can't finish until the predecessor task finishes. For example, you have to wait until everyone finishes eating dinner (Task 1) before you can finish washing the dishes (Task 2). In Figure 2-3, Task 1 is the predecessor task and Task 2 is the successor task in a finish-to-finish relationship. Notice that the link line starts at the finish of the predecessor task and connects to the finish of the successor task.

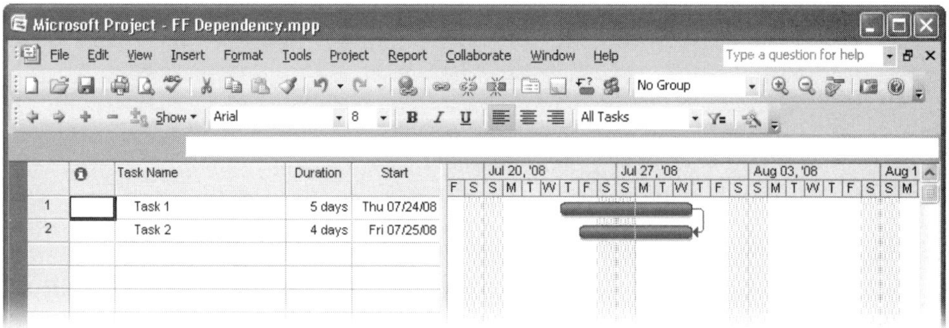

FIGURE 2-3 In the finish-to-finish relationship, the successor task can't finish before the predecessor task finishes.

Start-to-Finish Relationships

With the start-to-finish relationship, the successor task cannot finish until the predecessor task starts. Suppose, for example, that you're building a house and you have Task 1, Receive Framing Materials, and Task 2, Assemble House Frame. You don't need Task 1 to finish before beginning work on Task 2; you just need Task 1 to have started. In other words, you can always begin assembling the house frame even if *all* framing materials haven't arrived, so long as you have *some* of the materials. You can't finish Task 2 until Task 1 starts, so Task 1 is the predecessor task and Task 2 is the successor task. When you establish this kind of dependency, Project calculates the start date of the successor task by setting the finish date of the successor task equal to the start date of the predecessor task and then subtracting the duration of the successor task. Figure 2-4 shows a start-to-finish relationship. Notice that the link line starts at the beginning of the predecessor task and connects to the finish of the successor task.

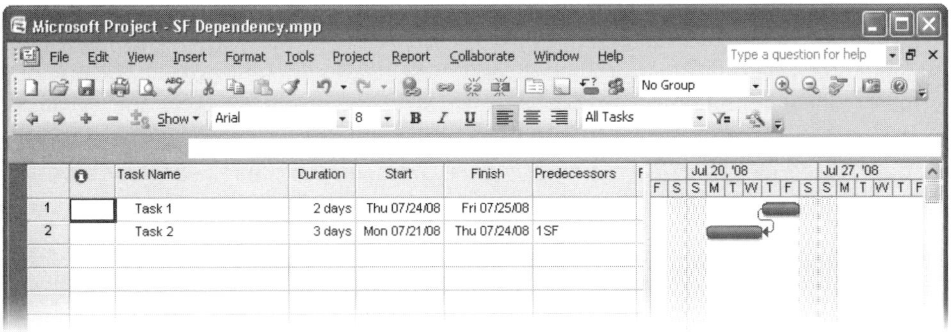

FIGURE 2-4 In the start-to-finish relationship, the successor task can't finish until the predecessor task starts.

> **NOTE** There's a fine line conceptually between finish-to-start relationships and start-to-finish relationships. For example, if you set up a finish-to-start relationship for the two tasks in the house-building project, you'd be saying that you couldn't start assembling the frame until you received all the framing materials. In the start-to-finish relationship, you can't finish assembling the frame until you start receiving the materials, but there's the potential to do part of the assembly as you're receiving materials—and you can make this kind of relationship visible using lead and lag time; see the section "What Are Lag and Lead Time?" later in this chapter for more information.

Setting Dependencies

Setting a finish-to-start dependency is quick and easy; I like to use the Link Tasks button shown in the margin. Select the row number of the predecessor task. Then press and hold the Ctrl key while you click the row number of the successor task. When you click the Link Tasks button, Project creates a finish-to-start link. The order in which you select the tasks you want to link does matter; Project establishes the first task you select as the predecessor and the second task as the successor.

> **TIP** ✓ You can select as many tasks as you want to create dependency links. Project links the tasks in the order you select them.

If you prefer, you can create the links using the Predecessors column of the Gantt chart's Entry table. Figure 2-5 displays enough of the Entry table so that you can see the Predecessors column. To establish a link, click on the row of the successor task and, in the Predecessors column, type the row number of the predecessor task. If you want to create any relationship other than a finish-to-start relationship, also type the letters that abbreviate the relationship (such as SF for start-to-finish). In the figure, the relationship between Tasks 1 and 2 is a start-to-finish relationship, and the relationship between Tasks 3 and 4 is a finish-to-start relationship.

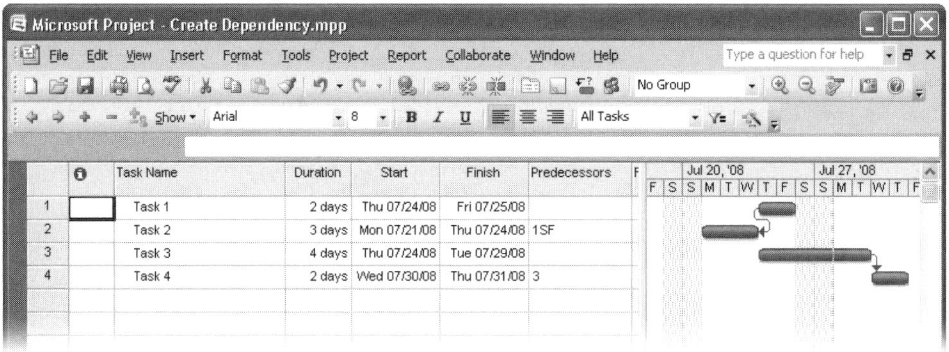

FIGURE 2-5 You can create dependencies using the Predecessors column.

Some people find dialog boxes more reassuring to use. You can set a dependency on the Predecessors tab of the Task Information dialog box (see Figure 2-6). Follow these steps:

1. Double-click the successor task.

2. When the Task Information dialog box appears, click the Predecessors tab.

3. In the Task Name column, type or select the name of the predecessor task.

4. In the Type column, select the type of dependency relationship you want to create.

5. Click OK.

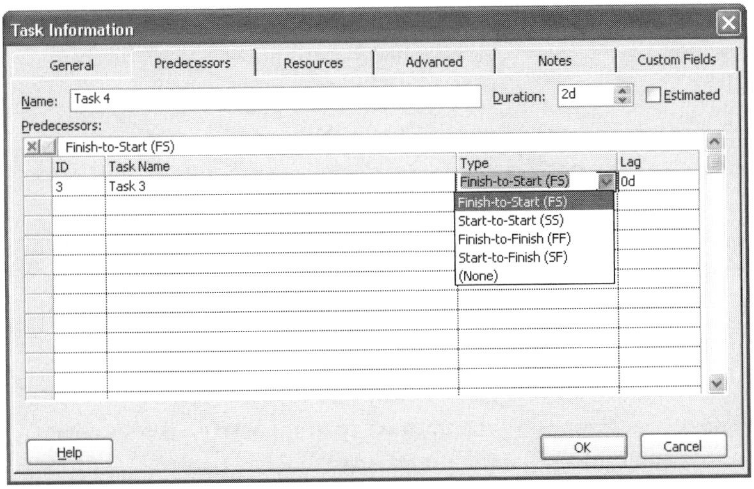

FIGURE 2-6 You can use the Task Information dialog box to set dependencies.

You can use the Task Dependency dialog box to change the existing relationship between two tasks. Just double-click the link line between the two tasks to display this dialog box and make your changes.

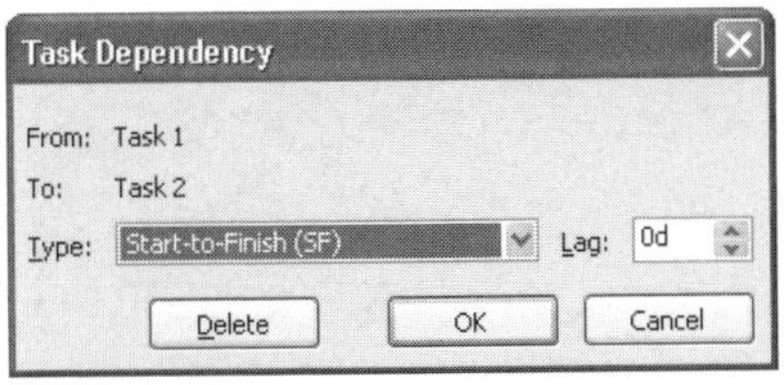

> **SEE ALSO**   Are you tempted to set dependencies using summary tasks? Please don't. See the section "How Many Dependencies Are Too Many?" later in this chapter for more information.

What Are Lag and Lead Time?

Okay, so Project lets you define the relationship between two tasks using dependencies that relate the tasks using their start dates, finish dates, or some combination of the two dates. But how can you indicate that one task should start a short time after another task starts—not when the other task finishes or at the same time the other task starts? Essentially, how do you indicate delay time or overlap time—often called *lag* and *lead time*—between tasks?

Enter the Lag field in Project. It works in conjunction with the type of dependency you select to add delay or overlap time between tasks. To create lag or lead time, you work with the successor task and enter a positive or negative duration value in the Lag column of the Task Information dialog box or the Task Dependency dialog box. The trick is determining whether to enter a positive or a negative value to incorporate delay or overlap. With some dependency types, using a positive value adds delay, while in other cases it incorporates overlap. Let's look at examples.

If you enter a positive value in the Lag column of a successor task that has a finish-to-start relationship with its predecessor, Project adds a delay to the start of the successor task and you see a gap between the end of the predecessor and the beginning of the successor. If you enter a negative value in the Lag column for the same type of relationship, Project adds overlap between the two tasks. In Figure 2-7, I entered a positive value in the Lag column and incorporated lag time between Tasks 1 and 2, forcing Task 2's start to be delayed two days after Task 1 finishes. Between Tasks 3 and 4, I entered a negative value in the Lag column and incorporated lead time that makes Tasks 3 and 4 overlap in timing, causing Task 4 to start while Task 3 is in progress.

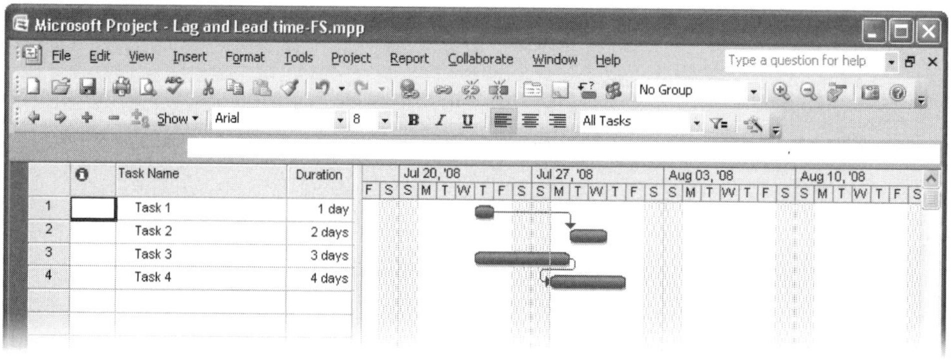

FIGURE 2-7 Adding delay and overlap to finish-to-start dependencies.

But suppose that the relationship between the tasks is a start-to-start dependency. As you can see in Figure 2-8, I entered a positive value in the Lag column for the first pair of tasks and a negative value in the Lag column for the second pair of tasks. A positive value in the Lag column of the successor task in a start-to-start dependency creates an overlap between the tasks, while a negative value creates a delay between the tasks.

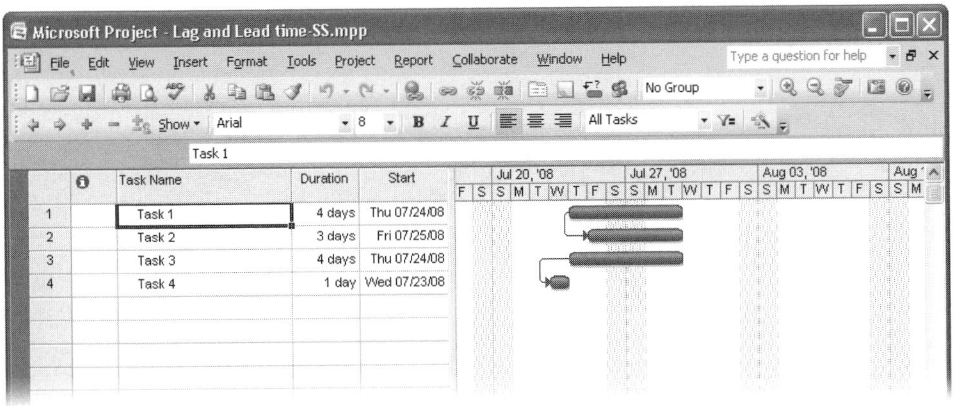

FIGURE 2-8 Adding delay and overlap to start-to-start dependencies.

In Figure 2-9, the relationship between Tasks 1 and 2 and Tasks 3 and 4 is a finish-to-finish dependency. Again, I entered a positive value in the Lag column for the first pair of tasks and a negative value in the Lag column for the second pair of tasks. As you can see, a positive value in the Lag column of the successor task in a finish-to-finish relationship creates an overlap between the tasks, while a negative value creates a delay between the tasks.

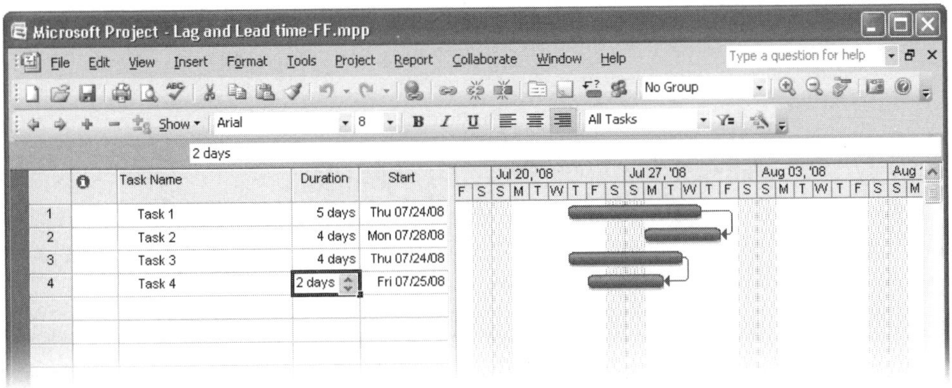

FIGURE 2-9 Adding delay and overlap to finish-to-finish dependencies.

I've repeated the experiment in Figure 2-10, this time using a start-to-finish dependency between Tasks 1 and 2 and Tasks 3 and 4. I entered a positive value in the Lag column and incorporated overlap between Tasks 1 and 2, causing Task 2 to start while Task 1 is in progress. Between Tasks 3 and 4, I entered a negative value in the Lag column and incorporated delay time, forcing Task 3's start to be delayed one day after Task 4 finishes.

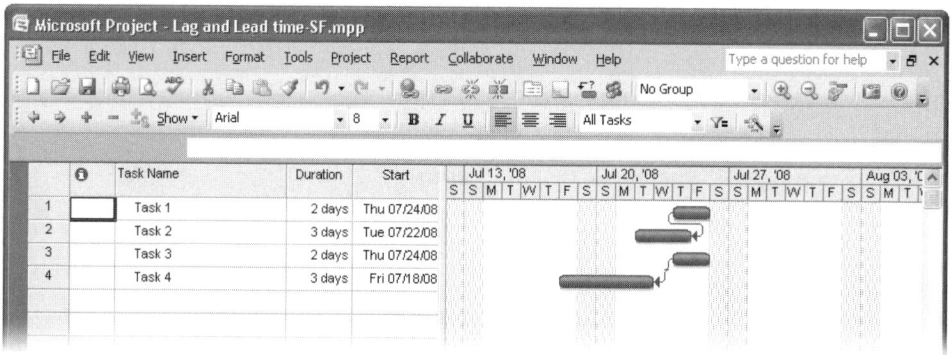

FIGURE 2-10 Adding delay and overlap to start-to-finish dependencies.

> **NOTE** In situations where you want to build delay between two tasks, you can simply create a task that represents the delay. For example, suppose that you need two days after a conference ends to write up a report of the conference. You can add a delay between the Write Final Report task and its predecessor, the Conference task, using the Lag column of the Write Final Report task, or you can add a task between them, naming it something like Conference Wrap-Up, and give it a duration of two days. The method you choose is a matter of personal preference.

How Many Dependencies Are Too Many?

It's quite possible to make one task the successor of many predecessors. Similarly, you can make one task the predecessor of many successor tasks. But you can get caught in the trap of over-thinking your dependencies.

Take a look at this simple example: Suppose that you need to photocopy, fold, and mail a flyer. You could create a finish-to-start dependency between the Photocopy task and the Mail task that indicates that you can't mail the flyer before you photocopy it. But you don't need that dependency.

If you set up a finish-to-start dependency between the Photocopy task and the Fold task, and another finish-to-start dependency between the Fold task and the Mail task, the dependency between the Photocopy and the Mail tasks is built into your schedule—you can't mail the flyer before you photocopy it (see Figure 2-11).

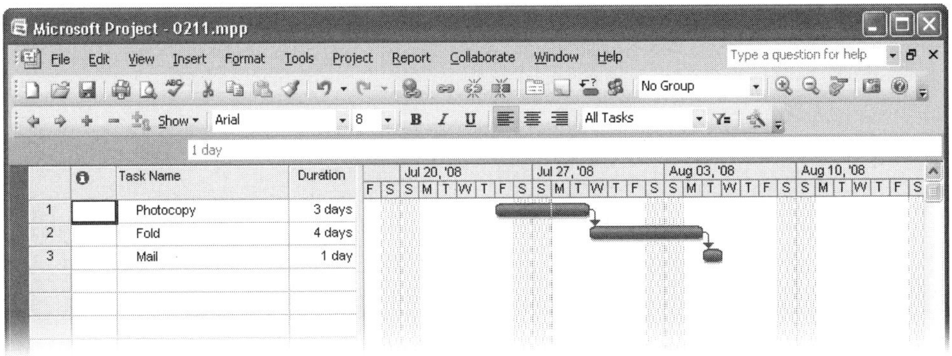

FIGURE 2-11 Don't over-think dependencies.

Also in the arena of avoiding too many dependencies, don't create links between summary tasks or summary tasks and subtasks. Remember that summary tasks in Project are not productive tasks in and of themselves. Instead, they serve the purpose of providing a visual summary of the timing of the subtasks below them, along with a data summary of the cost of those subtasks.

Can you link summary tasks? That is, will Project let you link summary tasks? Project won't stop you, but you shouldn't. Why not? Many circular reference errors in Project ultimately are most often related to links between summary tasks and between subtasks below different summary tasks. The flow of your dependency logic can become very complex and even confusing, particularly if a summary task link conflicts with a subtask link. So, in general, avoid linking summary tasks. Just let them serve their intended purpose: to summarize.

TIP ✓ Outdenting a linked subtask can create a linked summary task. In this case, delete the link from the new summary task as described later in this chapter.

Viewing Dependencies

You can view the dependencies you set in your schedule in a couple of ways—and visualizing the dependencies can help you get a handle on the structure of your project.

Throughout this chapter, I've shown you dependencies in the Gantt Chart view, and we've focused on the position of the link lines and the arrows. You also can use the Task Drivers feature to help you evaluate dependencies in your project. On the Project menu, click Task Drivers, and Project displays information that describes what affects the start date of the currently selected task in the Task Drivers pane at the left edge of the project (see Figure 2-12). The task driver information can include the currently selected task's start date, the number of the predecessor task, the type of link that exists between the two tasks, the amount of lag or lead time between the tasks, leveling delay information, constraint information, and assignment information.

> **TIP** ✓ Don't forget that the Entry table in the Gantt Chart view contains the Predecessors column by default and supplies you with predecessor information.

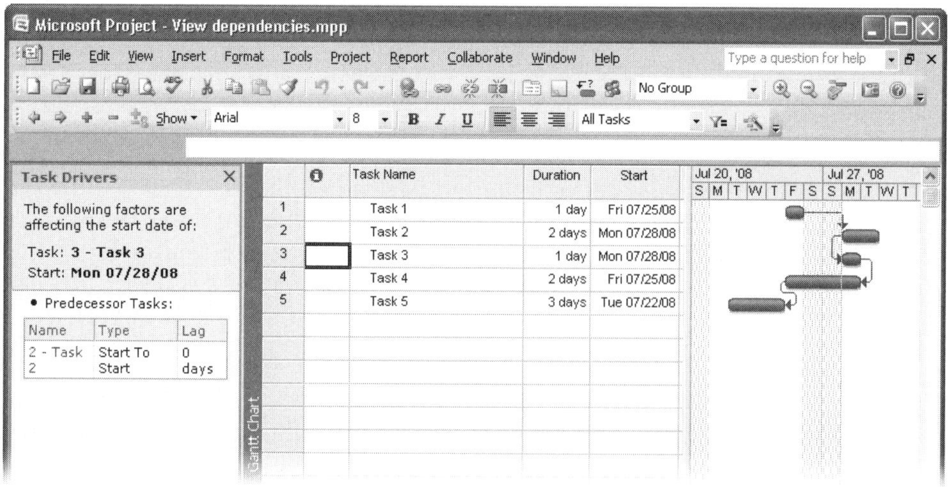

FIGURE 2-12 You can get information that helps you determine what affects the start date of any given task using the Task Drivers feature.

If you want to focus on the flow of your project, use the Network Diagram view. Figure 2-13 displays a Network Diagram view of the same project shown in Figure 2-12. To display this view, on the View menu, click Network Diagram.

Each box in the Network Diagram represents a task in your project and displays information about that task. By default, you'll find start and finish dates, task duration, task ID, and resource information, but you won't find the type of dependency that exists between tasks. The arrows on the Network Diagram do imply predecessor/successor relationships, but the lines don't by default indicate the type of dependencies linking the tasks.

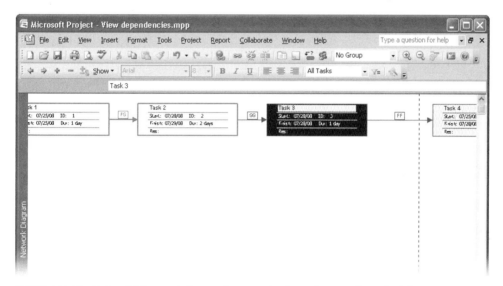

FIGURE 2-13 The Network Diagram helps you focus on the flow of your project schedule.

If you want to view dependency information while using the Network Diagram view, you have two choices:

- You can display the Task Drivers pane by clicking Task Drivers on the Project menu, or

- You can add link labels to the lines between the Network Diagram boxes, as I did in Figure 2-13.

To add link labels to the boxes on the Network Diagram, right-click any white area in the Network Diagram view and click Layout. In the Layout dialog box (see Figure 2-14), select the Show Link Labels check box and click OK. Project adds codes representing the type of dependency to the lines in your Network Diagram.

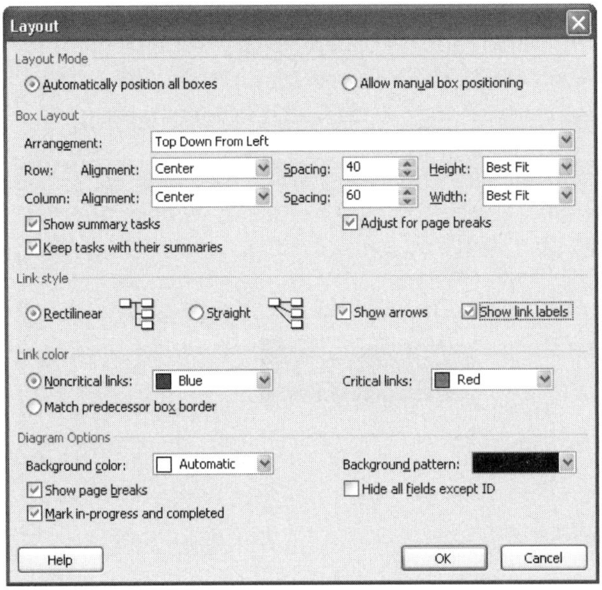

FIGURE 2-14 Add link labels to Network Diagram boxes.

Dependency Actions That Affect Your Plan

In addition to assigning dependencies, you can take a few other actions with respect to dependencies that can affect your project plan. For example, you can delete and create dependencies to an external project. Both these actions can change the timing of tasks in your plan.

TIP ✓	If you turn on Change Highlighting, you can see the tasks affected by actions you take when you make changes to dependencies. To turn this on, click Show Change Highlighting on the View menu.

Deleting Dependencies

As you evaluate your project plan, you might find that you added a dependency that really isn't needed. And, since that dependency might be adding time to your schedule, you'll want to delete it. For example, suppose that your project contains five tasks like those shown in Figure 2-15. As you re-evaluate the schedule, you realize that Task 4 really isn't dependent on the completion of Task 3. As such, you don't need that dependency. No problem—you can easily disconnect the link between the tasks.

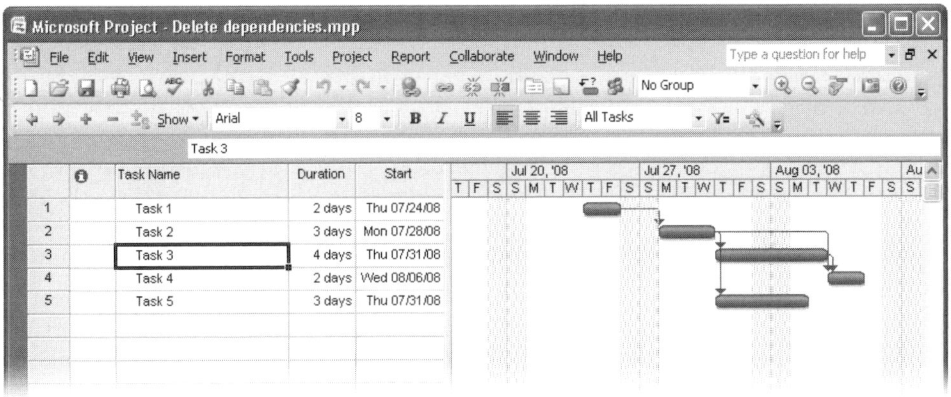

FIGURE 2-15 Task 4 is the successor of both Tasks 2 and 3.

Select the predecessor and successor tasks you want to disconnect by clicking one, pressing and holding Ctrl, and clicking the other one. Then click the Unlink Tasks button on the Standard toolbar. If you turned on Change Highlighting, Project highlights any changes to task start dates due to deleting the dependency.

WARNING Make sure that you select *both* tasks involved in the dependency relationship. If you accidentally select only one of the tasks, Project deletes *all* dependences for the selected task. Should you happen to make this mistake, remember to click the Undo button on the Standard toolbar or press Ctrl+Z.

When you delete the dependency between Task 3 and Task 4, your schedule becomes shorter. If you turned on Change Highlighting, you can see the new start date for Task 4 (see Figure 2-16).

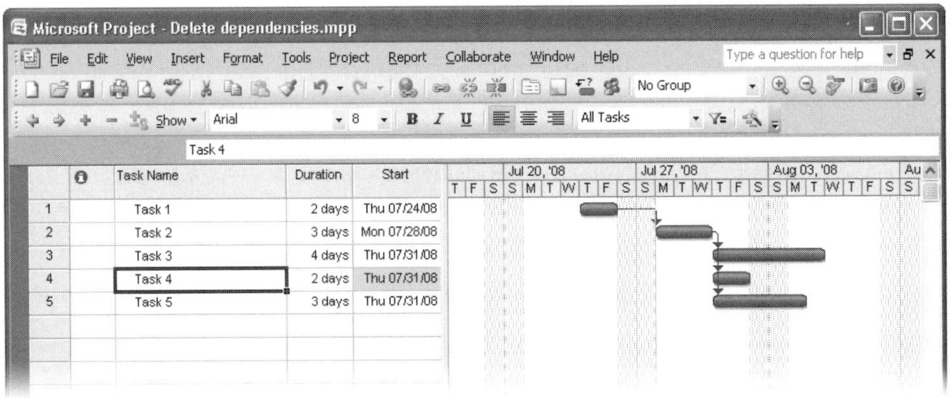

FIGURE 2-16 Removing a dependency can shorten the schedule.

Creating Dependencies to External Projects

It isn't the least bit uncommon to find out that your project actually affects or is affected by other projects. Perhaps a task in one project not only drives the tasks that follow it in that project but also drives the start of another project or a task in another project. Sometimes projects share resources.

To reflect these relationships, you can use consolidation techniques to create a link from a task in one project to a task in another project.

SEE ALSO	You can read about consolidation techniques in Chapter 13, "Managing Cross-Project Conflicts."

Working with Constraints

So far in this chapter, you've seen how dependencies tie the timing of one task to the timing of another task. Dependencies alone do not determine the timing of a task. Unless you assign fixed start and finish dates for a task, Project determines the timing of a task using the task duration, calendars, dependencies, and constraints.

WARNING Should you assign start and finish dates to tasks? More often than not, no. If a task has immutable timing, such as a July 4 celebration on July 4th, use the Start and Finish fields. In most cases, however, you know how many work days you need to complete a task, but you don't know when the work will be done. In these cases, supply a duration and let Project calculate the actual work dates based on the calendars, dependencies, and constraints.

Unlike dependencies, which tie the timing of one task to the timing of another task, *constraints* tie the timing of a task to the start or end of your project or to a specific date.

Understanding the Types of Constraints

If you select Project Start Date in the Schedule From field of the Project Information dialog box discussed in Chapter 1, "Scoping Out Your Project's Details," Project assigns, by default, an As Soon As Possible constraint to every task that you create. If you don't set any dependencies for a particular task, it will, by virtue of the As Soon As Possible constraint, start on the first day of the project.

If you select Project Finish Date in the Schedule From field of the Project Information dialog box, Project assigns, by default, an As Late As Possible constraint to every task that you create. If you don't set any dependencies for a particular task, it will, by virtue of the As Late As Possible constraint, finish on the last day of the project.

> **NOTE** Project sets the constraint automatically when you create a task, so changing the method of scheduling your project from Project Start Date to Project Finish Date, or vice versa, does not affect the constraint.

You can set other constraints:

- If you set an As Late As Possible constraint, Project forces the task to start on the last date possible so that the task ends no later than the end of the project.

- If you set a Finish No Earlier Than constraint or a Finish No Later Than constraint, Project makes sure that the task finishes no sooner or later than a date you supply.

- If you set a Must Start On constraint or a Must Finish On constraint, Project forces the task to start or finish on a date you supply.

- Finally, if you set a Start No Earlier Than constraint or a Start No Later Than constraint, Project makes sure that the task starts no sooner or later than a date you supply.

The Must Finish On constraint and the Must Start On constraint are inflexible constraints—sometimes called *hard constraints*—that force a task to start or end on a particular date. All of the other constraints are flexible constraints—sometimes called *soft constraints*—that force the task to occur within a certain time frame. This distinction is important, because soft constraints allow Project to change the start and finish dates of a task within the parameters of the constraint. Project cannot change the start or finish date of a task with a Must Start On or Must Finish On constraint.

Why do you care? You care because when you run into scheduling conflicts and have Project recalculate your schedule after you make changes to alleviate those problems, Project must work within the confines of all constraints you set. If you set any constraint other than As Soon As Possible or As Late As Possible, Project displays an icon in the Indicators column to alert you to the existence of the constraint. If you place your mouse pointer over the icon, Project displays a tip that describes the constraint (see Figure 2-17).

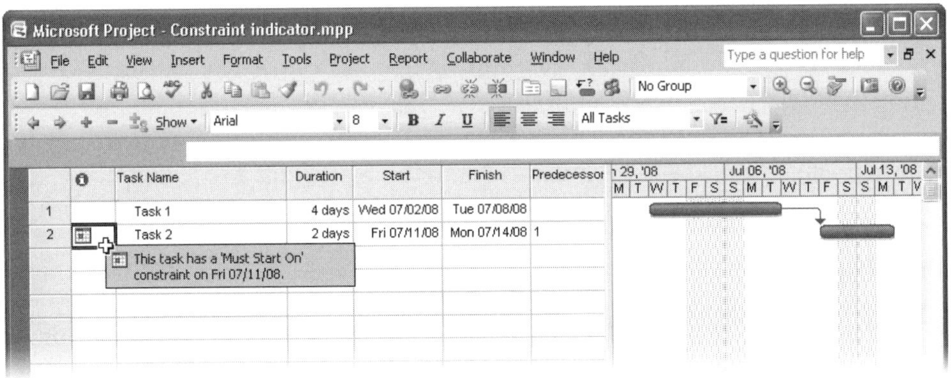

FIGURE 2-17 You can easily identify a task's constraint using the icon in the Indicator column.

WARNING Don't set constraints on summary tasks for the same reasons you shouldn't set dependencies for them. Let summary tasks do their job and summarize the information of the subtasks below them.

How Constraints and Dependencies Affect Each Other

Suppose that your company is moving into new offices that are currently being constructed. You've decided to move people into the offices in groups so that you can deal with problems that arise on a smaller scale without inconveniencing everyone. You've been told that the building will be complete on July 15, so you set up a task in your project to begin moving the first group of people on July 15—and you set a Must Start On constraint for that task; the moves of subsequent groups of people will depend on when the first group finishes moving.

In the new offices, each person will have a cubicle, and each cubicle needs to be assembled. You want the cubicles assembled before you move in the first group of people, so you set a finish-to-start relationship between Assemble Cubicles for Group 1 and Move Group 1. Let's examine the possibilities that can occur if you go ahead and use that Must

Start On constraint. Suppose that cubicle assembly finishes on July 10. In this case, you'll sit around for five days doing nothing, because you can't start the move, based on the Must Start On constraint, until July 15.

But what happens if cubicle assembly can't begin until July 17? In this case, the constraint causes a conflict with the dependency timing, and Project displays a Planning Wizard dialog box to let you know (see Figure 2-18).

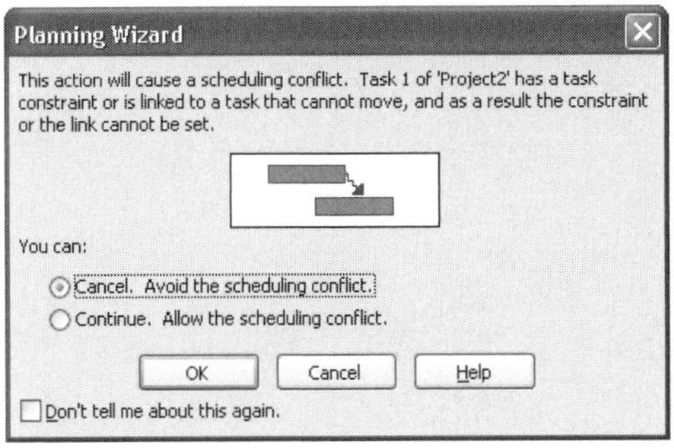

FIGURE 2-18 The Planning Wizard dialog box appears when a constraint causes a conflict with dependency timing.

Choosing Between Dependencies and Constraints

It's important to understand that Project, by default, views constraints as more important than dependencies. If, while calculating your schedule, Project must choose between honoring a constraint and honoring a dependency, Project will honor the constraint. You can change this behavior and make Project honor dependencies over constraints. On the Tools menu, click Options, and click the Schedule tab (see Figure 2-19). Then clear the Tasks Will Always Honor Their Constraint Dates check box.

A better approach, however, is to avoid setting constraints unless they are absolutely necessary. In this example, you might consider using a deadline date instead of a constraint.

SEE ALSO   You'll find information about deadline dates in the next section.

Suppose that you're closing the local office and offering severance packages to employees who don't relocate. If an employee chooses to relocate, you need to make all the arrangements for the employee to move. If an employee opts to leave the company, you need to make the financial arrangements for the severance package.

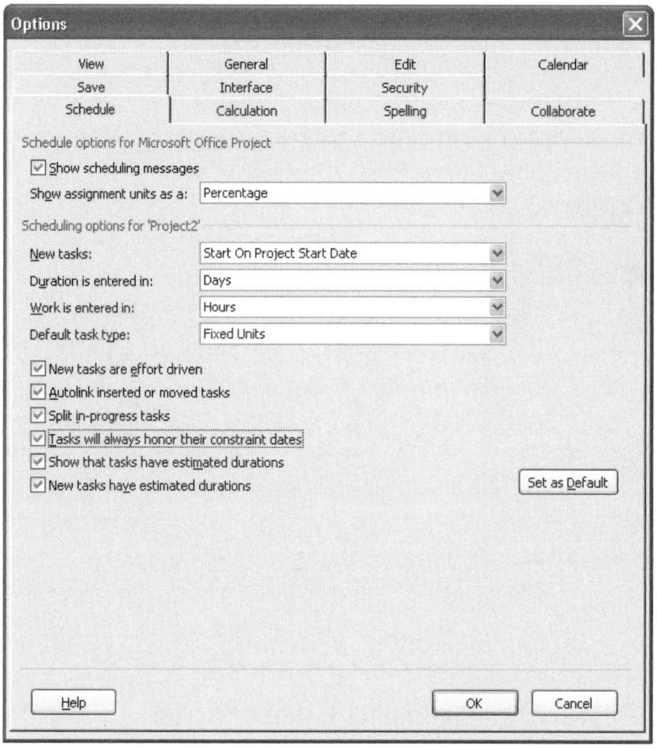

FIGURE 2-19 Project can honor dependencies over constraints.

After you identify all of the tasks associated with relocating and preparing severance packages, you can determine the date by which you must have an answer from each employee. Setting a Must Finish On constraint for the Evaluate Employee Responses task would be appropriate to ensure that you close the local office on time.

Using dependencies, though, truly is the best technique to get an accurate idea of the length of your project. By their very nature, constraints introduce timing factors into your project that might be artificial.

How Do Deadline Dates Work?

Project doesn't use deadline dates when calculating the project schedule for tasks with the As Soon as Possible constraint, so deadlines don't really affect the timing of tasks or of your project. They are instead visual indicators that appear in the chart portion of the Gantt Chart view to help you identify a date important to your project. For example, in the Office Move scenario, you might set the expected starting date for the move—July 15—as a deadline date.

The deadline date indicator appears as a downward pointing arrow on the date you set for the deadline; in Figure 2-20, the deadline date for Task 1 in Phase 2 (on Row 6 of the project) is August 1, and you can see the arrow in the chart portion beside the Gantt bar. You can place your mouse over the deadline date indicator to see a tip containing the deadline date information (I didn't show this in the figure, because the tip would have blocked the deadline indicator).

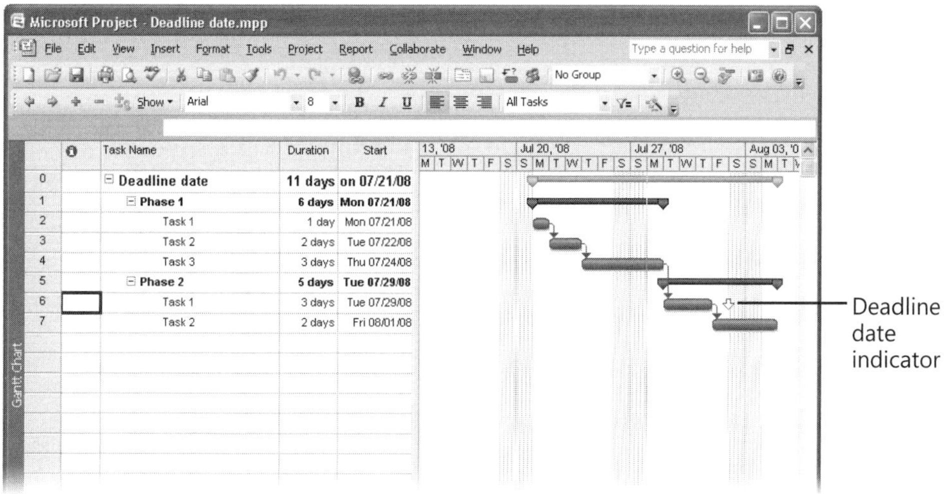

FIGURE 2-20 The deadline date indicator, a downward pointing arrow, appears in the chart portion of the Gantt Chart view on the date set for the deadline.

If the task finishes after the deadline date, Project displays an icon in the Indicators column to alert you that you missed the deadline.

> **NOTE** Project doesn't display an icon in the Indicators column if you complete the task prior to the deadline date.

Although in most cases Project doesn't use deadline dates when calculating a project schedule, deadline dates do affect a Late Finish date and the calculation of total slack for the project. In a project that you schedule from a beginning date, a deadline date has the same effect as a Finish No Later Than constraint when Project calculates slack. If you assign deadline dates to tasks in projects that you schedule from an ending date, those tasks will finish on their deadline dates unless a constraint or a dependency pushes them to an earlier date.

Setting Constraints and Deadlines

You can set constraints and deadline dates on tasks in your project from the Advanced tab of the Task Information dialog box (see Figure 2-21).

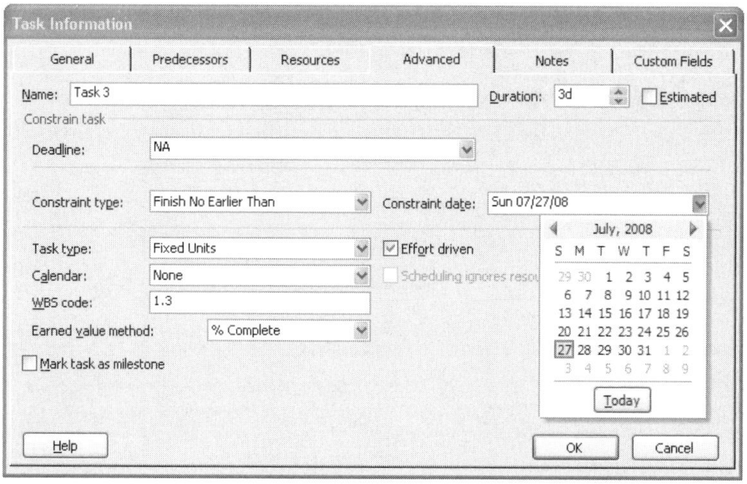

FIGURE 2-21 Set both constraints and deadline dates from the Advanced tab of the Task Information dialog box.

To set a constraint for a particular task, double-click the task, click the Advanced tab, and select a constraint type from the Constraint Type list. For all constraints other than As Late As Possible and As Soon As Possible, designate a date by selecting a date from the calendar that appears when you click the arrow in the Constraint Date field.

Set a deadline date by clicking the arrow next to the Deadline field and choosing a date from the calendar that appears.

What Causes Unexpected Start Dates?

So you've plowed through this chapter, working on dependencies and constraints in your project, and you notice that a successor task's start date doesn't match the predecessor's finish date. You've stuck to simple finish-to-start dependencies, so what's happening?

It's important to remember that a finish-to-start dependency tells Project only that the successor cannot start before the predecessor finishes. The dependency doesn't necessarily drive the successor task's start date.

First, it's possible that you incorporated lag or lead time between the tasks. It's also possible that your project is set to calculate manually and you've made changes without recalculating your project. Press the F9 key to calculate your project.

SWITCHING FROM MANUAL TO AUTOMATIC CALCULATION

You can change calculation from manual to automatic using the Options dialog box. On the Tools menu, click Options, and then click the Calculation tab. For the Calculation Mode setting, select Automatic.

Some people prefer to use manual calculation on large projects so that Project doesn't spend time recalculating the schedule for every change you make. Others prefer to see the effects of every change as it happens. If you find calculation eating up lots of your time, set it to Manual and press F9 when you need to recalculate the schedule.

It's also possible that the successor task's start date doesn't match the predecessor task's finish date because you set a Must Start On, Must Finish On, Start No Later Than, or Finish No Later Than constraint on the successor task. By default, Project honors constraints over dependencies and so will not move the successor task's start date based on dependencies.

Project also won't adjust a successor task's start date if you've recorded any progress on the task. In this case, Project fixes the successor task's start date as its actual start date.

In cases where you've linked two tasks using a finish-to-start dependency, the successor task's start date could be later than the finish date of the predecessor task because:

- The successor task has two predecessors and one is longer than the other; in this case, the successor task's start date will be driven by the finish date of the predecessor that finishes latest.

- You've set a Start No Earlier Than constraint or a Finish No Earlier Than constraint on the successor task.

- The successor task is a subtask of a summary task and you've set a constraint, a dependency, or both on the summary task that forces the summary task's start date.

That last reason, by the way, is one more good reason not to set constraints or dependencies on summary tasks.

CHAPTER 3

Pinning Down Your Budget

ALTHOUGH YOU DON'T ALWAYS NEED TO develop and monitor budgets and costs for projects, understanding how to calculate project costs can make you a better project manager. And, most likely, someday someone will ask you to develop a budget for a project and then monitor the progress of the project to determine how well projected costs matched actual costs. So even if you aren't required to develop and monitor costs for projects, you might want to do so to prepare for the future.

To calculate how much a project will cost, Microsoft Office Project 2007 uses the cost of resources you assign to tasks. In general, if you don't assign resources to tasks, Project won't be able to determine how much your project will cost.

Resources come in different "flavors," and the type of resource you establish determines how Project calculates the cost of the resource. In some cases, the amount of the resource you use affects the cost and possibly the duration of the project; in other cases, the amount of the resource you use affects only the cost but not the duration of the project. In addition, the availability of a resource can affect both the cost and the duration of your project. In this chapter, we'll review the basics of working with resources during the planning phase of your project.

Identifying the Resources You Need

Once you establish the tasks in a project and figure out the order in which they need to happen, you've got a blueprint in place that you can use to help you identify resources you need for your project. Evaluate each task and identify the skills needed to complete the task. Make a list of required skills by task; it helps.

Matching Skill Sets to Skills Needed

If you work in a large organization where you use Microsoft Office Project Server 2007, your organization has probably created a global resource pool. You can let Project match generic skill sets to the global resource pool to determine who could fill the needs for any particular project task. We'll review the "how" of that soon.

But what if you work in a smaller organization where you don't use Project Server, so you don't have a global resource pool that can tell you who has the skills needed to perform a job? Well, on a smaller scale you can create what I like to think of as a skills inventory.

You just made that list of skills per task. Now add a legend to the list that individuals can use to help them rank their proficiency in each skill. For example, you might use 1 for above average, 2 for average, and 3 for limited or minimal proficiency. In addition to ranking proficiency, ask each person to provide an "interest level" for each skill. You might set up an alphabetic scale for interest: you could use use A for exceedingly interested, B for average interest, and C for minimal interest. For example, John might be very proficient (a "1" on the proficiency scale) at research, but he may have little or no interest in doing it because he's done it so much that he finds no challenge in it (a "C" on the interest level scale). Mary, who's slightly less proficient but exceedingly inter-ested in conducting research, might be a better candidate for the job in the long run.

Next, make enough copies of the list so that you can give it to all of the people who might work on your project as well as their direct supervisors. Ask all potential team members to evaluate themselves, and ask each supervisor to evaluate each person who reports to him or her. When they finish and return the forms to you, group the forms you receive for each team member together so that you can compare each individual's assessments of himself or herself with the supervisors' assessments. You'll need to resolve discrepancies before you compile the skills inventory. Talk to both parties to try to determine the true skill and interest levels.

Now you're ready to compile your skills inventory; you can see a sample in Table 3.1. List the skills down the side and the people across the top, or vice versa if it fits better on the paper; you choose. At the intersection of various boxes, use graphics to represent skills and interest. In the figure, I've used an X to represent a primary skill for a person ranked as above average, a circle to represent a secondary skill for a person ranked as average, and I used no symbol at all to represent minimal or limited skills. For interest, I used a square—and I placed it around either a primary or secondary skill if one exists so that I can determine where interest intersects skill. I included the square for each person who indicated an A (exceedingly interested); if I were pressed for resources, I'd probably include another symbol for those who indicated only average interest.

TABLE 3.1 Skills Inventory

	JOHN	JIM	MARY	SUE
Research	X	☐	◉	☒
Writing/documentation		☒	☐	X
Programming	X	◉		
Testing			X	◉

X Primary Skill   ● Secondary Skill   ☐ Interest

It's important to understand that interest can be a driving factor, even when a person has no experience in the area. Suppose, for example, that you need two people to work on writing and documentation, but you don't need two experts. You could assign either John or Sue and add Mary to the team. She can learn from the expert, and given that she's interested, she'll probably be eager for the assignment. I've found that when someone is eager for an assignment, he or she excels at it.

Your skills inventory can help you identify assignments for people who are likely to commit fully to them, further increasing the likelihood that your project will succeed.

If the people you identify to work on your project don't report to you directly, don't forget to follow your company's policy to get those people assigned to your project. You'll probably need to supply the person's name, title, and the skills or knowledge needed for your project. As you begin to make assignments in Project, you'll also be in a position to identify when you're going to need each person.

Don't Forget About Those Non-Human Resources

In addition to identifying the skills you need to complete tasks, also identify non-human resources. For example, you'll need a laboratory if you're performing chemical tests. Or, if your company charges your project for each long-distance call made from a team member's phone, make sure you identify long-distance calling as a resource.

To plan for using these resources, first use your list of tasks and assign the resource to each task, estimating the amount of the resource you'll need. You can create a matrix that lists the tasks down the side and the resources across the top, and at the intersection you can identify the amount that you need; see Table 3.2 for an example.

TABLE 3.2 Proposed Use of Non-Human Resources

	LABORATORY TIME (IN HOURS)	COPIER (NUMBER OF COPIES)	WATER (NUMBER OF GALLONS)
Task 1	2	60	10
Task 2	1	60	15
Task 3	3	60	25

To identify when you'll need these resources, you can create individual charts for each resource that list the tasks down the side and the week in the project across the top, filling in the amount needed in the appropriate intersection. Then you can create a summary chart from the individual charts that shows the resources down the side, the week in the project across the top, and the number of units needed for each non-human resource. But before you manually create these charts, consider adding these non-human resources to your project and then using the Resource Usage report in Project. The Resource Usage report provides the same information as the summarized version you'll have if you prepare the reports manually and includes both human and non-human resources (see Figure 3-1).

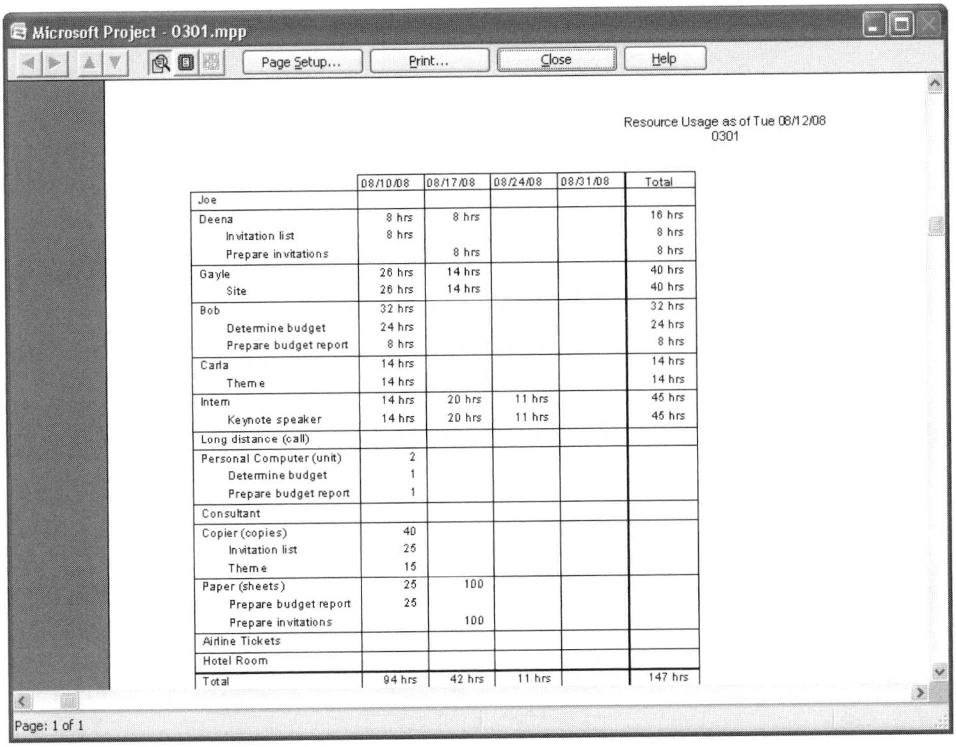

Microsoft Project - 0301.mpp

Page Setup...   Print...   Close   Help

Resource Usage as of Tue 08/12/08
0301

	08/10/08	08/17/08	08/24/08	08/31/08	Total
Joe					
Deena	8 hrs	8 hrs			16 hrs
Invitation list	8 hrs				8 hrs
Prepare invitations		8 hrs			8 hrs
Gayle	26 hrs	14 hrs			40 hrs
Site	26 hrs	14 hrs			40 hrs
Bob	32 hrs				32 hrs
Determine budget	24 hrs				24 hrs
Prepare budget report	8 hrs				8 hrs
Carla	14 hrs				14 hrs
Theme	14 hrs				14 hrs
Intern	14 hrs	20 hrs	11 hrs		45 hrs
Keynote speaker	14 hrs	20 hrs	11 hrs		45 hrs
Long distance (call)					
Personal Computer (unit)	2				
Determine budget	1				
Prepare budget report	1				
Consultant					
Copier (copies)	40				
Invitation list	25				
Theme	15				
Paper (sheets)	25	100			
Prepare budget report	25				
Prepare invitations		100			
Airline Tickets					
Hotel Room					
Total	94 hrs	42 hrs	11 hrs		147 hrs

Page: 1 of 1

FIGURE 3-1 The Resource Usage report summarizes the needs for various resources during your project.

SEE ALSO   See Chapter 9, "Determining How to Communicate with Your Team," for information on printing reports.

UNDERSTANDING DIRECT AND INDIRECT COSTS

When you hear accountants talk about costs, they often refer to direct costs and indirect costs. *Direct costs* refer to costs incurred specifically for your project. Equipment you rent to complete your project and the salaries of your team members while they work on your project are direct costs of your project. Think of determining direct costs this way: If your project weren't happening, would the costs be incurred? If the answer is no, you're probably looking at a direct cost.

Indirect costs, on the other hand, are the costs that your company incurs and would incur even if your project weren't happening. For example, your company probably rents an office location where everybody works. If your project weren't happening, your company would still rent that office and incur the rent and utilities costs associated with the office.

Direct costs are fairly easy to identify, but identifying indirect costs can be tricky. Some organizations develop a rate to represent these indirect costs; in these cases, you'll have additional costs on your project that allocate to your project its share of the cost of running the company. The indirect cost rate is usually built in to the amount per hour your company assigns to each human resource who works on your project, and you won't need to do anything to account for these costs. If the indirect cost rate isn't built in to the amount per hour your company assigns to each human resource, and you're expected to account for indirect costs in your project budget, ask your financial people for guidance on how you should make the calculation.

Choosing the Right Resource Type

Distinguishing between human and non-human resources is fairly straightforward and easy: if it breathes, it's human. However, although you still want to account for all the resources you'll use on your project, when you set up resources in Project, you don't make the distinction quite that directly.

Project lets you define three types of resources: Work, Material, and Cost. Work resources are usually people. Costs for Work resources are always calculated based on some increment of time. You can think of Material resources as resources consumed during your project. Costs for Material resources are calculated based on some unit of measurement other than time. Cost resources don't have a unit of measure that allows you to calculate cost easily. People—Work resources—typically cost money per hour. Photocopies—Material resources—cost money per copy. Airline Tickets—Cost resources—are typically treated as a total cost.

The gray area appears when you consider resources such as long-distance phone calls, which cost money per minute. Obviously, long-distance phone calls aren't people (using my previous loose definition for Work resources concerning breathing). But in Project, long-distance phone calls, for which you pay by the minute, are considered Work resources because Project reserves costs for all time-related unit measurements for Work resources. So when setting up your resource, your rule of thumb for choosing between a Work resource and a Material resource is to determine by the unit measurement associated with the resource. If you incur costs for the resource per second, minute, hour, day, week, month, or year, set it up as a Work resource. If you use some other measurement, such as per copy or per gallon, set it up as a Material resource.

> **NOTE** If your organization allocates the cost for long-distance charges using a flat rate, such as $.25 per call, you can set up long-distance phone calls as a Material resource. As a rule of thumb, try to set up only labor resources as Work resources whenever possible.

A Cost resource, the third type of resource available in Project, is a resource for which the cost you incur doesn't depend on the amount of work or the duration of a task. Airline tickets and hotel expenses for a trip needed to complete a task are Cost resources. You'll find more information about these expenses in Chapter 7, "Taming That Monster Budget."

> **NOTE** You also can assign a fixed cost to a task and a cost per use to a resource, but assigning these types of costs doesn't depend on establishing a particular resource type. I'll talk about using these costs in the section "Assigning Resource Costs" later in this chapter.

Creating Resources in a Project

If you are using Project Standard or Project Professional without Project Server, you can set up the resources available to you for the project using the Resource Sheet view.

NOTE If your organization shares resources among projects, the information that follows still applies to you, but you might also want to take advantage of resource pooling. See Chapter 13, "Manging Cross-Project Conflicts," for more information before you set up resources in your project.

You can create any of the three types of resources using the same basic approach:

1. On the View menu, click Resource Sheet to display the Resource Sheet view shown here:

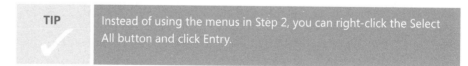

2. If you don't see the Entry table shown in the above graphic, on the View Menu, point to Table, and then click Entry.

TIP Instead of using the menus in Step 2, you can right-click the Select All button and click Entry.

3. In the Resource Name column, type the resource's name.

4. In the Type column, select a resource type (Work, Material, Cost).

5. For a Material resource, use the Material Label column to type the unit in which you measure the resource.

6. For Work and Material resources, type their standard rate (per unit of measure) in the Std. Rate column. For Work resources, if an overtime rate applies, type it in the Ovt. Rate column. The Overtime Rate field is not available for Material resources, which makes sense because there is no way of distinguishing how many units (based on the Material unit of measure) would be considered regular and how many would be overtime.

Project fills in the Initials column and the Max. Units column automatically, assumes standard overtime rates, and sets cost per use rates at $0. Project also sets all resource costs to accrue on a prorated basis and assigns the calendar used by the project to each resource. You can make changes to most of these fields, depending on the type of resource you define. For example, for a Cost resource, you can change the initials and the way Project accrues costs, but you can't change the Max. Units field, any of the rate fields, or the Base Calendar field. For Material resources, you can change all of the fields except for ones that relate to working time, such as the Max Units field, the Ovt. Rate field, and the Base Calendar field. For Work resources, you can change any of the fields.

> **TIP** ✓ You can create generic resources, like the Intern resource you see in the graphic in step 1. You use generic resources when you don't know the exact person who's going to perform the job. Instead, you name the resource using a job title or description. In the Project Server environment, you can select the Generic check box in the Resource Information dialog box and use the Enterprise Global Resource Pool (discussed in the following section) and the Resource Substitution wizard to help you find people who meet the qualifications of the generic resource.

Resources and Project Server

If your organization uses Project Server, you can take advantage of the Enterprise Resource Pool, which provides a list of all resources that are owned by your organization. Instead of creating resources in your project as described in the preceding section, you can select resources for a project using the Team Builder feature and the Enterprise Resource Pool.

BOOKING TYPES

If you're setting up resources in a project that will eventually end up in the Project Server database, you can use the Booking Type list in the Resource Information dialog box shown in the graphic below to describe a resource's assignment to all tasks in your project. If you click Committed in the Booking Type list, you officially assign the resource to the project. If you click Proposed, you indicate that the resource is not yet officially assigned to the project. If you then load your project into the Project Server database, any Proposed resource's calendar isn't affected by your project. If another project manager chooses to commit the resource to a different project for the same timeframe, Project will permit it and not identify the resource as being overallocated.

To assign resources to a project using the Enterprise Resource Pool, log on to Project Server and open the project to which you want to assign resources. Then on the Tools menu, click Build Team From Enterprise to display the Build Team dialog box (see Figure 3-2).

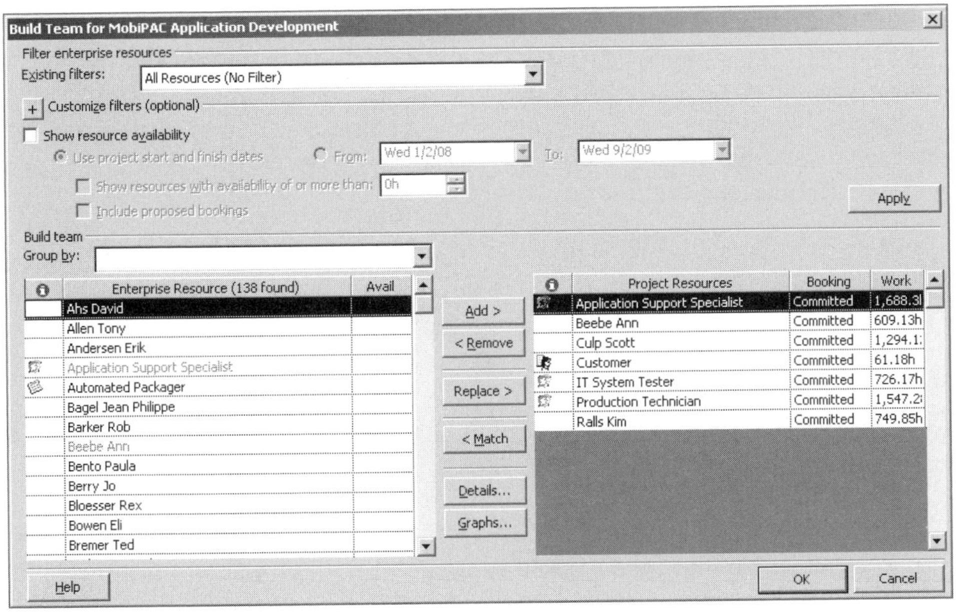

FIGURE 3-2 This dialog box helps you select resources from the Enterprise Resource Pool for your project.

By default, Project displays all resources in the Enterprise Resource Pool, but you can limit the resources that you see by applying filters using the Existing Filters list. You also can create custom filters by clicking the plus sign (+) beside the Customize Filters field. And you can use the Show Resource Availability section to filter for resources that are available on a set of dates.

Once you select resources and click OK, the resources you selected appear on the Resource Sheet of your project. You're now ready to assign resources to tasks.

Assigning Resources to Tasks

By assigning a standard rate to a resource, you've taken the first basic step to assigning costs to your project. Although there are several other ways to assign costs, let's take a look at the effects of the simplest case, where you assign a resource with a standard rate to a task. In Project, the cost of your project is a mathematical calculation. Project applies the cost of each resource assigned to a task and calculates a cost for each task. The cost of your project is the sum of all of the tasks' costs.

The method you use to assign resources to tasks doesn't depend on whether you are working on a stand-alone project or an Enterprise project stored in the Project Server database. You can assign resources to tasks from most of the Task views; in this example, I use the Gantt Chart view. The table you select isn't important, but I've selected the Cost table so that you can see the effects on costs when you add resources to a task. Follow these steps to add resources to a task:

1. In the table portion of the view, click the name of the task to which you want to assign a resource.

2. Click the Assign Resources button or, on the Tools menu, click Assign Resources to open the Assign Resources dialog box:

3. In the Resource Name column, click the resource that you want to assign.

> **TIP** If you forgot to define a resource, you can define it here; just type the name of the resource in a blank cell in the Resource Name column.

4. Use the Units column to identify the amount of the resource you need.

> **NOTE** By default, Project assigns 100%—one unit—of Work resources, so you don't need to type anything if you want to assign a Work resource full-time to the task. To assign a resource to work half-time on the task, type 50; you don't need to supply the percent sign (%). For Material resources, Project assigns one unit of the resource by default.

5. Click Assign. Project displays a check mark beside the resource's name to indicate that the resource is assigned to the selected task. Project also calculates the resource's cost using the cost you supplied when you defined the resource.

6. Repeat Steps 3, 4, and 5 to assign additional resources to the selected task, or click Close.

> **TIP** ✓ If you're using Project Server and you intend to use the Resource Substitution wizard, use the R/D field to indicate whether you need a specific resource or any resource with the required skills. Type **R**—for Request—to indicate that you can use any resource with the skills required for the task, or type **D**—for Demand—to indicate that you need a specific resource.

Assigning Resource Costs

In many cases, the costs you define for Work and Material resources on the Resource Sheet are sufficient. In some cases, however, you need more flexibility. Suppose that your project involves printing brochures, and there's a $50 fee each time you set up the press to print along with the per-copy cost. Or suppose you need to rent a van for a day to transport tools from one location to another, and the van rental fee is a flat $19.95 for the day (it's probably an old used van, but since it runs and you only need it for the day, you don't care). And then there's the issue of determining when Project assigns costs to your tasks. In this section, we'll explore assigning a cost per use to a resource, adding fixed costs to a project or task, and setting cost accrual methods.

> **SEE ALSO**   Because Cost resources are really their own breed, you can find more
> information about them in Chapter 7.

Assigning a Cost per Use to a Resource

Suppose that a particular medical procedure requires the use of a particular instrument. The instrument costs $100 per hour to use, but there's a calibration fee of $500 to use the instrument. The instrument would be a Work resource (remember, you can't assign "per hour" rates to a Material resource) with an associated cost of $100 per hour plus a Cost Per Use fee of $500.

If you hire a consultant who charges you a fixed price to perform a task, regardless of the amount of work or the time involved in doing the work, you can set up the consultant as a Work resource with no hourly rate in the Std. Rate column; instead, supply the fixed price of the consultant in the Cost/Use column. This approach allows you to assign a cost to a task without affecting its duration. In addition, you can at some future time change the resource's rate or availability, and Project will factor in the change.

Establishing a cost per use is a simple matter; supply the value in the Cost/Use column on the Resource Sheet view. But can you establish different costs per use for a resource? Yes, you can, using the technique described in Chapter 7.

Assigning Fixed Costs

Fixed costs are typically single costs you add to a task or a project to account for some charge that doesn't depend on a resource. For example, suppose that one task in your project involves testing three chemicals for their reactions under certain conditions, and your own laboratory is very busy and can't schedule the tests in a timely fashion. You make some calls and find out that you can hire the services of an outside laboratory to do the job when you need it done for $1,000, and delaying the project to use your own lab will force other resources to sit around and do nothing, costing your project about $1,500 in lost time. So you hire the outside laboratory for a fee of $1,000. You set up a Perform Laboratory Tests task in your project to account for the time needed to perform the tests, but you don't need to assign any of your own resources to it. To account for the $1,000 cost of the task, you add a fixed cost to the Perform Laboratory Tests task.

WARNING Suppose that you hire a consultant who charges you a fixed price to perform a task; you might be tempted to account for the consultant's cost as a fixed cost assigned to the task. But if you use this approach and the consultant's availability or rate changes partway through the task, you won't be able to account for the change. Instead, for this scenario use the Cost Per Use approach described in the preceding section.

To assign a fixed cost to a task, follow these steps:

1. On the View menu, click Gantt Chart to display your project in the Gantt Chart view.

2. Right-click the Select All button and click Cost. Project displays the Cost table of the Gantt Chart:

3. Select the task to which you want to assign the fixed cost.

4. Type the amount of the cost in the Fixed Cost column.

> **NOTE** You can assign only one fixed cost to a task. If you need to assign multiple fixed costs to a task, consider using Cost resources as described in the next section.

You can assign a fixed cost to your entire project. You might use this approach if your organization tells you to account for overhead costs for your project using a lump sum number that they supply. To assign a fixed cost to your entire project, select the Project Summary task in Step 3 above. If you don't see the Project Summary task, on the Tools menu, click Options to display the Options dialog box shown in Figure 3-3. Click the View tab, select the Show Project Summary Task check box, and click OK.

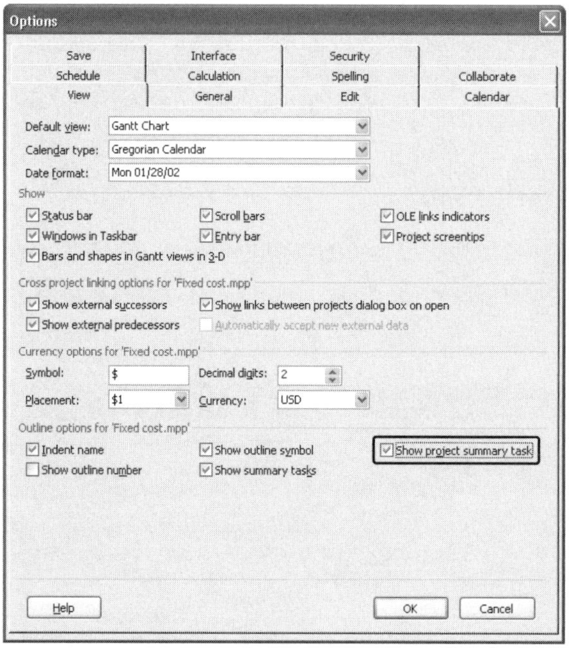

FIGURE 3-3 In the Options dialog box, on the View tab, you can select Show Project Summary Task.

How Cost Accrual Methods Work

The way you accrue costs controls the timing Project uses to apply costs to your tasks. Although accruing costs differently won't change the overall cost of your project, the accrual method you choose can make your project seem to be over or under budget at any particular point in time.

By default, Project accrues the cost of each resource by prorating the cost—distributing it evenly—over the life of the task to which you assigned the resource. You can opt, however, to have Project calculate the cost of the resource at the beginning or the end of the task. For example, if the month-long Create Report task culminates in producing 50 copies of the report, you might want to accrue the cost of the copier—a Material resource—at the end of the task, since that's when you'll actually use it.

To change the timing Project uses to accrue the cost of a resource, use the Resource Sheet view (on the View menu, click Resource Sheet). For the resource for which you want to change the timing of cost accrual, click the Accrue At field. Project displays a list box arrow; click it to display your choices and make a selection (see Figure 3-4).

	❶	Resource Name	Type	Material Label	Initials	Group	Max. Units	Std. Rate	Ovt. Rate	Cost/Use	Accrue At	Base Calendar
1		Joe	Work		J		100%	$25.00/hr	$0.00/hr	$0.00	Prorated	Standard
2		Deena	Work		D		100%	$25.00/hr	$0.00/hr	$0.00	Prorated	Standard
3		Gayle	Work		G		100%	$20.00/hr	$0.00/hr	$0.00	Prorated	Standard
4		Bob	Work		B		100%	$30.00/hr	$35.00/hr	$0.00	Prorated	Standard
5		Carla	Work		C		100%	$25.00/hr	$0.00/hr	$0.00	Prorated	Standard
6	📝🖊	Intern	Work		I		200%	$10.00/hr	$0.00/hr	$0.00	Prorated	Standard
7		Long distance	Material	call	L			$0.00			$0.25	Prorated
8		Personal Computer	Material	unit	P			$0.00			$25.00	Prorated
9		Consultant	Work		C		100%	$0.00/hr	$0.00/hr	$1,500.00	Prorated	Standard
10		Copier	Material	copies	C			$0.10		$0.00	Prorated
11		Paper	Material	sheets	P			$0.10			Start
12		Airline Tickets	Cost		A						Prorated
13		Hotel Room	Cost		H						End

FIGURE 3-4 Use the Accrue At column to change the timing Project uses to accrue costs for a resource.

Be aware that Project uses the accrual timing you select for a resource for every task to which you assign the resource. So if you use that copier throughout another task, you might want to create two versions of the copier so that you can accrue its costs in two different ways.

How Organizational Structure Affects Resource Availability

In Project, resource availability is driven by calendars. But in reality, resource availability is driven by your organization's structure. Before we dive in and examine Project and resource availability, let's examine how organizational structure can affect resource availability.

Managing Projects from a Central Office

Some organizations that manage projects use a traditional hierarchical structure with an executive office and departments of finance, operations, and sales, with individuals running these departments. To accommodate projects, these organizations have one central "Department of Special Projects," which is staffed to meet the needs of projects in the organization. As a project manager in this environment, you work in a specialty unit and all of the staff in this unit do nothing but work on projects. You typically have a specific staff that works just for you on all projects you manage. You set priorities for this staff and resolve assignment conflicts. You evaluate your staff's performance and control performance appraisal, and approve raises, promotions, and requests for leave.

Handling Projects As They Arise

Some organizations that manage and complete projects use a hierarchical organizational structure that addresses project management on a project-by-project basis. In this organization, you'll find the typical executive office and departments of finance, operations, and sales, with individuals running these departments. When it comes to completing projects, there's no "Department of Special Projects." Instead, projects are staffed by people from varying functional areas in your company. In this environment, you might find yourself with people whom you manage administratively—that is, you control administrative activities such as performance appraisal and approving raises, promotions, and requests for leave. You might also find yourself with different people whom you manage in a project environment, where you oversee their day-to-day work but have little or no input on administrative issues.

Managing Projects Within Each Functional Unit

Some organizations use a hierarchical structure and, within each department area, they establish a "Department of Special Projects." This organization matches the traditional hierarchical structure in the way things occur: As a project manager in this environment, you work in a specialty unit within a functional department and you typically have a specific staff that works for you on projects. You set priorities for this staff and resolve assignment conflicts. You evaluate your staff's performance and control administrative activities such as performance appraisal and approving raises, promotions, and requests for leave.

How Organizational Structures Impact Project Management

Each of the three above-mentioned company organizations has pros and cons for getting the job done. For example, the organization that has a company-wide special projects department tends to select projects to perform using consistent criteria, and the project team reports to the same manager for daily work and for administrative activities such as performance appraisal. However, in this situation the project team may not be completely familiar with the functional requirements of the unit that requested the project, making the project take longer to complete. And the workflow of the Department of Special Projects tends to be a "feast or famine" situation—either there's too much work or not enough work.

The organizations that handle projects as they arise typically can assemble teams quickly and usually gain support from the various functional units because supplying personnel to those projects helps the functional unit see the benefits of the project. On the other hand, this same structure makes team members report to two managers and requires coordination between a project manager and an administrative manager.

The organizations that set up a Department of Special Projects in each functional unit have the same advantages as organizations with a single, company-wide Department of Special Projects. No "two manager" problems here. In the disadvantage column, these organizations don't fare well when a project crosses over functional unit lines. Further, the chances increase for overlap and duplication in projects because multiple functional units might try to tackle the same project.

But we're not here to reorganize your company's structure. Instead, we need to work within it. As long as you recognize what structure your company uses, you'll be in a good position to understand how to deal with the people who work on your projects.

Understanding How Availability Affects Your Project

Many of the resources you use on a project affect the length of time needed to complete a task. On these effort-driven tasks, one person might complete the job in 30 days, while two people might be able to complete the job in half the time, and three people in one third of the time. If the cost of all three resources is the same, using one or three people won't affect the cost of your project; rather, the number of people you use will affect only the project's duration. That's the simple, straightforward, mathematical approach.

In a perfect world, you'd have all the resources you need to complete your project exactly when you need them. But we don't live in a perfect world. So when you're planning a project, you need to recognize that you won't have all of the resources you need all of the time. Some resources might be available to work on your project only for a certain time period. Other resources might have vacation time scheduled. If you identify a resource's availability in Project, you can use the information to make sure that you don't accidentally assign a resource to a task when the resource isn't available.

> **NOTE** If your organization shares resources among projects, the information that follows still applies to you, but you may also want to take advantage of resource pooling. See Chapter 13 for more information on sharing resources.

Accounting for Availability

You are bound to run into cases in which a resource is available to you for only some portion of the time your project will be running. Suppose that your project begins on August 1 and a particular resource won't become available to you until September 1. To account for the resource's availability, use the Resource Information dialog box.

On the Resource Sheet view (on the View menu, click Resource Sheet), double-click the resource to display the Resource Information dialog box (see Figure 3-5). Use the Resource Availability table on the General tab to set dates that describe when the resource will be available. You can set both starting and ending dates or set just a starting date. And if the resource will be available to you only part-time, use the Units column to specific a percentage less than 100 percent.

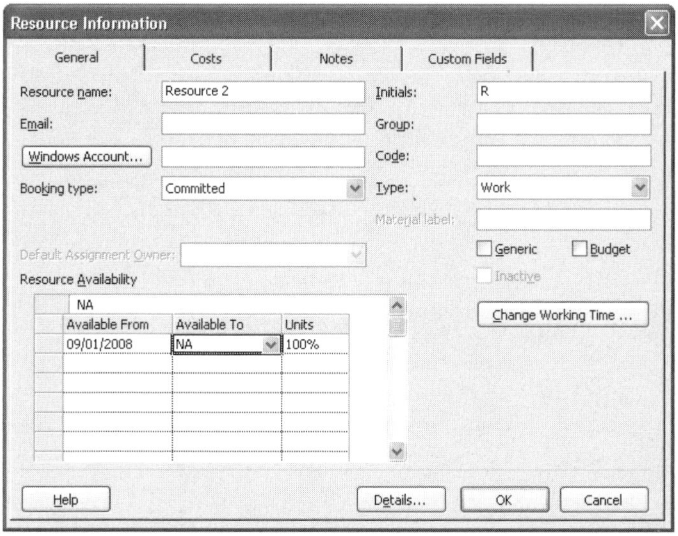

FIGURE 3-5 Use the Resource Availability table to identify the dates a resource is available.

Setting Resource Calendars

You use a resource's calendar to set exceptions to working time for a particular resource. Don't get crazy here; if a resource is taking a half day off once for a doctor's appointment, you really don't need to set the exception on the resource's calendar; in all likelihood, the resource will make up the time over the life of the project.

But if a resource has a two-week vacation planned in the middle of your project, you should set up that exception on the resource's calendar to avoid assigning work to that resource during that period. Or if a resource's work week doesn't match the calendar assigned to the project—suppose that the resource works a 32-hour week, Monday through Thursday—you should set up all Fridays as non-working days on the resource's calendar.

To set up an exception to a resource's calendar, follow these steps:

1. Double-click the resource on the Resource Sheet to open the Resource Information dialog box.

2. On the General tab, click the Change Working Time button. Project displays the resource's calendar with today's date selected.

3. On the Exceptions tab, type a name in the Name column that helps you remember the purpose of the exception.

4. In the Start column, select the date on which the exception starts from the calendar that appears.

5. In the Finish column, select the date on which the exception ends. Project sets every day between the starting and ending dates as an exception on the calendar:

SETTING UP A WORK WEEK EXCEPTION

To set up a work week exception for a resource who, for example, doesn't work on Fridays, use the Work Weeks tab. Type a name for the exception such as "Off Fridays," set starting and ending dates, and then click the Details button. Project displays the Details For dialog box.

Select the Set Days To Nonworking Time option and click OK. When Project redisplays the Change Working Time dialog box, all of the days you specified between the beginning and ending dates appear underlined on the calendar; all Fridays appear shaded darker than Mondays through Thursdays.

Checking Availability While Assigning Resources

Once you establish a resource's availability, you can take advantage of your work while you assign resources. Earlier in this chapter, I showed you the basics for assigning resources. But now that you've factored in resource availability, let's see how you can use the availability information while making assignments to avoid assigning an unavailable resource.

Let's examine a simple case—you've got Tasks 1, 2, and 3 in your project, which begins on August 1, and you've got Resources 1 and 2 set up in the project. While working in the Gantt Chart view (on the View menu, click Gantt Chart), you select Task 1 and then click the Assign Resources button to display the Assign Resources window. Initially, both resources appear in the window (see Figure 3-6).

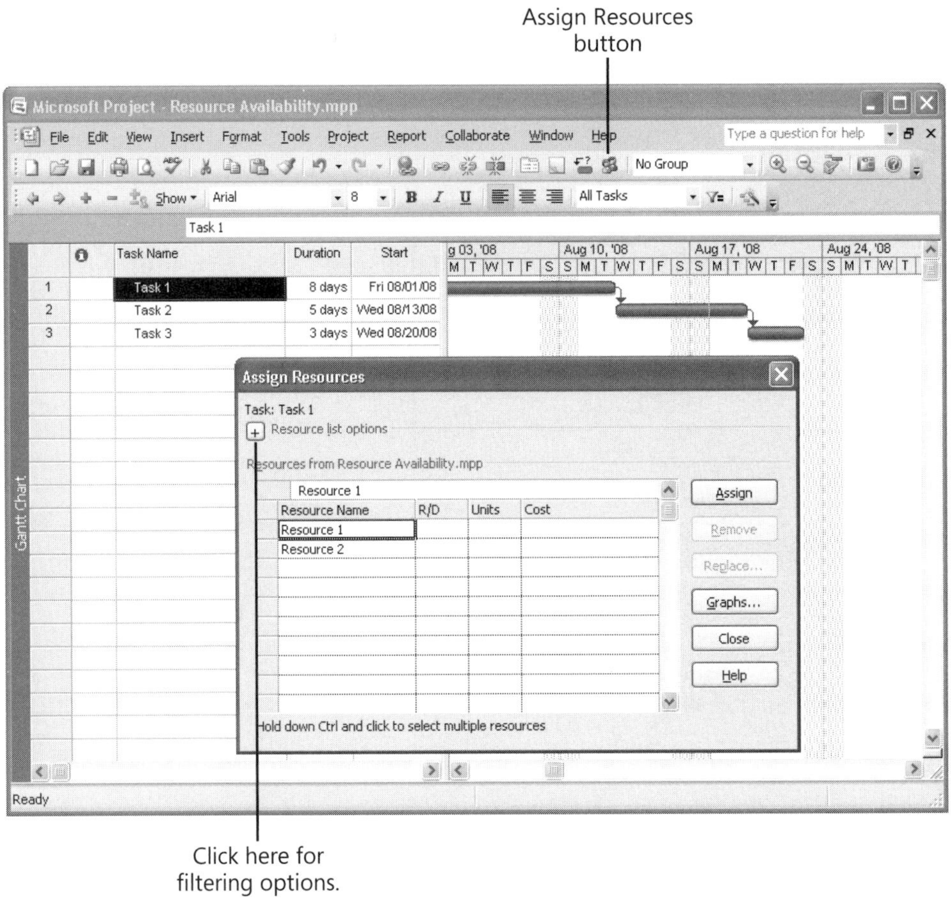

Assign Resources
button

FIGURE 3-6 Click the Resource List Options plus sign (+) to hide and display options you can use to filter available resources.

You can check availability before you make an assignment if you click the Resource List Options plus sign (+). Then select Available To Work and specify the number of hours per day a resource needs to be available for the task you selected. Project hides any resources not available to work in the timeframe of Task 1 based on examining their availability and their resource calendars and comparing that information to the duration of the selected task (see Figure 3-7).

In this example, when you filter for resources available to work 80 hours—the 10 days the task is scheduled to last—Project shows you that neither resource is available. In this example, Resource 1 is scheduled for a two-week vacation running from August 11 to 22, and Resource 2 doesn't become available to work on the project until September 1. However, in the real world, I won't be around to tell you why resources are not available. But you don't need me; you can find out why these resources aren't available for yourself.

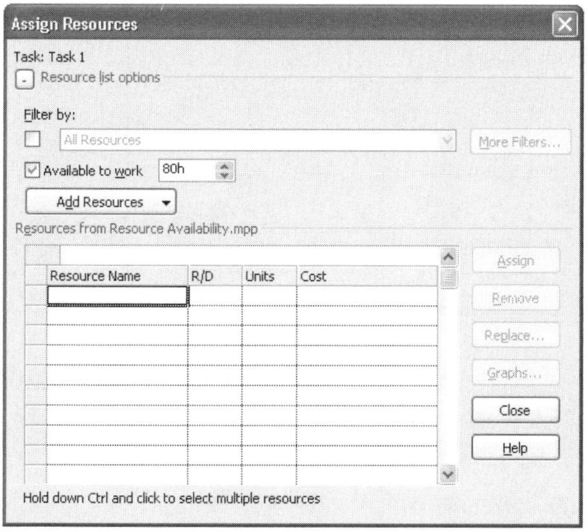

FIGURE 3-7 Filter for resources available to work the 10-day duration of the task.

To see what's going on with your two resources, you can use the Graphs button in the Assign Resources window. First, clear your Available To Work filter so that you can see your resources; then click a resource and click the Graphs button.

> **TIP** You can display the graphs described below for more than one resource at a time. Press and hold the Ctrl key as you click each resource you want to graph. Then click the Graphs button.

Three graphs, which relate to the resource you selected and not to the task for which you're considering assignment, are available in the Graphs window that appears:

- The Work graph shows the amount of work that is assigned to the selected resource on a day-by-day basis.

- The Assignment Work graph breaks down the total workload of the resource that you're considering, showing you the resource's workload on the selected task, other tasks, and the resource's total availability based on the calendar. Using this graph helps you to see whether you'll overallocate the resource by assigning it to this task.

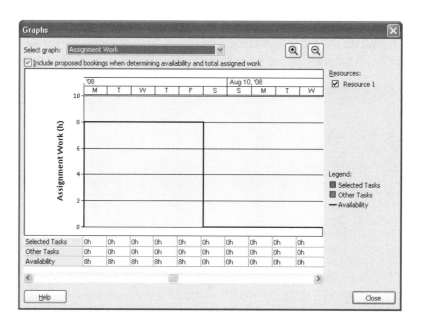

- The Remaining Availability graph shows you only the resource's unassigned time.

TIP   You also can view the Remaining Availability graph from the Resource Center in Project Web Access if your organization uses Project Server.

Because the Assignment Work graph shows you what's going on with the resource's work-load on both the selected task and other tasks, you often can spot an overallocation situation before it happens. In this example, Resource 1 isn't assigned to any tasks beginning August 11, but Resource 1 also is not available. That information tells you that something is going on with the resource's availability or calendar, and helps you avoid making an assignment that can't be completed by this resource.

Using Overtime Wisely

Sometimes you can avoid overallocating a resource. Assign overtime sparingly for two reasons:

- Typically, a resource's overtime rate is higher than the resource's regular rate, so assigning overtime can make your project more expensive to complete.

- Assigning overtime as a regular practice causes people to burn out and their work to suffer.

While you might think that you can simply replace a burned-out employee who quits, people are actually your most costly resource. You invest money to train them and get them up to speed on the way your company operates, so replacing an employee costs your company money. So don't make assigning overtime a regular practice—make it the exception to the rule.

> **SEE ALSO** For details on assigning overtime, see Chapter 6, "Solving Resource Conflicts."

Printing Cost Reports

You've already seen that you can use the Cost table to view costs on-screen. There are a couple of reports related to project costs you might want to print, such as the Cash Flow report (see Figure 3-8) and the Budget report (see Figure 3-9), which might be most useful after you set a baseline and begin tracking actual costs in your project.

Microsoft Project - Budgeting.mpp

Page Setup... | Print... | Close | Help

Cash Flow as of Mon 08/18/08
Budgeting.mpp

	08/10/08	08/17/08	08/24/08	08/31/08	Total
Budgeting					
Meeting					
Planning					
Determine budget	$745.00				$745.00
Prepare budget report	$267.50				$267.50
Invitation list	$202.50				$202.50
Prepare invitations		$230.00			$230.00
Identify Basic Components					
Theme	$351.50				$351.50
Site	$997.75	$537.25			$1,535.00
Keynote speaker	$702.50	$85.00			$787.50
Select & Reserve					
Caterer					
Bartenders					
Security					
Photographers					
Cleanup Crew					
Entertainment					
Baseball Game					
Opera					
Media					
Alert community					
Press release					
Rent Equipment					
PA System					
Total	$3,266.75	$852.25			$4,119.00

Page: 1 of 1

FIGURE 3-8 The Cash Flow report shows you task costs in a week-by-week view.

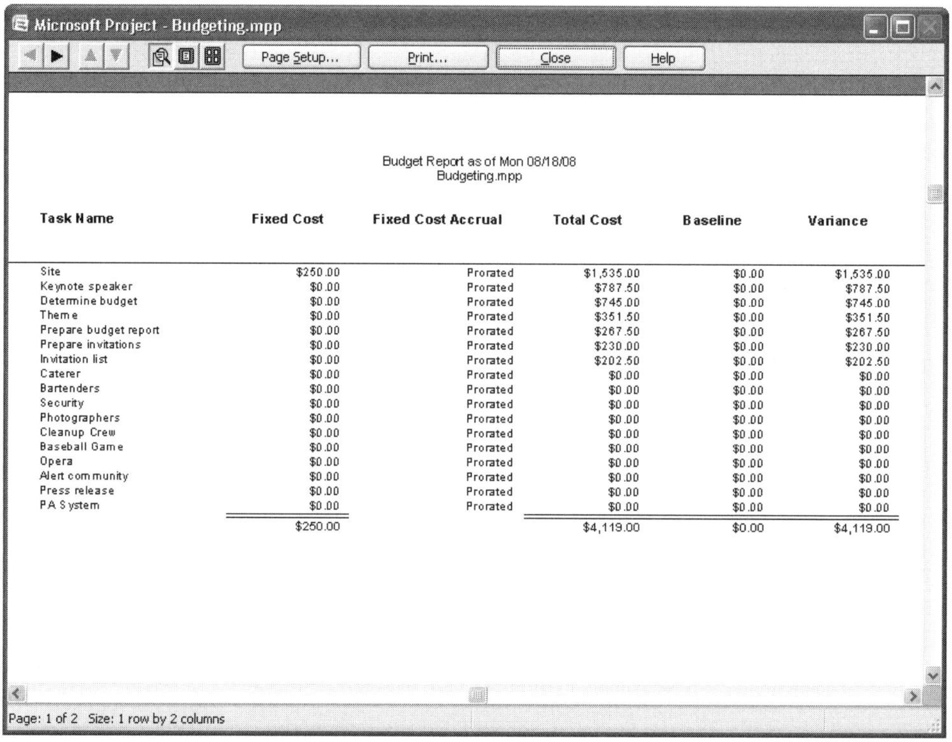

Budget Report as of Mon 08/18/08
Budgeting.mpp

Task Name	Fixed Cost	Fixed Cost Accrual	Total Cost	Baseline	Variance
Site	$250.00	Prorated	$1,535.00	$0.00	$1,535.00
Keynote speaker	$0.00	Prorated	$787.50	$0.00	$787.50
Determine budget	$0.00	Prorated	$745.00	$0.00	$745.00
Theme	$0.00	Prorated	$351.50	$0.00	$351.50
Prepare budget report	$0.00	Prorated	$267.50	$0.00	$267.50
Prepare invitations	$0.00	Prorated	$230.00	$0.00	$230.00
Invitation list	$0.00	Prorated	$202.50	$0.00	$202.50
Caterer	$0.00	Prorated	$0.00	$0.00	$0.00
Bartenders	$0.00	Prorated	$0.00	$0.00	$0.00
Security	$0.00	Prorated	$0.00	$0.00	$0.00
Photographers	$0.00	Prorated	$0.00	$0.00	$0.00
Cleanup Crew	$0.00	Prorated	$0.00	$0.00	$0.00
Baseball Game	$0.00	Prorated	$0.00	$0.00	$0.00
Opera	$0.00	Prorated	$0.00	$0.00	$0.00
Alert community	$0.00	Prorated	$0.00	$0.00	$0.00
Press release	$0.00	Prorated	$0.00	$0.00	$0.00
PA System	$0.00	Prorated	$0.00	$0.00	$0.00
	$250.00		$4,119.00	$0.00	$4,119.00

FIGURE 3-9 The Budget report shows you fixed and total costs, along with baseline and variance amounts.

To review and print both of these reports, on the Reports menu, click Reports and then double-click the Costs button. You'll also find the Overbudget Tasks, Overbudget Resources, and Earned Value reports in this report category. For more information on earned value, see Chapter 7.

2 Working Out the Kinks

CHAPTER 4

Finding the Information You Need

PUTTING INFORMATION INTO A PROJECT IS FINE, but you put information into Microsoft Office Project 2007 so that you can get information out of Project. You can use reports—and Project comes with a boatload that you can read about in Chapter 9, "Determining How to Communicate with Your Team"—but you don't always need to print something to find the information you need. For example, when you want to focus on resource overallocations, there are a number of ways to look at your project data. This chapter describes seeing project information on-screen using views and tables, and filtering, sorting, and grouping project information to focus on particular aspects of it. I also cover using custom fields in Project; custom fields give you a great deal of flexibility in viewing and tracking information.

Understanding Views

Using views, you can enter and organize information. You can also use views to examine information from various perspectives. For example, use task views when you want to focus on the tasks in your project, but when you start to evaluate resource allocations, use resource views.

Project contains more than 27 standard views. To display any of them, on the View menu, click More Views. In the More Views window (see Figure 4-1), select the view you want and click Apply.

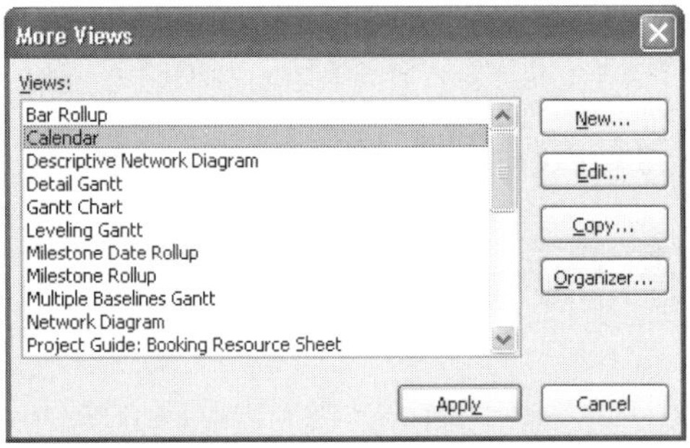

FIGURE 4-1 Use this window to select a view.

It's important to understand that each view focuses either on tasks or on resources. Some views, such as the Task Usage view and the Resource Usage view, combine information about tasks and resources, but each view has a primary focus. Understanding this concept will help you select the right view to get the information you need and will also help you understand custom fields, which also depend on the task orientation or resource orientation of a view. You can read more about custom fields later in this chapter, in the section "Using Custom Fields."

| NOTE | The New button in the More Views window lets you create your own views. But I suggest you explore all of the standard views before you start creating your own views; the chances are quite good that you'll find what you need without creating a new view. |

Picture Views

In addition to having either a task orientation or a resource orientation, views come in various flavors; for example, you'll find picture views such as the Resource Graph view, which presents a resource's allocation using a bar chart (see Figure 4-2). The Calendar view, shown in Figure 4-3, lays out tasks on a calendar, providing a visual representation of task duration against a familiar backdrop. The Network Diagram view also falls into this family of views, showing how your tasks connect to each other.

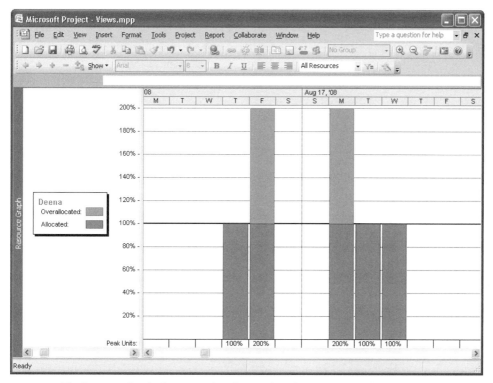

FIGURE 4-2 The Resource Graph view uses a bar chart to describe a resource's allocation.

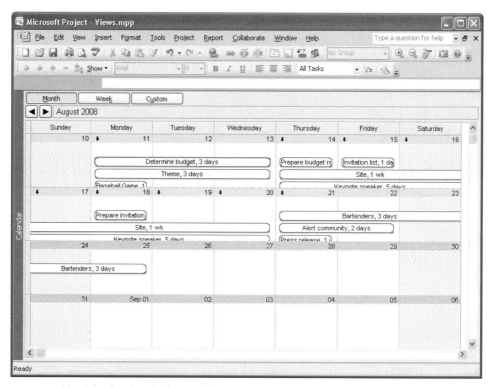

FIGURE 4-3 The Calendar view displays task durations against a monthly or weekly calendar.

Form Views

Form views present information about a single task or resource, and you can use them to view or edit information. The Resource Form view (see Figure 4-4) shows the tasks to which one resource is assigned. When you display the Task Form view, you'll see the information from the opposite perspective—for a single task, the view displays the resources assigned to the task.

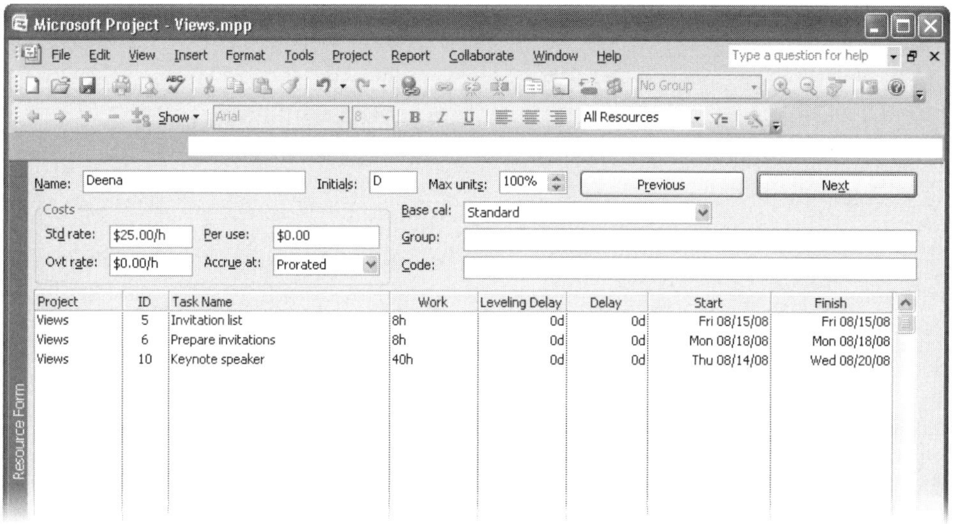

FIGURE 4-4 The Resource Form view shows the tasks to which a single resource is assigned.

Sheet Views

Sheet views, such as the Resource Sheet view or the Task Sheet view, present information in a table that includes a Name column that identifies the resource or task, and information about each resource or task appears across the rows (see Figure 4-5). One sheet view can actually present a variety of information, depending on the table you select; see the section "Understanding Tables" later in this chapter for more information about tables.

	ⓘ	Resource Name	Type	Material Label	Initials	Group	Budget Category	Max. Units	Std. Rate	Ovt. Rate	Cost/Use	Accru
1		Joe	Work		J		Work/Material	100%	$25.00/hr	$0.00/hr	$0.00	Prora
2	◇	Deena	Work		D		Work/Material	100%	$25.00/hr	$0.00/hr	$0.00	Pror:
3		Gayle	Work		G		Work/Material	100%	$20.00/hr	$0.00/hr	$0.00	Prora
4	◇	Bob	Work		B		Work/Material	100%	$30.00/hr	$35.00/hr	$0.00	Pror:
5		Carla	Work		C		Work/Material	100%	$25.00/hr	$0.00/hr	$0.00	Prora
6	✎ ☞	Intern	Work		I		Work/Material	200%	$10.00/hr	$0.00/hr	$0.00	Prora
7		Long distance	Material	call	L		Work/Material		$0.00		$0.25	Prora
8		Personal Computer	Material	unit	P		Work/Material		$0.00		$25.00	Prora
9		Consultant	Work		C		Work/Material	100%	$0.00/hr	$0.00/hr	$1,500.00	Prora
10		Copier	Material	copies	C		Work/Material		$0.10		$0.00	Prora
11		Paper	Material	sheets	P		Work/Material		$0.10		$0.00	Prora
12		Airline Tickets	Cost		A		Cost					Prora
13		Hotel Room	Cost		H		Cost					Prora
14		Budget-Labor/Materials	Work		B		Work/Material					Prora
15		Budget-Costs	Cost		B		Cost					Prora

FIGURE 4-5 A sheet view presents information in table format.

Combination Views

The Gantt Chart view and its relatives—the Tracking Gantt, the Leveling Gantt, the Detailed Gantt, and the Multiple Baselines Gantt views—are views that display a table on the left side of the view and a picture-oriented view on the right side. The Resource Usage and Task Usage views are views that display a table on the left and a Details portion on the right that displays usage information—resource time or task duration—on a timescale, which displays daily information by default, but you can change the timescale to display information over weeks or months.

TIP ✓   You can change the timescales used in the usage views and the various Gantt Chart views by right-clicking the timescale and clicking Timescale.

While the Gantt Chart views and the usage views are views that combine a table and some other type of view, Project officially considers the views that appear when you use the Split command (on the Window menu) as *combination views*, which display one view in the top pane of the window and either the Task Form view or the Resource Form view in the bottom pane. The form view that Project displays in the bottom pane depends on the view you displayed before you split the window. If you display a task-oriented view, such as the Gantt Chart view, and then split the window, Project displays the Task Form view. If you display a resource-oriented view, such as the Resource Graph view, and then split the window, Project displays the Resource Form view.

Start in the Gantt Chart view, and on the Window menu, click Split. Project displays the Task Form view in the bottom of the window. When you work in a combination view, whatever you select in the top portion of the view controls the information Project displays in the bottom portion of the view. So, as shown in Figure 4-6, the Task Form view in the bottom of the window displays the details of the resources assigned to the task appearing on Row 3 of the Gantt Chart view in the top portion of the window.

You can use the Split bar to split any view and to remove the split. In a view that doesn't contain a split, the Split bar appears as a small, flat, horizontal bar just below the vertical scroll bar arrow on the right side of the window. When you move the mouse pointer over the Split bar, the mouse pointer appears as a pair of parallel horizontal lines with arrows pointing up and down. Drag the Split bar up to create a split view. In a view you've already split, the Split bar runs horizontally across the entire window and separates the top view from the bottom view. Drag the Split bar down to remove a split view.

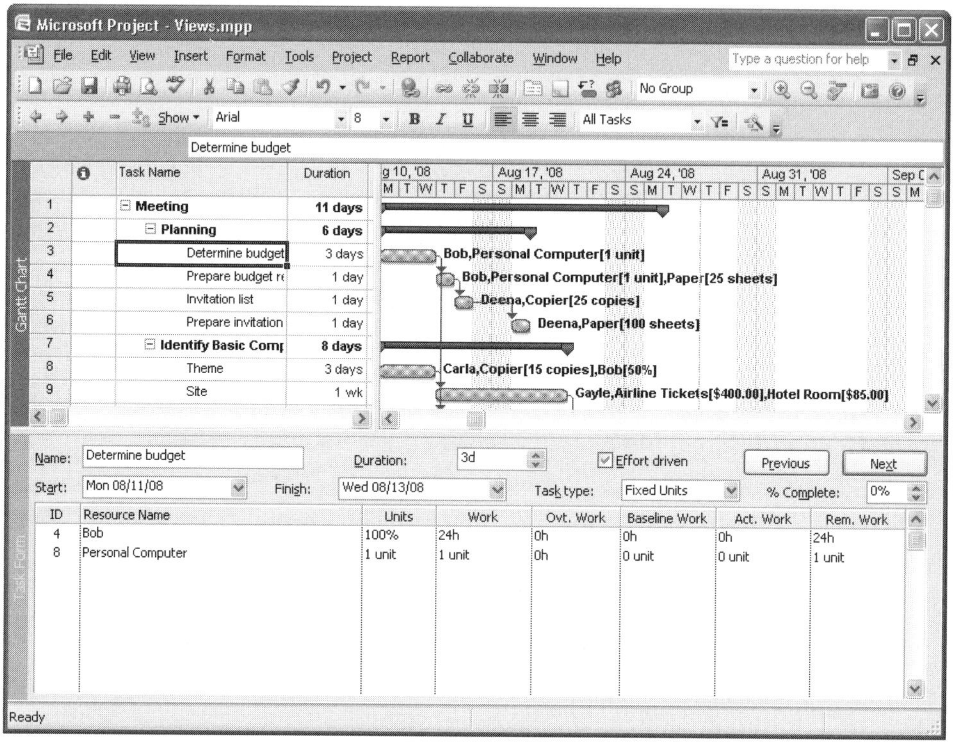

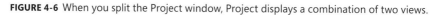

FIGURE 4-6 When you split the Project window, Project displays a combination of two views.

You can work in either view by clicking that view. You also can change the view that appears in either pane by clicking that pane and then selecting a different view—which is the true distinction between a combination view and a view like the Gantt Chart or the Resource Usage view. In the Gantt Chart view or the Resource Usage view, you can display different tables on the left, but you cannot select a different view to appear on the left or right side of the screen.

When you finish working in a combination view like the one shown in Figure 4.5, you can, on the Window menu, click Remove Split. Project always hides the view that appears in the bottom portion of the window.

■ **REMEMBER** You can remove a split by dragging the Split bar down.

Understanding Tables

Tables appear in many views, and sheet views are made up entirely of tables. But the table you see when you display a view isn't the only table available—that is, you can switch the table to view different information in the view. For example, Figure 4-7 shows the Entry table of the Gantt Chart view. Figure 4-8 shows the Cost table for the same view.

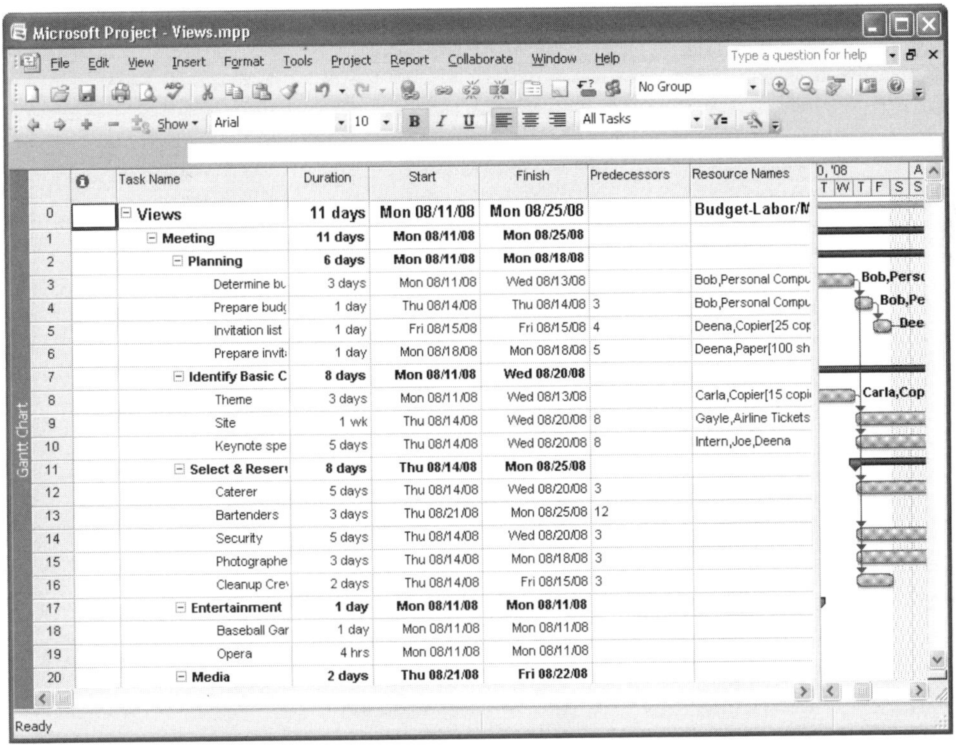

FIGURE 4-7 The Entry table of the Gantt Chart view.

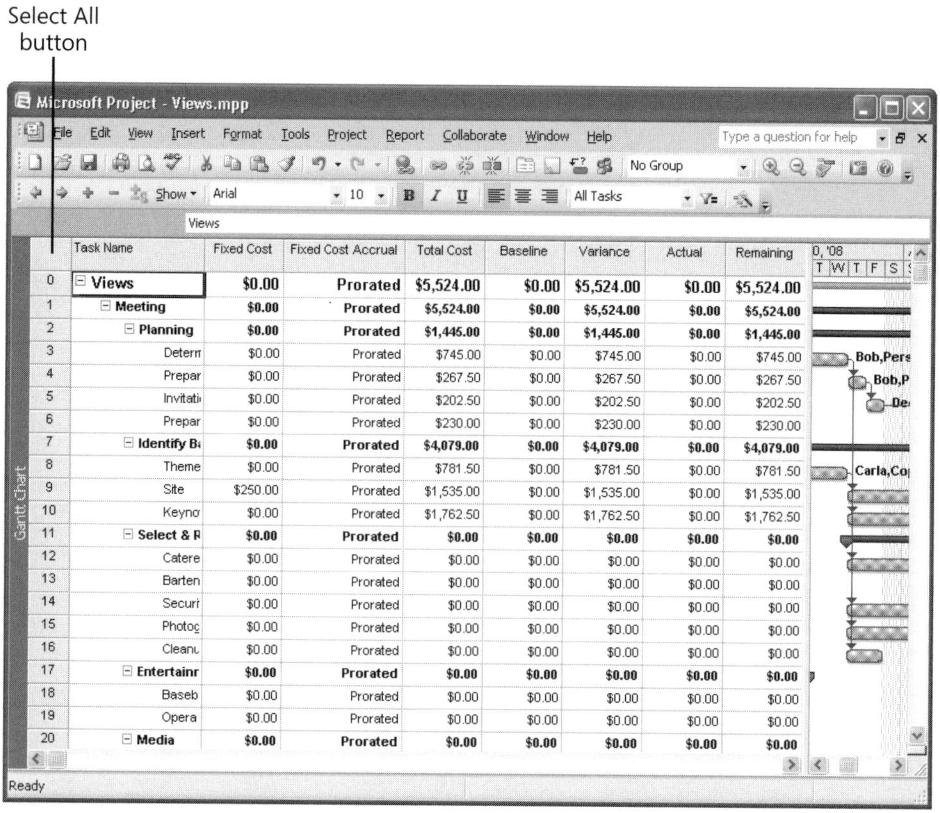

Select All
button

FIGURE 4-8 You can use the Select All button to switch to the Cost table of the Gantt Chart view.

You'll see different sets of fields on the tables of task-oriented views than you see on the tables of resource-oriented views. But the fields that appear on task-oriented tables don't change from view to view, and the fields that appear on resource-oriented tables don't change from view to view. That is, the Entry table for all task-oriented views contains one set of task-related fields, and the Entry table for all resource-oriented views contains one set of resource-related fields.

To switch to a different table, right-click the Select All button (as shown in Figure 4-8) and select a table. If the table you want to view doesn't appear on the shortcut menu, click More Tables. In the More Tables window, select the table you want to view and click Apply.

Adding a Field to a Table

In addition to using the tables as they appear on-screen, you can add fields to a table or hide fields that you don't want to view. Fields are the elements Project uses to store information you enter into your project. Every column heading in every table associated with any view represents a field in Project.

To hide a field, right-click the column heading for that field. Project selects that column and displays a shortcut menu. Click Hide Column (see Figure 4-9). Remember, the information remains in your Project file; it's just hidden from view.

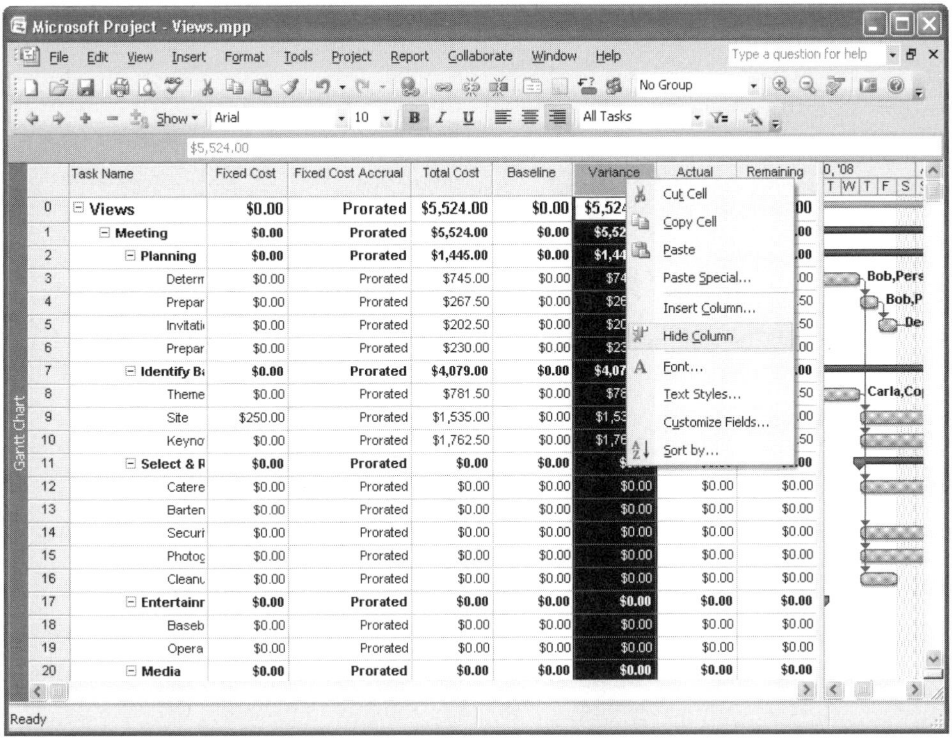

FIGURE 4-9 Hiding a field on a table.

To display a field, right-click the column heading of the column that should appear to the right of the new field. On the shortcut menu that Project displays, click Insert Column, and Project displays the Column Definition dialog box (see Figure 4-10).

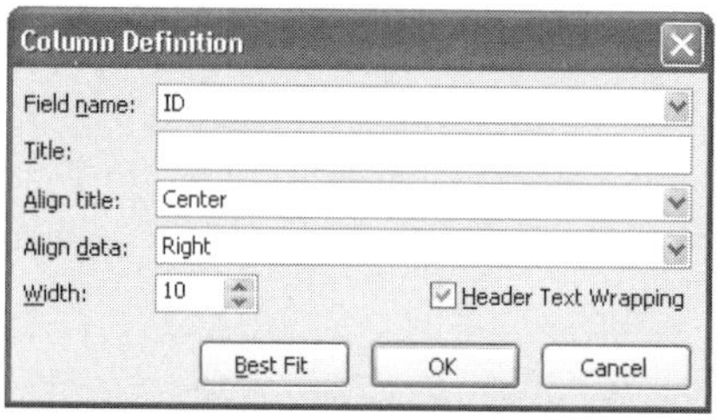

FIGURE 4-10 The Column Definition dialog box.

In the Field Name list, type a few characters of the name of the field that you want to add to the table or use the list box to select the field. Then click OK. Project adds the new field to the left of the field you originally right-clicked.

> **TIP**
> ✓
> You can change the row height or column width of any row or column in a table by dragging a border. To adjust any row's height, move the mouse pointer into the row number area and drag the row's lower border up or down. To adjust any column's width, move the mouse pointer into the column heading area and drag the column's right border to the left or right.

Working with the Details Portion of a Usage View

While we're talking about tables, let's review the Details portion of the Task Usage and Resource Usage views. The table portion of these views appears on the left side of the screen, and the Details portion, another type of table, appears on the right side of the screen. In the Details portion of these views, you find assignment information distributed over time—Project calls this information *timephased* information.

You can display additional information in the Details section. Unlike the tables we just reviewed, where you add fields as columns in the table, you add fields to the Details section by adding rows. By default, Project displays the Work field in the Details section of both usage views. To add fields to the Details section, right-click anywhere in the Details section and then click the appropriate field from the shortcut menu that appears (see Figure 4-11). Rows in the table of the view get wider to accommodate fields you add to the Details section.

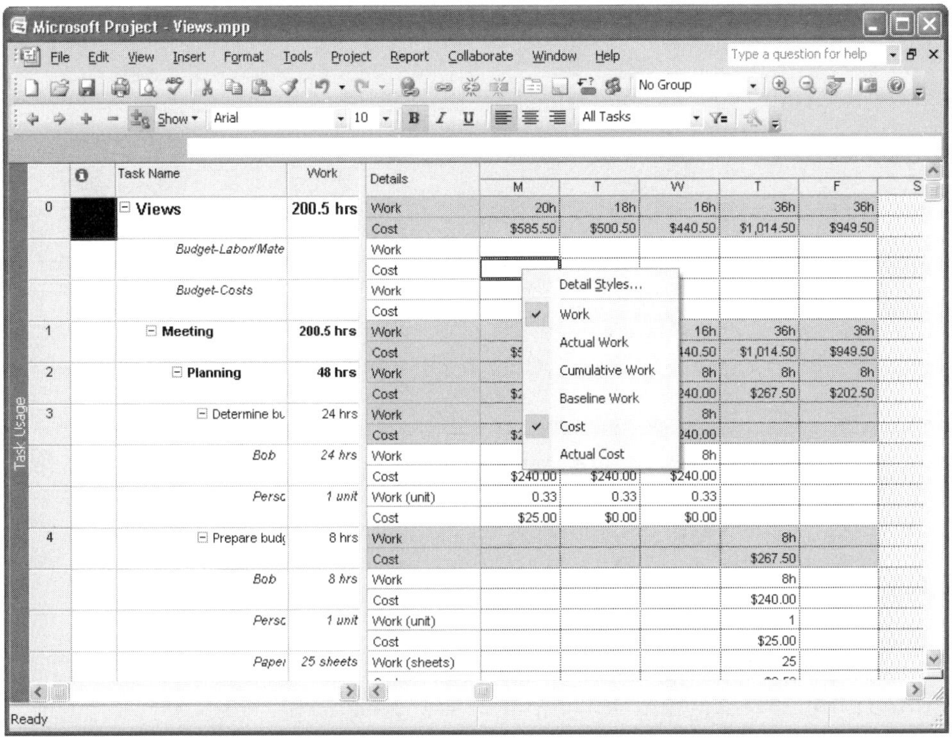

FIGURE 4-11 You can add fields to the Details section using a shortcut menu.

If the field you want to add doesn't appear on the shortcut menu, click Detail Styles on the shortcut menu to display the Detail Styles dialog box (see Figure 4-12). In the Available Fields list, click a field and then click the Show button.

> **TIP** ✓ If you add a particular field to the Details section often, add it to the shortcut menu by selecting the Show In Menu check box in the Detail Styles dialog box. For example, if you use budget resources regularly, you might want to add the Budget Work and Budget Cost fields to the shortcut menu to have easy access to them.

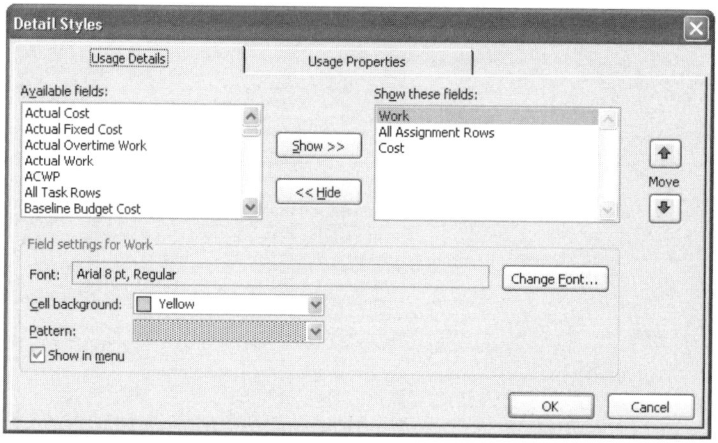

FIGURE 4-12 Adding a field to the Details portion of a usage view.

You hide fields in the Details section of a usage view the same way you display them: right-click anywhere in the Details section to display a shortcut menu of available fields and click the field you want to hide. Project removes the field from the Details portion of the view.

> **NOTE** The appearance of fields—displayed or hidden—on the shortcut menu is controlled by the Show In Menu check box in the Detail Styles dialog box.

Sorting Information

You can sort tasks in your project schedule to organize the information in your project in a way that helps you focus on particular aspects of the project. In Chapter 6, "Solving Resource Conflicts," you can read about establishing priorities for tasks before you level the project to resolve resource conflicts. The priorities you set identify for Project the order it should use to select tasks to delay or to split. After you set priorities, but before you level a project, you can sort the tasks in Priority order to see the tasks Project is most likely to select to level in any given phase; Figure 4-13 shows a project's Task Sheet view sorted in Priority order; notice that the Task ID numbers no longer appear in order from lowest to highest, and Project sorts the tasks by default from highest priority number to lowest priority number within each summary task heading.

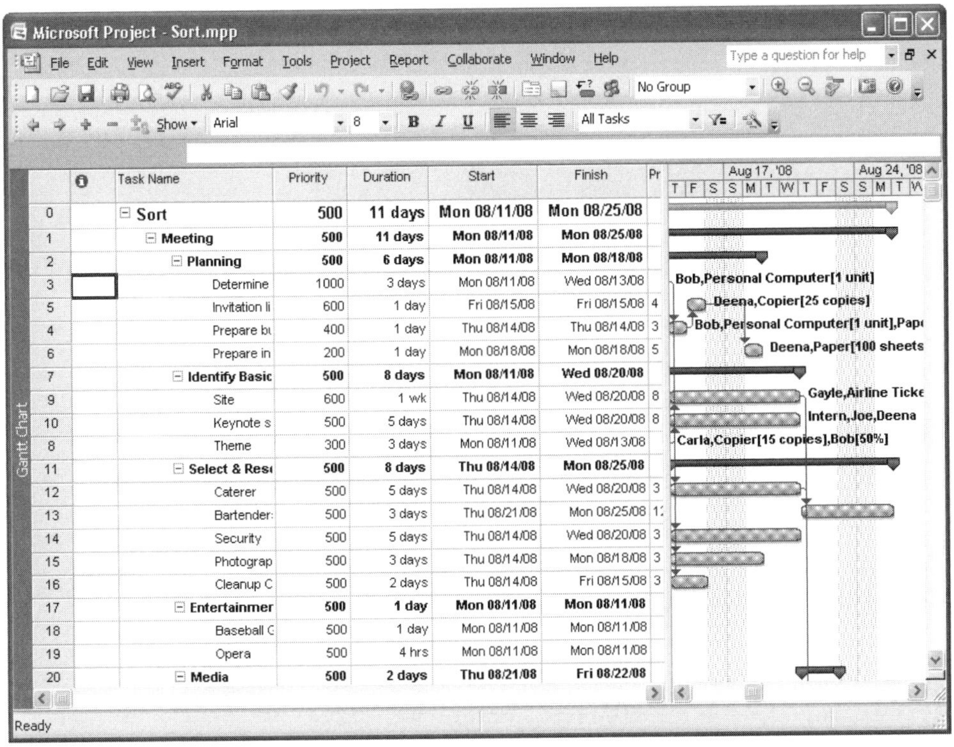

FIGURE 4-13 A Task Sheet view sorted in Priority order.

In the leveling scenario, Project delays tasks with lower priority numbers before it delays tasks with higher priority numbers. You might, though, prefer to sort from lowest to highest instead of from highest to lowest. Or you might dream up your own way in which you want to sort tasks. To make these kinds of changes, on the Project menu, point to Sort. From the submenu that appears, you can select one of the more typical sorts. Or to control sort order or select some field not shown on the submenu, click Sort By. Project displays the Sort dialog box (see Figure 4-14), where you can control sort order and select fields on which to sort your project.

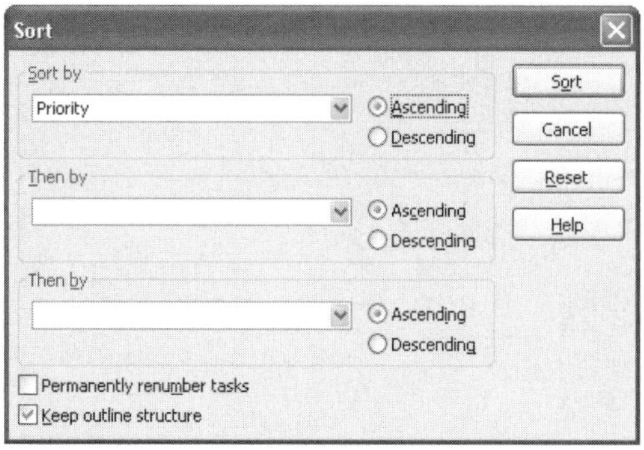

FIGURE 4-14 The Sort dialog box.

If you want to sort tasks by Priority order, regardless of position within summary tasks in a project, clear the Keep Outline Structure check box—you might want to try this approach for the Priority sorting example. To make the new sort order permanent, select Permanently Renumber Tasks; when you select this option, project reassigns Task ID numbers according to sorted position. Most of the time, though, you don't want to make the sort order permanent.

Filtering to Find What You Need

Filtering can also help you focus on a particular aspect of your project because it limits the information you see in a view or highlights information that meet criteria you specify. The filters available in any given view depend on the type of view. Resource views contain filters associated with resources, while task views contain filters associated with tasks. For example, you might find it really helpful when resolving resource conflicts to filter a resource-oriented view such as the Resource Usage view for overallocated resources. When looking for ways to shorten a project or avoid delaying it, you might want to filter a task-oriented view such as the Gantt Chart view or the Calendar view to display only or highlight tasks on the critical path.

Using Built-in Filters

Depending on your purpose for filtering, select either a task-oriented view or a resource-oriented view, and then on the Project menu, point to Filtered For. From the submenu that appears, select a filter or click the More Filters command to display the More Filters window (see Figure 4-15).

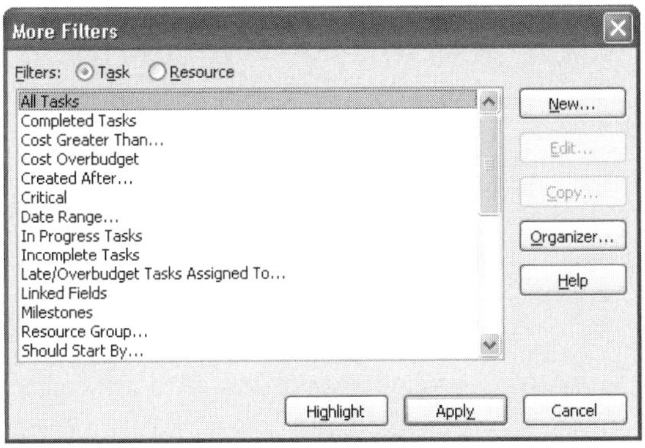

FIGURE 4-15 The More Filters dialog box.

Although you can select either Task or Resource at the top of the window and view all filters, the Apply button won't be available unless you select a filter associated with the type of view you selected before you opened the window. Select a filter in the list and click either Apply or Highlight. If you click Apply, Project hides information that doesn't meet the filter's criteria. If you select Highlight, Project continues to display all tasks or resources in the view but highlights the ones that meet the criteria of the filter.

Using AutoFilters

Using the AutoFilters feature, you can make quick filtering changes in the table portion of any view containing a table. You can turn on AutoFilters by clicking the AutoFilters button on the Formatting toolbar.

When you turn on AutoFilters, Project displays a list box arrow at the right edge of each column heading on any table view; when you click the arrow, Project displays a list of values available for that column. When you select a value, Project filters the information in the table to display only those tasks that meet the filter's criteria (see Figure 4-16).

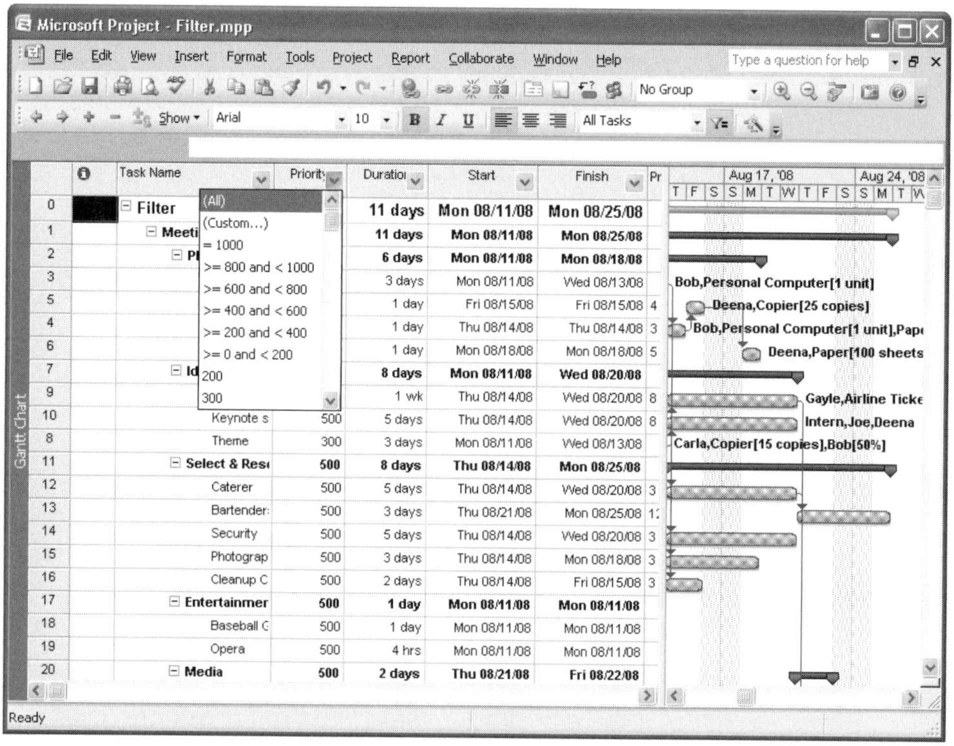

FIGURE 4-16 AutoFilter lists contain available values for each column of a table.

Grouping Information

Grouping is another feature you can use to help you focus on particular information. For example, when you want to review budget information, you can display the Budget Work and Budget Cost fields in a resource view and then group resources by the budget category to which you assign them. In Figure 4-17, I've set up two budget categories—Cost and Work/Material—and grouped resources based on the budget category to which I assigned them so that I can compare budgeted work and costs to assignments I've made in the planning stage of a project.

	❶	Resource Name	Budget Work	Budget Cost	Work	Cost		Details	
		⊟			**0 hrs**	**$0.00**		Work	
		⊞ Unassigned			0 hrs	$0.00		Work	
		⊟ **Cost**		**$800.00**		**$485.00**		Work	
	12	⊟ Airline Tickets				$400.00		Work	
		Site				*$400.00*		Work	
	13	⊟ Hotel Room				$85.00		Work	
		Site				*$85.00*		Work	
	15	⊟ Budget-Costs		$800.00				Work	
		Budgeting		*$800.00*				Work	
		⊟ **Work/Material**	**272 hrs**		**147 hrs**	**$3,384.00**		Work	
	1	⊟ Joe			22.5 hrs	$562.50		Work	
		Keynote speaker			*22.5 hrs*	*$562.50*		Work	
	2	⊟ Deena			16 hrs	$400.00		Work	
		Invitation list			*8 hrs*	*$200.00*		Work	
		Prepare invitations			*8 hrs*	*$200.00*		Work	
	3	⊟ Gayle			40 hrs	$800.00		Work	
		Site			*40 hrs*	*$800.00*		Work	
	4	⊟ Bob			32 hrs	$960.00		Work	
		Determine budget			*24 hrs*	*$720.00*		Work	
		Prepare budget report			*8 hrs*	*$240.00*		Work	
	5	⊟ Carla			14 hrs	$350.00		Work	

FIGURE 4-17 When you group resources, Project displays yellow highlighting around each group.

SEE ALSO	To learn more about using Budget Resources, turn to Chapter 7, "Taming That Monster Budget."

Like filters, the groups available to you in any view depend on the type of view you select. You'll find one set of groups for task-oriented views and another for resource-oriented views. To establish a grouping, select the view you want to use and on the Project menu, pont to Group By. From the submenu that appears, select the grouping you want to use. Or you can click Customize Groups By to display the Customize Group By dialog box (shown in Figure 4-18), which you can use to create your own custom grouping.

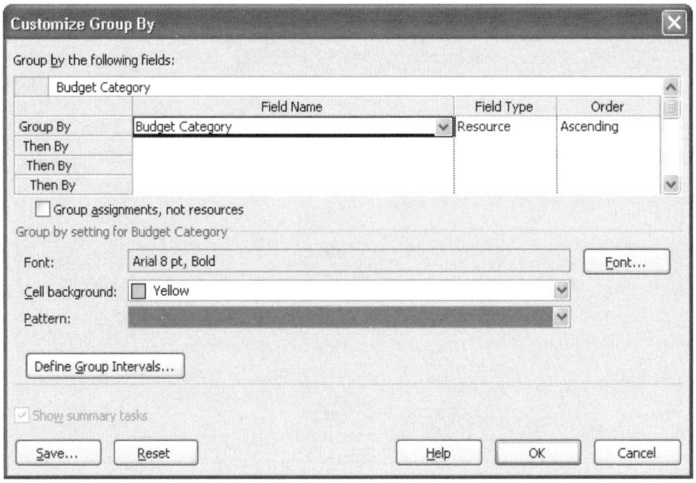

FIGURE 4-18 Use this dialog box to create custom groups.

In this dialog box, you select the field by which you want to group and then select a sort order for items within the group. As you can see, you also can create groups within groups, but remember not to get too crazy here—having too many groups defeats the purpose of organizing information in a way that helps you find what you're looking for.

> **NOTE** Depending on the type of grouping you select, you can click the Define Group Internals button to further refine the grouping. For example, if you group a task-oriented view by Duration, you can change the default grouping from Each Value to group tasks instead by Days and then set a range. Project then displays two groups: tasks with a duration within the range you specified and tasks outside the range you specified.

Using Custom Fields

Custom fields are one of Project's most powerful features—using them, you can track, view, and report on a wide variety of information that Project stores but either doesn't make visible to you by default or doesn't present in quite the way you want. When would you use a custom field? You can use custom fields, for example, when you want to:

- Create lists from which to select values to ensure accurate data entry,
- Store additional data about a task or resource,

- Create formulas to perform calculations on data, and

- Insert icons that present information graphically.

In Chapter 7, for example, I present an example of creating a resource-oriented custom field to track budget resource information. Before you dive in and start defining custom fields, there are a few concepts that are important to understand.

Understanding Custom Fields

How do custom fields differ from fields? As I described earlier in this chapter in the section "Adding a Field to a Table," fields are the elements Project uses to store information you enter into your project. Every column heading in every table associated with any view represents a field in Project. In dialog boxes, the text boxes you fill, the check boxes you select, the option buttons you click, and the selections you make from list boxes are stored in fields. You display fields using the Column Definition dialog box; on the Insert menu, click Column to display this dialog box (see Figure 4-19). Every item in the Field Name list is a field in which Project stores information about your project.

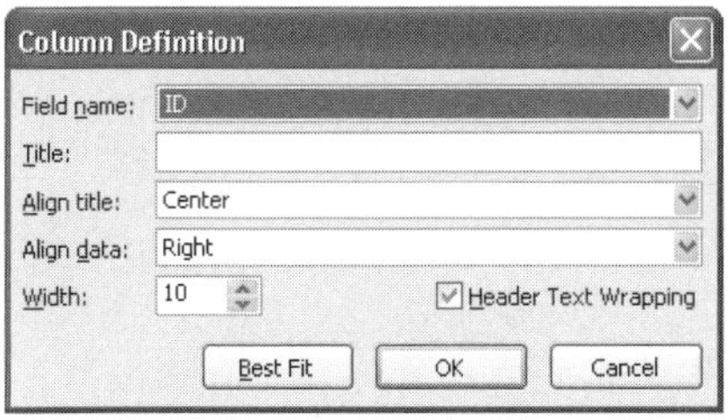

FIGURE 4-19 All fields Project uses to store project data appear in the Field Name list.

NOTE To be technically accurate here, when you make selections in, for example, the Options dialog box, Project stores your choices in fields, but you can't display these fields on views, and you won't find those fields in the Column Definition dialog box. However, the choices you make in the Resource Information, Assignment Information, and Task Information dialog boxes are all stored in fields that you can display on views.

Project stores task-related data in task fields and displays task-related data on task-oriented views. Similarly, Project stores resource-related data in resource fields and displays resource-related data on resource-oriented views.

> **NOTE** Assignment data matches resources to tasks; you can best view assignment data in either the Task Usage view or the Resource Usage view.

Custom fields are actually empty fields, waiting for you to define them. Once you define them, you display them in views the same way you display fields. When your custom fields are visible, you can store information in them. Since you display custom fields in views, it's important to recognize that you'll be able to create and use task-oriented custom fields only in tables on task-oriented views, including the Task Usage view. Similarly, you'll be able to create and use resource-oriented custom fields only in tables on resource-oriented views, including the Resource Usage view.

Creating a Custom Field That Includes a Data Entry List

Project organizes the custom fields using nine types, and you'll find these same nine types of custom fields whether you create a resource custom field or a task custom field: Cost, Date, Duration, Finish, Flag, Number, Outline Code, Start, and Text.

Each of these types of custom fields has rules associated with the kind of information you can enter in the field—so selecting the correct type of field can affect the functionality of your custom field. For example, use a Text custom field to include alphanumeric characters in the field and any selection list you create for the field. If you create a Date, Start, or Finish custom field, you can include only valid dates in the field and in any selection list you create for the field. If you create a Duration custom field, you can include duration or work values in the field and in any selection list you create for the field. If you create a Flag custom field, you can include only Yes or No in the field and in any selection list you create for the field. If you create a Number or Cost custom field, you can include only numbers in the field and in any selection list you create for the field.

> **NOTE** Outline codes are a special breed of custom field; you can read more about them in Chapter 9.

Suppose that the education level of your resources plays a role in whether you assign them to certain tasks. You can create a custom field called something like "Education" and create a list of accepted entries for that custom field. After you create the field, you can establish a value for each resource and then display the field as you make assignments. For this example, I'll create a Text custom field using these steps:

1. On the Tools menu, point to Customize, and click Fields to display the Custom Fields dialog box:

2. In the Field section, select Task or Resource to specify whether the custom field you want to create will contain task or resource information—I chose Resource for this example.

3. Open the Type list to select the type of custom field you want to create—I chose Text for this example.

4. Click Rename and type a new name for the field so that you'll recognize it when you want to add it to a view. You can't use any name that Project is already using.

> **TIP** ✓ Any custom fields you already created and renamed appear with their new names in the list; the ones you did not rename or have not created appear as generic names that include their type and a number.

5. To create a selection list that you can use to enter data consistently, click the Lookup button. Project displays the Edit Lookup Table window:

6. In the Value column, type the names of the elements you want to appear in the list; remember, if you are creating a type of custom field other than text, you need to enter the kind of elements appropriate for that list.

> **TIP** ✓ You can set a default value for the list by selecting Use A Value From The Table As The Default Entry For The Field. Then click the value you want to use as the default and click the Set Default button.

WARNING Although you can use the Data Entry Options section to allow users to make entries other than the ones you enter into the list, that approach can get you into trouble if you try to filter or group based on the custom field, because users might misspell entries or not use them consistently.

7. Click Close to redisplay the Custom Fields dialog box.

8. Click OK.

Storing Information in a Custom Field

You're now ready to enter information into the custom field you just created. Start by displaying it as a column in a sheet view. If you defined a task custom field, display any task-oriented view containing a table. If you defined a resource custom field, display any resource-oriented view containing a table and follow these steps:

1. Click the title of the column that you want to appear to the right of the custom field. Project selects the column.

2. On the Insert menu, click Column to display the Column Definition dialog box:

3. Open the Field Name list box and select the custom field that you defined, using the name that you supplied when you defined the field.

4. Click OK. The custom field appears on screen:

		Resource Name	Education	Type	Computer skills needed	Material Label	Initials	Group	Budget Category	Max. Units	Std. Rate
1		Joe	College	Work	Data entry		J		Work/Material	100%	$25.00/h
2		Deena	College	Work	Word processing		D		Work/Material	100%	$25.00/h
3		Gayle	Postgraduate	Work	Spreadsheet		G		Work/Material	100%	$20.00/h
4		Bob	Postgraduate	Work	Data entry		B		Work/Material	100%	$30.00/h
5		Carla	College	Work	Data entry		C		Work/Material	100%	$25.00/h
6		Intern	High School	Work	Programming		I		Work/Material	200%	$10.00/h
7		Long distance		Material	N/A	call	L		Work/Material		$0.0(
8		Personal Computer		Material	N/A	unit	P		Work/Material		$0.0(
9		Consultant	College	Work	Data entry		C		Work/Material	100%	$0.00/h
10		High School		Material	N/A	copies	C		Work/Material		$0.1(
11		College		Material	N/A	sheets	P		Work/Material		$0.1(
12		Postgraduate		Cost	N/A		A		Cost		
13		Hotel Room		Cost	N/A		H		Cost		
14		Budget-Labor/Materials		Work	N/A		B		Work/Material		
15		Budget-Costs		Cost	N/A		B		Cost		

5. Click any entry in the custom field's column; Project displays a list box arrow.

6. Open the list box to display the value list that you created.

7. For each row of the table, select values from the list, or simply type them.

> **NOTE** When you created the custom field, if you didn't allow any values in the field except the ones you supplied in the list, you can enter only values in the list. If you try to enter a value that doesn't exist in the list, Project displays an error message instructing you to use a value from the list.

Custom Fields, Formulas, and Indicators

Sometimes a visual cue is more helpful in a table than staring at the numbers. You can set up formulas in custom fields and use them to flag you when certain conditions arise. For example, suppose that you want to know when fixed costs on any task exceed a certain dollar value. You can set up a custom field containing a formula that refers to the Fixed Cost field and then, to make spotting overages easy, assign a graphical indicator to the field. Follow these steps:

1. On the Tools menu, point to Customize, and click Fields. Project displays the Customize Fields dialog box.

2. For this example, select Task and Cost.

    WARNING The type of field that you select from the Type list matters. If you select a type that doesn't match what you're trying to calculate in a formula, Project lets you create the formula but displays #ERROR in the custom field column when you display it in a table.

3. Click the Rename button and type the new name for the custom field; in this example, I named the field Monitor Cost and clicked OK to redisplay the Customize Fields dialog box.

4. Click the Formula button to display the Formula dialog box:

5. Create a formula in the text box by selecting fields or functions. To select a field, click the Field button; Project displays a list of field categories. Select the appropriate field category, and Project displays a list of the available fields. To select a function, click the Function button and follow the same process. For this example, I simply identified the field I want my custom field to monitor. If you need to make a calculation, use the operators that appear above the Field and Function buttons.

6. Click OK. Project warns you that it will discard any information that was previously stored in the custom field you selected and will replace the information with the calculated values based on the formula.

> **NOTE** If you click OK at this point and display a column for the custom field on a table, Project displays the result of the formula—in my example, Project displays the fixed cost of each task, which isn't the goal.

7. In the Customize Fields box, click the Graphical Indicators button. Project displays the Graphical Indicators dialog box:

8. Choose the type of row to which you want to assign an indicator: Nonsummary Rows, Summary Rows, or Project Summary.

9. In the Test For section, set up the tests that you want Project to use based on the formula's result, and select a graphic indicator for each test. In the Value(s) column, you can compare the custom field's formula result to the value of another field or to a numeric value. In my example, if a task's fixed cost is greater than or equal to $250, I want to see a red flag. However, if the task's fixed cost is less than $250, things will be fine, so I want to see a green dot.

10. Click OK to redisplay the Customize Fields dialog box.

11. Click OK again to redisplay your project in a view where the custom field is available.

12. If necessary, display the column for the custom field as described earlier in the section "Understanding Custom Fields."

When you display the custom field, it will contain an indicator (see Figure 4-20).

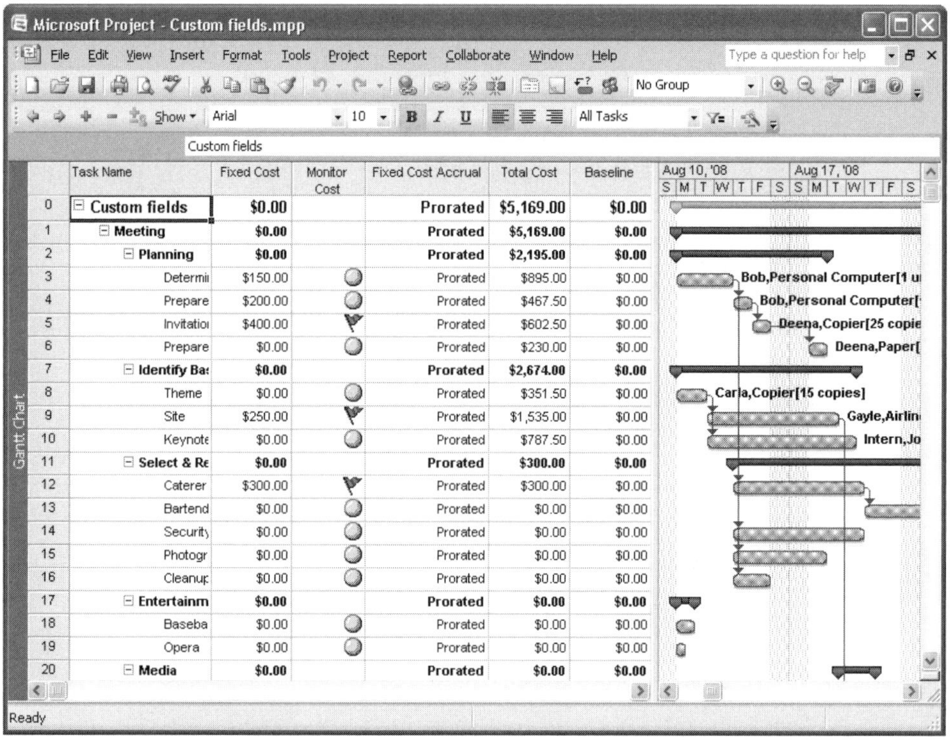

FIGURE 4-20 A custom field displaying an indicator.

CHAPTER 5

Controlling an Out-of-Control Schedule

HERE YOU ARE, in the final stages of the planning phase, and your schedule is longer than you anticipated. Or your schedule seems to be fitting into the time allotted for your project, but you're just not sure that you've set everything up correctly. This chapter helps you evaluate the factors that affect the timing of the tasks in your project.

Focusing on Tasks

When you begin to evaluate the timing of your project, you should look at a couple of different views in Microsoft Office Project 2007 to help you get a handle on project timing. At the same time, you might want to take a look at what tasks are driving other tasks.

In Chapter 4, "Finding the Information You Need," I covered views in general; let's take a quick look at some of the views that can help you focus on tasks. First is the Gantt Chart view, shown in Figure 5-1. From this view, the table, with its outline organization, helps you identify the general organization of your project by displaying parent tasks in bold print and indenting subtasks. The table also contains other information about the tasks, and since you can change tables, you can view a wide variety of information. The chart portion of the view presents a visual representation of a task's duration, and the link lines help you identify what tasks depend on other tasks.

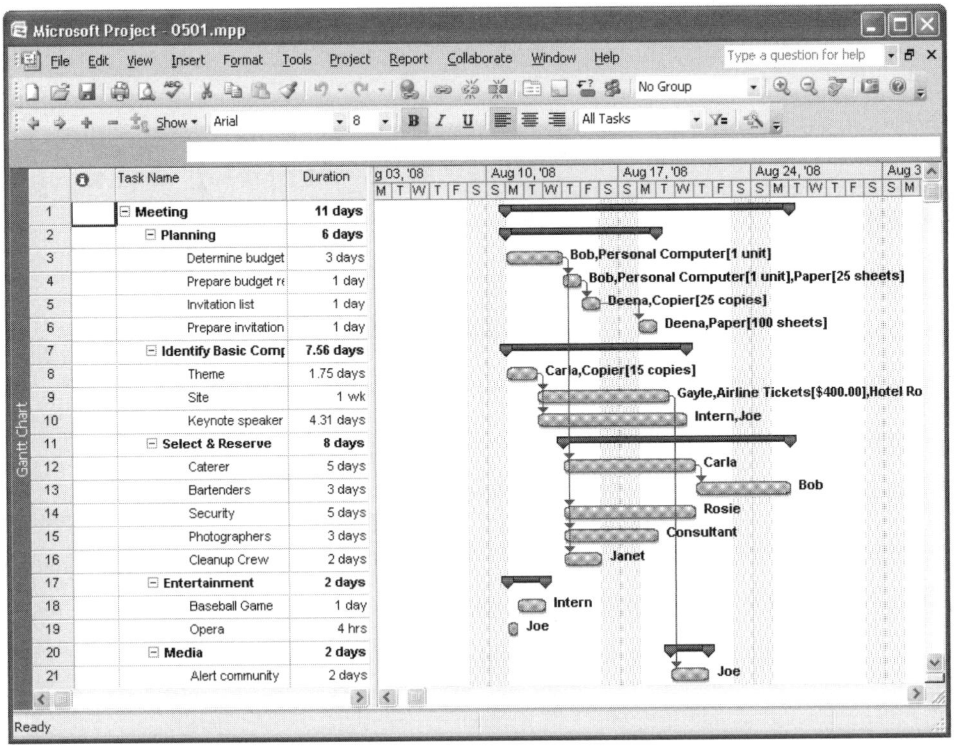

FIGURE 5-1 The Gantt Chart view helps you visualize organization, duration, and task dependencies.

The Calendar view, shown in Figure 5-2, can help you visualize a project's duration in a familiar environment. Using the buttons above the view, you can focus on a particular week's tasks or a particular month's tasks, or you can set up a custom date range to view.

As you proceed through this chapter, you'll find some other views that help you in specific situations when working with tasks in your schedule.

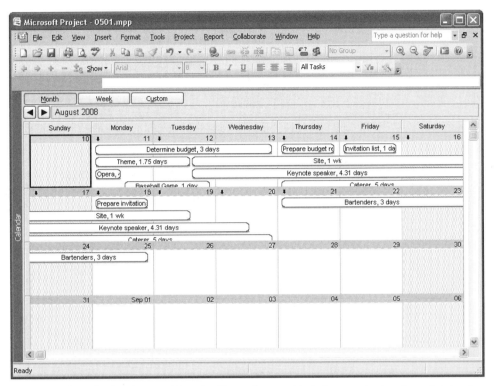

FIGURE 5-2 The Calendar view provides a familiar environment to help you get a handle on the duration of a project.

Tasks and Timing

The timing of the tasks in your project is affected by several factors. For example, the duration of a task affects the timing in your schedule, along with the start and finish dates of the project. In addition to those factors, you'll find that whatever type of task you select, the dependencies you create between tasks and the constraints you might have placed on tasks all affect task timing. In addition, resource availability and calendars in your project can affect task timing.

Identifying Task Drivers

The Relationship Diagram view (see Figure 5-3) and the Network Diagram view (see Figure 5-4) focus on the dependencies between tasks, helping you focus on identifying task dependencies. The Relationship Diagram view displays only task names, task ID numbers, and link lines that include designations for the type of dependency that exists between two tasks. In Figure 5-3, the FS that appears on the link lines of the five tasks on the right stands for "finish-to-start" and means that none of the five tasks on the right can begin until the task on the left ends.

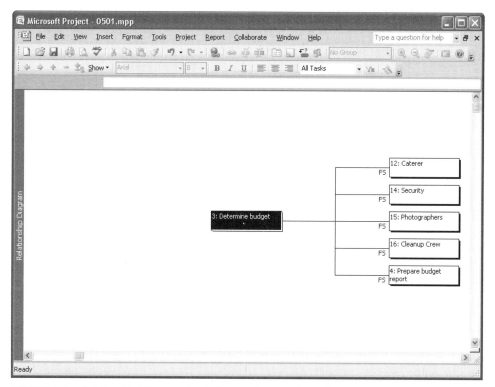

FIGURE 5-3 The Relationship Diagram view helps you focus on dependencies between tasks.

In addition to focusing on task dependencies, the Network Diagram view displays critical tasks in red, making them easy to identify, and provides details such as the start and finish dates and the duration for each task.

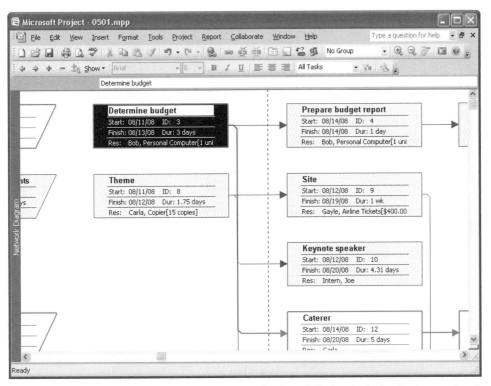

FIGURE 5-4 The Network Diagram view identifies critical tasks and displays basic details about each task.

You also can take advantage of Project's Task Drivers pane to help you quickly and easily identify task predecessors and successors; the Task Drivers pane can be particularly helpful when you've got a lot of dependency links in your project. The Task Drivers pane identifies for the selected task the factors that, well, drive the task: the ID and name of the selected task, its start date, subtasks, predecessors, resources, and task or resource calendars associated with the task. To display the Task Drivers pane, on the Project menu, click Task Drivers. Project adds the Task Drivers pane to the left side of any task-oriented view (see Figure 5-5).

In the Task Drivers pane, you also see predecessor information that identifies the task type of the predecessor as well as any lag time. If you've entered any actual information, such as the actual start date, that information also appears in the Task Drivers pane.

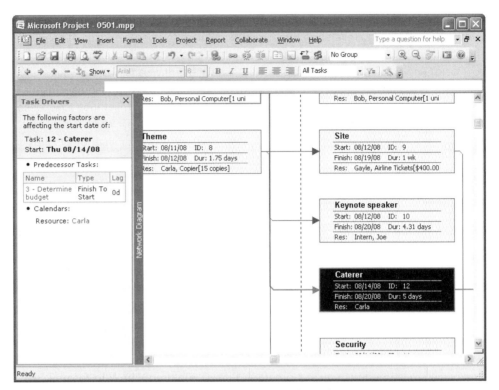

FIGURE 5-5 The Task Drivers pane can help you identify task relationships.

How Task Types Affect Task Timing

The task type you select when you create a task affects the way Project calculates the project schedule. In some cases, adding resources changes the way Project handles the scheduling of the task, while in other cases, adding resources doesn't affect Project's calculation of the schedule.

> **NOTE**   For all of the examples that follow, I've used the Standard calendar, which assumes a work week consisting of five days, and each working day consisting of eight hours.

By default, when you create a task, Project creates a fixed units task. When you assign a resource to a fixed units task, you specify the assignment as a percentage, such as "100%" for full-time or "25%" for one quarter of the resource's time. For fixed units tasks, Project doesn't change the assignment percentage if you change the duration of the task.

In Figure 5-6, I've assigned Resource 1 to work half-time on Task 1, which is a 10-day fixed units task. In Figure 5-7, I've changed the duration of Task 1; notice that Project doesn't change the half-time work assignment of Resource 1.

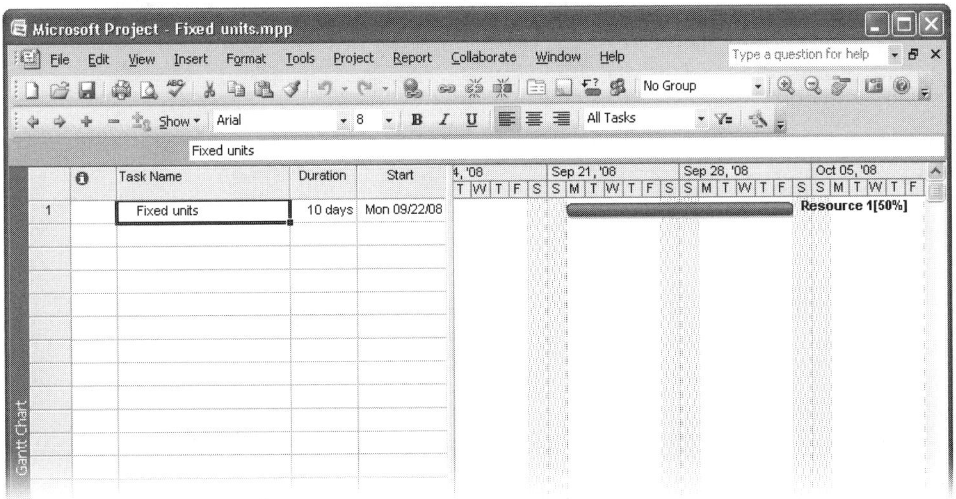

FIGURE 5-6 A fixed units task with a resource assigned to work half-time on the task.

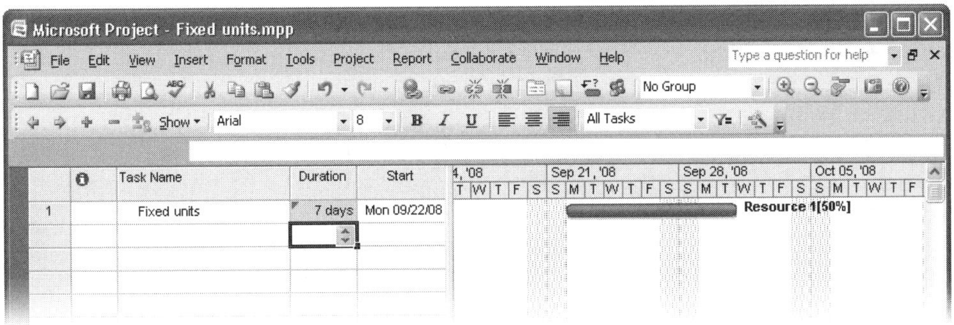

FIGURE 5-7 The assignment percentage doesn't change when you change the duration of a fixed units task.

When you use a fixed duration task, you indicate that a task will take a particular amount of time, regardless of the number of resources working on the task. When you pour a concrete slab foundation for a house, the concrete needs a specified amount of time to cure before you can proceed to frame the house. In Figure 5-8, I've set up a five-day fixed duration task and assigned Resource 1 to it. In Figure 5-9, I've added Resource 2 to the task; because the duration is fixed, Project doesn't change the five-day period needed to accomplish the task.

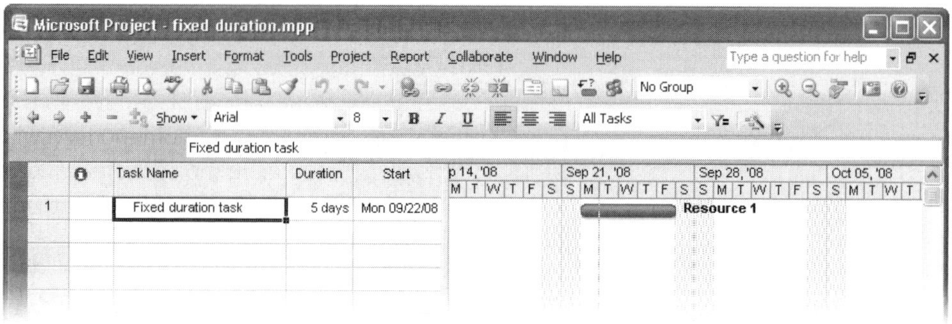

FIGURE 5-8 A five-day fixed duration task with one resource assigned.

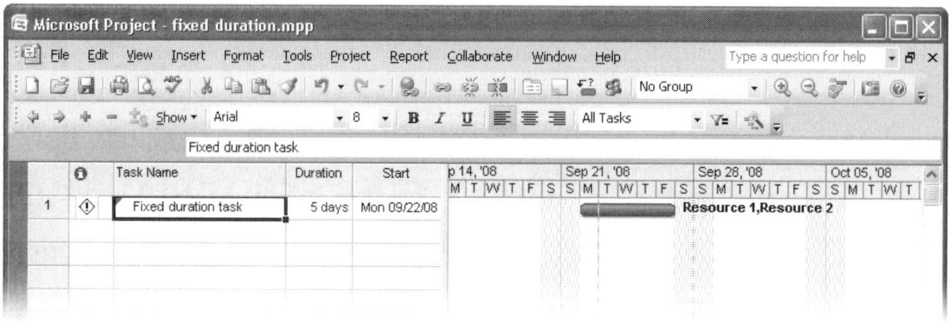

FIGURE 5-9 When you assign a second resource to a fixed duration task, Project adjusts the resource assignment value of the first resource but doesn't change the task's duration.

When you create a fixed work task, you supply a duration that represents the total amount of work needed to complete the task. When you assign a resource to that task at a particular assignment percentage level, Project assumes that the task requires that level of effort to complete in the time you specified as the duration. For example, if you create a fixed work task that takes eight days to complete, and you assign one resource to work full-time on the task, Project calculates that the task will be completed in eight days. If you initially assign one resource to the task to work half-time on an eight-day task, Project assumes that the task requires eight days for a resource working half-time to complete it. In either case, if you assign a second resource to work on the task using the same effort level as the first resource, Project reduces the amount of time needed to complete the task to half the initial amount required. The amount of work required to complete the task doesn't change, but the duration of the task does. In Figure 5-10, I've created two fixed work tasks that are each eight days long. I assigned Resource 1 to work full-time on the first task and Resource 2 to work half-time on the second task.

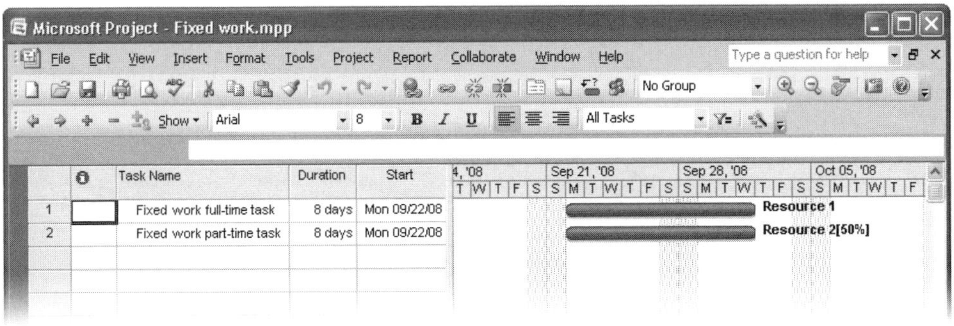

FIGURE 5-10 Two fixed work tasks.

In Figure 5-11, I have assigned a second resource to each task; in each case, the second resource is providing the same level of effort as the first resource. Note that Project reduces the duration of both tasks to four days. If I had assigned the second resource using a different level of effort, Project would have adjusted the duration of the task accordingly without changing the amount of work required to complete the task.

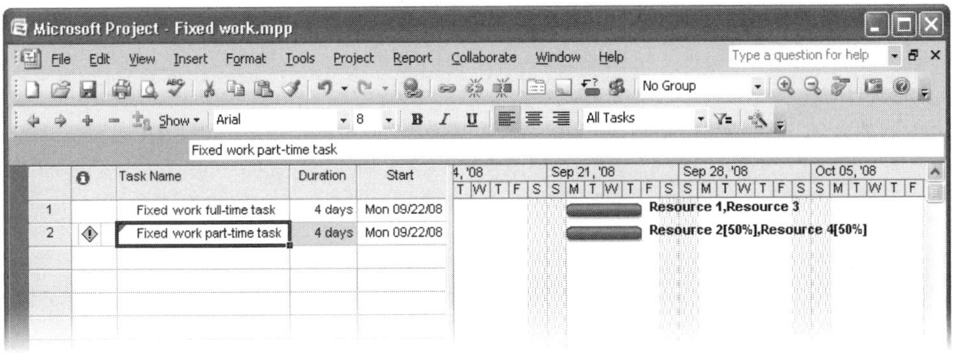

FIGURE 5-11 The duration of a fixed work task changes when you add resources to it.

In Figure 5-12, I have displayed the Task Usage view of this project; notice that Task 1 still requires 64 hours of work (eight days) to complete, although I've assigned two resources and, as shown in Figure 5-11, the task will finish in four days. Similarly, Task 2 still requires 32 hours of work to complete (eight days at half-time or four hours per day).

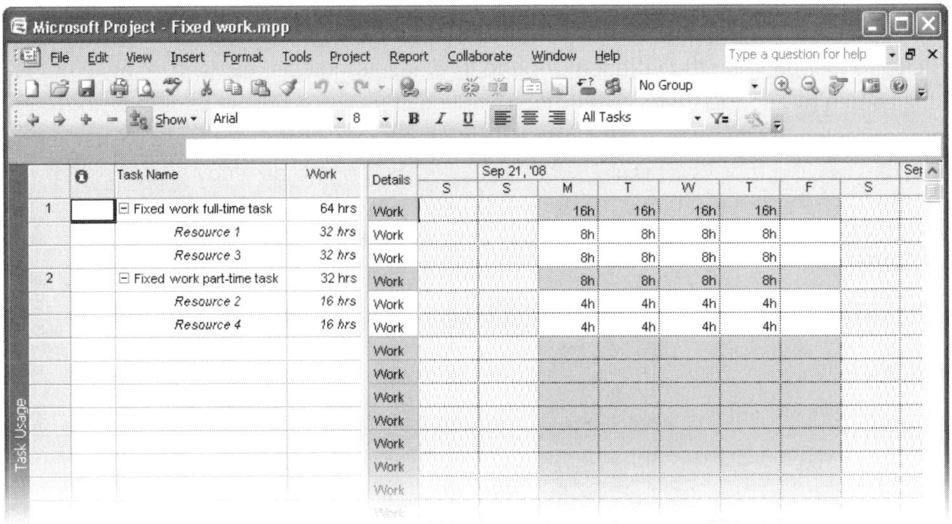

FIGURE 5-12 The amount of work required doesn't change when you add resources to a fixed work task, even though Project reduces the task's duration.

Exploring the Effort-Driven Equation

An *effort-driven* task is one that is affected by the number of resources you assign to it. By default, all fixed work tasks are effort-driven and you can't change that behavior. If it takes one person an hour to wash a car, this fixed work, effort-driven task could be accomplished by two people in half the time, assuming they don't stop for a water fight.

> **NOTE** The changes Project calculates for any effort-driven task are strictly a mathematical calculation. For example, Project calculates that three people get work done in one third of the time it takes one person to do the job. In real life, however, the time you save is rarely a straight, mathematical calculation. After all, people on a job talk to each other, take breaks, and so on.

In the preceding section, you saw how changing the duration of a fixed units task did not change the amount of effort assigned to a resource working on the task. When you create a fixed units, effort-driven task, the same rule holds true; Project doesn't change the effort level you assign to the resources. However, Project does change the duration of the task. In Figure 5-13, I've created a fixed units, effort-driven task that is four days in duration, and I've assigned Resource 1 to work on the task half-time.

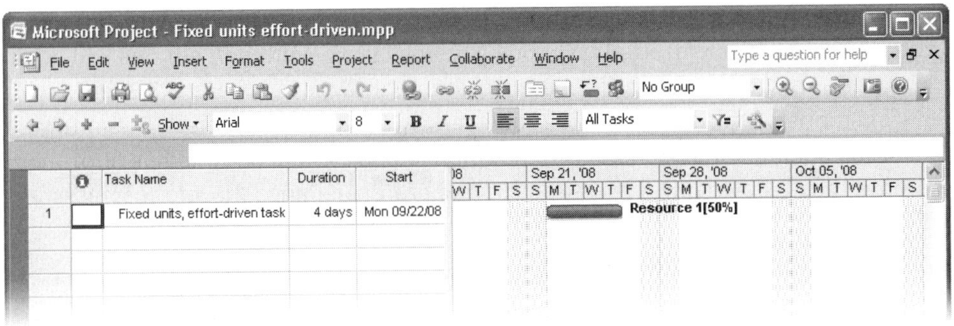

FIGURE 5-13 A fixed units, effort-driven task with a resource assigned at half-time.

In Figure 5-14, I've added another resource to work on the task half-time, and Project has reduced the duration of the task by half, because two people can accomplish in half the time what one person accomplishes in the originally specified duration. If I were to change the duration of that task by simply typing a new duration, Project would not change the assignment level of either resource.

> **NOTE** I assigned these resources to work half-time instead of full-time simply to make it easier to see that Project doesn't change the assignment level on this type of task.

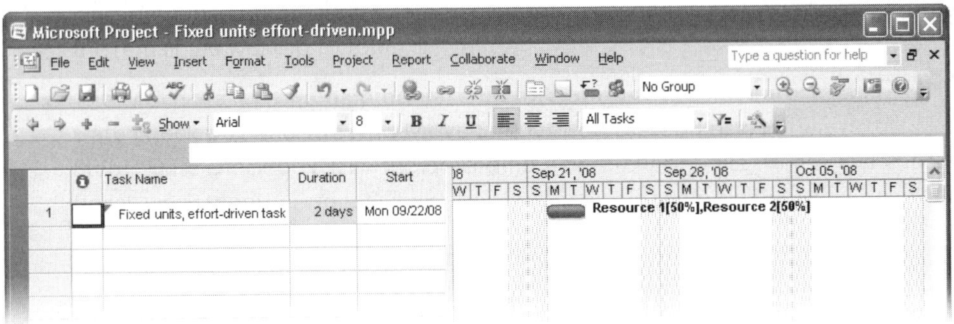

FIGURE 5-14 Adding a resource to a fixed units, effort-driven task reduces the duration of the task without reducing the amount of work required to complete the task.

When you change the number of resources assigned to a fixed duration, effort-driven task, Project modifies the percentage of total work allocated to each resource working on the task but doesn't change the amount of work that's required to complete the task. In Figure 5-15, I've created a four-day fixed duration, effort-driven task and assigned Resource 1 to work on the task full-time.

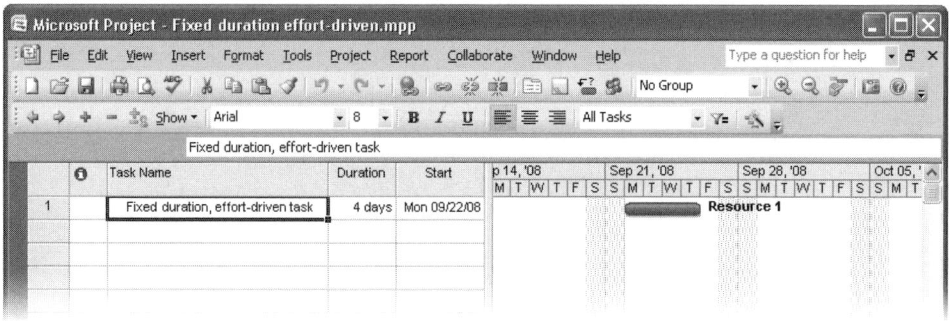

FIGURE 5-15 A four-day fixed duration, effort-driven task with one resource assigned full-time.

In Figure 5-16, I've added another resource to work on the task full-time. In this case, Project doesn't change the duration of the task, but Project reduces the amount of the assignment of each resource to 50 percent, indicating that two resources can accomplish the same amount of work by working half the time for the duration of the task that one resource can accomplish by working full-time for the duration of the task.

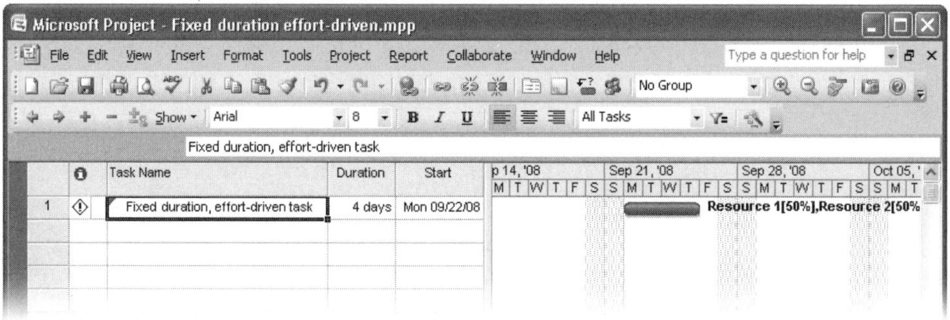

FIGURE 5-16 When you add a resource to an effort-driven, fixed duration task, Project reduces the amount of effort required from all resources assigned to the task.

By default, Project creates fixed units, effort-driven tasks. And all fixed work tasks are effort-driven by default. To create a fixed duration task that is also effort-driven, double-click the task in question to display the Task Information dialog box for that task. Then click the Advanced tab and select the Effort Driven check box (see Figure 5-17).

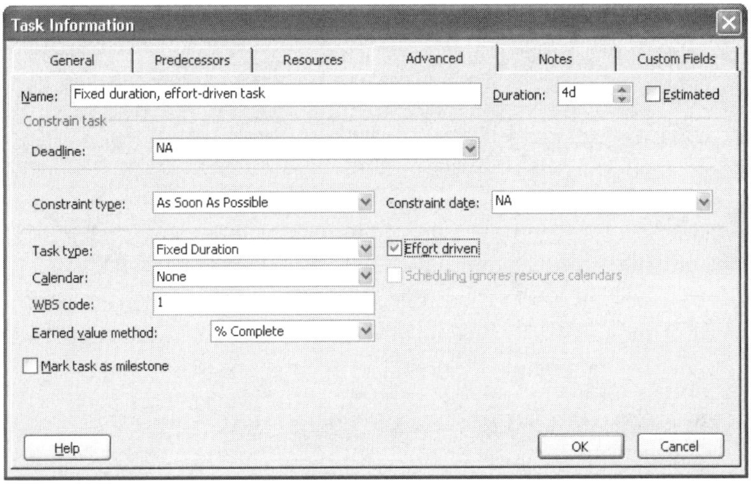

FIGURE 5-17 Use the Task Information dialog box to create a fixed duration, effort-driven task.

When Should You Use a Task Calendar?

Back in Chapter 3, "Pinning Down Your Budget," I explained that resource calendars help you establish availability for a resource. Using a resource calendar, you can assign a resource to a task and Project won't plan the resource to work when the resource isn't available. In essence, a resource calendar provides a way to make exceptions to the ordinary working schedule on a resource-by-resource basis.

Task calendars work in much the same way. You can create a task calendar and assign it to a task to ensure that Project doesn't allow the task to be scheduled during a period of non-working time or to make non-working time be working time for a particular task. Suppose, for example, that your project uses the Standard calendar, which designates Monday through Friday, 8:00 A.M. to 5:00 P.M., as working time. Further suppose that one task in your project involves performing routine maintenance on equipment. If you perform the routine maintenance during regular business hours, all work stops because the equipment isn't available. However, if you perform the routine maintenance at night, when most people don't work, you get the job done without impacting the work of others on your project. In this case, you'd create a calendar for the Equipment Maintenance task and set working hours on the calendar from 5:00 P.M. to 8:00 A.M.

> **NOTE** In the preceding example, you don't need to create a special calendar if you can fit your maintenance into the working hours available on the Night Shift calendar, which is one of the three calendars that automatically come with Project. You can simply assign that calendar to your task.

When you create a new calendar, you can base it on one of the existing calendars: the Standard calendar, the Night Shift calendar, or the 24 Hours calendar. Or you can create a new base calendar; when you do, Project assigns the Standard calendar settings to your new calendar and you can change them. To create a new calendar, on the Tools menu, click Change Working Time to display the Change Working Time dialog box (see Figure 5-18).

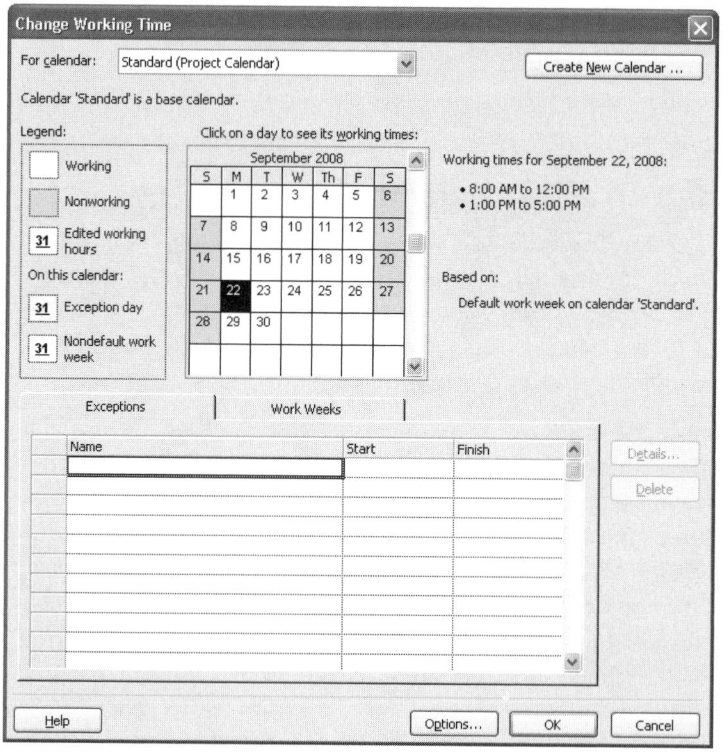

FIGURE 5-18 Begin the process of creating a new calendar in the Change Working Time dialog box.

Click the Create New Calendar button to display the Create New Base Calendar dialog box (see Figure 5-19).

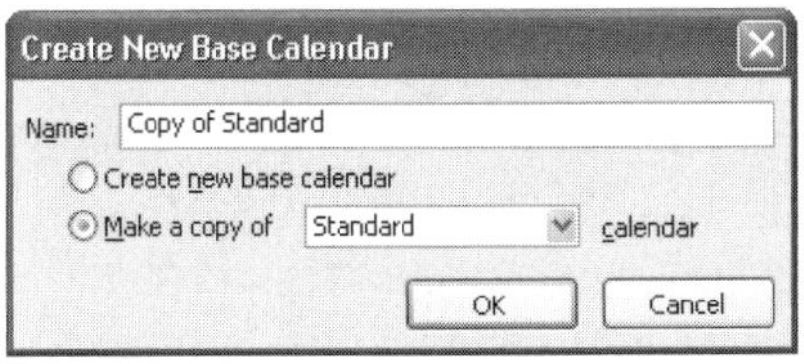

FIGURE 5-19 Use this dialog box to create a new calendar.

In the Name box, type a name for the calendar you want to create. If you want to use one of the existing base calendars as your model, select the Make A Copy Of option and click the base calendar in the list. When you click OK, Project displays the Change Working Time dialog box again, and your new calendar's name appears in the For Calendar list.

> **SEE ALSO**   For details on modifying the work week hours or to set exceptions for, say, company holidays, see Chapter 1, "Scoping Out Your Project's Details."

Once you've set up your calendar, you need to assign it to the appropriate task in your project. Double-click the task to display the Task Information dialog box. Click the Advanced tab, and select from the Calendar list the calendar you want to assign to your task (see Figure 5-20). Click OK, and you're done.

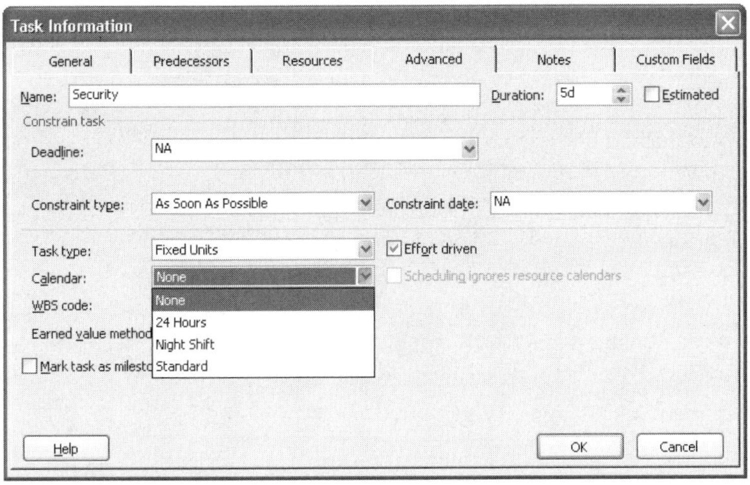

FIGURE 5-20 Assign a calendar to a task.

What Are Your Task Constraints Doing to Your Schedule?

In addition to using task duration, dependencies, and calendars to determine the timing of a task, Project also uses constraints. Unlike dependencies, which tie the timing of one task to the timing of another task, constraints tie the timing of a task to the start or end of your project or to a specific date. Every time you set a start date for a task, you create a Start No Earlier Than constraint, assuming that you set your project to schedule from the project start date. By default, Project honors constraints over dependencies, so if you set that start date, Project won't let the task start until the date you select. Essentially, Project can't adjust your schedule automatically when you use constraints. In addition, when you use constraints, you will in all probability understate or overstate the amount of time needed to complete a project. Suppose that you have two tasks linked together with a finish-to-start dependency—Task 1 and Task 2—and Task 2 needs to start after you finish Task 1. If you set a start date for Task 2 of, say, October 15, and then realize that Task 1 will be able to finish on October 10, your schedule is automatically five days longer than it needs to be. But what happens if Task 1 won't be able to finish until October 20? Now your schedule is actually five days *shorter* than it needs to be.

Although you can change Project's behavior and remove the requirement to honor constraints over dependencies, in general you'll find that you produce better project schedules using dependencies over constraints because Project *can* adjust your schedule automatically when conditions change and you've used only dependencies. If you had simply set a finish-to-start dependency between the two tasks in the example, Project would have automatically adjusted the start date of Task 2 for you, based on the finish date of Task 1.

NOTE The Must Finish On constraint and the Must Start On constraint are inflexible constraints, sometimes called *hard constraints*. They force a task to start or end on a particular date. All of the other constraints are flexible or *soft constraints* and force a task to occur within a certain time-frame. This distinction is important, because Project can change the start and finish dates of a task that uses a soft constraint using the parameters of the constraint. Project cannot change the start or finish date of a task with a Must Start On or Must Finish On constraint.

WARNING Don't set constraints on summary tasks for the same reasons you shouldn't set dependencies for summary tasks. Let summary tasks do their job and summarize the information of the subtasks below them.

There are times when you need to use a constraint. But you also can minimize your use of constraints by simulating constraints using dependencies.

For example, suppose that you're closing the local office and offering severance packages to employees who don't relocate to the company headquarters in Houston. You need to identify the type of financial offer you will make to those who choose to leave the company. You also need to identify the type of financial offer that you'll make to those who decide to relocate; for example, you need to decide how you want to handle moving expenses and how involved you will be in an employee's effort to sell a local home. If you plan to offer moving and home sale benefits, you need to work out details; you might, for example, identify the mover and the real estate agency you want employees to use.

Because you understand the emotional upheaval this decision will cause, you want to be as fair as possible to your employees and give them as much time as possible to make their decisions. Essentially, you want to set up the tasks that lead up to requiring a response from your employees to end as late as possible.

Although you might be tempted to use As Late As Possible (ALAP) constraints in your schedule, you can avoid the problems associated with using constraints by minimizing them. In Figure 5-21, I've set up a sample schedule that uses start-to-finish dependencies to model this "just in time" scenario; this approach avoids using ALAP constraints.

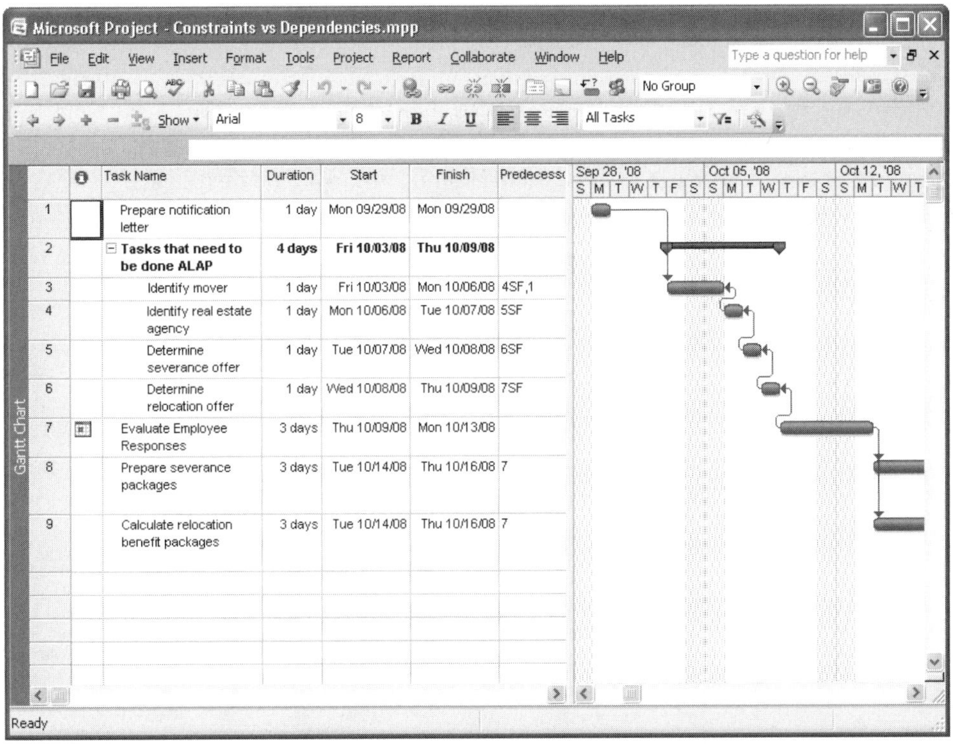

FIGURE 5-21 Using start-to-finish dependencies to create a "just in time" scenario.

Task 7 is the only task that uses a constraint; in this example, I used a Must Finish On constraint. But before I set that constraint, I set up Tasks 3 through 6, setting their durations, and created start-to-finish relationships between them. That approach says, essentially, that Task 4 won't start until Task 3 finishes. Project calculated the finish date for each task based on its duration. When I set up Task 7, I used its calculated finish date as the Must Finish On constraint date.

Yes, I could have linked Tasks 3 through 6 in finish-to-start relationships and then set constraints on them to make them finish as late as possible, but I chose the alternate approach of using start-to-finish relationships because there are times when the late finish date that Project calculates for an ALAP task may actually be later than its successor tasks' dates, and then the dependencies won't hold true because Project honors constraints over dependencies. By using start-to-finish relationships, I achieve the same result as using the ALAP constraint, but my schedule isn't subject to the issues that ALAP constraints can add.

Scheduling from Start or Finish

In Chapter 1, I showed you how to use the Project Information dialog box to set the start date for your project. As you work on planning your project, Project uses the start date as the beginning point for all schedule calculations. Typically you don't change the project start date during your planning; it simply isn't practical, nor is there any real reason to change it until you're ready to set a baseline and begin working on the project.

Understanding Scheduling

When you are ready to begin working on your project, on the Project menu, click Project Information to display the Project Information dialog box and set a beginning date for your project (see Figure 5-22).

When you make a change to the project start date, Project automatically adjusts the tasks in your project to accommodate that start date, assuming that you didn't use constraints or set start dates when you created the tasks in your project.

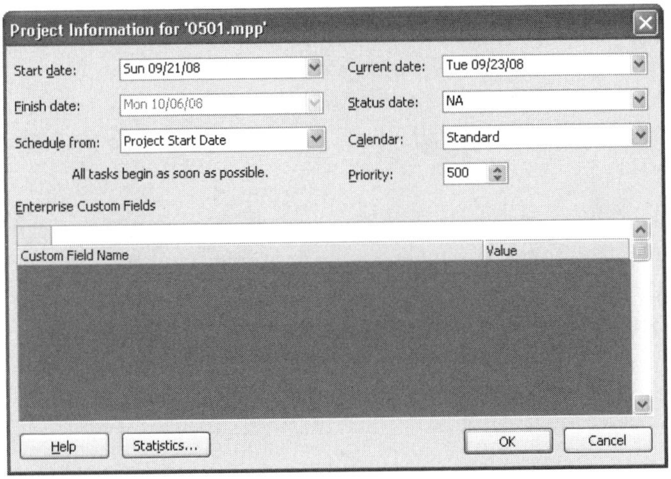

FIGURE 5-22 Set the beginning date for your project.

Most of the time, people set a start date for a project and all of the task timing flows from that date. After you set up all of the tasks in the project, Project tells you when the project will finish, based on its start date.

In some cases, it makes more sense to drive a project from its ending date. For example, in the scenario I set up in the section "What Are Your Task Constraints Doing to Your Schedule?" it might make sense to schedule a project that closes the local office on a target date using that target date as the project's finish date, because you need to know when to start the project to make sure that it finishes on time. In this case, you use the Project Information dialog box to establish a finish date for the project instead of a start date. When you schedule from the finish date, Project tells you when you have to start to complete the project by the specified finish date.

The Schedule From list in the Project Information dialog box controls whether you can set a start date or a finish date. By default, Project assumes you want to schedule from the project's starting date, but if you want to schedule from an ending date, in the Schedule From list, click Project Finish Date. Project then makes available the Finish Date field and you can select a finish date; at the same time, Project disables the Start Date field.

What about Scheduling Backwards?

If you schedule a project from its start date, Project automatically assigns the flexible As Soon As Possible (ASAP) constraint to each task you create. If you schedule a project from its finish date, Project automatically assigns the flexible As Late As Possible (ALAP) constraint to each task you create.

Be aware that although Project adjusts task dates automatically if you switch from scheduling using the project start date to scheduling using the project finish date, Project doesn't change the ASAP constraint of tasks that already exist in your project—instead, those tasks continue to use the ASAP constraint instead of using an ALAP constraint. In addition, you'll remove all leveling delays and splits that Project previously calculated.

In most cases, try to schedule your project from a start date, even if you know when the project should finish. You're more likely to build a more realistic schedule if you schedule from a start date and let Project tell you how long the project will take to complete.

If you find out after you've begun working on setting up a project that you need to use backward scheduling, you can change the ASAP setting on tasks most easily if you display the Constraint Type column in any Gantt Chart view table. Place the cell pointer in the column that you want to appear to the right of the Constraint Type column, and then on the Insert menu, click Column. In the Column Definition dialog box (shown in Figure 5-23), in the Field Name list, click Constraint Type.

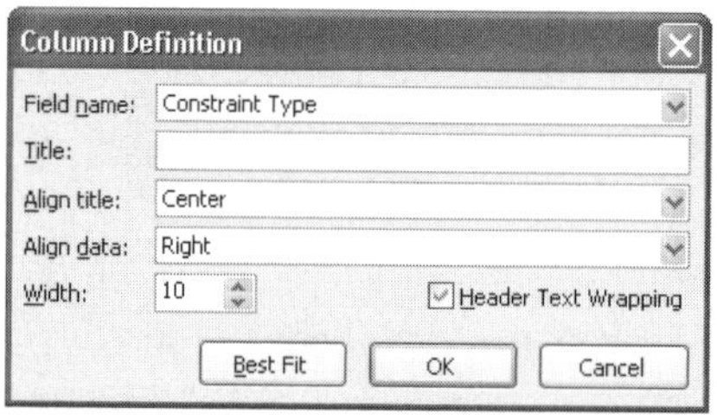

FIGURE 5-23 Add the Constraint Type field using the Column Definition dialog box.

When you click OK, Project adds a column to the table that identifies the constraint type assigned to each task (see Figure 5-24). When you click any row in the Constraint Type column, you'll see a list arrow; click the arrow to see the available constraint types and select As Late As Possible to change each task's constraint type.

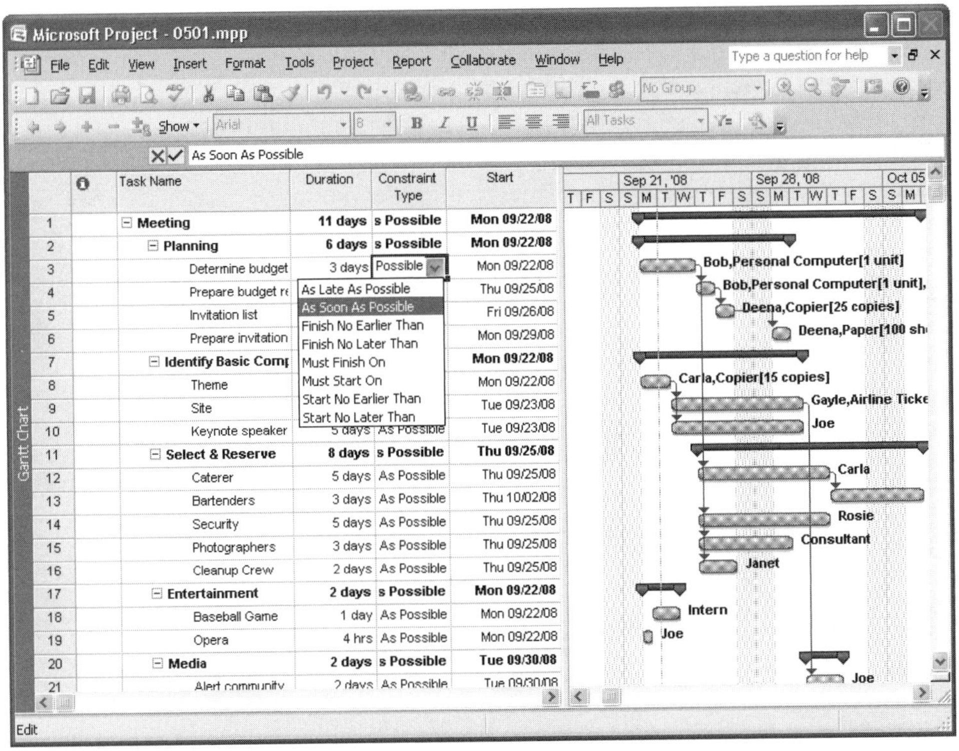

FIGURE 5-24 Using the Constraint Type list, you can quickly change from one constraint type to another.

Understanding What Calendar Settings Actually Do

Project contains several different types of calendars: base, project, resource, and task calendars. Project uses these calendars when calculating your project schedule and resource availability. If you understand how these calendars interact with each other, you'll also understand why Project calculates the schedule that you see. Using this information, you might be able to find ways to change the schedule.

The *base calendar* in Project serves as a model for all other calendars. Project comes with three base calendars: the Standard calendar, the 24 Hours calendar, and the Night Shift calendar. They each contain a fairly standard set of working times and non-working times, based on their names. You can use any of these base calendars directly in your project, you can create copies of these base calendars to use in your project, or you can create your own base calendars.

You use the *project calendar* to define your company's working and non-working times. By default, Project assigns the Standard base calendar to your project; you can make changes to it to reflect holidays and other company-specific working time information. If you prefer, you can create your own base calendar and assign it to your project in the Project Information dialog box (see Figure 5-25). If you don't use any resource or task calendars, Project uses the project calendar to calculate your project's schedule. See Chapter 1 for details on working with project calendars.

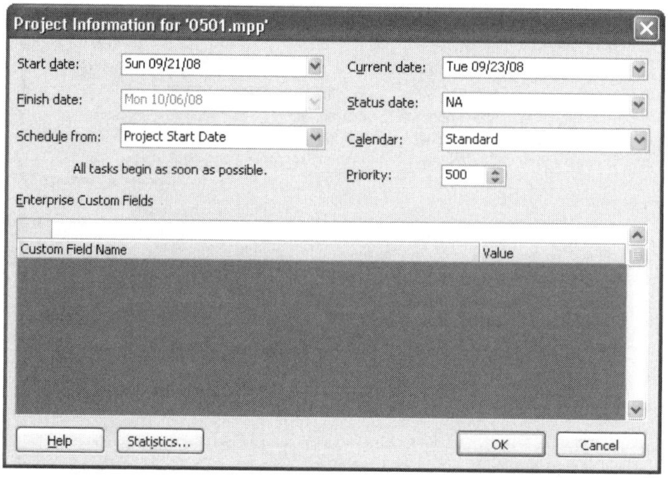

FIGURE 5-25 Set the project calendar in the Project Information dialog box.

If you change a resource's working time and then assign that resource to a task, Project schedules the task in the project using the *resource calendar* over the project calendar for tasks that do not have a fixed duration. So if September 1 through 14 are working days in your organization and Mary is on vacation during that time, Project won't schedule Mary for any tasks during that time, although some work might occur on the task if you schedule other people to work on it. See Chapter 3 for details on working with resource calendars.

You use a *task calendar* to schedule a task using time that differs from the project calendar. For example, you might create a task calendar to schedule a task to be performed over a weekend when your project calendar designates weekends as non-working time. If you assign a task calendar to a task, Project schedules the task in the project using the task calendar over the project calendar. See the section "When Should You Use a Task Calendar?" earlier in this chapter for more information on task calendars.

So what happens when you use both a task calendar and a resource calendar? Project schedules the task to occur during hours common to both calendars. Suppose that you create a resource calendar for John that has him working Tuesday through Saturday.

You then create a task calendar for Equipment Maintenance so that it will happen over a weekend. When you assign John to the Equipment Maintenance task, Project schedules the task to occur only on Saturday. You can then make the task calendar take precedence over the resource calendar. Double-click the task so that the Task Information dialog box appears and then click the Advanced tab. Next to the Calendar drop-down list, select the Scheduling Ignores Resource Calendars check box.

> **NOTE** If you use Project Professional connected to Microsoft Office Project Server 2007, calendars reside in the Project Server database. Check with your Project Server administrator to find out if you can create task and resource calendars locally.

Managing Slack

Tasks that appear on the critical path are called critical tasks. By default, Project 2007 defines critical tasks as tasks without slack (also called *float*). Project calculates a task's slack by calculating the difference between early finish and late finish dates; when these two dates are the same, the difference is zero, the task has no slack, and Project identifies the task as a critical task.

When a task has slack, you can afford to delay the task up to the amount of slack it has without placing the task on the critical path of your project. Generally speaking, if you delay a task that has slack, you won't delay your project unless you delay the task beyond the amount of slack it has and don't make up for this delay elsewhere.

Project tracks both free slack and total slack. *Free slack* is the amount of time you can delay a task without delaying its successor task. You can use the Free Slack field to help you determine if you can delay a task without impacting your schedule. If a task has free slack, you can allow resources working on it more time to complete the task. Or you might consider reassigning a resource from a task with free slack to a critical task to help ensure that your project stays on schedule.

Total slack is the amount of time you can delay a task without delaying the project finish date. When the total slack value is positive, it represents the amount of time that you can delay the task without affecting the project finish date. If the total slack is negative, you're looking at the amount of time you need to save to avoid delaying the project finish date. Negative slack is usually caused by a constraint placed on the task.

Ways to Identify Slack

So how do you find slack in your project? The easiest way is to use the Detail Gantt view. By default, Project displays critical task Gantt bars in red in this view, but because this book isn't in color, I've changed the appearance of critical task Gantt bars to use a crosshatch pattern so that you can identify them (see Figure 5-26).

Critical tasks, by definition, have no slack. Next to the Gantt bars of non-critical tasks that have free slack, lines appear that represent the task's free slack, and the numbers beside those bars tell you the amount of free slack associated with the task.

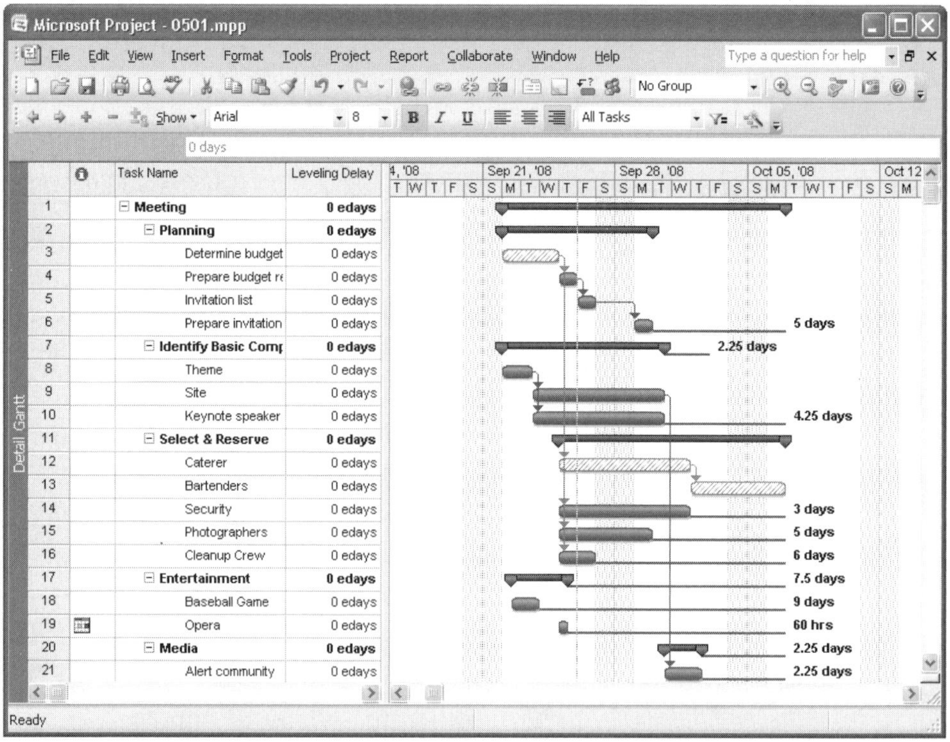

FIGURE 5-26 The Detail Gantt view shows you slack associated with tasks.

You also can add the Free Slack and Total Slack fields to any task-oriented table view. Right-click the heading of the column that you want to appear to the right of the Free Slack column, and then on the Insert menu, click Column. In the Column Definition dialog box, in the Field Name list, click Free Slack.

When you click OK, Project adds a column to the table that shows you how much free slack you have for each task in the project (see Figure 5-27). You can add the Total Slack field using the same technique.

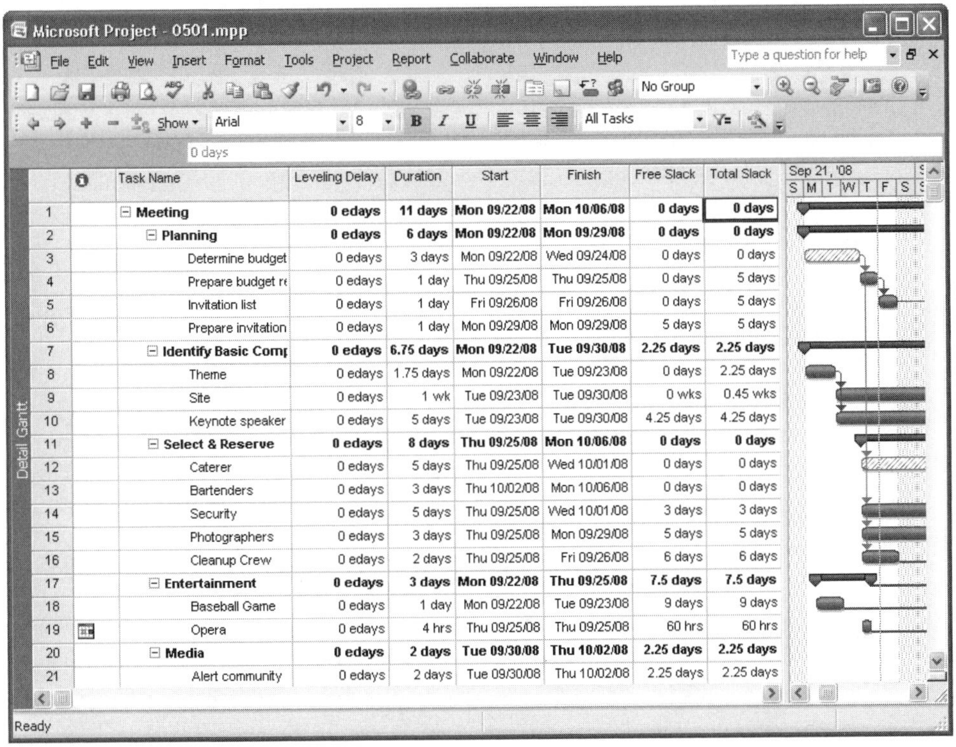

FIGURE 5-27 You can add the Free Slack and Total Slack fields to any task-oriented table to view slack associated with each task.

Some other fields might help you in your analysis of slack in your project, and you can add them to a task-oriented table view the same way you add the Free Slack and Total Slack fields:

- The Start Slack field shows the duration Project calculates between the early start date and the late start date. Correspondingly, the Finish Slack field shows the duration Project calculates between the early finish date and the late finish date. The smaller value—Start Slack or Finish Slack—is the free slack value that Project calculates for the task.

- The Early Start field shows the earliest date that a task could possibly begin if all of its predecessor and successor tasks also begin on their early start dates, considering constraints and leveling delays. Initially, Project sets the early start date equal to the task's scheduled start date, which is the project start date, and then recalculates the early start date as you link the task to predecessors and successors and apply constraints.

- The Early Finish field shows the earliest date that a task could possibly finish if all of its predecessor and successor tasks also finish on their early finish dates, considering constraints and leveling delays. Initially, Project sets the early finish date equal to the task's scheduled finish date, which is the task's scheduled start date plus its duration, and then recalculates the early finish date as you link the task to predecessors and successors and apply constraints.

- The Late Start field shows the latest date that a task could possibly begin without delaying the project if all of its predecessor and successor tasks also begin and end on their late start dates and late finish dates, considering constraints and leveling delays. Initially, Project sets the late start date equal to the project finish date minus the task's duration, and then recalculates the late start date as you link the task to predecessors and successors and apply constraints.

- The Late Finish field shows the latest date that a task could possibly end without delaying the project if all of its predecessor and successor tasks also start and end on their late start dates and late finish dates, considering constraints and leveling delays. Initially, Project sets the late finish date equal to the project finish date and then recalculates the late finish date as you link the task to predecessors and successors and apply constraints.

Project determines slack by calculating the difference between the early finish date and the late finish date. For critical path tasks the early finish date and late finish date are identical, so they have no slack.

Ways to Build in Slack

A wise project manager builds slack into the tasks of a project to try to account for the little things that go wrong. And there are always little things that go wrong. Not long ago, Hurricane Ike shut down Houston. If project managers in Houston built slack into their tasks, their projects might not be delivered quite as late as they would be without slack built in. Of course, Hurricane Ike is an extreme case, but if your suppliers go on strike, you won't get much work done until a new supply chain is established. With slack built into your project, that delay might become a tiny bump in the road instead of automatically making your project run past its scheduled end date.

That said, there's no concrete rule about how to build slack into your project. Like much of project management, building slack into a project is more art than science.

Some people like to add slack by exaggerating the duration of each task in the project. In this case, the slack in the schedule isn't visible to anyone, and even you might not know how much slack your tasks contain. This technique might really extend a project's schedule. Think about it; if the project contains 30 tasks and you add one day to each task, you just extended the project by 30 days.

Some people like to add a "slack task" to the project or to each phase of the project. That is, they create a task with an innocuous name like Phase I Finish-Up and assign it a duration of, say, five days. If other tasks in the phase slip, you can safely reduce the duration of this "non-task" without hurting your schedule. Project doesn't associate any slack with this task, so again you won't see any values in the Free Slack or Total Slack fields for this task.

If you schedule your project from its finish date, you can add breathing room by setting a deadline date on the last task in the project. You'll have a deadline indicator on the project schedule, but again Project won't display any slack values in the Free Slack or Total Slack fields. If you miss the deadline, you still have more time to complete the project, and Project simply displays an indicator in the Indicators column that tells you that the deadline date passed before the task was completed.

Another approach you can use is to increase the amount of slack a task must have to be considered critical. Using this approach, tasks become critical sooner, so more tasks appear on the critical path. If you're paying close attention to the critical path like you should, you'll become aware of approaching difficulties for a task earlier because you'll be watching those critical tasks. And in reality, you'll have some breathing room because you made some of these tasks critical before they really are critical. You can use the Calculation tab of the Options dialog box; on the Tools menu, click Options, and then click the Calculation tab (see Figure 5-28). In the Tasks Are Critical If Slack Is Less Than Or Equal To box, change the value from 0 to the number of slack days you want to add to each task. So for example, if you set the value to 1, a task becomes critical when it has one day or less of slack.

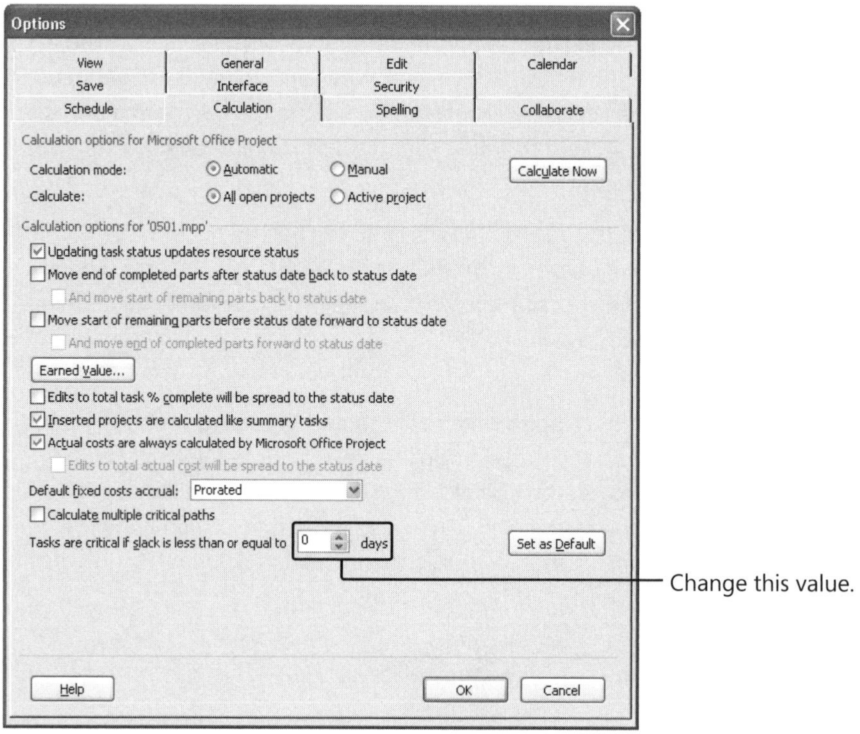

Change this value.

FIGURE 5-28 You can add slack days to add to each task.

In Figure 5-29, I set the value equal to three days; if you compare this figure with Figure 5-26, you'll see that more tasks now appear on the critical path.

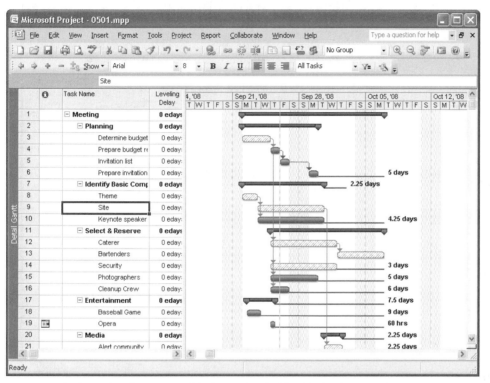

FIGURE 5-29 By increasing the amount of slack associated with critical tasks, I added more tasks to the critical path.

In cases where you want to build slack into only some tasks, you can use lag time, which is a delay between two linked tasks. In Figure 5-30, I set a finish-to-start dependency between all three tasks, and then I set a two-day delay from the finish of Task 1 to the start of Task 2. Although all three tasks are on the critical path, I actually have two extra days to finish Task 1 before I delay the project. Lag time doesn't appear as slack in the Free Slack or Total Slack fields.

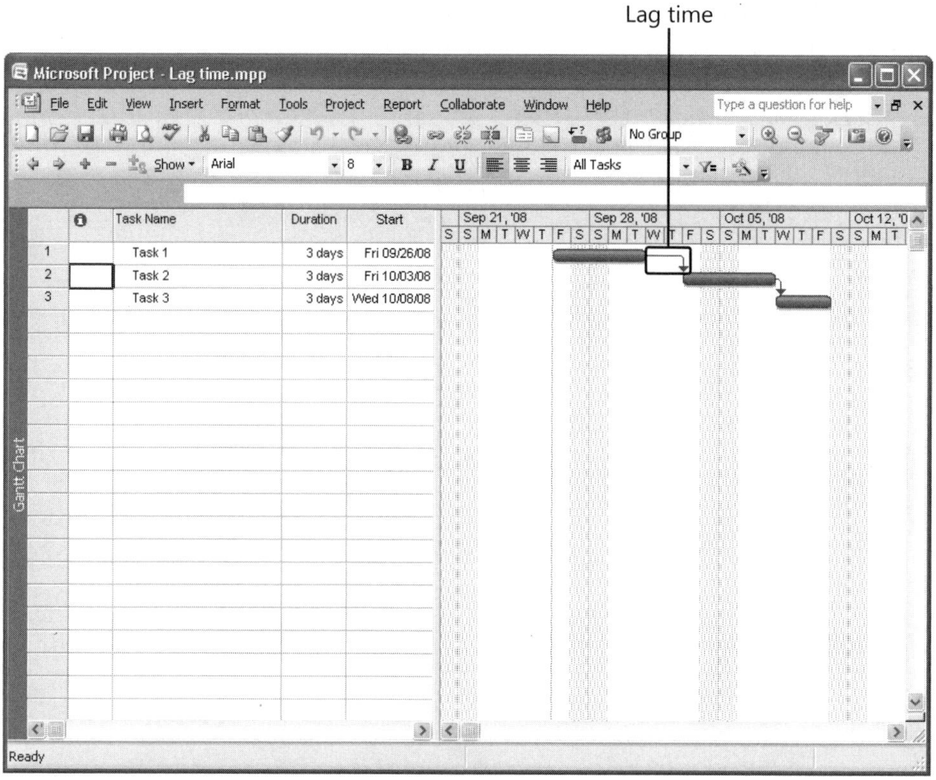

Lag time

FIGURE 5-30 Adding lag time delays the start of a task that has a finish-to-start relationship with its predecessor.

To add lag time, double-click the successor task—in my example, Task 2—and click the Predecessors tab. In the Lag column, enter a positive value either in days or as a percentage of the duration of the predecessor task (see Figure 5-31).

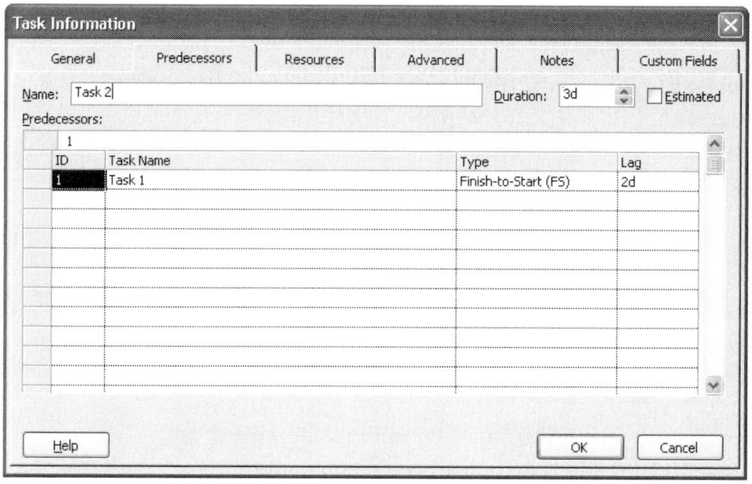

FIGURE 5-31 Adding lag time.

TIP   If you enter a negative value in the Lag column, you add lead time between the tasks. When the two tasks have a finish-to-start relationship, lead time creates an overlap between the finish of Task 1 and the start of Task 2, indicating that Task 2 can start before Task 1 finishes.

CHAPTER 6

Solving Resource Conflicts

OKAY, YOU'VE ENTERED A LOT OF INFORMATION into your project, and you entered it using your best estimates about the effort needed to complete the tasks. In the world of limited resources, it's highly likely that some of your resources are over-committed. In this chapter, we explore ways you can deal with overallocated resources to make your plan reflect reality.

What Causes Resource Conflicts?

Resource conflicts occur whenever you assign a resource to more work than that resource's standard calendar permits. Because projects can get very complicated, with numerous tasks scheduled for completion at various times, you can inadvertently create resource conflicts.

For example, suppose that you have two fixed units or fixed work tasks, which we'll call Task 1 and Task 2. These two tasks run concurrently; Task 1 is five days in duration and Task 2 is 10 days in duration. You also have two resources (Resource 1 and Resource 2), and you have assigned Resource 1 to Task 1 and Resource 2 to Task 2. When you add Resource 1 to Task 2, Microsoft Office Project 2007 reduces the duration of Task 2 by 50 percent and creates an overallocation situation for Resource 1. This becomes readily apparent in the Resource Usage view; in Figure 6-1, you can see the Resource Allocation view that shows the Resource Usage view on the top of the screen and the Leveling Gantt Chart view on the bottom of the screen.

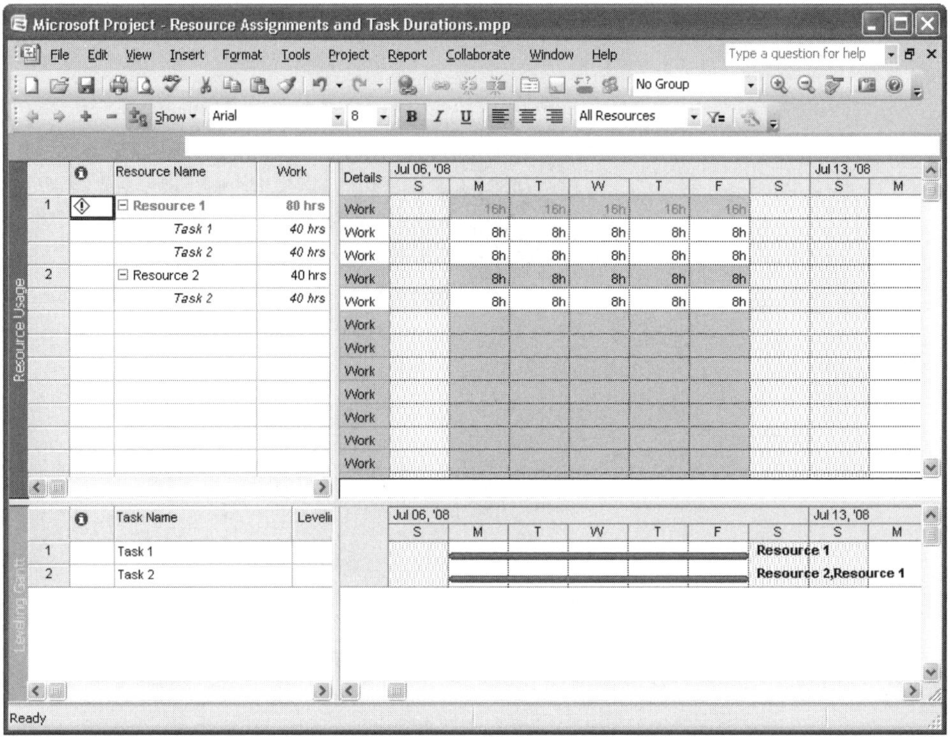

FIGURE 6-1 After assigning Resource 1 to both Task 1 and Task 2, Project reduces the duration of Task 2 and overallocates Resource 1.

> **NOTE**   Project adjusts the duration of fixed units and fixed work tasks when you add resources; Project does not adjust the duration of fixed duration tasks when you add resources.

You might have expected Project to understand that Resource 1 frees up during the second week, and will just assign Resource 1 to Task 2 during the second week. If Project did that and left Resource 2 to continue working on Task 2, why, between the two of them they'd finish Task 2 in seven and a half days: Resource 2 would work five days the first week, and Resources 1 and 2 would each work on the task during the second week, putting in eight hours each on the first two days, and four hours each on the third day.

So why doesn't Project set up Task 2 to finish in seven and a half days?

You need to understand that Project looks only at the assignments on a particular task when it recalculates the schedule; it doesn't look at a resource's assignments throughout the project. So that means that Project doesn't know that Resource 1 is assigned to Task 1 when you add Resource 1 to Task 2; instead, Project treats Task 2's resource assignments and scheduled duration independently of Task 1's resource assignments and duration, and recalculates Task 2's duration without considering conflicts in resource allocation.

In this chapter, we'll explore the many ways you can resolve such conflicts.

Identifying Resource Conflicts

In Chapter 4, "Finding the Information You Need," I discussed among other things the concepts of views and how they help you as you work in Project. When you're trying to evaluate resource information and resolve resource conflicts, certain resource views can help you identify conflicts.

The Resource Graph View

The Resource Graph view displays a vivid representation of each resource's allocation (see Figure 6-2) and makes it easy for you to find overallocated resources. Each vertical bar represents a resource's allocation percentage on a particular day, based on the working hours for the resource. There's a thick horizontal line that represents the 100% allocation mark. The bars below that line are blue and indicate 100 percent or less allocation. The bars above the line are red and indicate that the resource is overallocated and by what percentage. You also see the resource's total allocation for any given day at the bottom of that day's bar on the row labeled Peak Units. Any overallocated resource's name appears in bold red letters.

You view resources one at a time in this view; press the Page Down key or Page Up key to scroll through your resources. Use the scroll bar across the bottom of the right side of the view to display the resource's allocation over time.

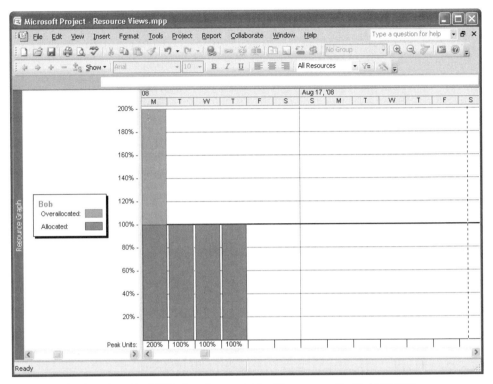

FIGURE 6-2 Any bar above the 100% allocation mark identifies an overallocated resource.

The Resource Allocation View

The Resource Allocation view consists of two panes and combines a Gantt chart in the lower pane with the Resource Usage view in the upper pane. Using this view, you can see the allocated work hours in the upper pane and simultaneously use the visual representation provided by the Gantt task bars to see the task timing and dependencies. If you select a resource in the upper pane, Project displays the tasks assigned to that resource in the Gantt Chart view that appears in the lower pane. Tasks that start at the same time overlap in the Gantt Chart pane, helping you to pinpoint the tasks that are causing the resource's overallocation. In Figure 6-3, Bob is overallocated on Thursday, August 14; he's scheduled to work 16 hours that day. When you examine the Gantt Chart view in the lower pane, you'll notice that Bob is assigned to work on two tasks that overlap on that day.

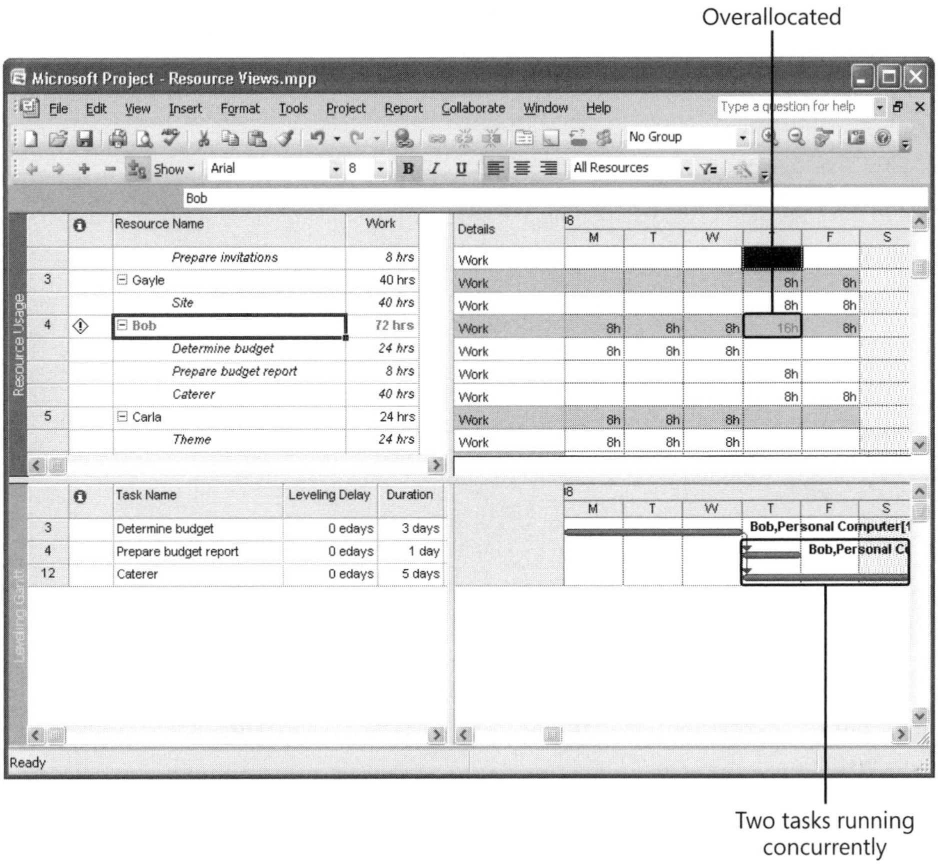

Overallocated

FIGURE 6-3 You can use the Resource Allocation view to help you spot and track down overallocations.

The top pane of the Resource Allocation view provides a few other clues that help you find overallocations: the names of overallocated resources appear in bold red type and a Caution icon appears in the Indicators column beside their names.

The Resource Usage View

In the Resource Usage view, the names of overallocated resources appear in bold red type and a Caution icon appears in the Indicator column beside their names. If you move the mouse over the Caution icon, you can see a message about the overallocation.

You can filter this view to display only overallocated resources and then modify the view to display the extent of each resource's overallocation. The names of overallocated resources appear in bold red type, and overallocated hours appear in red type. Follow these steps:

1. On the View menu, click Resource Usage to display the view.

2. In the Filter list on the Formatting toolbar, click Overallocated Resources to display only those resources that are overallocated:

3. To determine the amount of each overallocation, on the Format menu, point to Details, and click Overallocation. Project adds a row to the timescale portion of the Resource Usage view to show you the number of hours that you need to eliminate to correct the overallocation:

Techniques to Resolve Conflicts

There are several approaches you can take to resolve resource conflicts. Some of the approaches work regardless of whether the task is effort-driven. Other techniques work only if the task is effort-driven. Remember, Project adjusts the duration of an effort-driven task based on the number of resources you assign to the task, but Project leaves the duration unaffected by resource assignments if a task is not effort-driven. In some cases, shortening the duration of an effort-driven task might eliminate an overallocation for a resource, but if the task isn't effort-driven, you can't shorten the task's duration.

If a task is not effort-driven, you can try any of the following to resolve a resource conflict:

- Swapping out resources
- Using overtime

If a task is effort-driven, you can try those techniques along with these techniques:

- Adding a resource to a task to shorten its duration and possibly resolve a conflict
- Using part-time work assignments to smooth out a resource's allocation to several tasks
- Controlling the date a resource starts working on a task
- Contouring a resource's assignment on a task to resolve a conflict
- Leveling resource assignments

It's also important to understand that you might decide to do nothing about an over-allocation. If a resource is overallocated by two hours a day for two or three days, you might decide to permit the overallocation. Just remember that you really can't permit an overallocation for any extended period of time or your resources will burn out and you won't be successful as a project manager. And if the overallocated resource is a person who earns overtime for work beyond the standard day, you do need to account for the extra hours in the day as overtime hours to correctly estimate the cost of your project.

Swapping Out Resources

When you've got an overallocated Work resource working on a task, you can swap out that resource for another with the same qualifications that isn't overallocated.

> **NOTE**   Overallocation applies only to Work resources, not to Cost or Material resources.

Let's assume that you used the Resource Allocation view to identify an overallocated resource and the task that is causing the conflict. If you swap the top and bottom panes of this view, you can select a task in the top pane and see all resources assigned to it in the bottom pane, along with overallocations. So let's set up a view to show the Gantt Chart view on top and the Resource Usage view on the bottom. Switch to the Gantt Chart view and then on the Window menu, click Split. Click anywhere in the bottom pane, and on the View menu, click Resource Usage. Your screen will look something like the one shown in Figure 6-4.

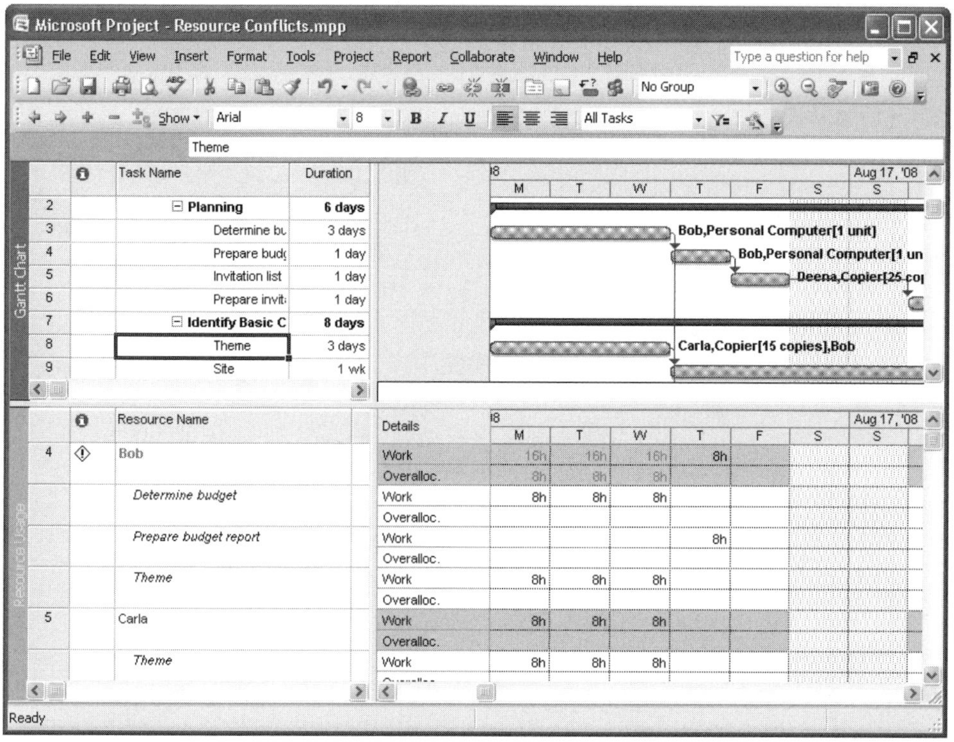

FIGURE 6-4 Display the Gantt Chart view in the upper pane and the Resource Usage view in the lower pane.

Follow these steps to swap one resource for another:

1. In the upper pane, click the task containing the resource you want to swap out. In the bottom of the window, Project displays all the assignments for every resource assigned to the task selected in the top pane.

2. Click the Assign Resources button to open the Assign Resources window:

3. Highlight the resource you want to swap out.

4. Click the Replace button. The Replace Resource dialog box appears:

5. Select the resource you want to use on the task.

6. Fill in the Units column only if you want to change the number of units of the new resource assigned to the task. If you leave the Units column blank, Project assumes you want the same number of units of the replacement resource as you had assigned to the original resource.

7. Click OK in the Replace Resource dialog box.

> **NOTE** You might see a message from the Planning wizard. Read the message and click OK to continue.

8. Click Close in the Assign Resources window.

Project will change the assignment without affecting historical actuals, and no resources are affected other than the ones involved in the switch.

REMOVING RESOURCES

Occasionally, you might need to remove a resource from a task. During the planning stage, when no work has been performed, you can safely remove a resource assignment from a task. If the task is effort-driven, Project will adjust the duration of the task, just as you'd expect. However, once you've started tracking, don't remove a resource from an assignment if the resource has done any work on that assignment. Instead, make sure that you replace the resource with another resource as described in the preceding section. When you *replace* a resource, Project maintains historical actual information. But if you *remove* a resource for which you've recorded historical actual information, Project removes that information as well. Project shows the task as completed, but you won't see any work or actual work values at the task level.

Using Overtime

In Project, overtime is the amount of work that you schedule for a resource beyond the resource's regular working hours. Overtime work represents the amount of time a resource spends on a task during non-regular hours; overtime work does not represent additional work on a task. By scheduling overtime, the resource might finish the task faster and therefore eliminate an allocation conflict.

Project charges overtime hours to the project using the resource's overtime rate, so for overallocated resources that are not salaried and cost extra when working overtime, assigning overtime hours helps you correctly estimate the cost of your project in addition to possibly resolving a resource conflict.

In Figure 6-5, Mary is overallocated on Thursday, August 28, by four hours. I've decided to give her four hours of overtime that day to resolve the conflict. For me to do this, I use the Task Entry view, which is a combination of the Gantt Chart view and the Task Form view, to schedule overtime. Here's how I handle it:

1. To display the Task Entry view, on the View menu, click More Views. In the More Views window, select Task Entry, and click Apply.

2. Click the Task Form to make it the active pane.

3. On the Format menu, point to Details, and click Resource Work. Project displays the Ovt. Work column in the Task Form pane. In this column, "0h" means that you have not yet assigned overtime.

4. In the top pane, select the task to which you want to assign overtime.

5. In the bottom pane, fill in the amount of overtime you want to assign to the appropriate resource.

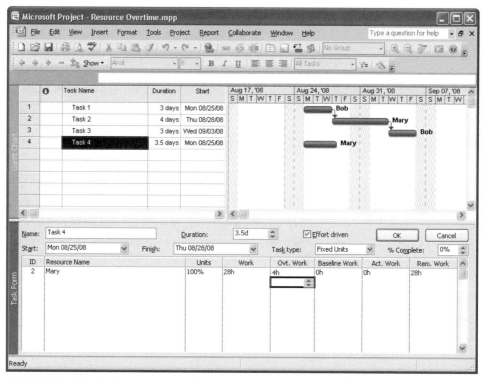

FIGURE 6-5 Use the Task Form view and display the Overtime column to add overtime to an assignment.

Adding Resources

You can try adding a resource to resolve an overallocation. If the task isn't effort-driven, adding a resource doesn't reduce the duration of the task, but it can reduce the amount of effort you need from the overallocated resource by spreading the effort out over two resources. And if you're able to reduce that overallocated resource's effort on the conflicting task, you just might be able to eliminate the conflict. Essentially, you're assigning part-time work to an overallocated resource; you can read more about assigning part-time work in the section "Part-Time Assignments" later in this chapter.

When you add a resource to an effort-driven task, you shorten the duration of the task and it's possible that you'll eliminate the overallocation if the task is completed more quickly.

| **SEE ALSO** | See Chapter 3, "Pinning Down Your Budget," for details on adding a resource. |

Using a Shared Resource

What, you've run out of resources of your own? You might be able to borrow a resource from another manager. If your organization uses the same resources to work on multiple projects and doesn't use Microsoft Office Project Server 2007, you might consider setting up a resource pool, which is nothing more than a set of resources that are available to any project. Using a resource pool is closely tied to the topic of managing multiple projects, so you'll find information about it in Chapter 13, "Managing Cross-Project Conflicts."

If your organization uses Project Server, you'll share resources using the Enterprise Resource Pool, and you can use the Resource Substitution wizard to resolve resource conflicts. The Resource Substitution wizard is usually used to substitute real people for generic resources, but you also can use it to help you find someone with the right skills who is also available to work on your project.

You can select one or more projects and have the Resource Substitution wizard reallocate the resources in those projects to better utilize their time. To find a resource with the skills needed to complete a particular task, you can use the Resource Substitution wizard in conjunction with the Resource Breakdown Structure (RBS) code.

The RBS code is a custom outline code—a type of custom field—with an attached value list; in many cases, each value in the list represents a skill or set of skills. The person in your organization who manages the Enterprise Resource Pool assigns to each resource in the pool an RBS code that describes the resource's skills. The Resource Substitution wizard can use the RBS code to review the skills of resources that are already assigned to tasks and then substitute other resources with the same RBS code.

> **SEE ALSO** For information on custom fields, see Chapter 4.

To run the Resource Substitution wizard, on the Tools menu, click Substitute Resources. Then complete the pages that the wizard presents. You can select multiple projects and resources for the wizard to consider while making substitution suggestions.

Part-Time Assignments

Here's the situation: You've assigned a resource to several concurrent tasks, and in the process, you've overallocated the resource. You don't have any other resources to add to the tasks or substitute for the overallocated resource, and you're trying to avoid using overtime to keep costs down.

In this situation, you can assign the resource to work part-time on each of the tasks to solve the conflict. Since the amount of work isn't changing, the tasks will take longer to complete.

> **TIP** ✓ If you have additional resources available, you can use part-time assignments in conjunction with adding resources to tasks and probably complete the task on time.

When you assign a resource to work part-time, you change the number of units of the resource that you apply to the task. Since Project sets task types to Fixed Units by default, and fixed units tasks are effort-driven, changing the amount of time that a resource works on a task also changes the duration of the task. So if you reduce the number of resource units assigned to the task, Project lengthens the task to accommodate the effort required.

Let's take a look at an example. In Figure 6-6, I've assigned Resource 1 to work at 100-percent capacity on Task 1, a five-day task.

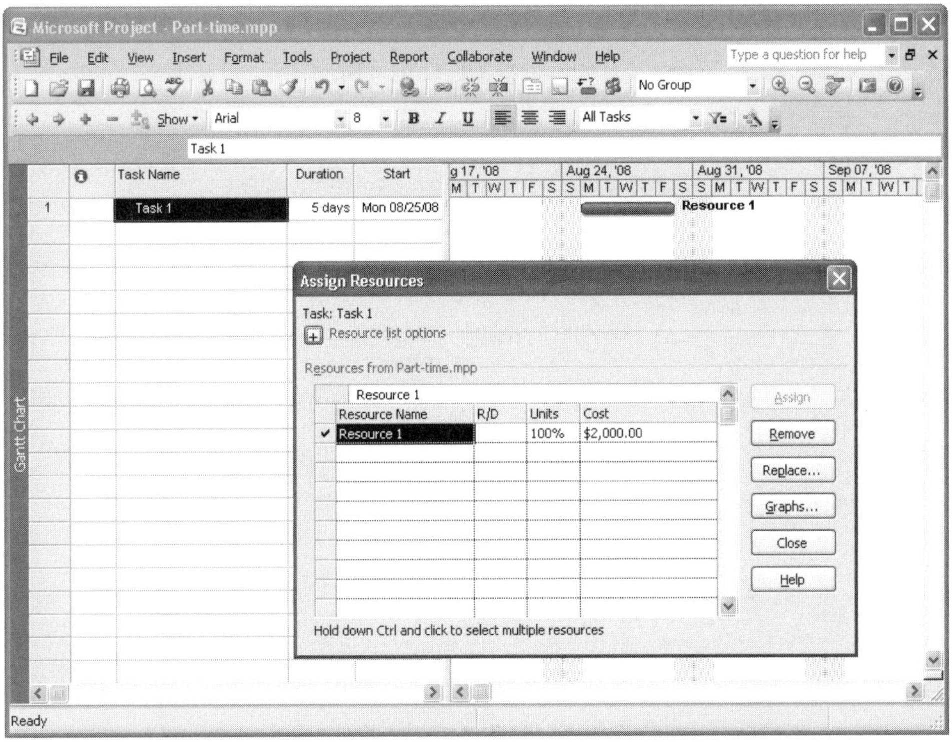

FIGURE 6-6 A typical situation, where a resource is assigned to work full-time on a task.

In Figure 6-7, I've reduced the number of units of the resource assigned to the task, setting the resource to work half of the time on the task. Project correspondingly doubles the duration of the task. Notice that using this approach doesn't change the cost of your project, so you don't need to worry about any budget considerations. You only need to consider what happens to the end date of your project. If this task isn't on your project's critical path, the solution is an excellent one, since lengthening the task won't affect the end date of your project. If, however, the task is on the critical path, you need to confirm with management that the added time needed to complete your project is acceptable.

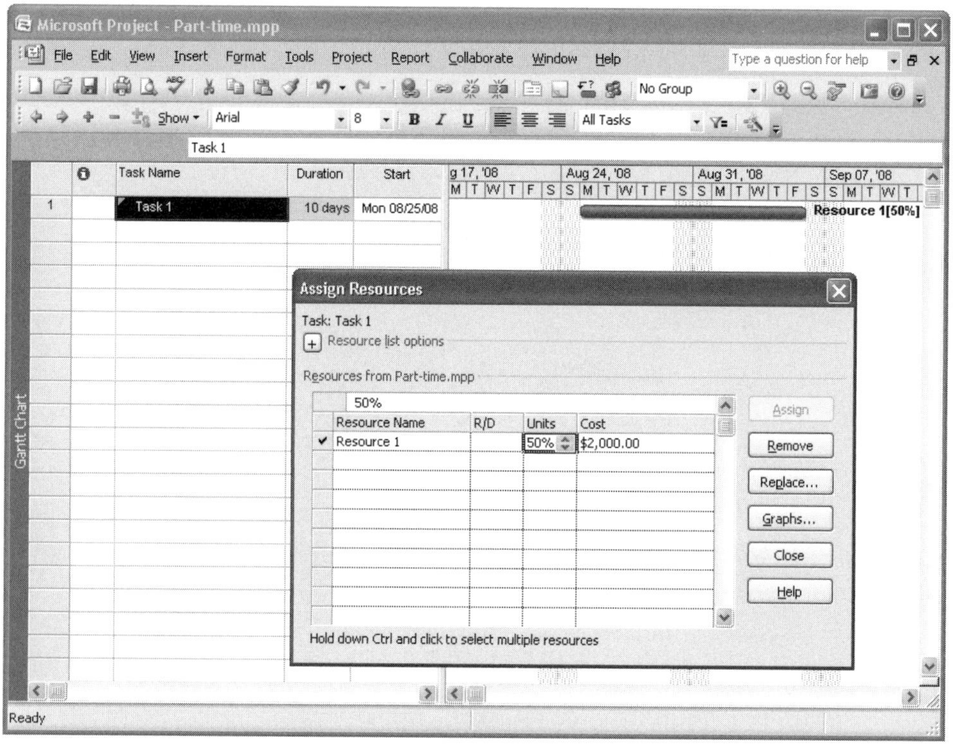

FIGURE 6-7 Having a resource work part-time on an effort-driven task lengthens the amount of time needed to complete the task.

NOTE	You might be tempted to change the task type to Fixed Duration to avoid changing the task's duration when you assign a resource to work part-time on it. By making this change, however, you imply that the task can be completed by the resource in less time than you originally allotted—effectively, you are shortening the amount of time that it takes to complete the task because you're applying less effort during the same timeframe. If the total amount of effort to complete the task doesn't change, resist the temptation to use a fixed duration task.

Staggering Work Time

Sometimes controlling when a resource works on a task can resolve a conflict. For example, if you've assigned more than one resource to a task, you might be able to delay one resource's start on a task to resolve a conflict. Or you might be able to change a resource's work contour to eliminate a conflict.

Changing When a Resource Begins Working on a Task

Back in the beginning of this chapter, I posed a situation that created an overallocation. In that example, your project had two fixed units or fixed work tasks that we called Task 1 and Task 2. The two tasks ran concurrently, with Task 1 being five days in duration and Task 2 being 10 days in duration. You also had two resources (Resource 1 and Resource 2), and you assigned Resource 1 to Task 1 and Resource 2 to Task 2. When you added Resource 1 to Task 2, Project reduced the duration of Task 2 by 50 percent and created an overallocation situation for Resource 1 (see Figure 6-8).

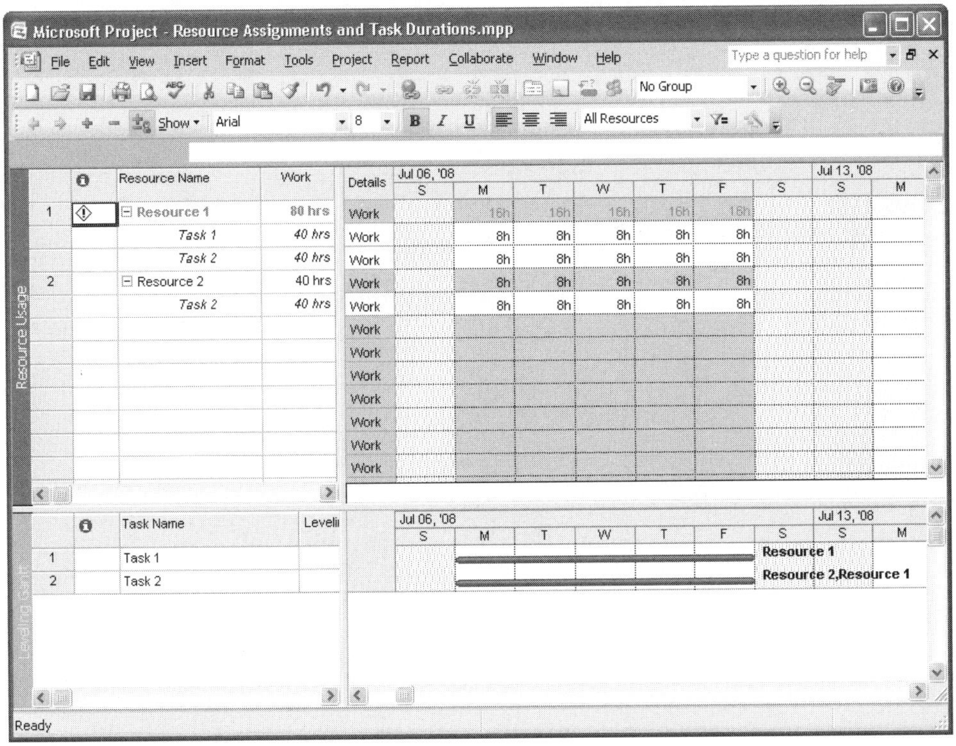

FIGURE 6-8 Project reduces the duration of Task 2 and overallocates Resource 1.

You might have expected Project to recognize that Resource 1 frees up during the second week and would have assigned Resource 1 to Task 2 during the second week, enabling both resources to finish Task 2 in seven and a half days. But Project didn't make that adjustment because Project looks only at the assignments on a particular task when it recalculates the schedule; it doesn't look at a resource's assignments throughout the project.

Although this technique isn't the most common approach to making an adjustment, you can resolve the resource conflict by changing the dates Resource 1 works on the task using these steps:

1. Display the Resource Usage view or the Resource Allocation view, where you can easily identify the resource overallocation.

2. Double-click the name of the task below the resource whose start you want to delay—in this example, Task 2 under Resource 1. Project displays the General tab of the Assignment Information dialog box:

3. Change the Start and Finish fields below the Work Contour list to reflect the actual start date and actual finish date that Resource 1 will work on during Task 2.

> **NOTE** I set the Finish field to the end of that week, not the last day that Resource 1 would work on the task.

4. Click OK to save the change, and Project moves Resource 1 (full-time) to work on the task during the second week. Resource 1 is no longer overallocated, and both resources are working full-time during the second week on Task 2.

5. On the Sheet portion of the view, use the Work column to reallocate the hours each resource works on Task 2 from 40 for Resource 1 and 40 for Resource 2 to 20 for Resource 1 and 60 for Resource 2 (see the graphic below). You can see that Project has reset the duration of the task to seven and a half days, with everybody working just the way you thought they would.

NOTE	As an alternative method to resolving this resource conflict, you can create two tasks to represent Task 2; you'd assign Resource 2 to the part that runs concurrently with Task 1, and you'd assign both resources to the second part. You'd need to calculate the durations for each of these parts of Task 2 separately based on the total effort required and the effort still needed when Resource 1 joins in to work on the task. This approach would net you the same result as shown in the previous graphic.

There are no technological downsides to making an adjustment like this one, except that an experienced Project user might notice the manipulations and wonder how and why you did that. From a conceptual perspective, though, consider this: When you allow Project to schedule as it typically does and correct the overallocation situation for Resource 1 using leveling—which is the most usual way to correct the overallocation, and the method you'll read about later in this chapter in the section "How Resource Leveling Really Works"—Project extends the duration of Task 2 back to the 10 days you originally estimated (instead of the seven and a half days you thought). In addition, Resource 1 has assignments for the total 10 days, working Task 1 during Week 1 and Task 2 during Week 2, while Resource 2 has an assignment on Task 2 only during Week 1. Although the resource assignments might look strange to you, there is an advantage to leaving things the way Project calculates: If you leave the duration of Task 2 at 10 days, you build two and a half days of slack into your schedule; and if you finish early, you might look like a hero. If you make the manual adjustment and you miss the deadline, well . . . management probably won't be really happy with you.

Using Contours

You can use contours to adjust the way Project assigns a resource's time, along the way eliminating the conflict. An assignment's contour refers to the shape of a resource's work assignment over time. The default contour Project assigns is the Flat contour; when you use this contour, the resource works on a task for the maximum number of hours that he or she is assigned to the task throughout the assignment.

Project includes several other contours; the most commonly used contours, beside the Flat contour, are the Front Loaded, Back Loaded, and Bell contours. When you use a Back Loaded contour for a particular assignment, Project assigns the majority of the resource's work at the end of the assignment. Using a Front Loaded contour tells Project to assign most of the resource's work at the beginning of the task. Using a Bell contour tells Project to assign most of the resource's work in the middle of the task.

In Figure 6-9, the Resource Usage view shows that Mary is overallocated by four hours on Thursday, August 28. If you could reduce her work on that day by delaying some of her work on Task 2 using a Back Loaded contour, you might be able to eliminate the overallocation, or at least reduce it to something acceptable.

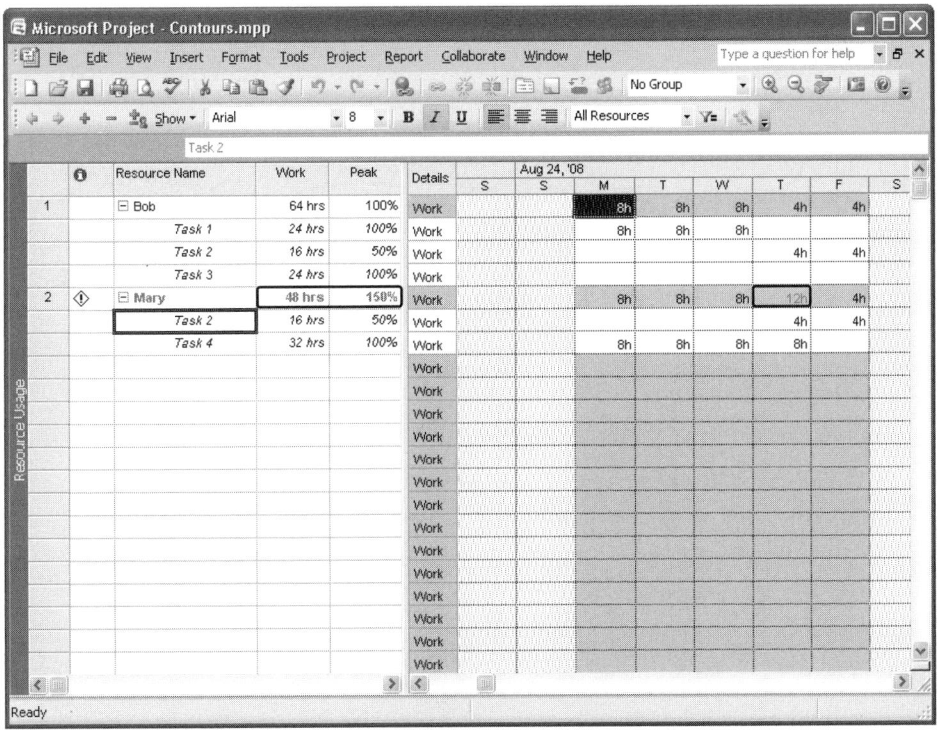

FIGURE 6-9 Mary is scheduled to work a 12-hour day on August 28.

DISPLAYING THE PEAK COLUMN

In Figure 6-9, I added the Peak column to the view so that I could easily see the maximum effort distributed over time that a resource is assigned to work. You might find this field useful when you use a contour other than the default Flat contour. To display this field, right-click any other field—I right-clicked the Work heading in the sheet area—and click Insert Column. Project displays the Column Definition dialog box. In the Field Name list, type a few characters of the field you want to display until Project displays the correct field. Press Enter and then click OK. Project adds the field to the right of the field you right-clicked; you can drag the field right or left to change its position.

To change Mary's assignment on Task 2 to use a Back Loaded contour, follow these steps:

1. Display the Resource Usage view (on the View menu, click Resource Usage).

2. In the Resource Name column, double-click the name of the task below the resource whose assignment contour you want to change. Project displays the General tab of the Assignment Information dialog box:

3. In the Work Contour list, click Back Loaded.

4. Click OK.

When Project redisplays the Resource Usage view (see Figure 6-10), you see that Mary's workload during the first week of her assignment to Task 2 has been redistributed, almost completely eliminating the conflict. In fact, Mary is overallocated less than a half hour on August 28. That's an overallocation that you can accept. Remember, though—if Mary is not a salaried employee and she earns overtime at a higher rate than her standard rate, assign her extra .47 hour on August 28 to overtime to keep your estimated project costs accurate.

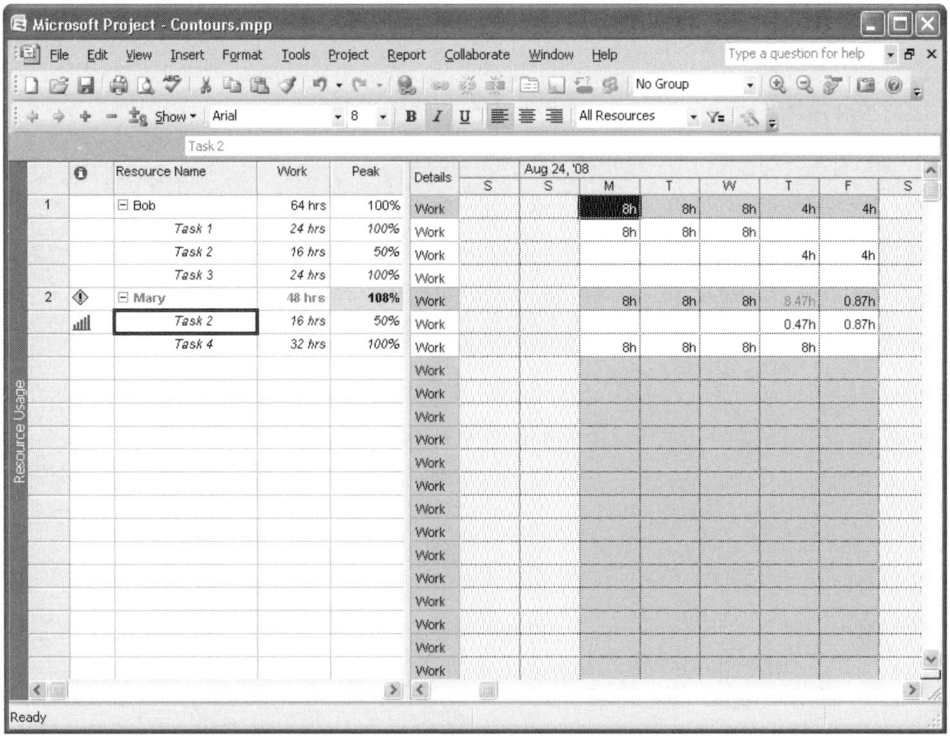

FIGURE 6-10 Using a contour reduces an overallocation to an acceptable level.

> **TIP**
> ✓
> The icon in the Indicators column next to the task reminds you that you selected a contour other than Flat. Move your mouse over the icon to see what contour you assigned.

You should be aware of the ways contours behave when you make changes to tasks. If you increase the duration of a task, Project stretches the contour to include the new duration. And if you set a contour and then change the start date of the task or the start date of a resource's work on the task, Project preserves the pattern of the original contour by automatically shifting the contour and reapplying it to include the new date.

If you apply a contour other than the default Flat contour to a task and later add new total work values to the task, Project automatically reapplies the contour pattern to the task and the resources. Project first distributes the new task work values across the affected time span and then assigns new work values to the resources assigned to the task.

How Resource Leveling Really Works

If you have scheduled several tasks to run concurrently and you now find resource conflicts in your project, you can spread out the resource workload by using Project's leveling feature. When you level resource loads, Project resolves resource conflicts by delaying or splitting tasks to take into consideration the schedules of assigned resources.

You can let Project level your project whenever a conflict arises, or you can control when Project levels to resolve resource conflicts. Regardless of when Project levels, you can choose to level the entire project or only selected resources, and you can choose a date range for Project to use to level resource assignments.

How Project Selects Tasks to Delay or Split

Project assesses each task to determine if it is the cause of a resource overallocation. For each task that is causing an overallocation, Project evaluates the task to determine if it has a priority of 1000, which tells Project not to level the task. For more information on priorities, see the section "Using Priorities to Control Leveling" later in this chapter.

Next, Project evaluates the task for constraints. Project won't level tasks with a Must Start On or Must Finish On constraint. If you are scheduling your project from the start date, Project won't level tasks with an As Late As Possible (ALAP) constraint. Similarly, if you are scheduling your project from the finish date, Project won't level tasks with an As Soon As Possible (ASAP) constraint.

Finally, Project determines whether you've recorded any "actual" information for a task. Project won't level a task with an actual start date unless you select a leveling option that permits Project to split any remaining work.

Understanding Leveling Order

By default, Project uses the following criteria in the order listed to select tasks to delay or split:

1. Project looks at predecessor relationships and selects tasks that do not have successor dependencies before those that have successor dependencies.

2. Project selects tasks with more total slack before those with less total slack.

3. Project selects tasks that start later before those that start earlier. If you're scheduling from the finish date of your project, Project selects tasks that finish earlier before selecting those that finish later.

4. Project selects tasks with lower priority values before selecting those with higher priority values.

5. Project selects tasks without inflexible constraints before selecting those with inflexible constraints.

This set of criteria is called the Standard leveling order. You can also choose to level using the Priority, Standard leveling order. In this case, Project uses the same criteria to select tasks to delay or split, but it moves Number 4 in the list above into the Number 1 slot.

Project offers one other leveling order—the ID Only leveling order. When you choose this leveling order, Project delays tasks with higher ID numbers before considering any other criteria.

Using Priorities to Control Leveling

You can use the Priority field to control the order in which Project selects tasks to delay. The values you can use in the Priority field range from 1 to 1000; Project avoids delaying tasks with higher priority values. For example, suppose that you've assigned a priority of 500 to Task 1 and a priority of 700 to Task 2. During leveling, Project will delay Task 1— the task with the lower priority number—before it delays Task 2.

TIP Assigning a priority of 1000 tells Project not to delay a task.

By default, Project assigns a priority of 500 to every task, and you can change the priority value on the General tab of each task's Task Information dialog box (see Figure 6-11).

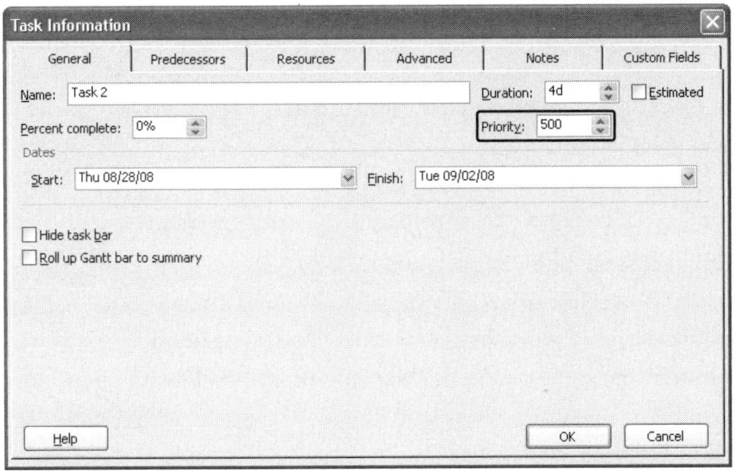

FIGURE 6-11 You can use the General tab of the Task Information dialog box to change a task's priority.

You might prefer to add the Priority field to the table portion of the Gantt Chart view or the Task Usage view; that way, you can easily see the priorities of other tasks (see Figure 6-12). To add the field, right-click the field you want to appear to the right of the Priority field and click Insert Column. In the Field Name list of the Column Definition dialog box that appears, type a few letters of the Priority field name until Project highlights it. Press Enter and then click OK.

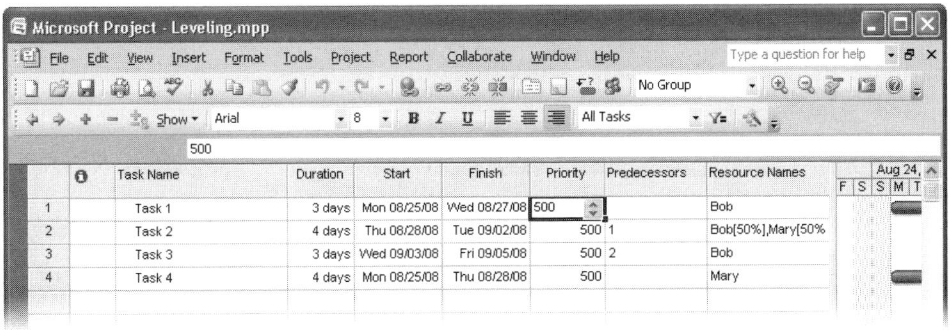

FIGURE 6-12 Add the Priority column to a table view to set task priorities.

> **NOTE** In addition to setting priorities for tasks, you can set a priority for the project in the Project Information dialog box (on the Project menu, click Project Information), which is useful if you work with resources in multiple projects.

After you prioritize tasks, you can sort them by priority to see the tasks Project is most likely to level. On the Project menu, point to Sort, and click By Priority.

Setting Leveling Options

You set leveling options using the same dialog box that you use to level resource assignments in your project. On the Tools menu, click Level Resources to display the Resource Leveling dialog box shown in Figure 6-13.

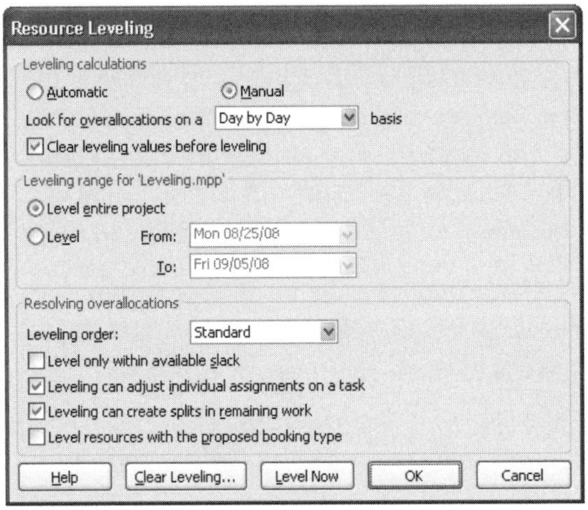

FIGURE 6-13 Set the options that control the way Project levels resources.

From the Resource Leveling dialog box, you can set the following resource leveling options:

- In the Leveling Calculations area, select the Automatic option button if you want Project to level resources if necessary whenever you make a change to your schedule. Select Manual to perform leveling only when you click the Level Now button in this dialog box. Many people prefer to use the Manual option, as automatically leveling your project can slow down schedule calculations when projects are large.

- In the Look For Overallocations list, select a timeframe that you want Project to use when determining whether leveling is necessary. The icon in the Indicators column of the Resource Usage view may contain a note that suggests the appropriate basis. The timeframe you select controls how sensitive Project is to recognizing an overallocation. For example, if you select Day By Day, Project considers a resource overallocated if scheduled to work more than eight hours a day based on the Standard calendar. But if you select Week By Week, a resource won't be considered overallocated unless his or her work week exceeds 40 hours based on the Standard calendar. Under these conditions, the resource could be scheduled to work 10 hours in one day but only six hours the next day and not be flagged as overallocated for leveling purposes.

- Select the Clear Leveling Values Before Leveling check box to make Project reset all delays previously established as a result of leveling or manually entering a leveling delay. If you don't select this box, Project builds upon previously established leveling values. Under these circumstances, Project probably won't change the scheduling of previously leveled tasks but will focus on new overallocations. If you opted to use Automatic leveling, you'll find that performance will improve if you do not select this check box because Project will not need to consider your entire schedule each time it levels.

- In the Leveling Range For area, select either to level the entire project or to level only for dates you select.

- In the Leveling Order list, click the order that you want Project to use when leveling your project. See the section "Understanding Leveling Order" earlier in this chapter for details on how these options work.

- Select any of the following check boxes in the Resolving Overallocations area:

  - Select Level Only Within Available Slack to avoid changing the end date of your project when Project splits and delays tasks.

  - Select Leveling Can Adjust Individual Assignments On A Task to allow leveling to adjust one resource's work schedule on a task independent of other resources that are working on the same task.

  - Select Leveling Can Create Splits In Remaining Work to allow leveling to split tasks to resolve resource conflicts.

- Select Level Resources With The Proposed Booking Type if you want Project to level tasks containing proposed resources. Typically, if a resource is not committed to a task in your project, you don't want to level the resource's assignments.

TIP ✓	Selecting Leveling Can Adjust Individual Assignments On A Task and Leveling Can Create Splits In Remaining Work affects your entire project. You can, however, apply these settings to only those tasks you select by adding the Level Assignments field and the Leveling Can Split field to a table in a task view and then setting the value for these fields to Yes. You add these fields by adding columns to the table. (See the discussion of adding fields in the section "Using Priorities to Control Leveling" earlier in this chapter.)

When you finish setting your leveling options, click Level Now to level using those options. Figure 6-14 shows a project in the Leveling Gantt view in which Mary is over-allocated because she's simultaneously assigned to both Task 2 (a four-day task) and Task 4 (a seven-day task).

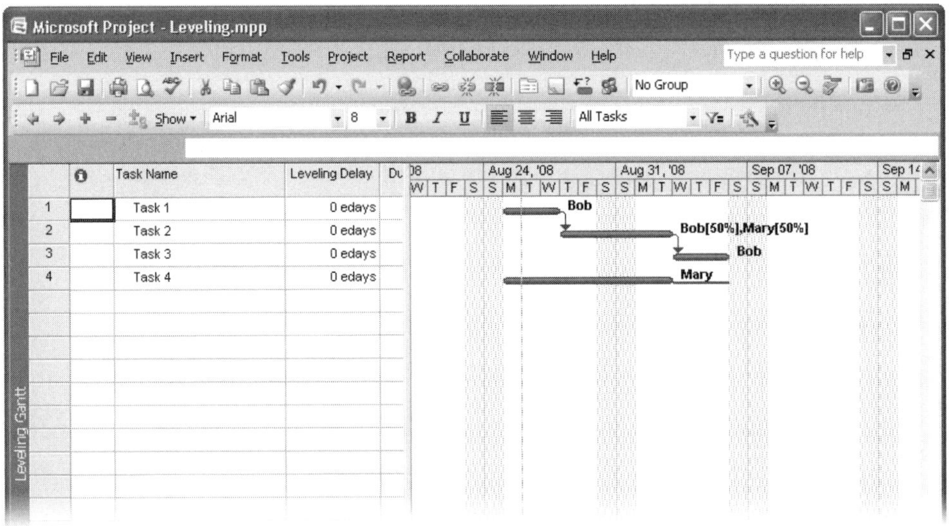

FIGURE 6-14 The Leveling Gantt view of a project before leveling.

Figure 6-15 shows the same project after leveling. After you level a project, Project adds green bars to the Leveling Gantt view; the green bars represent the tasks before leveling.

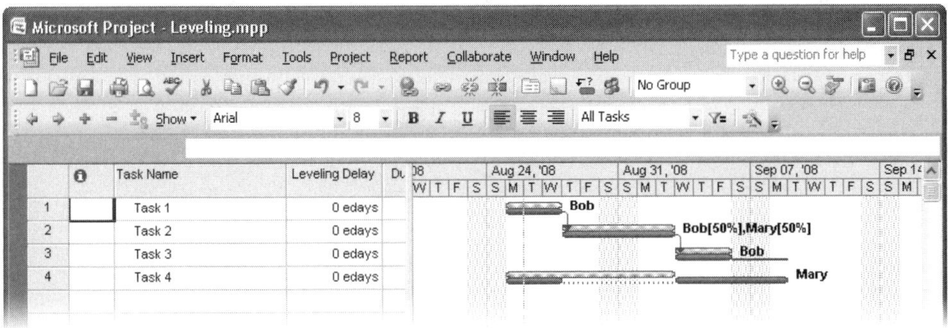

FIGURE 6-15 The Leveling Gantt view after leveling.

Not happy with what you see? No problem. Simply remove the effects of leveling by reopening the Resource Leveling dialog box (on the Tools menu, click Level Resources) and click the Clear Leveling button. Project displays another dialog box where you can choose to clear leveling for the entire project or for selected tasks only.

Handling Leveling on Your Own

Suppose that you're *mostly* happy with the results of leveling and that you just want to make a few changes on your own. Or suppose that you've got a very small amount of adjusting that needs to happen. You don't need to level resources from the Resource Leveling dialog box. Instead, you can manually enter delays on tasks. Sometimes the leveling that Project applies produces results you don't like—for example, you might not want to split work on a task to resolve an overallocation; instead, you might want to delay the start of another task.

First, you need to display the Resource Allocation view. To do this, on the View menu, click More Views. From the More Views window that appears, highlight Resource Allocation, and click Apply. In the Resource Allocation view, select the task that you want to delay in the top pane. In the bottom pane, enter an amount in the Leveling Delay field. Project delays the task accordingly and reduces the resource's conflict. In Figure 6-16, Mary is overallocated because she is simultaneously assigned part-time to Task 2, a four-day task, and full-time to Task 4, a five-day task.

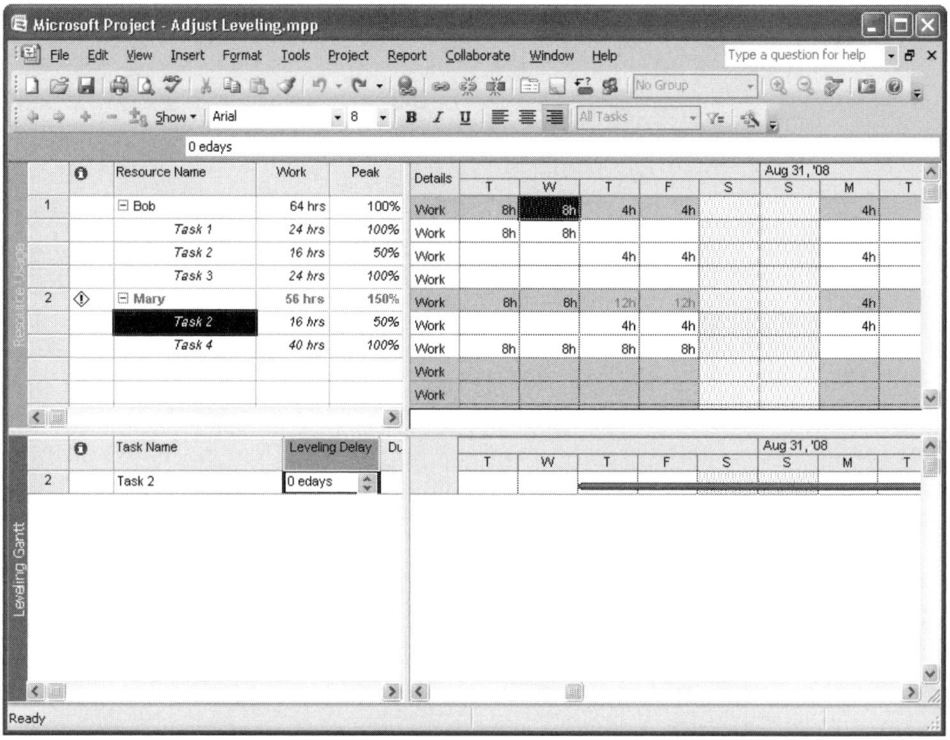

FIGURE 6-16 Mary is overallocated on Thursday and Friday, August 28 and August 29.

To eliminate the overallocation, I selected Task 2 in the top portion of the view and then, in the Leveling Delay field in the bottom portion of the view, I delayed the task by two days (see Figure 6-17).

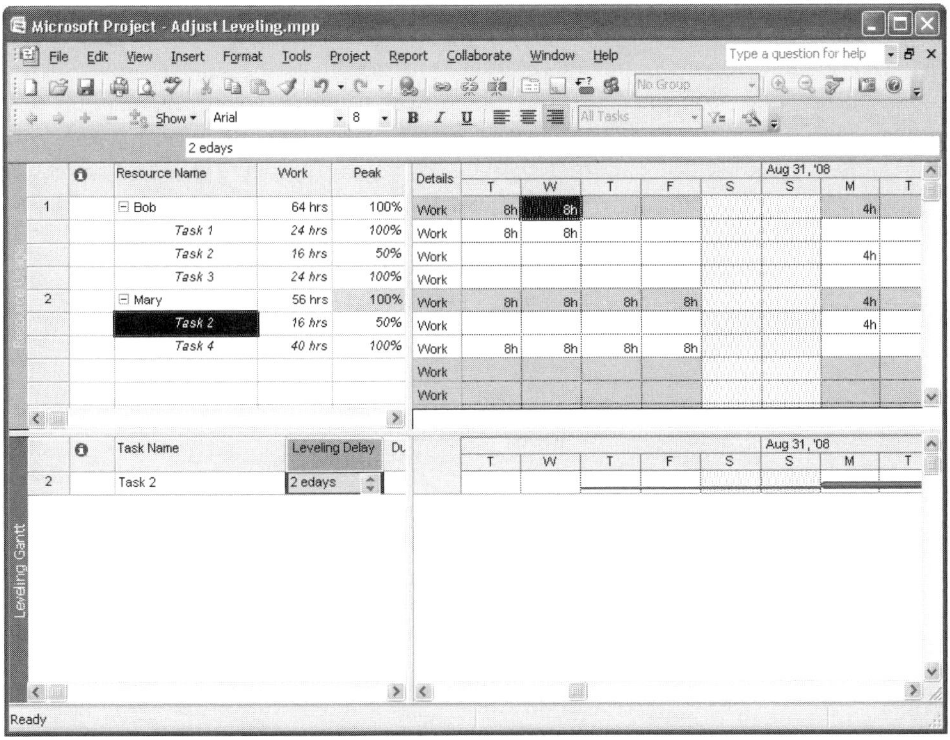

FIGURE 6-17 Mary's allocations after delaying the start of Task 2.

TIP Even though you might not use the Resource Leveling dialog box to apply leveling, you can use the dialog box to clear leveling. On the Tools menu, point to Level Resources, and then click Clear Leveling. Project removes all leveling applied, whether you used the Resource Leveling dialog box or you used the Resource Allocation view to apply the leveling.

What If You Had More Time?

When all else fails, you can always ask for more time to complete a project. By adding time to the schedule, you can adjust the durations of tasks to avoid overallocating resources. But before you go off and request more time for the project, you need to evaluate the project's critical path to determine just how adding time to the schedule will affect the schedule and the cost of the project. For more information on working with the critical path, see Chapter 8, "Completing the Planning Phase in Project." You might also want to review Chapter 5, "Controlling an Out-of-Control Schedule," to look for and address factors that might be affecting the schedule.

CHAPTER 7

Taming That Monster Budget

MOST PEOPLE INITIALLY PLAN A PROJECT without considering costs—and that's appropriate. Doing so helps you make honest estimates concerning the work that needs to be done and the resources needed to complete the work. Toward the end of the planning stage of your project, you can begin to review the costs involved. At this stage, there are some cost-related issues you need to address, along with some tools that Microsoft Office Project 2007 offers that you can use to help you get a handle on costs in the likely event you'll need to find ways to cut back.

How to Use Cost Resources Effectively

In Chapter 3, "Pinning Down Your Budget," I discussed Work and Material resources. Cost resources are the third type of resources available in Project. You use a Cost resource when the cost you incur doesn't depend on the amount of work or the duration of a task. Cost resources usually aren't people; they are things you need to complete a task. Airline tickets, meals while working, and hotel expenses needed to complete a task are Cost resources.

NOTE   You also can assign a fixed cost to a task and a cost per use to a resource, but assigning these types of costs doesn't depend on establishing a particular resource type. I talked about using these costs in the "Assigning Resource Costs" section in Chapter 3.

For example, suppose that your company is based in Atlanta, Georgia, with employees scattered in Georgia and North Carolina, and it is developing a Web site to aid travelers who are planning weekend getaways. You and your employees are the idea and marketing people, and you have hired a highly recommended Web design company in Austin, Texas, to help you develop the look and feel of the site. The Web design company has come up with some preliminary designs that you need to review, and its designers have a number of ideas to discuss with you. So a few members of your team are going to travel to Austin for a meeting with the Web design people. In addition to the human resources from your company, the Review Preliminary Design task in your project needs to include Cost resources to account for the cost of the airline tickets, meals, and hotel rooms.

Let's assume that you've already created the Cost resources on the Resource Sheet view. Now you need to assign costs to the Cost resources. To assign a cost to a Cost resource, follow these steps:

1. Assign the Cost resource to a task.

2. On the View menu, click Task Usage to switch to the Task Usage view. Optionally, you can display the Cost table to see the effects of assigning a cost to a Cost resource:

Assignment Information button

3. Select the Cost resource under the task to which it is assigned and click the Assignment Information button. Project displays the Assignment Information dialog box.

4. In the Cost text box, type an amount for the Cost resource.

5. Click OK.

Anticipating Cost Hikes Realistically

Suppose that the annual pay raise cycle occurs during your project. That means that the cost of employees will change over the life of your project. So you need to assess the cost of employees working on your project using one set of standard and overtime rates before a particular date, and another set after that date. Or suppose that you need to account for an increase in the price of a Material resource at a particular point in time. Or you might use different grades of paper—at differing costs—for various reports you prepare. To set up these different costs, you use cost rate tables, available in the Resource Information dialog box.

To set up cost rate tables, display the Resource Sheet and double-click the resource in question. Then click the Costs tab. The five tabs that appear, A through E, represent different cost rate tables you can apply; by default, Project uses the values displayed on Cost Rate Table A for any particular resource. On any tab, you can create different rates that become effective on different dates. For example, if you need to account for those pay raises, you can set up different rates on different lines of the A tab, setting different effective rates for each date (see Figure 7-1). If you need to account for a price increase for a particular Material resource, you'd use the same technique.

But suppose that you need to charge different rates for different grades of paper. In this case, you don't supply the different rates on the same tab; instead you assign them on different tabs. In Figure 7-2, I used Cost Rate Table A to establish a default cost of

$0.10 per sheet for the Material resource Paper; in Figure 7-3, I used Cost Rate Table C to establish a rate of $0.30 per sheet. Although I don't show it, I also supplied a cost rate of $0.20 per sheet on Cost Rate Table B.

Resource Information

| General | Costs | Notes | Custom Fields |

Resource Name: Deena

Cost rate tables

For rates, enter a value or a percentage increase or decrease from the previous rate. For instance, if a resource's Per Use Cost is reduced by 20%, type -20%.

| A (Default) | B | C | D | E |

Effective Date	Standard Rate	Overtime Rate	Per Use Cost
--	$25.00/h	$0.00/h	$0.00
Wed 10/01/08	$30.00/h	$0.00/h	$0.00

Cost accrual: Prorated

Help   Details...   OK   Cancel

FIGURE 7-1 To account for changes in rates controlled by an effective date, set up the various rates using the same cost rate table.

Resource Information

| General | Costs | Notes | Custom Fields |

Resource Name: Paper

Cost rate tables

For rates, enter a value or a percentage increase or decrease from the previous rate. For instance, if a resource's Per Use Cost is reduced by 20%, type -20%.

| A (Default) | B | C | D | E |

Effective Date	Standard Rate	Overtime Rate	Per Use Cost
--	$0.10		$0.00

Cost accrual: Prorated

Help   Details...   OK   Cancel

FIGURE 7-2 To establish different rates that don't depend on an effective date, use different cost rate tables.

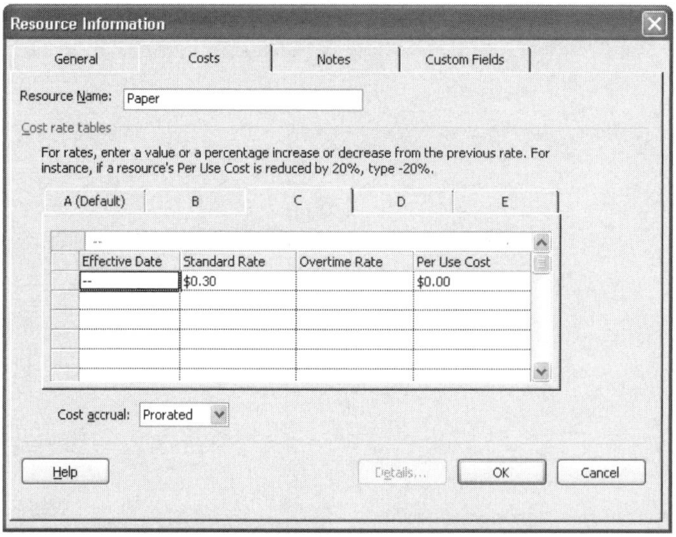

FIGURE 7-3 Using different cost tables, you can assign costs to varying grades of materials, for example.

Okay, once you set up the cost rate tables, what do you do with them? Well, if you established different effective dates for costs using the same cost rate table, you don't need to do anything else. Project will automatically assign the appropriate cost to the resource, based on the dates the resource is assigned to a task.

When you establish different cost rate tables, as in the example of using different grades of materials, you need to select the appropriate cost rate table after you assign the resource to a task. To select the correct cost rate table, on the View menu, click Task Usage, and in the Task Usage view, select the resource under the task in question (see Figure 7-4). Then click the Assignment Information button on the toolbar.

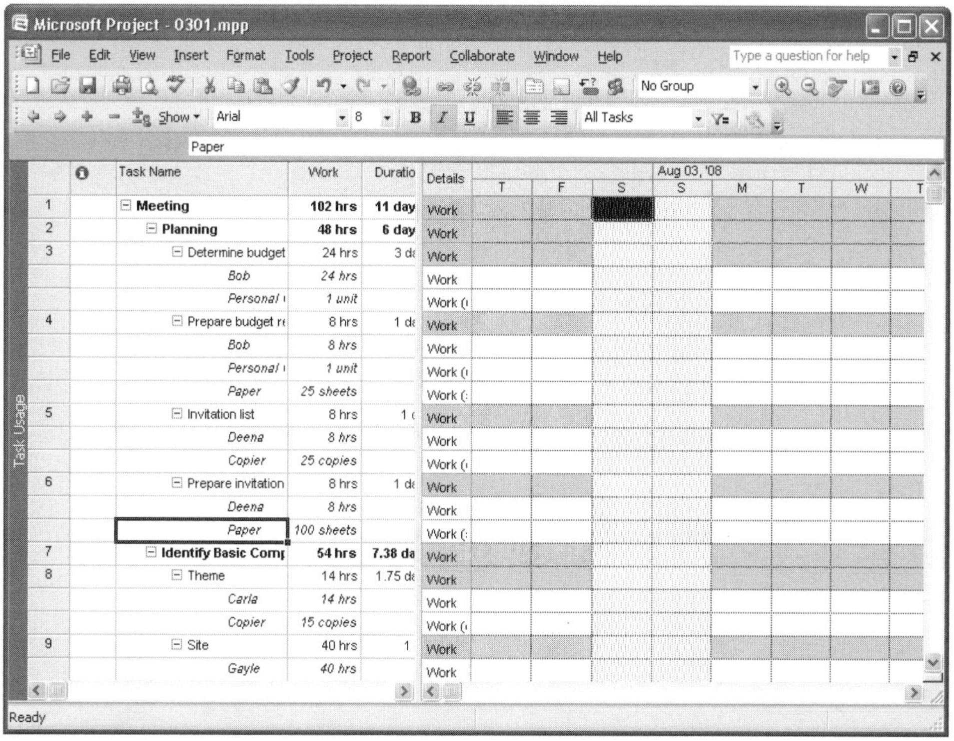

FIGURE 7-4 Use the Task Usage view to find the task and select the resource whose cost rate table you want to change.

In the Assignment Information dialog box that appears, in the Cost Rate Table list on the General tab, select the table containing the appropriate rate for the resource (see Figure 7-5).

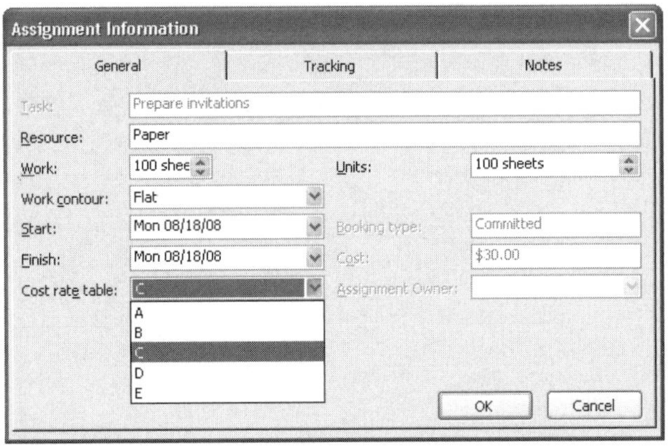

FIGURE 7-5 Use the Cost Rate Table list to select the appropriate cost rate table to assign to the resource for the selected task.

> **NOTE** For those of you who were wondering, cost rate tables don't apply to Cost resources. See the "Assigning Resource Costs" section in Chapter 3 for details on establishing costs for Cost resources.

What Are Budget Resources and When Do You Use Them?

Budget resources are, well, exactly what their name implies. They are resources you set up to budget for work or costs during a project. Using a budget resource, you can compare amounts you want to budget for Work, Material, and Cost resources to the amounts you actually assign to those resources, helping you see where you stand after you make resource assignments.

Creating Budget Resources

To use budget resources, you create them and assign them to the project summary task to allocate your budget across the entire project. When you create budget resources, you typically set up budget categories that are meaningful to you. In my example, I'll set up two budget categories: Labor/Materials and Costs. Later in this process, I'll assign each non-budget resource on my Resource Sheet to one of these budget resources.

Be aware that Project contains two budget fields you can use to establish budget values: Budget Work and Budget Cost. And Project tracks both Work resources and Material resources in the Budget Work field. If you want, you can segregate Work and Material resources for purposes of examining their costs separately; I simply opted to combine them in this example. The point is you can create any budget resources you want to help you compare budgeted amounts to amounts assigned.

> **NOTE** When you create budget resources, you don't assign rates to them; see the section "Establishing the Value of Budget Resources" later in this chapter for details on how you establish budget amounts.

To create a budget resource, follow these steps:

1. On the View menu, click Resource Sheet to display the Resource Sheet view.

2. In the Resource Name column, type the name of the budget resource; I called mine Budget-Labor/Materials.

3. In the Type column, click the type of resource that corresponds to the type of resource the budget resource will track, but don't bother filling out any other fields for the budget resource. For example, click Work or Material for a budget resource that will track work or materials. For a budget resource that will track costs, click Cost.

4. Double-click the budget resource to display the Resource Information dialog box and select the General tab.

5.   Select the Budget check box to establish the resource as a budget resource and click OK.

Next, assign your budget resources to the project summary task. Switch to the Gantt Chart view, and if the project summary task isn't visible, display it by opening the Tools menu and clicking Options; then click the View tab. Then select the Show Project Summary Task check box. Finally, using the steps in the "Assigning Resources to Tasks" section in Chapter 3, select the project summary task and assign the budget resources to it.

Assigning Resources to Budget Resource Categories

After you create budget resources, you need to assign each resource—both budget resources and non-budget resources—to a budget category that represents the type of cost each resource will incur. To make this assignment, you use a custom field. In the steps below, I'm going to create a custom field called Budget Category with a lookup list so that when you make the assignment, you select from the list. This ensures that you assign only the allowed values to each resource. After creating the custom field, I'll show you how to assign a budget category to each resource.

1.   On the Tools menu, point to Customize, and click Fields to display the Custom Fields dialog box:

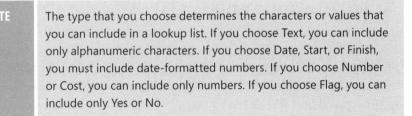

2. At the top of the box, select the Resource option button.

3. In the Type list, click Text.

> **NOTE** The type that you choose determines the characters or values that you can include in a lookup list. If you choose Text, you can include only alphanumeric characters. If you choose Date, Start, or Finish, you must include date-formatted numbers. If you choose Number or Cost, you can include only numbers. If you choose Flag, you can include only Yes or No.

4. Select an available text field—one that isn't already being used—and click the Rename button to provide a meaningful name for the custom field. Then click OK to redisplay the Customize Fields dialog box.

5. Click the Lookup button to display the Edit Lookup Table dialog box.

6. In the Value column, type each of the labels that should appear in the list.

7. Click Close to save the value list and redisplay the Customize Fields dialog box.

8. Click OK to redisplay your project.

You're now ready to assign resources to budget categories. Switch to the Resource Sheet view (on the View menu, click Resource Sheet) and insert a column for the Budget Category custom field you just created. Click the column heading that you want to appear to the right of the Budget Category column, and then on the Insert menu, click Column. In the Field Name box, type the first few letters of the custom field you created, and then select it from the list that appears. Click OK, and Project displays the column on the Resource Sheet view (see Figure 7-6).

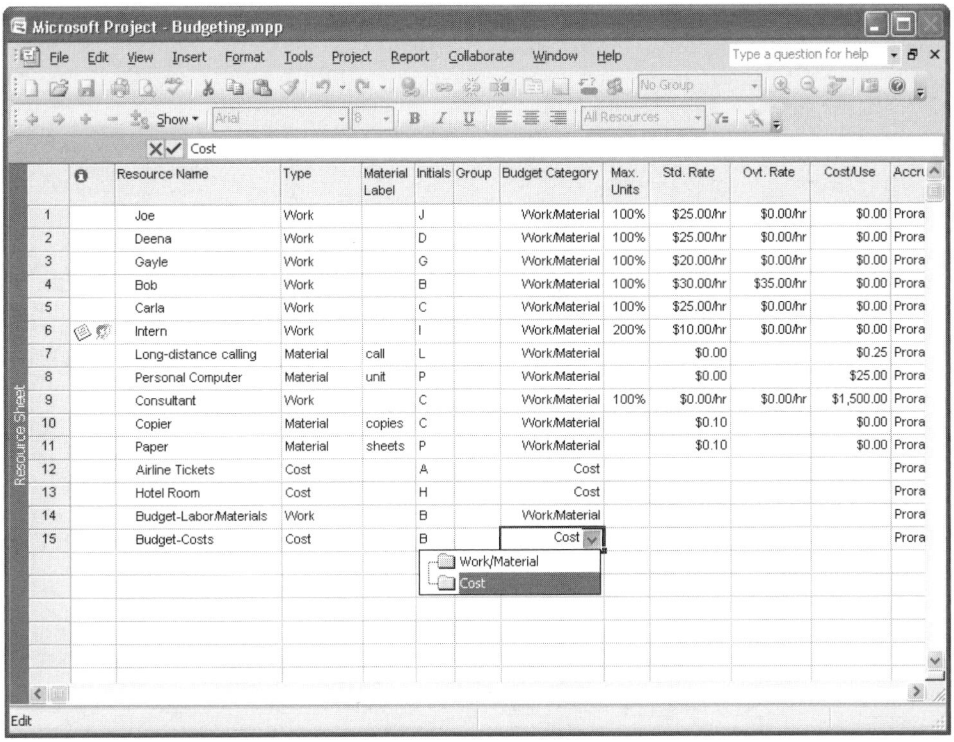

FIGURE 7-6 For each resource, select a budget category.

Click in the Budget Category column for each resource and use the list to select the appropriate category for that particular resource.

Establishing the Value of Budget Resources

You use the Resource Usage view to assign budget values to the budget resources using the Budget Cost and Budget Work fields. To add the budget amounts as a total for your project, you add these two fields to the view as columns. To budget the amounts in a specific timeframe of your project, you use the timephased portion of the view to assign the budget values.

To establish overall project budget values for your budget resources, without regard to when those budget values are in effect, follow these steps:

1. On the View menu, click Resource Usage.

2. Click in the Work column. (When inserting columns, Project places columns to the left of the selected column.)

3. On the Insert menu, click Column to display the Column Definition dialog box.

4. In the Field Name box, type a few letters of the name of the Budget Cost field. Project displays the field in the list that begins with the letters you type.

5. Select the Budget Cost field and click OK.

6. Repeat steps 3 through 5 to insert the Budget Work column.

7. Find the budget resources in the Resource Name column and select the task below them—the one that represents the project summary task.

8. In the appropriate column—Budget Work or Budget Cost—supply the amount that you want to budget:

If you prefer, you can assign budget values for time periods throughout your project. You still display the Budget Work and Budget Cost columns to help you track the totals that you assign, and you still make the budget value assignments on the project summary task. But you don't type the amounts into the Budget Work or Budget Cost columns. Instead, you add rows to the Details portion of the Resource Usage view and enter the amounts on these rows for the project summary task (see Figure 7-7).

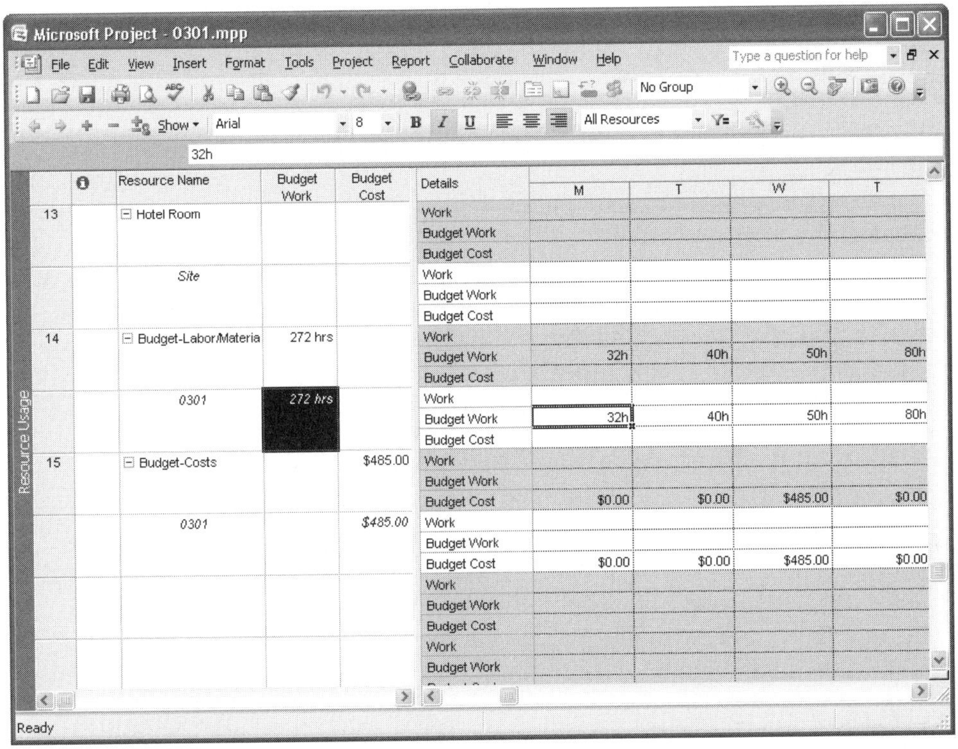

FIGURE 7-7 Enter values on the Budget Work and Budget Cost rows for the project summary task. Watch the Budget Work and Budget Cost columns update to display totals assigned.

To display these rows in the Details section, on the Format menu, click Detail Styles to display the Detail Styles dialog box (see Figure 7-8). In the Available Fields column, find and click the Budget Work field, and then click the Show button. Repeat this process for the Budget Work field and click OK.

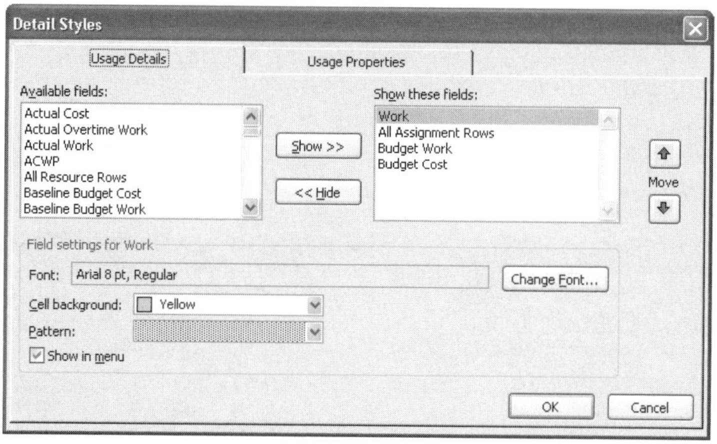

FIGURE 7-8 The Detail Styles dialog box.

Then in the Details portion, on the appropriate dates, type the values for which you want to budget. Remember, when you enter values for Budget Work, you're entering values for both Work and Material resources.

Reviewing Budget Amounts and Assigned Amounts

To view the amount you have budgeted and compare it to the planned amount you have assigned to tasks in your project, on the View menu, click Resource Usage. By default, Project displays the Usage table. Earlier in this chapter, in the section "Establishing the Value of Budget Resources," I added the Budget Work and Budget Cost columns. To make the comparison easy to understand, you might want to add the Cost column using the same technique.

Let's group the sheet portion of the Resource Usage view by the Budget Category field to easily compare budgeted costs to costs assigned, and budgeted work to work assigned. On the Project menu, point to Group By, and click Customize Group By. Project displays the Customize Group By dialog box (see Figure 7-9).

In the Field Name column, type a few letters of the Budget Category field name, and then select it from the list. Click OK, and Project groups the resources in your project based on the Budget Category (see Figure 7-10).

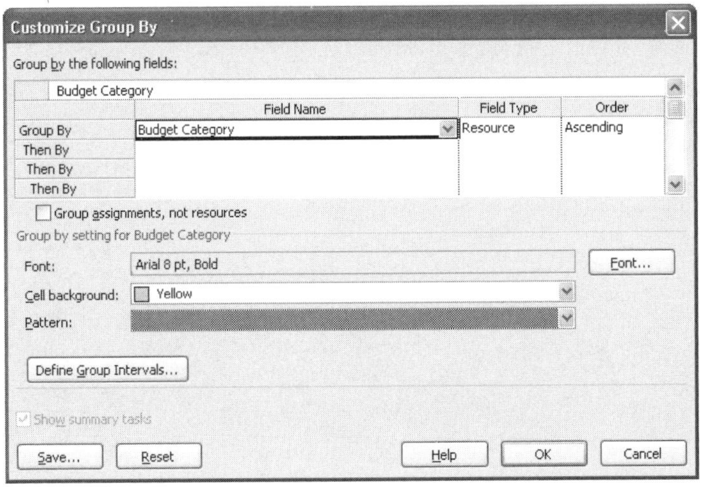

FIGURE 7-9 The Customize Group By dialog box.

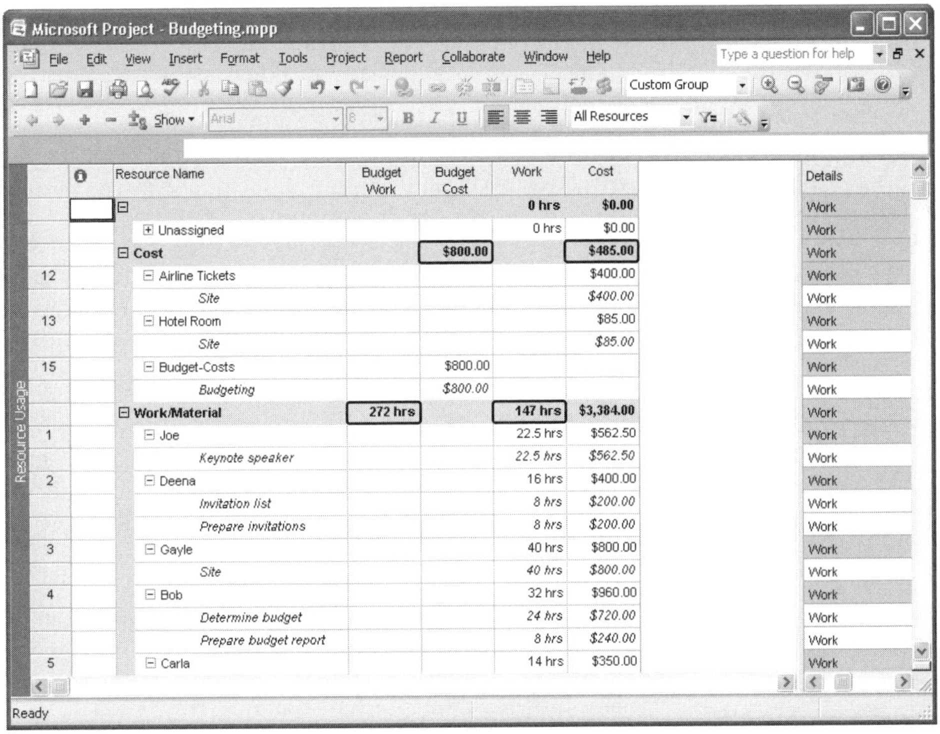

FIGURE 7-10 The Resource Usage view, grouped by budget category.

For the Cost budget category, compare the Budget Cost value with the planned Cost value; the details of what makes up the Cost value appear below it in the Cost column. Similarly, you can compare the Budget Cost for Work and Material resources with the planned amounts you have assigned.

Remember, we're in the planning stage here, so the amounts on-screen aren't actual amounts of work done or costs incurred; instead they are planned amounts of work and cost assigned in the project.

> **TIP** ✓ The technique for reviewing and comparing amounts works, though, when you get into actual amounts used; you simply need to display the Actual Work and Actual Cost fields in the Resource Usage view.

Tips for Trimming the Bottom Line

In the world of limited costs, to complete a project you'll probably be faced with the need to reduce the costs of your project. Here are a few areas you can consider:

- Lower travel costs. For example, if you've included five visits to a client site in another state, can you reduce the number of visits you make without reducing the quality of the product you deliver? Can you get cheaper airline tickets if you book farther in advance? Can you reduce the number of people traveling?

- Lower equipment costs. Can you find a vendor who will sell or rent equipment to you at a lower price than you allocated in your project? Can you rent equipment you planned to buy, and if so, will renting be less expensive than buying?

- Lower human resource costs. Can you substitute an employee who costs less to do a job than the consultant you planned on hiring? Although using a less-experienced resource might make a task take longer, will the additional time needed to complete the task by that less-experienced resource cancel out the benefit of using a lower-cost resource? Also, can you reduce overtime, which is typically more expensive than work done during regular hours?

- If you must use more expensive resources on fixed units, effort-driven tasks, can they get the job done faster than you've planned?

CHAPTER 8

Completing the Planning Phase in Project

AS YOU MOVE toward finalizing your plan and get ready to begin the "implementation stage" of your project, it's always wise to step back and review what you've got in your plan. As you work on this finalization of the project plan, you want to review the project's scope to make sure that the scope hasn't changed. You also want to review the project schedule from a variety of views, making sure you've addressed all possible concerns. You want to determine the critical path of the project plan so that you can keep a close eye on tasks on the critical path. Finally, you want to set a baseline for the plan so that later, after you've completed the plan, you can compare your estimates to what actually happened; this type of review helps you identify where your estimates were inaccurate so that you can improve your estimating skills for the next project.

Reviewing What You've Got

When you reach the final stages of the planning phase of a project, you want to review the project plan from a variety of perspectives. This review can help you determine whether you think you can implement the plan on time and within budget. In Chapter 4, "Finding the Information You Need," you will learn how to change views and change tables in views. You also can find information there on adding and removing information from tables in views.

While working with Microsoft Office Project 2007, it's not uncommon to spend a great deal of time in the Gantt Chart view, shown in Figure 8-1. The Gantt Chart view provides a visual representation of the timing of your tasks along with a variety of tables that help you review different types of information.

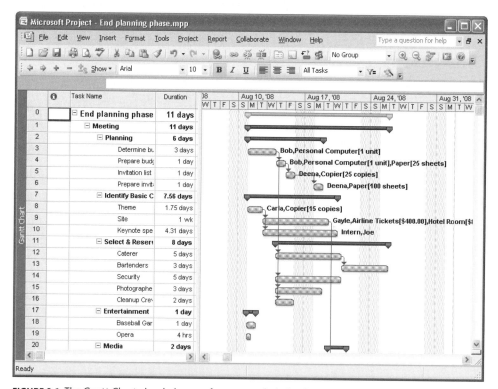

FIGURE 8-1 The Gantt Chart view helps you focus on task timing in your project.

The Relationship Diagram view, shown in Figure 8-2, is exceedingly helpful when you want to study task dependencies. Like the Network Diagram view, which also helps you study task relationships, this view has no table. Unlike the Network Diagram view, which does contain some task information such as start and end dates, duration, and resources assigned, the Relationship Diagram view has no distractions from the purpose of examining the relationships of tasks in your project. You select any task in your project, and the Relationship Diagram view shows you the task's ID, predecessor tasks, successor tasks, and the type of dependency that exists between tasks. Using this view, you might find a dependency you created that you don't need, or a dependency that you need but didn't create, or even a dependency of the wrong type.

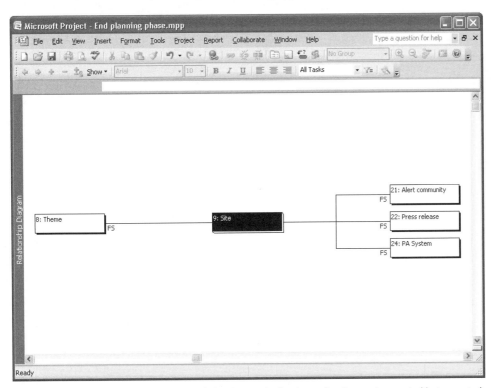

FIGURE 8-2 The Relationship Diagram view helps you study the dependencies you've created between tasks.

As you read in Chapter 6, "Solving Resource Conflicts," the Resource Graph view and the Resource Allocation view are both helpful when you are trying to find and resolve resource overallocations. The Resource Form view shows you not only the tasks to which any particular resource is assigned; you also see the resource's rate, maximum units, and calendar information, all on a single page (see Figure 8-3).

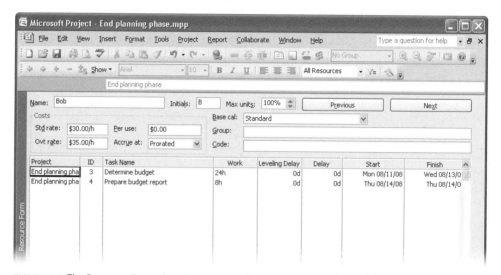

FIGURE 8-3 The Resource Form view shows you tasks for a resource, along with resource-specific information.

Tables are typically more helpful when you want to review costs on-screen, and the Cost table shows you just about everything you might want to know about costs during the planning phase of your project. You can view the Cost table from any view that has a table associated with it. If you start in a task-oriented view, and then apply the Cost table by right-clicking the Select All button and clicking Cost, Project displays the costs associated with each task. If you start from a resource-oriented view such as the Resource Sheet view, and apply the Cost table, Project displays your project's costs as they are associated with each resource. If you view costs from a usage view, such as the Resource Usage view shown in Figure 8-4, and apply the Cost table, Project breaks down the costs both by task and by resource.

> **NOTE** During the planning phase, the baseline cost and the actual cost are zero. Before you start tracking, you'll set a baseline as described later in this chapter. When you begin implementing your plan, you'll capture the actual costs and be able to make comparisons between planned costs and actual costs.

Resource Name	Cost	Baseline Cost	Variance	Actual Cost	Remaining	Details	T
⊞ Unassigned	$0.00	$0.00	$0.00	$0.00	$0.00	Work	
1 ⊟ Joe	$562.50	$0.00	$562.50	$0.00	$562.50	Work	2h
Keynote speal	*$562.50*	*$0.00*	*$562.50*	*$0.00*	*$562.50*	Work	2h
2 ⊟ Deena	$400.00	$0.00	$400.00	$0.00	$400.00	Work	
Invitation list	*$200.00*	*$0.00*	*$200.00*	*$0.00*	*$200.00*	Work	
Prepare invitai	*$200.00*	*$0.00*	*$200.00*	*$0.00*	*$200.00*	Work	
3 ⊟ Gayle	$800.00	$0.00	$800.00	$0.00	$800.00	Work	2h
Site	*$800.00*	*$0.00*	*$800.00*	*$0.00*	*$800.00*	Work	2h
4 ⊟ Bob	$960.00	$0.00	$960.00	$0.00	$960.00	Work	8h
Determine buc	*$720.00*	*$0.00*	*$720.00*	*$0.00*	*$720.00*	Work	8h
Prepare budge	*$240.00*	*$0.00*	*$240.00*	*$0.00*	*$240.00*	Work	
5 ⊟ Carla	$350.00	$0.00	$350.00	$0.00	$350.00	Work	6h
Theme	*$350.00*	*$0.00*	*$350.00*	*$0.00*	*$350.00*	Work	6h
6 ⊟ Intern	$225.00	$0.00	$225.00	$0.00	$225.00	Work	2h
Keynote speal	*$225.00*	*$0.00*	*$225.00*	*$0.00*	*$225.00*	Work	2h
7 Long-distance calling	$0.00	$0.00	$0.00	$0.00	$0.00	Work (call)	
8 ⊟ Personal Computer	$50.00	$0.00	$50.00	$0.00	$50.00	Work (unit)	0.33
Determine buc	*$25.00*	*$0.00*	*$25.00*	*$0.00*	*$25.00*	Work (unit)	0.33
Prepare budge	*$25.00*	*$0.00*	*$25.00*	*$0.00*	*$25.00*	Work (unit)	
9 Consultant	$0.00	$0.00	$0.00	$0.00	$0.00	Work	
10 ⊟ Copier	$4.00	$0.00	$4.00	$0.00	$4.00	Work (copies)	6.43

FIGURE 8-4 Use the Cost table on the Resource Usage view to review planned costs.

NOTE It's important to understand that the Cost table shows different fields for task-oriented views and resource-oriented views. You can see fixed costs and their effects on your project only from the Cost table in task-oriented views.

When you start tracking what really happens after you begin work on your project, as described in Chapter 10, "Establishing Guidelines for Tracking," you'll probably use the Tracking Gantt view most often. From this view, you can enter information about when tasks actually start and end, actual duration information, and actual work information. The Tracking Gantt view (see Figure 8-5) demonstrates visually where you stand in reality compared to the baseline project plan that shows where you thought you'd be.

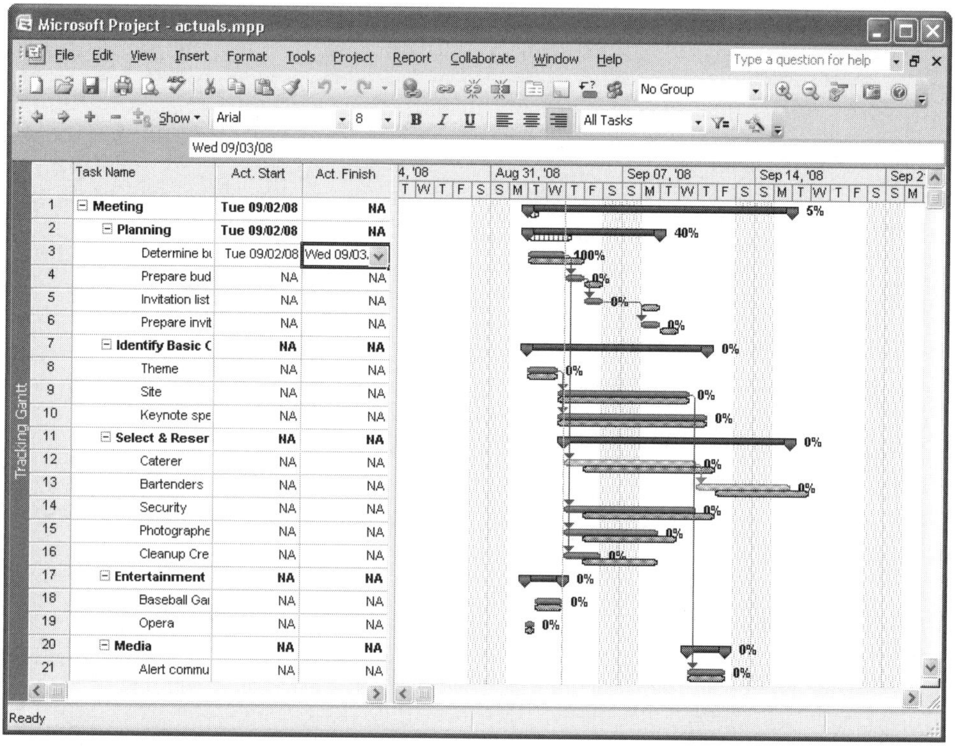

FIGURE 8-5 The Tracking Gantt view shows you where you stand in relation to where you thought you'd stand.

Redefining Project Scope

When you review your plan, you might find that you cannot complete your project within the allotted timeframe, the budget, or both. You can try redefining the scope of your project. The scope of your project defines where your project work starts and ends. For example, suppose your project is intended to develop a new computer system. Your scope statement might read something like: "This project involves designing, developing, and testing a new computer system. It does not include implementing the system or training people to use it."

After tugging at your project plan, let's say you simply can't find a way to finish the project within the allotted timeframe and budget. So you can re-evaluate the scope of your project. You might be able to reduce the number of products you are expected to deliver. For example, if the project stakeholders are willing to sacrifice some of the features of the computer system you're designing, you might be able to finish the project on time and within budget. In reality, you're reducing the products you plan to deliver if you take this approach of scaling down the computer system. If you change the scope, you might design and develop the computer system in one project, and establish a second project that handles testing.

Both approaches can help you fit your project within time and budget constraints, but you'll need to make sure that your project stakeholders understand and accept the changes you propose. If you propose to eliminate features, you effectively reduce the quality of the initial delivery. But if all the players can agree that the features can be added to the system later, this approach might be the way to please most of the people in the most cost-efficient manner. And it's entirely possible that your stakeholders will decide that some features were "nice but not essential" and that those features could be eliminated from the system or possibly revisited at some time down the road. Those features might not ever make it into the computer system.

If you change the scope of the project to eliminate a phase and establish another project to handle that phase, the chances are quite good that you'll need to sell the project stakeholders on a longer schedule. Why? Because the amount of work to be done before the computer system can be delivered hasn't been reduced; it's simply been split apart into two projects. However, your project stakeholders may want the complete system delivered, even if you need more time to deliver it in its entirety.

Regardless of the approach you take to resolving the issue, don't eliminate tasks until you copy them into another project. If you opt to eliminate products to deliver, it's quite possible that your next project might be to enhance the one you deliver with those eliminated products. If you opt to divide your project into two or more projects, you can save the work you've already done in another project, and you can even link the projects together to track the overall cost and time you need to complete the project at hand. See Chapter 13, "Managing Cross-Project Conflicts," for details.

| SEE ALSO | Chapter 11, "Dealing with Management," provides more information on managing change. |

Identifying the Critical Path

The critical path of any project marks the longest way through your project, identifying the tasks that cannot slip if you expect to finish your project on schedule. And if you're looking for ways to shorten the length of your project, look for ways to shorten the critical path. The critical path of your project can change as the project progresses. How? Tasks on the critical path might finish early, making what was the critical path shorter than some other path through your project. Or tasks on some other path through the project might be delayed, moving those tasks onto the critical path. So knowing which tasks can make or break your project's on-time completion is, well, critical!

Tasks that appear on the critical path are called *critical tasks*. Project treats a task as a critical task if it meets any of the following criteria:

- In a project scheduled from a start date, any task that has an As Late As Possible (ALAP) constraint or has a predecessor task with an ALAP constraint.

- In a project scheduled from a finish date, any task that has an As Soon As Possible (ASAP) constraint.

- Any task that has a finish date that is the same as or later than its deadline date.

- Any task that has a Must Start On or Must Finish On date constraint.

- Any task that has no slack (also called *float*).

> **NOTE** Project calculates a task's slack by calculating the difference between the task's early finish and late finish dates; when these two dates are the same, the difference equals zero and Project identifies the task as a critical task. You can change the default difference from zero to another number. For more information on slack, see Chapter 5, "Controlling an Out-of-Control Schedule."

You can view the critical path in a variety of ways from any task-oriented view. Perhaps the easiest way is to display the Detail Gantt view (on the View menu, point to More Views, click Detail Gantt, and click Apply). In the Detail Gantt view, critical tasks appear in red, while non-critical tasks appear in blue. Because this book doesn't show the figures in color, I've applied a pattern to the Gantt bars of critical tasks in the Detail Gantt view shown in Figure 8-6.

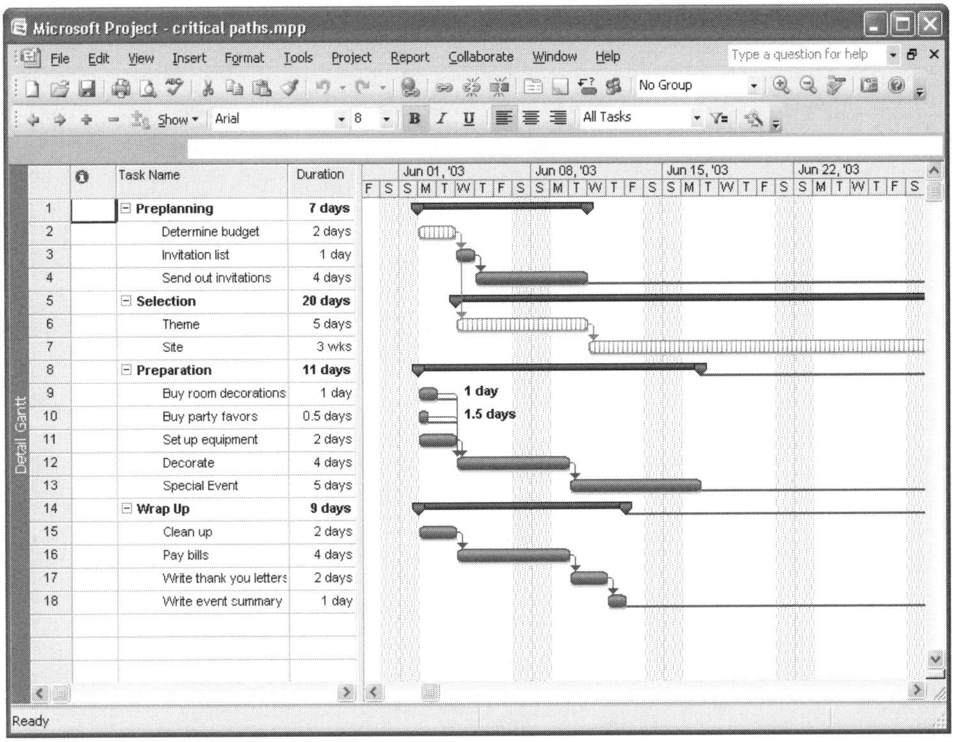

FIGURE 8-6 The Detail Gantt view uses red and blue to distinguish between critical and non-critical tasks; I added a pattern to critical tasks to make them easily visible in the figure.

You'll find the same kind of behavior in the both the Tracking Gantt view and the Network Diagram; that is, critical tasks appear in red by default.

You also can filter a view to display only critical tasks. In Figure 8-7, I displayed the Gantt Chart view, and in the Filter list, clicked Critical. Notice that Task ID numbers appear to be missing in the leftmost column of the view. The missing IDs belong to non-critical tasks that don't appear when I filter to display only critical tasks.

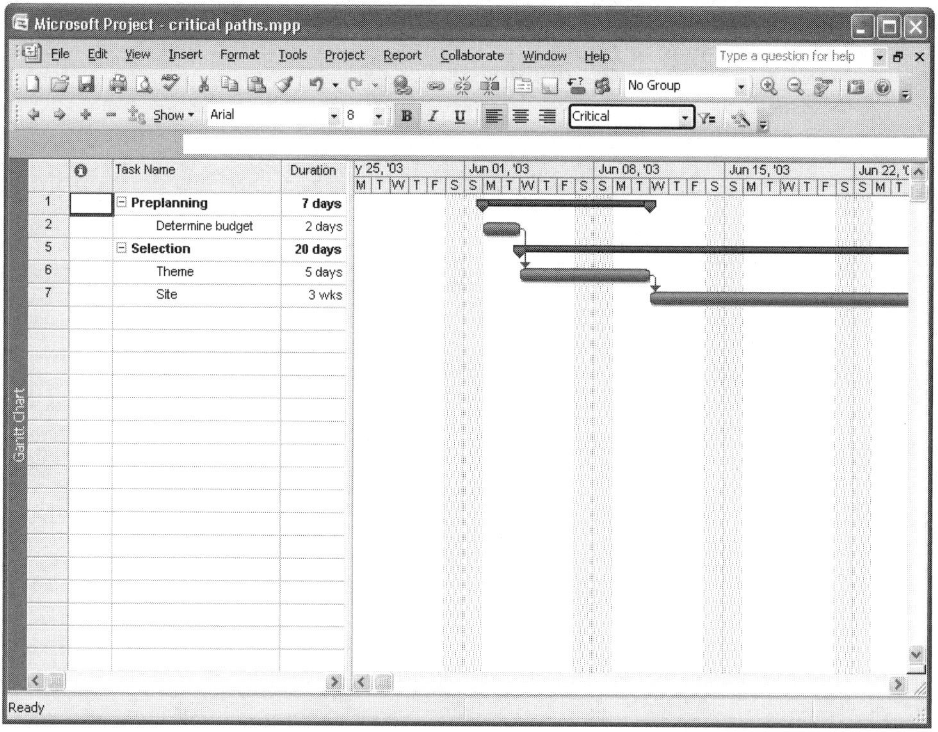

FIGURE 8-7 By filtering, you can display only critical tasks.

In any task-oriented view that contains a table, you can group tasks into two groups: critical and non-critical. On the Project menu, point to Group By, and click Critical. Project then organizes your tasks into two groups: non-critical tasks followed by critical tasks.

TIP   You also can use the Group list to select a grouping; it appears on the Standard toolbar just above the Filter list highlighted in Figure 8-7.

Your project can have multiple critical paths. Using Project's Display Multiple Critical Paths option, you can view the critical path within each network of tasks. Figure 8-6, shown earlier, contains four networks of tasks: Preplanning, Selection, Preparation, and Wrap Up. As you can see, the critical path for the project spans across the first two networks of tasks. In Figure 8-8, I've opted to view the critical path of each network. As you can see, the tasks within each network are all critical to their respective networks except the first two tasks in the Preparation network.

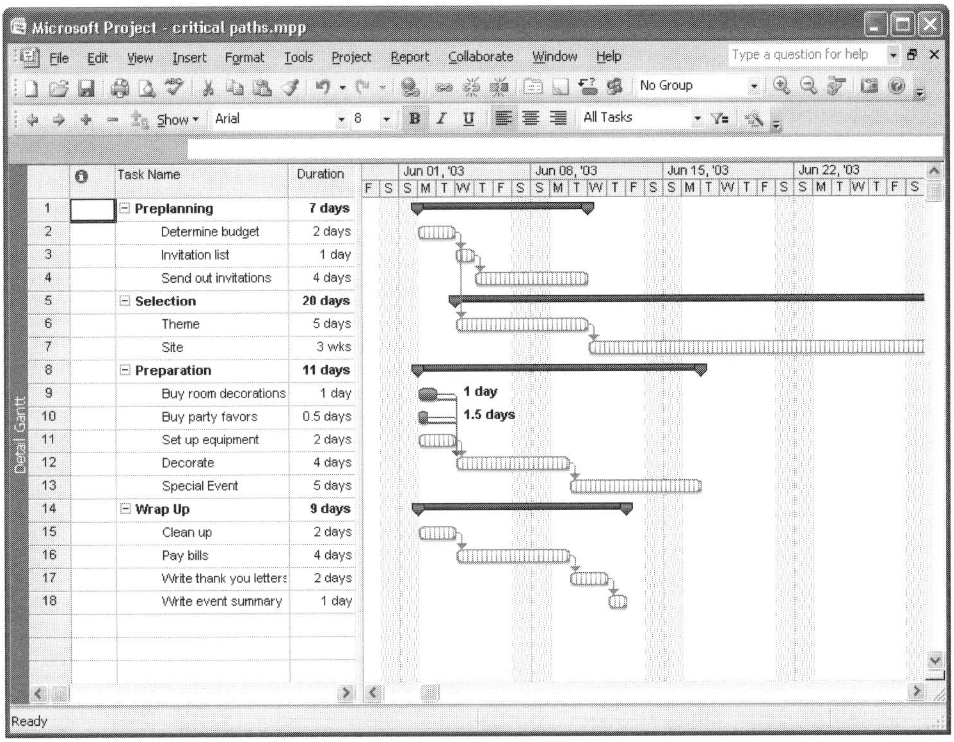

FIGURE 8-8 If you display multiple critical paths, Project shows you the critical path within each network of tasks.

To display multiple critical paths, on the Tools menu, click Options, and in the Options dialog box, click the Calculation tab. Then select the Calculate Multiple Critical Paths check box (see Figure 8-9).

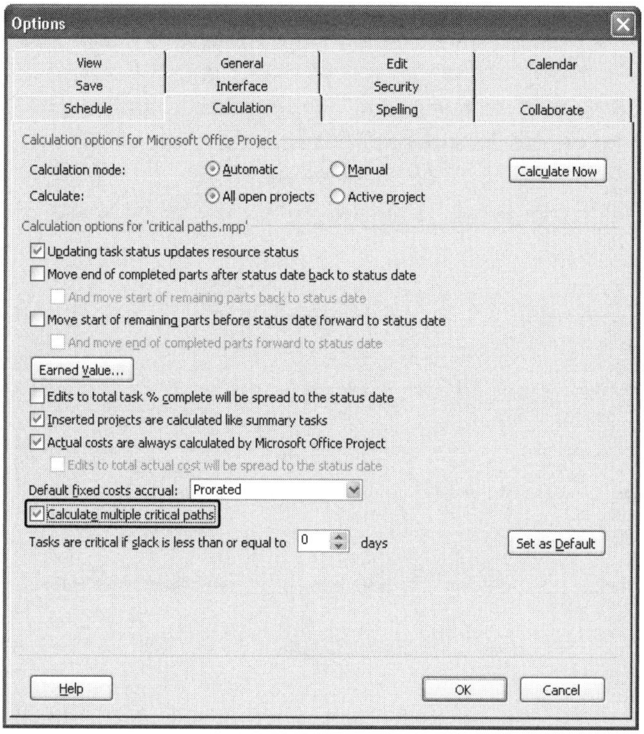

FIGURE 8-9 Tracking multiple critical paths.

Working with Baselines and Interim Plans

When you finally reach a plan you want to execute, your last step in the planning phase should be to create a *baseline* for your project. A baseline is a snapshot of your project at a moment in time. In a baseline plan, Project stores start and finish dates, duration, work, and cost information about tasks, resources, and assignments. You can use this information later, to compare your original estimates to what actually happens as you execute your project. By making this comparison, you can be alert for shifts in timing. Good project managers use these comparisons to become better project managers in the future by learning what worked and what didn't work. *Interim plans* are similar to baselines, but they contain less information. Because Project stores only a set of task start and finish dates in an interim plan, you can use interim plans for comparisons concerning progress or slippage but not duration, work, or cost information.

Setting a Baseline or an Interim Plan

You can set up to 11 baselines in a project; typically, you set a baseline at the end of the planning phase before you start recording information about what actually happens as you execute your project plan. You might also want to set additional baselines as you complete each phase of your project or as you reach milestones.

WARNING Just because you can save 11 baselines doesn't mean you should. Saving baselines increases the size of your Project file because Project adds a set of fields to your project file to store each baseline's information. Saving lots of baselines can slow down Project's calculation of your schedule and make the analysis work confusing and more difficult.

To set a baseline, save your project. Then on the Tools menu, point to Tracking, and click Set Baseline to display the Set Baseline dialog box (see Figure 8-10). Click the Set Baseline option and in the Set Baseline list, click the baseline that you want to set. Click OK, and Project creates the baseline information.

FIGURE 8-10 The Set Baseline dialog box.

When you save your project, Project saves the baseline information along with the rest of your project information. Figure 8-11 shows the Tracking Gantt view of a project before setting the baseline. Notice that each Gantt bar is only a single bar. Figure 8-12 shows the same project after setting a baseline. The bottom bar of each task represents the baseline information and the top bar represents the actual information.

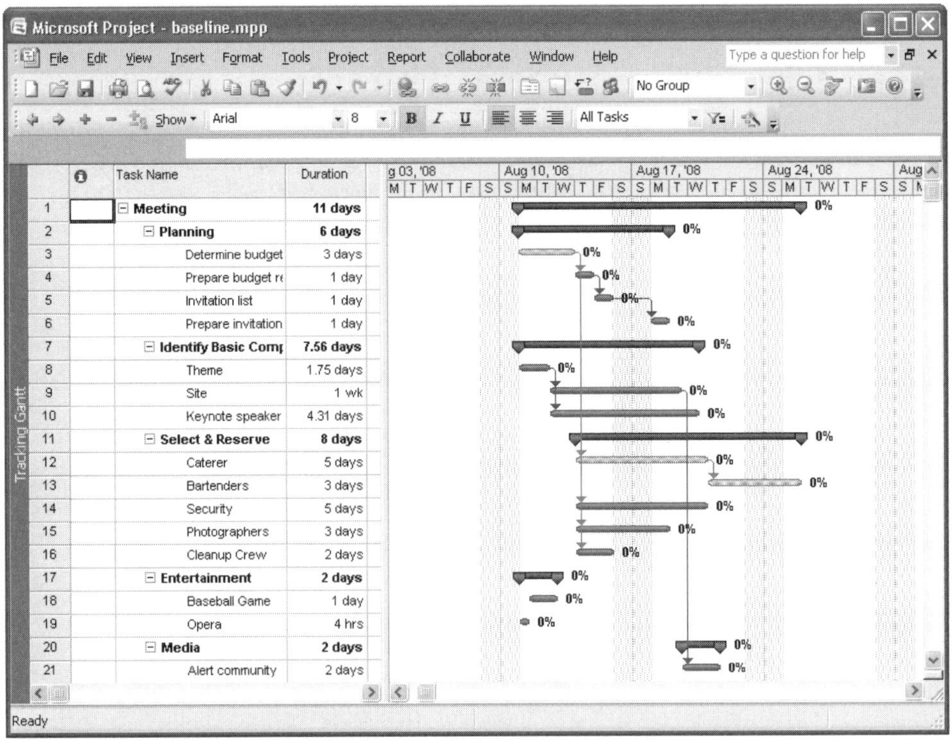

FIGURE 8-11 A project in the Tracking Gantt view before setting a baseline.

You save interim plans the same way that you set a baseline; in the Set Baseline dialog box, select the Set Interim Plan option. Then identify the start and finish dates you want to copy; you can copy start and finish dates from any of the baselines you created, from the current plan, or from any of the interim plans you created. You then select the fields into which you want to copy the information. For example, you might copy Start and Finish into Start1 and Finish1 for your first interim plan. Later, you can copy Start and Finish into Start2 and Finish2 to create another interim plan.

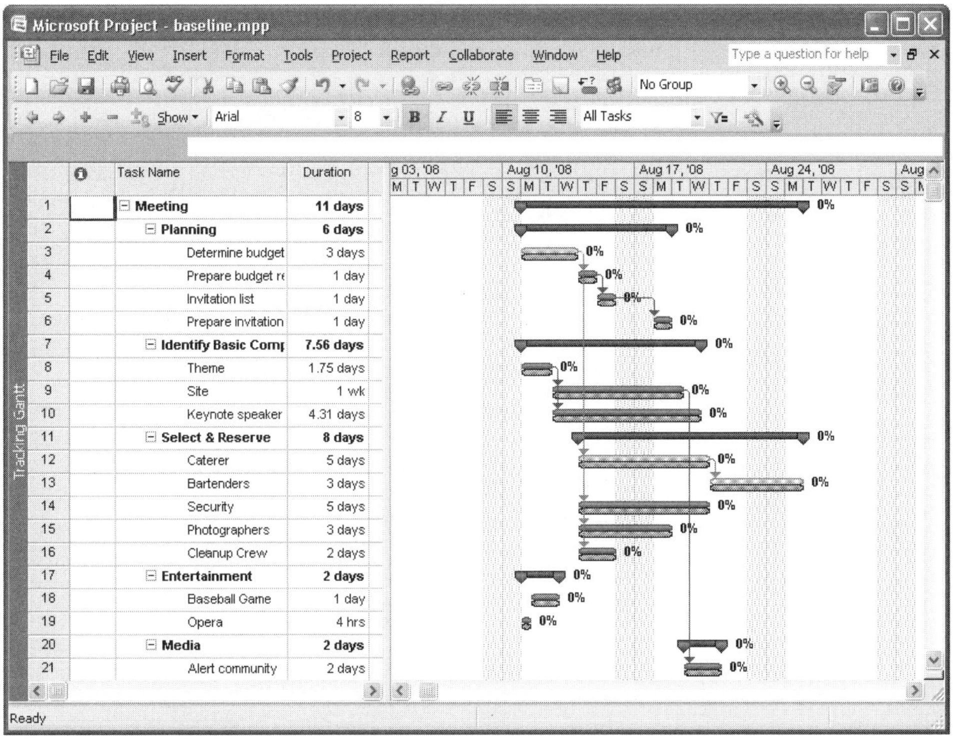

FIGURE 8-12 The same project in Figure 8-11 after setting a baseline.

Comparing Baseline and Actual Information

To analyze baseline and actual information for your project, you can use the Project Statistics window. On the Project menu, click Project Information, and then click the Statistics button (see Figure 8-13). This window helps you compare overall baseline information stored in the Baseline fields to overall actual information you've recorded.

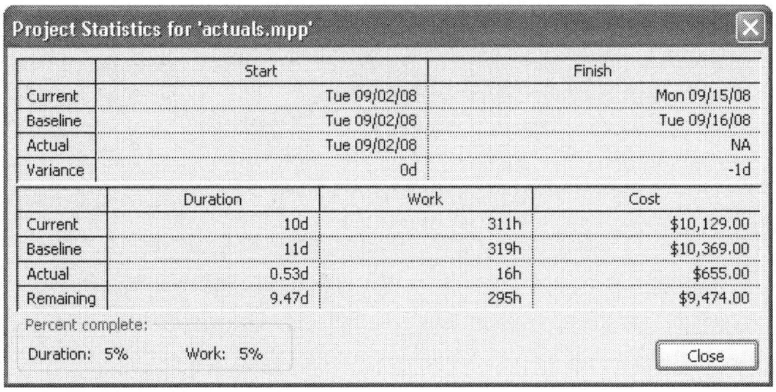
Project Statistics for 'actuals.mpp'

	Start	Finish
Current	Tue 09/02/08	Mon 09/15/08
Baseline	Tue 09/02/08	Tue 09/16/08
Actual	Tue 09/02/08	NA
Variance	0d	-1d

	Duration	Work	Cost
Current	10d	311h	$10,129.00
Baseline	11d	319h	$10,369.00
Actual	0.53d	16h	$655.00
Remaining	9.47d	295h	$9,474.00

Percent complete:
Duration: 5% Work: 5%

Close

FIGURE 8-13 Displaying project statistics.

You also can compare baseline and actual information in more detail using the Variance table of any task-oriented view that contains a table. Right-click the Select All button in the table and click Variance. The Variance table, shown in Figure 8-14, shows baseline and scheduled fields by default; you can add other baseline fields to the table if you want.

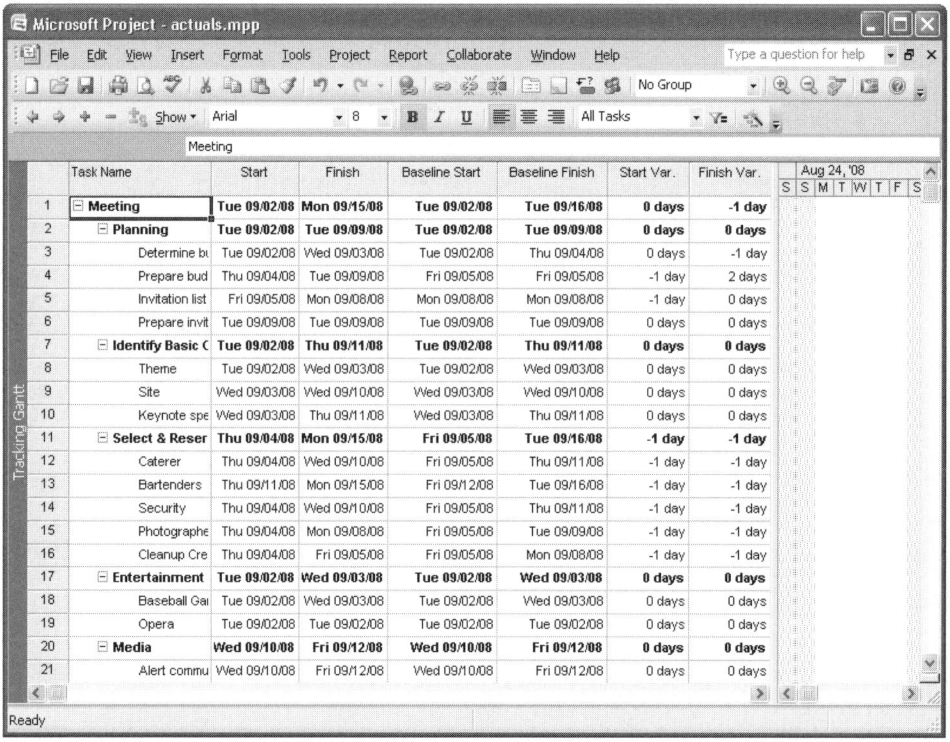

	Task Name	Start	Finish	Baseline Start	Baseline Finish	Start Var.	Finish Var.
1	**Meeting**	**Tue 09/02/08**	**Mon 09/15/08**	**Tue 09/02/08**	**Tue 09/16/08**	**0 days**	**-1 day**
2	**Planning**	**Tue 09/02/08**	**Tue 09/09/08**	**Tue 09/02/08**	**Tue 09/09/08**	**0 days**	**0 days**
3	Determine bu	Tue 09/02/08	Wed 09/03/08	Tue 09/02/08	Thu 09/04/08	0 days	-1 day
4	Prepare bud	Thu 09/04/08	Tue 09/09/08	Fri 09/05/08	Fri 09/05/08	-1 day	2 days
5	Invitation list	Fri 09/05/08	Mon 09/08/08	Mon 09/08/08	Mon 09/08/08	-1 day	0 days
6	Prepare invit	Tue 09/09/08	Tue 09/09/08	Tue 09/09/08	Tue 09/09/08	0 days	0 days
7	**Identify Basic C**	**Tue 09/02/08**	**Thu 09/11/08**	**Tue 09/02/08**	**Thu 09/11/08**	**0 days**	**0 days**
8	Theme	Tue 09/02/08	Wed 09/03/08	Tue 09/02/08	Wed 09/03/08	0 days	0 days
9	Site	Wed 09/03/08	Wed 09/10/08	Wed 09/03/08	Wed 09/10/08	0 days	0 days
10	Keynote spe	Wed 09/03/08	Thu 09/11/08	Wed 09/03/08	Thu 09/11/08	0 days	0 days
11	**Select & Reser**	**Thu 09/04/08**	**Mon 09/15/08**	**Fri 09/05/08**	**Tue 09/16/08**	**-1 day**	**-1 day**
12	Caterer	Thu 09/04/08	Wed 09/10/08	Fri 09/05/08	Thu 09/11/08	-1 day	-1 day
13	Bartenders	Thu 09/11/08	Mon 09/15/08	Fri 09/12/08	Tue 09/16/08	-1 day	-1 day
14	Security	Thu 09/04/08	Wed 09/10/08	Fri 09/05/08	Thu 09/11/08	-1 day	-1 day
15	Photographe	Thu 09/04/08	Mon 09/08/08	Fri 09/05/08	Tue 09/09/08	-1 day	-1 day
16	Cleanup Cre	Thu 09/04/08	Fri 09/05/08	Fri 09/05/08	Mon 09/08/08	-1 day	-1 day
17	**Entertainment**	**Tue 09/02/08**	**Wed 09/03/08**	**Tue 09/02/08**	**Wed 09/03/08**	**0 days**	**0 days**
18	Baseball Gai	Tue 09/02/08	Wed 09/03/08	Tue 09/02/08	Wed 09/03/08	0 days	0 days
19	Opera	Tue 09/02/08	Tue 09/02/08	Tue 09/02/08	Tue 09/02/08	0 days	0 days
20	**Media**	**Wed 09/10/08**	**Fri 09/12/08**	**Wed 09/10/08**	**Fri 09/12/08**	**0 days**	**0 days**
21	Alert commu	Wed 09/10/08	Fri 09/12/08	Wed 09/10/08	Fri 09/12/08	0 days	0 days

FIGURE 8-14 The Variance table helps you compare estimates with actuals.

Using the Tracking Gantt view, shown earlier in Figure 8-11, you also can compare what you planned with what's happening in the project.

NOTE In Figure 8-11, no progress had yet been recorded.

If you set multiple baselines, you can view them using the Multiple Baselines Gantt view (on the View menu, click More Views. In the More Views window that appears, click Multiple Baselines Gantt and then click Apply). From this view, you can see Baseline, Baseline1, and Baseline2 information. To view information from other baselines, use the Bar Styles dialog box (on the Format menu, click Bar Styles) to add additional baseline fields to the view.

Setting Up Your Infrastructure

CHAPTER 9

Determining How to Communicate with Your Team

A MAJOR PORTION of your job as a project manager is to keep your eyes and ears open to what's happening on your project. You can ensure the success of your project in two key ways:

- Document both your project plan and what ultimately takes place, and

- Keep communication open and encourage your team to keep you informed when things don't go as expected.

There are a number of ways to communicate project information. For example, depending on the size of the project and number of people involved, your organization may decide to use Microsoft Office Project Server 2007, which can facilitate communicating project information. And there are a number of additional products that can facilitate communication when you use Microsoft Office Project 2007 alone. You can also use Project's series of standard and visually oriented reports to communicate project information.

The Lines of Communication

If more than one person works on a project—and even small projects often involve more than one person—you are working in a team situation. Teams succeed through cooperation. Achieving cooperation involves building trust. And you can't build trust in an environment in which people are afraid to admit they've made a mistake.

We all know that communication is important, but we sometimes forget—most often when an unexpected problematic situation arises—that the goal of communication is to pass along information. It's often been said that information is power—the more you know, the more powerful you are. I'm not personally into power; I'm into problem solving. But regardless of your motivation, you need information to succeed, and you're certain to fail if you don't have information.

To be a successful project manager, you need to remember to encourage people to provide you with information. A major portion of your job is to ensure that you learn about problems at the earliest possible moment. Your reaction to a report of a major problem will often determine how quickly you get that information the next time a situation arises.

In recent times, I've seen people spend way too much time pointing the finger of blame. Not only does finger-pointing not solve the problem, but it also helps to ensure that information doesn't surface quickly in the future. By spreading blame, you undermine the team environment of cooperation and your team members begin to lose sight of the fact that you're all working together toward a common goal. Instead, they begin to protect themselves as individuals and disengage from the group. So if you're one of those people with a quick temper, you're going to have trouble maintaining an effective team unless you keep your temper under control. Try hard to focus on the fact that time spent blaming others could have been used more effectively to focus on solutions.

As any sports coach would tell you, "Keep your eye on the ball," and don't get distracted by side issues that aren't important to winning the game. You'll have plenty of time after you've solved the problem to determine if assigning blame is necessary and important to the future of your company. And you'll be able to make that assessment in a calm, rational way that won't demoralize your staff and disrupt the lines of communication that make your team work together effectively. Of course, it's sometimes necessary to address an employee's bad judgment call. But that employee is far more likely to learn how to correct that bad judgment call if you present your case privately instead of publicly, and in a manner not intended to intimidate and harass but rather intended to share experience. After all, you wouldn't be in the position of project manager if you didn't have experiences to share. So don't sabotage your project by losing your temper when bad news arrives. Present yourself as the example leader you want your team members to follow.

How Much Information Do You Need?

In the preceding section, I said that you need information to succeed and you're certain to fail if you don't have information. That raises the question, "How much information does one need?"

The answer to that question often depends on the audience and the purpose of the information. In a problem-solving situation, more information is typically better than less information, because you never know which tiny fact will impact the solution.

In a research situation, the researcher wants as much information as possible to ensure that he or she has looked at all the angles before making a decision. If the researcher isn't the decision-maker, it becomes the researcher's job to synthesize the information into manageable amounts to present to the decision-maker, making sure that the decision-maker has enough information on all aspects of the situation to make an informed decision.

Project management situations are much like research situations. Team members are typically the researchers who gather information and then present it to managers, who make decisions using whatever is presented to them. Team members need to be thorough and should present information on all aspects of a situation, but also they should learn how to sift through the information to present salient points. Yes, there is such a thing as "too much information."

Managers who receive information either act on it or pass it on to additional managers. The same concepts apply to managers who pass on information; they must balance the presentation, providing enough information on all aspects of a situation to ensure an informed decision, but not subjecting the decision-maker to information overload.

When presenting information, you must know your audience and the way in which the information will be used. If you're talking to the CFO and his or her staff, those reports containing lots of numbers will be of great interest. The marketing staff will be far more responsive to graphs and charts, which help synthesize large quantities of information into pictures; because sociologists often cite that approximately 70 percent of the world learns visually, pictures are effective, oh, about 70 percent of the time.

The Pros and Cons of Project Server and SharePoint

Some companies perform most or all of their work in projects. For example, consulting firms take on different clients with different needs; each need would be a project. Book publishers set up projects for each book they publish. The sheer number of projects these companies perform drives the need to manage the company's portfolio of projects with every bit as much effort and detail as is needed to manage individual projects.

Other companies may not perform all or even most of their work in projects, but the projects that they do perform are large, complex, and sometimes even far-flung geographically. For example, your company may decide to open international plants. Large, complex projects are usually a challenge to manage from a communications perspective, particularly if you have resources working in different parts of the world.

In situations like these, Project Server might work well in helping your organization manage its projects along with its limited resources. Using Project Server, your organization stores all projects and all resources in one central database on your company's local area network (LAN) or intranet so that project managers can match limited resources to projects. Project managers in the organization install and use Project Professional to create projects in the same way they use Project without connecting it to Project Server. Project managers also can use tools in Project Professional to search the Project Server Enterprise Resource Pool for resources and assign them to tasks in projects. Project managers publish their projects in the Project Server database and then receive updated project information in Project Professional as team members provide it in the Project Server database.

Team members use Microsoft Office Project Web Access (see Figure 9-1), a browser-based product, to view and update project data that is stored in the Project Server database. Team members can, for example, receive, refuse, and delegate work assignments and update assignments with progress and completion information using a familiar timesheet format. Team members also can send status reports to the project manager and attach supporting documentation, such as budget estimates or feasibility studies, to a project.

This browser-based interface, connected to a networked database of projects, eases communication between team members and project managers. In addition, because you store all projects and all resources in the Project Server database, management can use Project Web Access to assess how things are going across all of the company's projects.

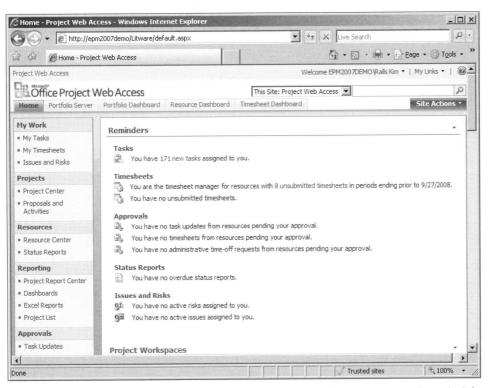

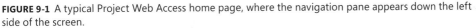

FIGURE 9-1 A typical Project Web Access home page, where the navigation pane appears down the left side of the screen.

Microsoft Windows SharePoint Services, which works with Project Server, provides a Web-based way to enhance collaboration between members of a project team. Using SharePoint, users can easily create workspaces for projects, where they can store project-related documents, record issues or project risks that arise during a project, and view or create a list of deliverables associated with a project—these deliverables can also be linked to Project Professional to manage dependencies across projects. Users can view or update a calendar of meetings, deadlines, and other important project-related events, and establish a task list to keep track of work a team needs to complete. In a project's SharePoint workspace, users also can hold newsgroup-style discussions. In Figure 9-2, you see a sample workspace Home page.

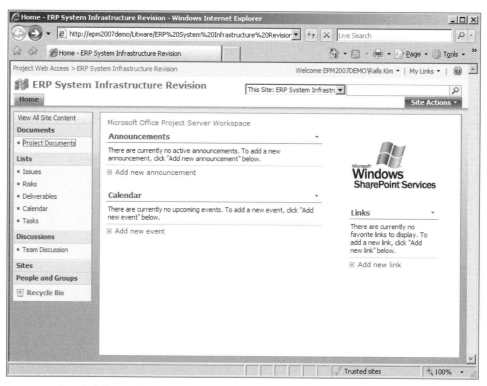

FIGURE 9-2 A typical SharePoint workspace for a project, in which the navigation pane appears down the left side of the screen.

So how do you decide if you really need Project Server? Project Server can help you if:

- Your organization manages large-scale projects or many different projects using the same resources.

- Your organization no longer wants project managers to spend time tracking down work information from resources and recording it into a project. Instead, your organization wants resources to record their time directly in project schedules.

- Your team members need access to project data outside your company's home office.

- Your organization is willing to invest in the configuration and maintenance of both the hardware and software required for project administration and the systems infrastructure.

- Your organization is willing to invest in and adopt a common approach to resource configuration and establish standards and conventions necessary to generate the types of reports or views desired.

Security and administration are serious issues if you decide to use Project Server and place all of the information about your organization's work into a centralized database. Although your LAN or intranet has been secure from the outside world from the moment you implemented it, Project Server introduces additional security needs. You need to secure the various projects within the Project Server database, since everybody working on projects stored in the database doesn't need to see every project. In fact, team members on the same project may need access to different information. So using Project Server also requires either a new employee or somebody in your organization to assume the additional responsibilities of the Project Server administrator, who, along with other administrative jobs such as establishing who can access the Project Server database, sets up security within the database to identify what each person accessing the database can see.

How Additional Software Can Help You Communicate

Although Project can stand on its own pretty well, there are other products out there that complement your use of Project and enhance communication with your team and with management.

Using Microsoft Office Outlook

One of the most obvious choices for communication, apart from regular team meetings, is e-mail. Microsoft Office Outlook is by far the most widely used e-mail program. Let's take a look at what you can and cannot accomplish with Outlook.

If you use Project without Project Server and Outlook, you don't have much flexibility in the way you communicate with your team members; Outlook and Project don't communicate in a direct way. You can store e-mail addresses for your team members in Project, but you can't get Project to open an Outlook e-mail message for you while you work in Project, nor can you attach task assignments to an Outlook e-mail message. Team members can send you assignment update information, but it isn't integrated seamlessly into Project; you'll need to manually record the assignment information in your project. E-mail workgroups, which gave you a lot of these features, were available up until Project 2003.

If your organization uses Project Server, users can communicate more directly using Outlook. If your Project Server administrator enables Outlook integration, you and your team members can synchronize Outlook with Project Web Access. Users can import assignments from Project Web Access to Outlook calendars, record work on tasks in Outlook, and export that information to Project Web Access. If your team members take advantage of Outlook integration, you won't really be aware of it, because Project Server sends assignment update information to Project Professional regardless of whether the team member entered the information using Project Web Access or uploaded assignment information from Outlook to Project Web Access. But if your organization enables Outlook integration, you can encourage your team members to use it to help ensure that you receive assignment update information in a timely fashion.

Sharing Files

If your organization doesn't use Project Server and SharePoint, or if your organization uses Project Server without using the collaboration tools offered by SharePoint, you can share files using a File Transfer Protocol (FTP) site.

If you use Project Server, you might want to take advantage of SharePoint to facilitate communication. Using a SharePoint workspace, you can store project-related documents. But SharePoint provides you with a much richer experience beyond sharing files. Anyone with access to the workspace can record project issues or risks that arise during a project, and view or create a list of deliverables associated with a project that they link to tasks in the project or to other projects. In the workspace, you can use the calendar functions to record project meetings and deadlines. Using the task list features of the workspace, you can track the work a team needs to complete. And team members can have newsgroup-style discussions.

Enhancing Reporting in Project

In addition to the standard reports available in Project, which you can read about in the section "Reviewing Reports" later in this chapter, you can use some additional products that enhance project reporting.

You can take advantage of WBS Chart Pro and PERT Chart EXPERT from Critical Tools (*www.criticaltools.com*). Project contains the information but not the capability to produce a Work Breakdown Structure (WBS) chart; the Critical Tools product solves that problem for you.

> **SEE ALSO** For more information on WBS charts, see the section "Using WBS Codes in Project Plans" later in this chapter.

Many compare Project's Network Diagram to a program evaluation and review technique (PERT) chart, but PERT Chart EXPERT gives you added capabilities that you won't find in Project. Using PERT Chart EXPERT, you can use data already stored in your project schedule to create a PERT chart. And when you update the project in PERT Chart EXPERT, all of your changes appear automatically in Project.

Using Milestones Project Companion from KIDASA Software, Inc., you can produce presentation reports for your Project schedules, customizing the results to meet your needs. This product contains a variety of reporting formats, including Gantt, Summary, Milestones, Resource, and Earned Value. You can create reports using multiple project schedules, and you can keep things up to date using the "refresh" feature in the software. You can refresh a Milestones Project Companion presentation schedule's dates and column fields with the latest information from a project schedule. You can create these reports in HTML, making them "Web ready," complete with features to view details behind the report.

Finally, you can use Microsoft Office Excel and Microsoft Office Visio to create visual reports—reports that use charts or other types of figures. To read more about these types of reports, see the section "Reviewing Reports" later in this chapter.

> **TIP** ✓ If you use Project 2007, you'll find it very worthwhile to also use Excel 2007 and Visio 2007, because the three products were designed to support each other. You might run into issues producing visual reports if you use Project 2007 with an earlier version of Visio or Excel.

Anticipating Reporting Needs

Reporting is one of the most common ways of communicating project information. Project contains reports containing numbers, and if you have Excel and Visio, you can also produce visual reports. But before you dive into producing reports, you might want to do a little planning.

Project supports two kinds of numbering schemes you can assign to tasks to help you quickly and easily identify the task's position in the hierarchy of your project: outline numbers and field codes, and WBS codes. Because you might want to include a numbering scheme to make discussion about tasks in your project easier, you might want to set up your project to include one or both of these numbering schemes.

Using Outline Numbers and Codes in Project Plans

Project enables you to use automatic outline numbering or outline field codes to number your tasks. Using outline numbers, you can't edit the outline numbers. You must simply accept the outline numbers Project assigns. If you want more control over how Project displays your outline numbers, use outline field codes.

Displaying Outline Numbers

The outline numbering system that Project uses closely resembles the numbering system you find in most legal documents. In a legal document, major headings are preceded by a whole number. Subordinate headings include the major heading's whole number, a period, and then a subordinate paragraph number. So the fourth major heading is numbered 4.0 (or just 4), and the third paragraph under the second major heading is numbered as 2.3.

When you display outline numbers in Project, you'll find that Project assigns whole numbers to tasks that are not indented, and Project assigns to subtasks numbers that start with their summary task's number. The actual number Project assigns to a subtask depends on how many times the subtask is indented from the left edge of the outline.

To display outline numbers, follow these steps:

1. While viewing any task-oriented view containing a table, on the Tools menu, click Options to display the Options dialog box.

2. Click the View tab.

3. Select the Show Outline Number check box:

4. Click OK.

Project displays outline numbers to the left of each task name (see Figure 9-3). The outline number Project assigns to a task depends on how much you have indented the task and the position of the task in the hierarchy.

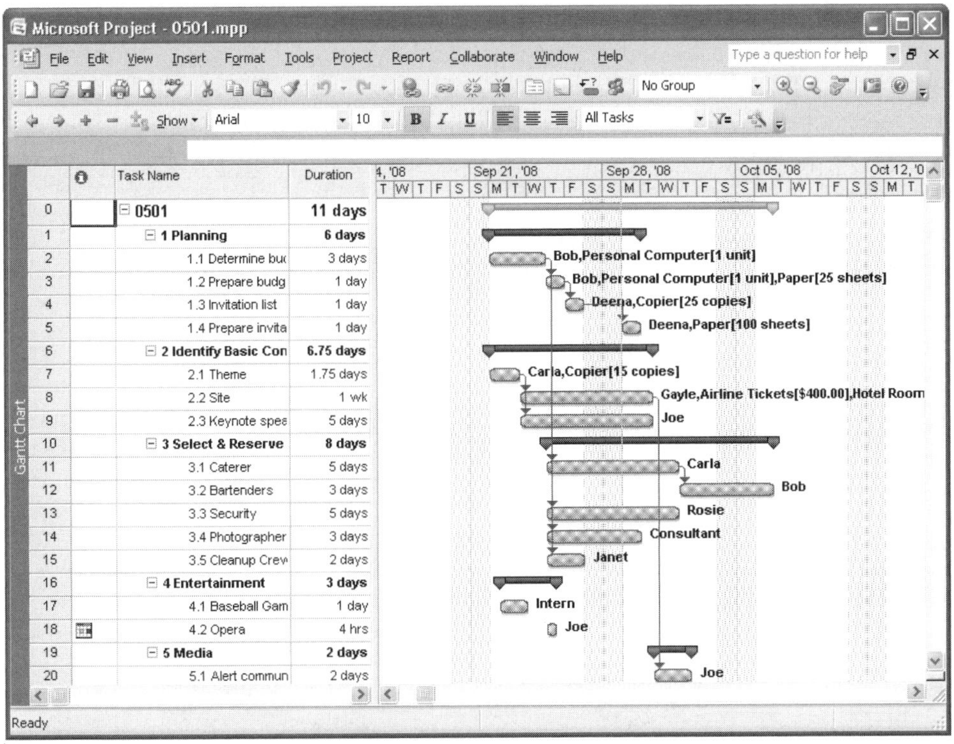

FIGURE 9-3 The outline number Project assigns to a task reflects its level in the outline.

Because the numbers Project assigns to each task depend on its position in the schedule, when you move a subtask in the outline, delete a task, or insert a task, Project renumbers all affected tasks. So if you move the third subtask in the first group of tasks so that it becomes the second subtask in the second group of tasks, Project renumbers the subtask you moved to 2.2; Project also renumbers all subtasks in the first group that appeared below the task you moved and all subtasks in the second group that appear below the new task you added to the group.

Using Outline Codes

Suppose that your organization has developed accounting codes that use an outline format and you want to assign these codes to the tasks in your project so that your tasks reflect the way that your organization does business. You can use a custom outline code field to create your accounting codes and assign them to each task.

> **NOTE** You don't need to choose between using automatic outline numbers and using custom outline codes—you can assign both to your tasks.

Outline codes don't depend on the structure of your project outline or on the number of times a task is indented. But outline codes can work in a hierarchical fashion. You create the hierarchy when you define the outline code, by establishing codes at the highest level and additional codes at various subordinate levels. Although Project won't limit you, don't define too many subordinate levels of outline codes because they simply become harder to use.

In addition to not relying on the structure of your project outline or the number of times a task is indented, outline codes differ from outline numbering in a few ways:

- You can control the form of outline codes but not the form of Project's automatic outline numbers.

- Outline codes are not tied to the hierarchical structure of your project like outline numbers are, but you can set up outline codes to use a hierarchical structure that you define.

- Outline numbers and outline codes behave differently when you move a task. When you use outline numbers, Project renumbers all affected tasks if you move, delete, or insert a task. If you use outline codes, the letters and numbers you assign are static, and Project doesn't renumber outline codes when you move, delete, or insert tasks.

You can enter outline code information randomly, but most people prefer to create a list of valid outline codes that Project displays as you assign codes to the tasks in your project. That way, the outline codes you assign to tasks are both consistent and meaningful.

Defining and using custom outline codes involves five major steps:

- Select one of Project's 10 outline codes to customize.

- Define the appearance of each portion of the code by setting up a code mask.

- Set up a lookup table that contains the valid values for the outline code that you can assign to tasks.

- Display the outline code field in your project.

- Assign the appropriate outline code value to each task in your project.

Follow these steps to select and rename an outline code, establish its appearance, and create a lookup table of valid values for it:

1. On the Tools menu, point to Customize, and click Fields to display the Custom Fields dialog box.

2. In the Type list, click Outline Code:

3. From the list of outline code fields, select one to customize.

4. Click the Rename button and type the new name for the outline code—one that will help you remember its purpose. Then click OK to redisplay the Custom Fields dialog box.

5. Click the Lookup button to display the Edit Lookup Table dialog box.

6. Click the plus sign (+) beside Code Mask to change it to a minus sign (-) and display the top portion of the Edit Lookup Table dialog box.

7. Click the Edit Mask button to display the Code Mask Definition dialog box:

8. In the list in the Sequence column, select whether the first part of the outline code should be numbers, uppercase or lowercase letters, or characters—a combination of uppercase or lowercase letters and numbers. If you choose Characters, Project initially displays asterisks for that part of the code mask in the Code Preview box, indicating that you can replace those asterisks with any characters that you want when you define values in the lookup table.

9. In the list in the Length column, specify a length for the first portion of the outline code.

10. In the list in the Separator column, select a character to separate the parts of your outline code. You can choose a period (.), dash (-), plus sign (+), or slash (/), or you can type in any character that is not a number or a letter (such as =).

11. Repeat steps 8 through 10 for each level you want to define in your outline code.

12. Click OK to redisplay the Edit Lookup Table dialog box.

13. Click the plus sign (+) beside Lookup Table, and Project expands the Edit Lookup Table dialog box so that you can define lookup table values.

Use these buttons
to indent and outdent.

14. In the first row of the Value column, type a permissible value for the first level of your outline code and press Enter. Optionally, you can type an explanation of the value in the Description column.

15. In the second row of the Value column, type an outline code for the second level that is permissible under the first level and press Enter.

16. Move the pointer back into the second row and click the Indent button to indent the value so that it appears indented under the first outline level.

17. Repeat steps 15 and 16 to establish additional values indented under the first outline level. You can create values indented to the third level using the same technique.

> **NOTE** To establish another different first-level outline code, type the code, place the pointer in the code's row, and click the Outdent button as many times as necessary, depending on the indentation of the last code that you entered.

18. Click Close to redisplay the Custom Fields dialog box.

19. Click OK to save your outline code settings.

Now you're ready to display and enter your outline codes. To display the outline code, switch to a task-oriented view that contains a table, such as the Gantt Chart view. Click in the column that you want to appear to the right of the outline code and on the Insert menu, click Column. In the Field Name list, click the outline code that you just created; Project still displays Outline Code1 in the Field Name list, but the name you assigned to the code appears in parentheses (see Figure 9-4).

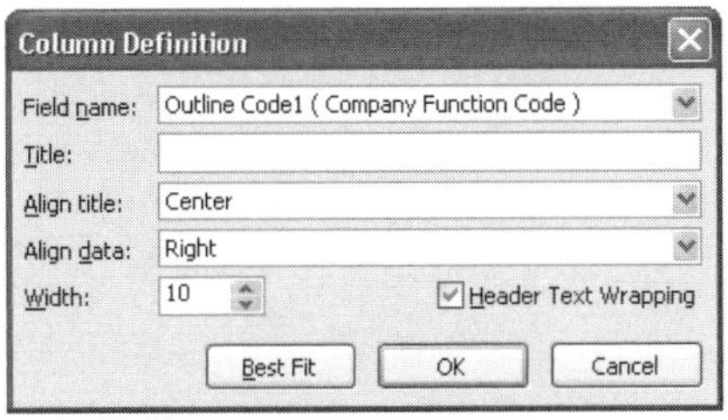

FIGURE 9-4 Adding the outline code to a table.

Click OK, and Project displays the column in the table. To enter values for the outline code, click in the outline code column. From the list that Project displays, you can select one of the entries you defined in the lookup table (see Figure 9-5).

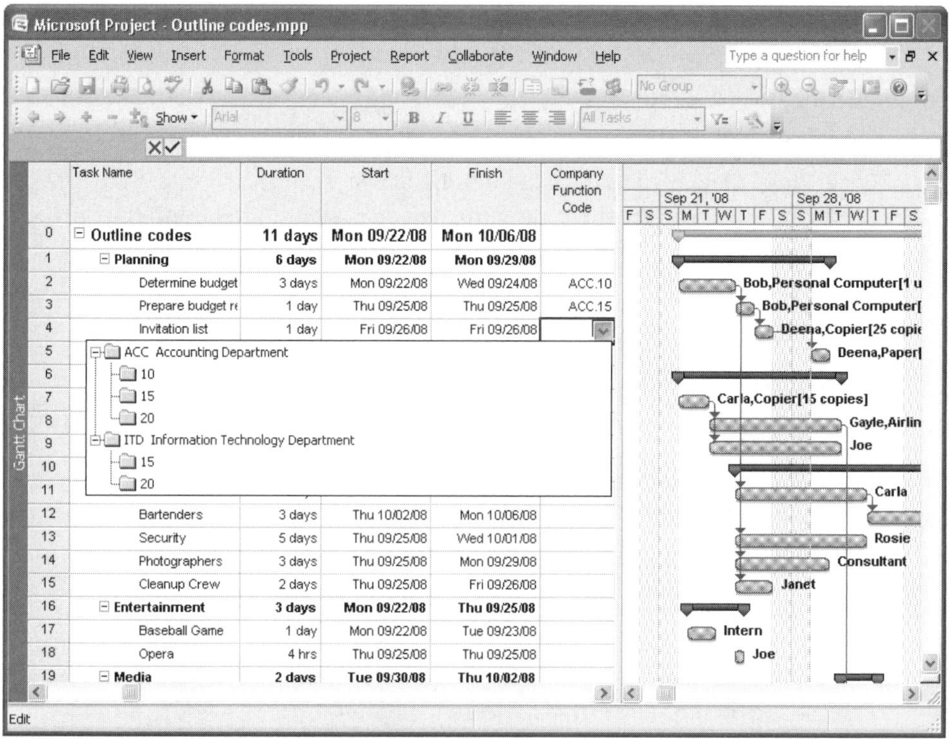

FIGURE 9-5 Enter outline codes using the entries from the lookup table you created.

Using WBS Codes in Project Plans

WBS codes provide another way to organize tasks in a project. These codes help identify the tasks in a project based on the phase in which the task occurs. WBS stands for *work breakdown structure*, and these codes were originally developed by the U.S. defense establishment.

The typical WBS chart would probably remind you of a company organization chart with boxes that organize tasks hierarchically. Each box contains the task's name along with a number that identifies the phase in which the task occurs and the phase's hierarchical relationship in the project; for example, the fourth task in the second phase of the project would have a WBS code of 2.4.

Project doesn't produce a WBS chart, but you can assign WBS codes to the tasks in your project.

TIP   You can use Visio or WBS Chart Pro to produce a WBS chart.

Project automatically assigns WBS codes that look like outline numbers to the tasks in your project; you simply need to display the WBS field to see them. Switch to a task-oriented view that contains a table, such as the Gantt Chart view. Click in the column that you want to appear to the right of the WBS code and on the Insert menu, click Column. In the Field Name list, click WBS, and click OK.

Project displays the WBS codes assigned to tasks in your project based on their position in the project outline (see Figure 9-6); a task with a WBS code of 1.4 is the fourth task in the first phase of the project. Whole numbers identify phases of the project.

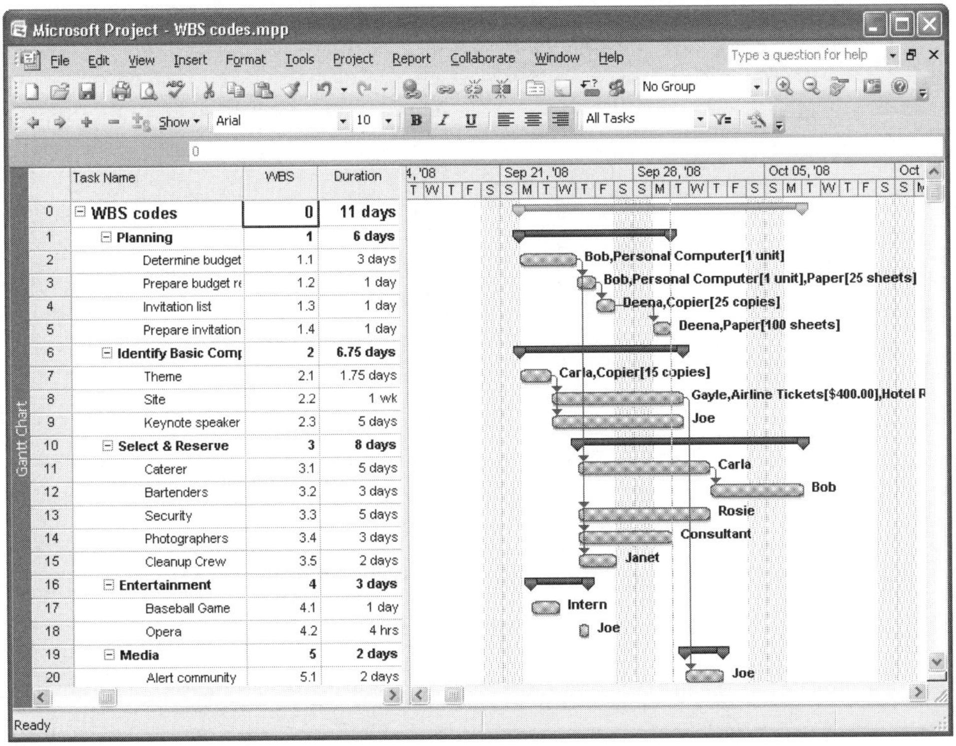

FIGURE 9-6 WBS codes closely resemble outline numbers.

Often, the default WBS numbers are all you need, but occasionally you might need to modify the appearance of the WBS code. For example, you might want to incorporate information that is meaningful to you and your client, such as the project name or a client number as a prefix for the WBS code. And you may want to include letters in the WBS code along with numbers.

You can customize the WBS codes that Project assigns by establishing your own code mask; like the code mask for outline numbers, the code mask for WBS codes defines the appearance of the code. When you define the code mask, you can use sequential numbers, uppercase or lowercase letters in alphabetical order, or numbers or letters in no order.

To create your own custom WBS codes, follow these steps:

1. On the Project menu, point to WBS, and click Define Code to display the WBS Code Definition dialog box:

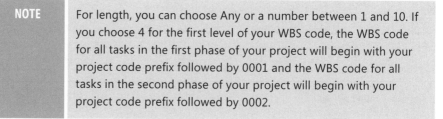

2. In the Project Code Prefix box, type any prefix that you want to appear at the beginning of all WBS codes, such as the initials of the project name or a client number.

3. Click the first blank row in the Sequence column to display an arrow, and select the type of character that you want to use for the first part of the WBS code.

4. In the Length column, identify a length for that portion of the WBS code.

> **NOTE** For length, you can choose Any or a number between 1 and 10. If you choose 4 for the first level of your WBS code, the WBS code for all tasks in the first phase of your project will begin with your project code prefix followed by 0001 and the WBS code for all tasks in the second phase of your project will begin with your project code prefix followed by 0002.

5. In the Separator column, select a character to separate the parts of your WBS code. You can choose period (.), dash (-), plus sign (+), or slash (/), or you can type any character that is not a number or a letter (such as =).

6. Repeat steps 3 through 5 for each level in your outline.

> **TIP** ✓ I suggest that you leave the check boxes at the bottom of the WBS Code Definition dialog box selected. Doing so ensures that Project assigns WBS codes to new tasks you insert in the project and that all WBS codes are unique.

7. Click OK to save your customized WBS code.

If you have already displayed the WBS field, Project updates the field with your newly designed WBS codes (see Figure 9-7).

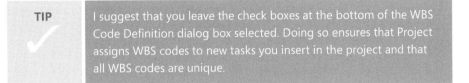

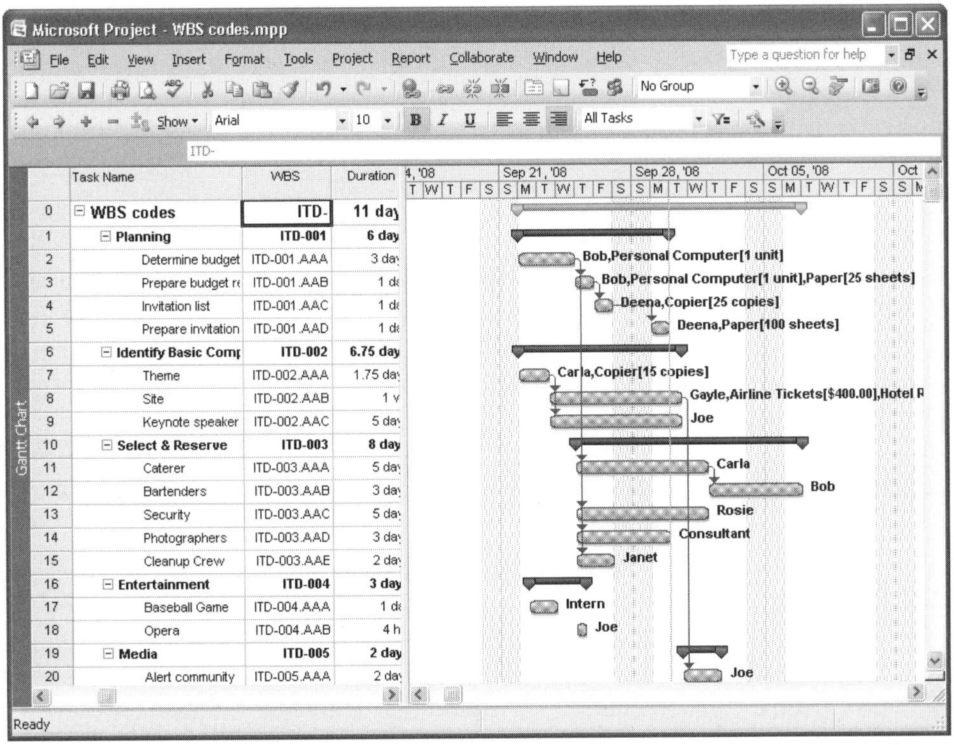

FIGURE 9-7 Use a customized WBS code to include information that describes a task's hierarchical position in the project outline.

Project's treatment of WBS code numbers changes, depending on whether you use the default WBS codes or customized WBS codes. If you use the default WBS codes that Project inserts without customizing them, Project renumbers affected WBS codes automatically if you move, insert, or delete a task.

If you use a custom code mask for WBS codes, Project doesn't automatically renumber when you move, insert, or delete a task. Project behaves this way because there are circumstances under which you don't want to renumber the WBS codes in your project.

Suppose, though, that you want to renumber tasks that use a customized WBS code. On the Project menu, point to WBS, and click Renumber. Project displays the WBS Renumber dialog box. Click OK, and Project renumbers the WBS codes in the project schedule. If you want to renumber the WBS codes for only some tasks, select those tasks before you open the WBS Renumber dialog box. Project then offers you the option of renumbering only the selected tasks or the entire project.

Reviewing Reports

Reports are an essential part of communication, providing information on paper that people can study and evaluate. You'll want to make sure that you review reports from Project so that you can ensure that the information in your project schedule accurately reflects the way things will happen.

Project's Standard Reports

You can print your Gantt chart and your Network Diagram and any other view you want by displaying that view; then on the File menu, click Print. Project also contains some standard reports that contain numbers in rows and columns primarily. To print any of the standard reports, on the Report menu, click Reports, and Project displays the Reports window shown in Figure 9-8.

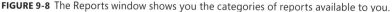

FIGURE 9-8 The Reports window shows you the categories of reports available to you.

Once you select a category, Project shows you the reports available in that category. Figure 9-9 shows the Top Level Tasks report from the Overview category, which helps you focus on "the big picture" by displaying information about the tasks that typically represent phases in your project. This report shows you the duration, start and finish dates, percentage complete, cost, and work for each of those tasks.

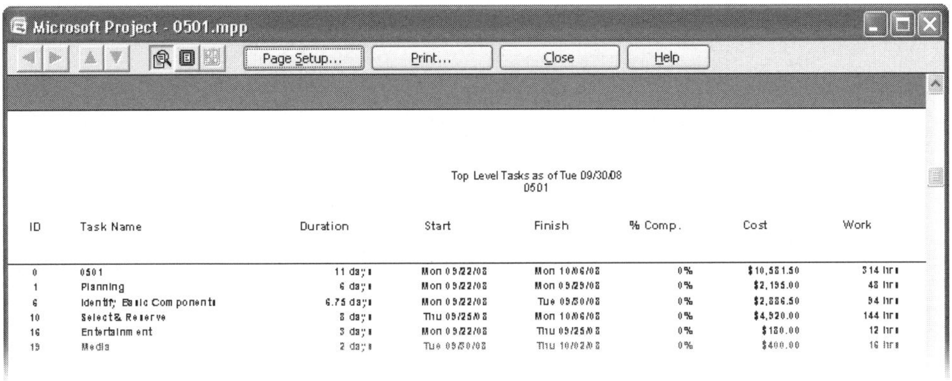

Top Level Tasks as of Tue 09/30/08
0501

ID	Task Name	Duration	Start	Finish	% Comp.	Cost	Work
0	0501	11 days	Mon 09/22/08	Mon 10/06/08	0%	$10,581.50	314 hrs
1	Planning	6 days	Mon 09/22/08	Mon 09/29/08	0%	$2,195.00	48 hrs
6	Identify Basic Components	6.75 days	Mon 09/22/08	Tue 09/30/08	0%	$2,886.50	94 hrs
10	Select & Reserve	8 days	Thu 09/25/08	Mon 10/06/08	0%	$4,920.00	144 hrs
16	Entertainment	3 days	Mon 09/22/08	Thu 09/25/08	0%	$180.00	12 hrs
19	Media	2 days	Tue 09/30/08	Thu 10/02/08	0%	$400.00	16 hrs

FIGURE 9-9 Standard reports typically present information in row/column format.

Each of the report categories provides reports that should be of interest to you. For example, also in the Overview category, you'll find a Critical Tasks report that singles out critical tasks, providing you with their duration, start and finish dates, predecessors, and successors. The Current Activities category provides you with reports that list tasks that haven't started, will start soon, are in progress, are completed, should have started, and are slipping from their anticipated ending dates. I recommend that you print each report for one project so that you can study the information provided on the report.

You can use the Custom category to print a variety of predefined reports such as the Base Calendar report. You also can edit any of the standard reports to customize them or create reports of your own.

Visual Reports

Visual reports use the numbers in your project schedule to create charts and graphs. Visual presentation is often helpful when trying to drive home a point. To use the visual reports available in Project, you need to install Excel 2007, Visio 2007, or both.

Project produces visual reports using a collection of Excel and Visio templates that use project information to produce workbooks that contain Excel PivotTables and Excel PivotCharts and files that contain Visio PivotDiagrams. Because the report information appears in Excel and Visio files, you can modify the report without affecting any data stored in your project schedule.

For those who are wondering, you don't need to start Excel or Visio before you produce a visual report in Project. Regardless of the visual report you choose to produce, follow these steps:

1. In the Project schedule on which you want to report, on the Report menu, click Visual Reports to display the Visual Reports – Create Report window:

2. The All tab displays all available visual reports; you can click the tab containing the type of report you want to produce to narrow your choices.

3. From the list, select a report to prepare.

4. Click View. Project displays the report in the appropriate program—Excel or Visio.

In a typical Excel-based visual report, you initially see the PivotChart Excel prepares using the project's data, but the workbook actually contains two tabs (see Figure 9-10).

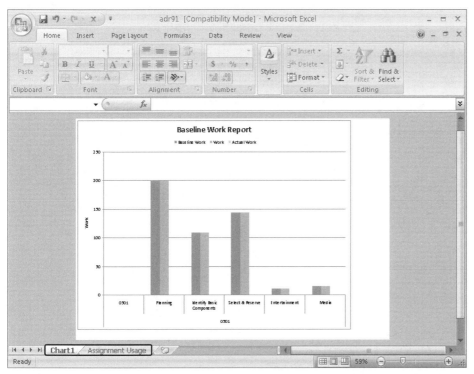

FIGURE 9-10 A workbook displaying an Excel visual report; the workbook contains two tabs.

The second tab contains the PivotTable on which the PivotChart was created (see Figure 9-11). Using the PivotTable Field List at the right side of the screen, you can change the information that appears in the chart. For example, you can control the fields that appear in the report by checking or removing checks from fields in the top portion of the pane. Use the information in the lower portion of the pane to rearrange the information in the chart. You also can filter the information that appears on the report using any lists that appear in the table.

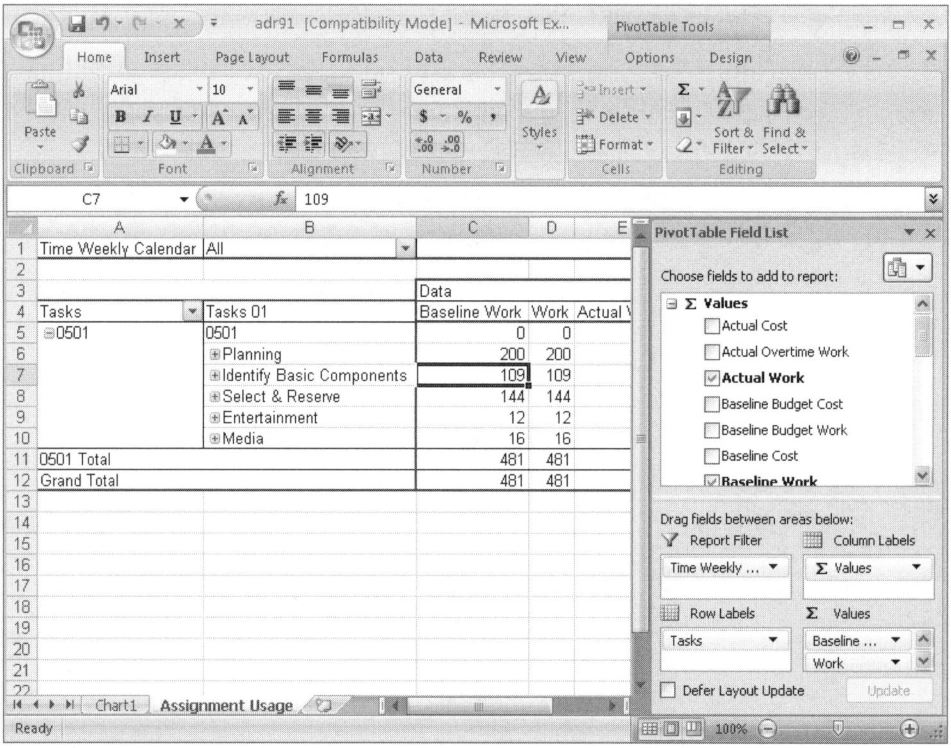

FIGURE 9-11 The PivotTable containing the data used to create the PivotChart.

Typical Visio-based visual reports are PivotDiagrams; I selected the Task Status report for the PivotDiagram shown in Figure 9-12 because, with a little fiddling in Visio, I can make this PivotDiagram into a WBS chart.

> **TIP** Initially, the PivotDiagram displays only top-level tasks that represent phases. You can display subordinate tasks by clicking each top-level task and then clicking Tasks in the Add Category portion of the pane on the left side of the screen.

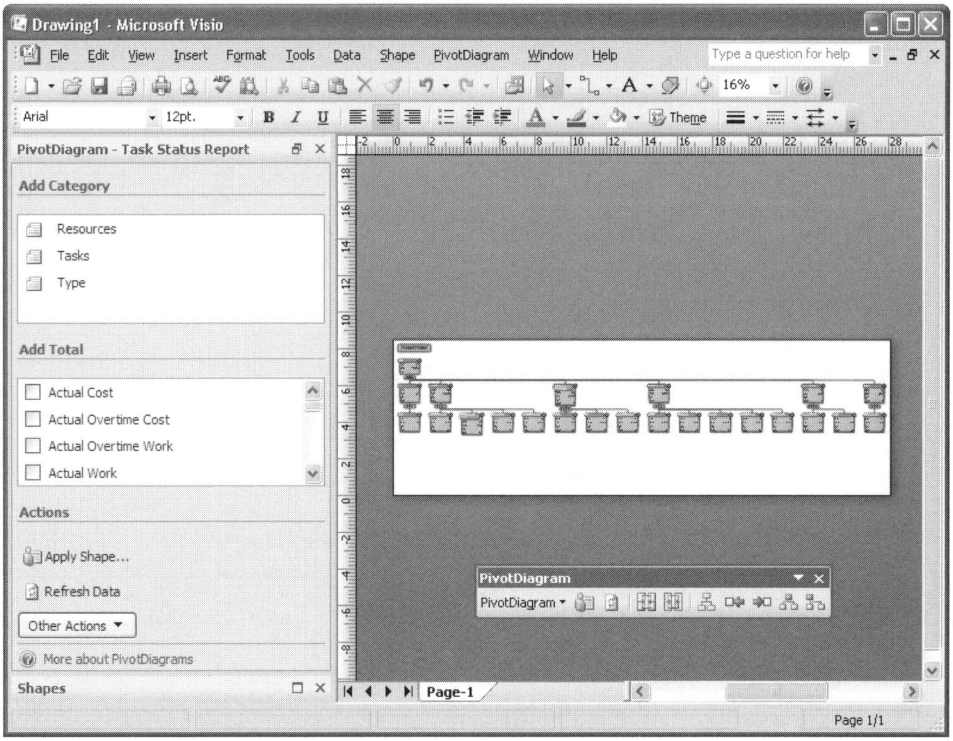

FIGURE 9-12 You can turn the Task Status report, generated in Visio, into a WBS chart.

To make this report into a WBS chart, add a new field in each box on the visual report; in the box, display the WBS number associated with the task. Right-click any box representing a task on the report, point to Data, and click Edit Data Graphic. In the Edit Data Graphic dialog box (see Figure 9-13), click New Item and click Text.

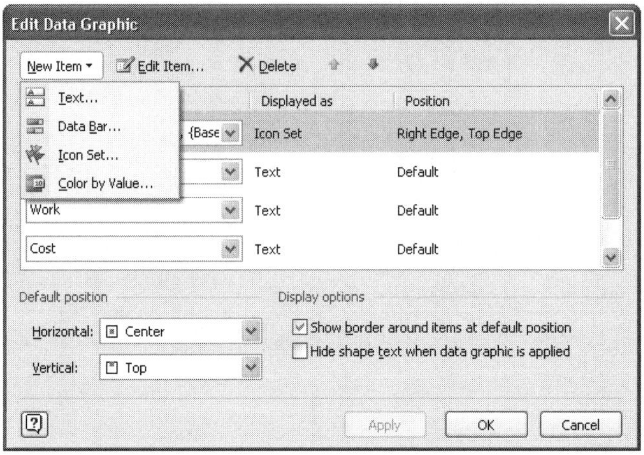

FIGURE 9-13 The Edit Data Graphic dialog box.

In the New Text dialog box (see Figure 9-14), in the Data Field list, click WBS.

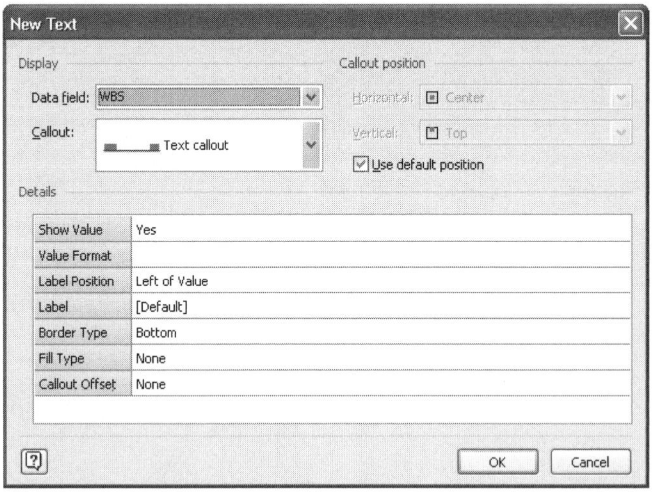

FIGURE 9-14 The New Text dialog box.

Click OK twice to redisplay the Visio PivotDiagram. Each task on the diagram will now display a WBS code.

CHAPTER 10

Establishing Guidelines for Tracking

YOU SHOULDN'T STOP WORKING WITH your project plan when you complete the planning phase. Successful projects revolve around project plans that receive the "TLC" (tender loving care) of monitoring. If you take advantage of your plan to monitor and track what happens on your project, you can use the information about what actually happens in a number of ways. For example, by monitoring your plan, you can predict deviations much earlier than if you don't track the project's progress—and you might be able to adjust the plan to accommodate those shifts before your project becomes hopelessly over budget or behind schedule.

You also can use the progress information to become a better planner for your next project by comparing what you thought would happen with what actually happened. After all, nobody can create project plans that predict the future with 100 percent accuracy. That's like trying to predict the weather; about all you can say with certainty is that it will be cooler at night than it was during the day. But your project plan represents what you believe to be a roadmap to successfully achieving your project's goals. And you build plans typically on foundations of experience. So when you begin a project, you have every right to believe that the project will happen as you expect. If you track what happens as your project progresses, you give yourself information that can help you improve your planning skills.

There are different ways to track progress in Microsoft Office Project 2007. If you identify the information you need from Project before you start tracking, you can choose a tracking method that best supports your needs.

Identifying the Information to Collect

When you record "actual" information in Project—and from this point forward, I'll refer to this type of information generically as *actuals*—you can enter it in a variety of ways. Project uses the information you provide to update several fields. For example, you can record a task's actual start date, actual finish date, and actual duration, and Project will update the task's remaining duration, percent complete, actual work, and remaining work fields. Or you can record actual work and remaining work, and Project will update the other fields I mentioned. The Tracking table, shown in Figure 10-1, contains the most common fields you can complete when recording actuals.

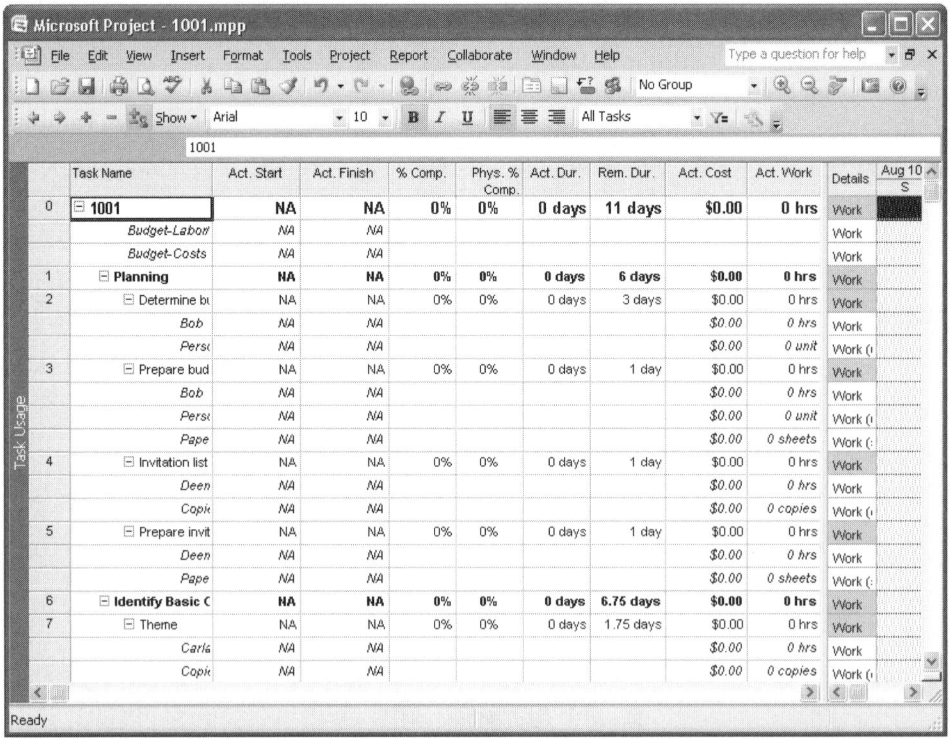

FIGURE 10-1 The Tracking table in any task view shows the fields most commonly used to record actual progress.

The type of information you choose to record determines the level of detail you need for information from team members. For example, if you want to be able to evaluate your project's progress and resource allocation using timephased views, you'll need hours worked on a task and dates the work was performed, along with the start and finish dates for the task. If, however, you're estimating percent complete, you need only an estimate of how much of the task is complete on the reporting date.

The level of detail you plan to track is often dictated by the amount of control you need to maintain your project's progress. For example, although recording percent complete is quick and easy, it can also mask the real progress on your project because, by its very nature, percent complete is an estimate and therefore may be inaccurate.

You can read more about tracking using the percent complete method and timephased fields later in this chapter in the sections "Estimating Percent Complete" and "Recording Actual Work."

Tracking Too Often or Not Often Enough

One question you should consider when monitoring your plan is, "How often should I record progress?" As with most questions of this nature, you need to find a balance. If you spend too much time tracking, you won't have time to manage the project. And considering that your team members will need to report progress to you, if you track too often, your team won't have time to work. On the other hand, if you don't spend enough time tracking, you really won't know what's going on in your project, and you might not be prepared to deal with the unexpected surprises that occur in every project.

To strike this balance, you need to combine your personal style with the complexity of your project. If you're a laissez-faire type of manager who prefers whenever possible to let things happen and you're working on a complex project, you'll do better if you modify your style to monitor your project more closely than you otherwise might. Consider tracking at least once each week and possibly more often.

On the flip side of that coin, if you're a Type-A, "get it done" manager who tends to be fairly "hands-on" and you're managing a fairly simple project, you might want to consider backing off and letting your staff take over some responsibility. In fact, these kinds of situations provide you with a perfect opportunity to test the management skills of those working for you, and you might consider turning over some of the tracking responsibilities to some of those people.

Another aspect to consider when deciding how often to track and update your project involves the length of the tasks you're tracking. In general, I encourage you to re-evaluate your plan and look for tasks with long durations such as six months. It's often difficult to measure progress on a long task, and I suggest that you avoid using tasks with long durations. Suppose that your long task involves designing and building a piece of equipment, and part of the task involves waiting for materials to arrive. If you wait the entire duration of the task before checking to ensure that the materials will arrive when you expect them, you won't like the surprise when they don't arrive on time. You might consider breaking a long task into smaller tasks, each of which lasts no longer than one month. That way, as you monitor progress, you'll find out much more quickly if there's a delay in receiving materials you need to complete a task. You can name the tasks Design 1, Design 2, Design 3, and so on if you can't find a good way to distinguish between the parts of the task. If anyone questions what you're doing, you can explain that you wanted a better way to manage a task with a long duration.

Like the level of detail you plan to track, the frequency with which you track is often dictated by the amount of control you need to maintain over your project's progress. When deciding how often to track, consider the overall length of the project, the risk of unexpected occurrences between tracking periods, and how close you are to major project milestones. You might opt to monitor some tasks daily, others weekly, and still others every two weeks. I suggest that you assess your project's overall progress at a minimum of once each month. Remember, monitoring progress helps you promptly identify any unexpected problems and address them, hopefully before they get out of hand.

Designating How Resources Report Activity

Once you identify the information that you want to track and determine how often you want to track progress, you'll need information about task progress from team members for each tracking period. During the tracking period, have team members track completed products or deliverables, successful acceptance tests, dates they reach milestones, dates they start and end tasks, number of hours they work on each task, amount of resources they use for each task, and any unplanned costs associated with each task. Ask your team members if they believe each task is on schedule. If it is not, ask them to revise the estimate for the duration of a task and the work required to complete the task. Ask your team members to provide you with the tracking information one business day after the tracking period ends.

If your team members record accomplishments when they occur, you're more likely to receive accurate data. And if your team members continually review their proposed schedules and record their accomplishments, they will be more aware of project goals and more likely to meet their commitments. Tracking can be more than an exercise in collecting data; it can help encourage your team members to perform.

Keep the reporting process as easy as possible for team members because you're more likely to get the information you request if you make it easy for team members to report.

Setting Up a Reporting Form

You might be tempted to create a form that your team members can use to supply tracking information. Giving in to this temptation is okay if your organization doesn't already have forms and processes in place. But don't give in to the temptation if your organization does have forms and processes team members can use to capture actual progress. Remember, you want to make the process of reporting progress as easy as possible for your team members, so take advantage of forms and processes your team members already use.

If you set up your own form or you want information not available on your organization's forms, look for ways that your team members can easily provide the information. Don't ask each team member to create a form; instead, set up a form for your team members. The form can include a list of tasks for the upcoming tracking period and columns for actual task start, finish, and milestone dates, along with any comments the team members might want to share. If you want information on your team members' reports that identifies whether a task is on the critical path, you can get that information from Project's Critical Tasks report and include it as a column on your form.

Using Timesheet Information

Your company's timesheets often contain information you might need to track task progress. You might consider asking your team members to provide you with a copy of their timesheets as part of the information you request for project tracking. That way, your team members need to complete the information only once. On your copy, you might ask team members to highlight the lines that apply to tasks on your project.

Explain to your team that you're using this information to help you determine when you may need to change aspects of the plan. When asked for details concerning the hours spent on specific assignments, some people might fear being criticized for not spending time exactly in accordance with the plan or for not spending enough hours on project work. If a team member doesn't understand your motives, you might end up with timesheets that reflect what your team member thinks you want to see instead of what he or she is really doing, and you can avoid this situation if you simply explain your purpose for collecting timesheet information.

Encourage team members to record the actual hours they work instead of making their total hours equal 40 hours per week. If your organization doesn't permit people to record more than 40 hours per week and members of your team work overtime, ask them to indicate the overtime hours on your copy of the timesheet so that you get accurate information that describes how long a task actually takes to complete.

Using Project Server for Tracking Information

If your organization uses Microsoft Office Project Server 2007, your team members can report progress electronically using Microsoft Office Project Web Access. Using Project Server, you can set the tracking method to one of the following methods, which determines the amount of detail you'll get from resources as they record progress:

- **Percent of Work Complete** Using this method, team members estimate and enter a percentage amount. While this method is the fastest way for resources to record time, it is also the least accurate because it is only an estimate.

- **Actual Work Done and Work Remaining** This "middle-of-the-road" approach provides a fairly accurate and fairly fast way for team members to enter the amount of work done in hours (or days, weeks, and so on) and the amount of work remaining to be completed.

- **Hours of Work Done per Time Period** Using this method, team members enter the actual hours worked on a task for a time period. This method is the most accurate method but also the most time-consuming.

In addition, your organization might decide for you just how detailed your tracking will be, since your organization can limit the tracking methods available to you.

Team members can report progress directly in Project Web Access using the tracking method you have chosen for the project. As a project manager, you can view and approve updates from team members using Project Professional or using Project Web Access. When you open a project for which team member updates exist, Project alerts you. Or when you log on to Project Web Access, your home page indicates how many task updates from re-sources are pending your approval. Using either product, you can preview the project plan to see the effects of the updates on the project plan and accept or reject the task updates.

Project Server also lets you set up status reports. You create the layout for the status report that you want to view from your team members and specify how often you want to receive status reports, when reporting should begin, which resources should report, and the sections you want included in the report. Project Web Access sends a skeleton of the status report to the team members you have identified as those who should provide the information you want to see in this report; the team members can fill in the skeleton and send it back to you.

Confirming the Plan for Each Reporting Period

At the beginning of each reporting period, revisit with all team members the tasks they agreed to perform, the dates they will start and finish these tasks, and the amount of effort needed to perform the tasks. This review helps team members clarify expectations, and you'll be helping to set the team member up for success rather than failure. You give the team member the opportunity to identify potential roadblocks that might prevent him or her from completing assignments on time and within budget. For example, during this review, you might discover that a team member has unexpectedly been assigned to work on another high-priority effort during the same time period. Together, you and the team member can work to develop a new plan for completing the assignment on your project.

Don't feel uncomfortable reviewing the plan with your team members. The review clari-fies expectations for both of you and opens the lines of communication. And if you do discover that the team member might not be available to work on your project, you'll find out before the project falls behind schedule—not after—and that gives you the chance to find another way to handle the situation.

Encouraging Team Members to Report

You can improve the accuracy of the information you receive in a number of ways. Tell team members how you plan to use the information they provide, because people are always more motivated to perform a task if they understand the reasons for it. After you use the information to update the project plan, provide copies of the updated plan to the people who give you the data so that they can see the results of their efforts.

Publicly acknowledge those people who report in a timely fashion and give you accurate information. Positive reinforcement is a strong motivator and makes your team members aware that they're meeting your expectations.

If you're collecting timesheet information, don't ask for timesheets before the period is over. Asking for timesheets early implies that guessing is acceptable.

Finally, make sure that you use all of the information that you collect and don't collect more information than you'll use.

How to Record Progress

Project uses the tracking information you provide to adjust both the schedule and the project's costs. If Project determines that you're running late on a task, Project moves dependent tasks into the future. And Project adjusts projected total costs using a combination of actual costs and remaining estimates.

Before you start recording tracking information in Project, you should set the status date and check your calculation options.

CONSOLIDATED PROJECTS AND TRACKING

When you create a consolidated project, you can choose to link the projects, as described in Chapter 13, "Managing Cross-Project Conflicts." If you link the projects and record progress in the consolidated file, Project retains the updates in the subproject files. Similarly, if you link the files and record progress in linked subproject files, Project retains the updates in the consolidated project. If you don't link the projects, changes you make to the consolidated project won't affect the individual subproject files and vice versa.

Setting the Project Status Date

In Project, you set a status date that you want Project to use when you record progress as percent complete or total work to date. Project uses the status date to determine where to place actual work and where to schedule the work that you still need to complete. If you don't set a status date, Project uses the current date. So if today is October 27 and you're recording progress for the week ending October 24, you might want to set the status date to October 24.

> **NOTE** Using the options on the Calculation tab, you can control the way Project uses the status date for placing actual work and remaining work where you want, particularly when assignments are completed earlier or later than scheduled. You can read about these options in more detail in the next section, "Reviewing Calculation Options."

To set the status date, on the Project menu, click Project Information. Project displays the Project Information dialog box for the current project (see Figure 10-2).

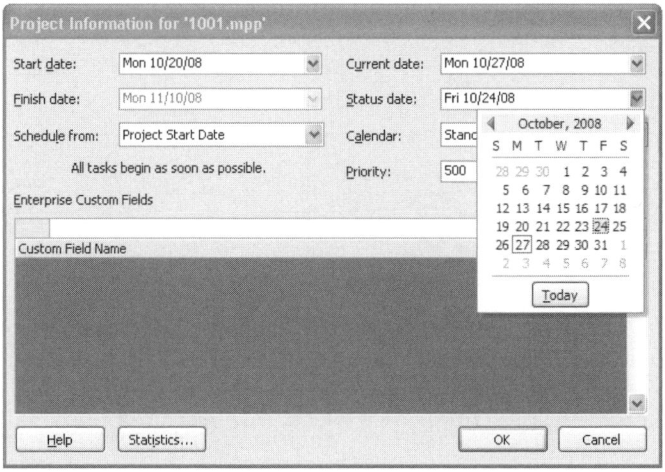

FIGURE 10-2 Set the status date before recording progress.

In the Status Date list, use the calendar that appears to select the date you want to use when recording progress; then click OK.

Reviewing Calculation Options

As you might expect, Project contains several options that affect the way Project calculates your project's schedule and costs, and you have control over these options. In particular, Project enables you to control several options that affect the way Project handles progress information when you record it.

To set calculation options, on the Tools menu, click Options to display the Options dialog box; then click the Calculation tab (see Figure 10-3).

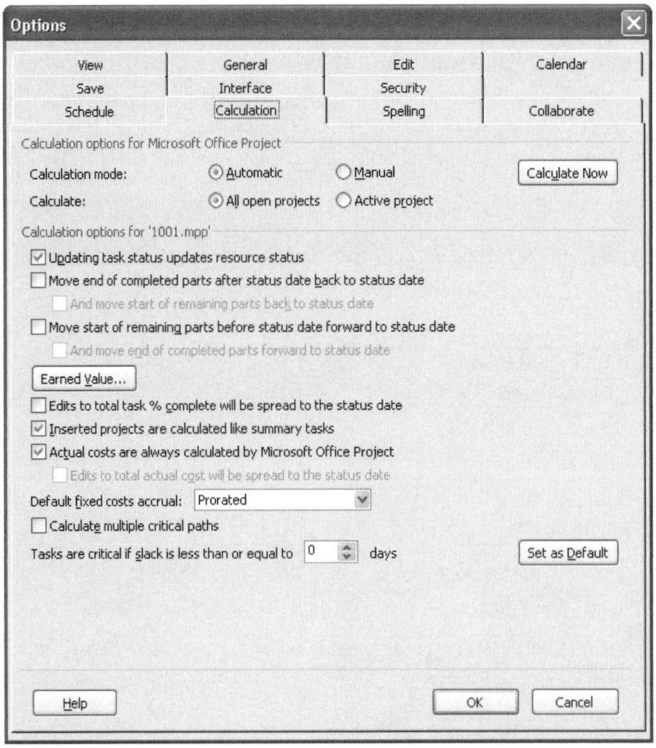

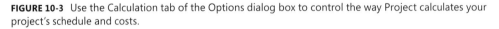

FIGURE 10-3   Use the Calculation tab of the Options dialog box to control the way Project calculates your project's schedule and costs.

You can set the following calculation options:

- **The Updating Task Status Updates Resource Status check box**   Selected by default, this option tells Project to update the corresponding resource status if you update a task's status. Similarly, Project also updates task status if you update a resource's status. For example, if you update the percentage of completion for a task, Project also updates the % Work Complete field for the resource and the assignment.

- **The Move End Of Completed Parts After Status Date Back To Status Date check box and the And Move Start Of Remaining Parts Back To Status Date check box** These two check boxes work together, so let's talk about them at the same time. These options apply only when you record progress by entering a task's total actual work, a task's actual duration, the total percent complete, or the percent of work complete; these options don't apply when you record progress in timephased fields, that is, when you enter the actual hours in the Details portion of the Resource or Task Usage view.

> **NOTE** These two options don't apply when you use timesheet information from Project Server to update your project.

By default, Project doesn't change the task start dates or adjust the remaining portions of tasks when tasks begin late or early. But if you select these check boxes, Project updates the tasks in relation to the status date. Suppose you set the status date to October 17 and you have a task with a start date of October 22 and a duration of four days. If the task actually starts early, on October 15, and you select the Move End Of Completed Parts After Status Date Back To Status Date check box, Project moves the task start date to October 15, sets the percent complete to 50 percent, and schedules the start of the remaining work for October 23, creating a split task. If you also select the And Move Start Of Remaining Parts Back To Status Date check box, Project makes all of the changes I just described but doesn't create a split task; instead Project moves the start of the remaining work to October 17.

- **The Move Start Of Remaining Parts Before Status Date Forward To Status Date check box and the And Move End Of Completed Parts Forward To Status Date check box** Like the preceding pair of check boxes, these two check boxes work together, so let's talk about them at the same time. Also like the preceding pair, these options apply only when you record progress by entering task total actual work, task actual duration, total percent complete, and percent work complete; these options don't apply when you record progress in timephased fields.

> **NOTE** These two options don't apply when you use timesheet information from Project Server to update your project.

By default, Project doesn't change the task start dates or adjust the remaining portions of tasks when tasks begin late or early. But if you select these check boxes, Project updates the tasks in relation to the status date. Suppose that the status date is October 17 and you have a task with a start date of October 11 and a duration of four days that actually starts on October 15. If you select the Move Start Of Remaining Parts Before Status Date Forward To Status Date check box, Project leaves the task start date at October 11, sets the percent complete to 50 percent, and schedules the remaining work to start on the status date, which is October 17, creating a split task. If you also select the And Move End Of Completed Parts Forward To Status Date check box, Project makes the changes I just described but doesn't create a split task; instead Project moves the task's actual start date to October 15.

- **The Edits To Total Task % Complete Will Be Spread To The Status Date check box** By default, Project distributes percent completion changes to the end of the actual duration of a task. But if you select this check box, Project instead distributes the changes evenly across the schedule to the project status date.

- **The Actual Costs Are Always Calculated By Microsoft Office Project check box** This option, selected by default, tells Project to calculate actual costs so you don't have to enter actual costs. If you clear this check box, enter costs and then reselect the check box; Project will overwrite any costs that you enter for any tasks that aren't 100 percent complete and will recalculate the costs for those tasks.

- **The Edits To Total Actual Cost Will Be Spread To The Status Date check box** This option becomes available if you don't select the Actual Costs Are Always Calculated By Microsoft Office Project check box. Select this option to have Project distribute changes to total actual cost evenly across the schedule to the status date. Suppose that you're entering $400 in costs for a four-day task scheduled to run from Monday through Thursday, and you've set the status date to Thursday. Further suppose that you've recorded, on Monday and Tuesday, two days in actual duration for this task. If you select this check box and enter the actual cost of $400 on the status date of Thursday, Project enters $100 for the task on Monday, Tuesday, Wednesday, and Thursday, spreading the cost across the task's schedule to the status date. If you don't select this check box, Project accrues the actual costs to the end of the actual duration of the task, and Project spreads the $400 of actual cost across the two days of actual duration, recording $200 on Monday and $200 on Tuesday. If you haven't entered any actual duration, Project records the actual cost at the beginning of the task, on Monday.

- **The Default Fixed Costs Accrual list** Use this option to indicate how you want Project to accrue fixed costs for new tasks. Project can accrue fixed costs at the start of a task or at the end of a task, or Project can prorate the costs throughout the duration of the task.

> **SEE ALSO** You can find information about earned value calculation options in Chapter 11, "Dealing with Management."

Making Notes As You Go

As you record progress, you might find it useful to make notes about unexpected events or circumstances—both positive and negative—that may affect the completion of a task. You can easily record a note for any task; simply select the task and click the Task Notes button on the Standard toolbar. Project displays the Notes tab of the Task Information dialog box (see Figure 10-4).

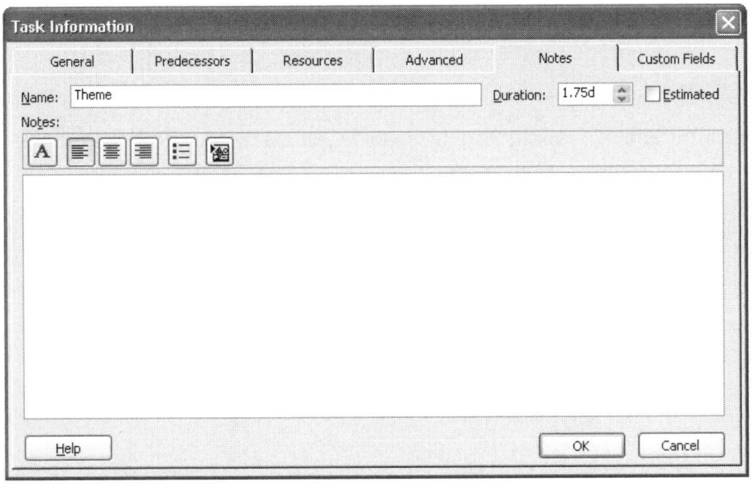

Task Information

| General | Predecessors | Resources | Advanced | Notes | Custom Fields |

Name: Theme   Duration: 1.75d   ☐ Estimated

Notes:

Help   OK   Cancel

FIGURE 10-4 Make notes about tasks in the Task Information dialog box.

When you record a note for a task, Project displays an icon in the Indicators column that looks like the one you see beside this paragraph. And you can print notes when you print views and some reports. For example, before you print the Gantt Chart view of your schedule, on the File menu, click Page Setup. On the View tab, select the Print Notes check box. Or when you print a report such as the Unstarted Tasks report or the Slipping Tasks report, you can click the Edit button; in the Task Report dialog box that appears, click the Details tab and select the Notes check box in the Task area (see Figure 10-5).

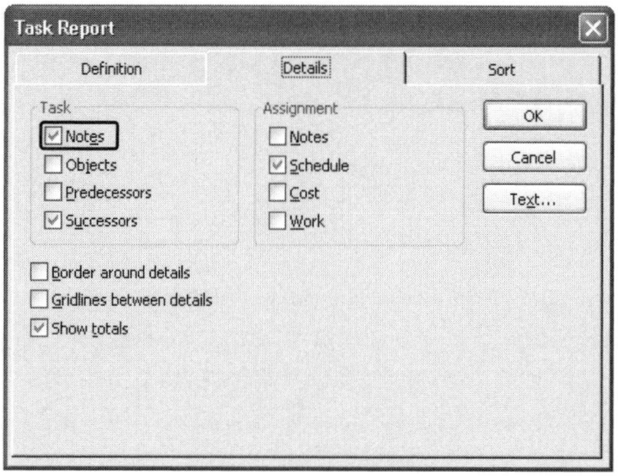

FIGURE 10-5 Select the Notes check box to include notes on the report when you print it.

Estimating Percent Complete

You can record progress on a task by assigning a Percent Complete value to the task. Enter any value less than 100 to indicate that the task is not complete. You can enter a Percent Complete value using the Tracking table on any task-oriented view. To display the Tracking table, right-click the Select All button and click Tracking.

The tools on the Tracking toolbar can help you enter percent complete values; right-click in the toolbar area and click Tracking to display the Tracking toolbar. In Figure 10-6, you see the Task Sheet view using the Tracking table along with the Tracking toolbar.

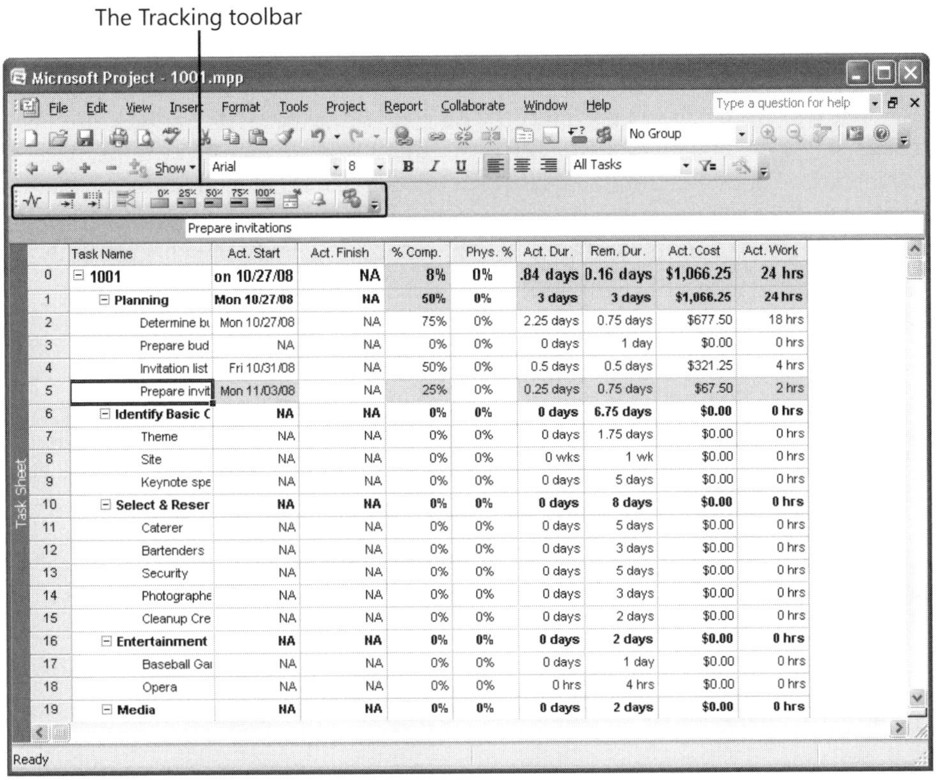

The Tracking toolbar

FIGURE 10-6 The Tracking table and the Tracking toolbar.

> **NOTE** You can use the Work table to enter the percent of work complete on a task. Enter the percentage value in the Percent Work Complete field (see the "Recording Actual Work" section later in this chapter.).

To record a percent complete progress value, click the task for which you want to record progress and enter the value in the % Complete column (or the % W. Complete column on the Work table). You can enter the standard values of 25%, 50%, 75%, or 100% using the Tracking toolbar. When you enter a Percent Complete value, Project assigns an Actual Start Date unless you entered one previously, and calculates the Actual Duration and Remaining Duration values. If your Calculation options call for updating resources when you update tasks, Project also calculates the Actual Cost and Actual Work values. Project assigns the planned finish date to the Actual Finish Date column if you enter **100** in the Percent Complete column. But if your task doesn't finish on the planned finish date, don't enter a Percent Complete value; instead enter an Actual Finish Date.

Entering the values isn't difficult; deciding what values to enter can be problematic. When a task produces something measurable, you can more easily estimate percent complete. For example, if the task calls for setting up 20 work cubicles and you've set up five, the task is probably 25 percent complete. Or if the task calls for doing telephone surveys to 30 employees and you've made 15 calls, the task is probably 50 percent complete.

If a task doesn't produce anything truly measurable, you can only enter your best guess, based on your experience and the information you get from the resources that provide you with information about a task's progress. For example, if your resources report spending two days on an eight-day task, the task might be 25 percent complete, but then again, it might not. You see, just because resources have put in 25 percent of the time you estimated doesn't mean that they've completed 25 percent of the work.

You might also be tempted to use costs to estimate completeness. If you estimate that three resources assigned to a three-day task will cost $3,000, you might be tempted to estimate that a task is 33 percent complete when the task's costs reach $1,000. But once again, just because costs have reached the 33 percent mark doesn't mean that 33 percent of the work on the task is complete.

I suggest that you use the percent complete approach only when you have a good way of measuring the task's progress. That way, you can rest easy in the knowledge that you're entering fairly accurate tracking information.

SEE ALSO   For information on the distinction between the % Complete field and the Physical % Complete field, see Chapter 11.

RECORDING PROGRESS QUICKLY

Suppose that you have several tasks that are on schedule or were completed on schedule. You can quickly and easily update the percent complete for several tasks or even your entire project at one time using the Update Project dialog box. Display any task-oriented view. If you plan to update only selected tasks, select them by clicking their ID numbers. Then on the Tools menu, point to Tracking, and click Update Project:

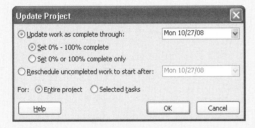

To update on-schedule tasks, select the Update Work As Complete Through option and click a date. Then do one of the following:

➤ Select the Set 0% – 100% Complete option to let Project calculate the percent complete on every task that should have begun by the selected date. Project assumes that tasks have started and are progressing according to your plan and sets the % Complete field value accordingly.

➤ Select the Set 0% Or 100% Complete Only option to have Project mark as finished all tasks that the baseline plan indicates would have been complete by the date you selected; Project leaves all other tasks as 0% complete.

You can choose to update your entire project or only selected tasks. When you update the entire project, Project sets the project status date to the date that you selected in the dialog box.

Recording Start and Finish Dates

You can record progress by entering task start or finish dates. If a task doesn't start or finish on time, you should enter an actual start date or an actual finish date; otherwise, if you mark a task complete, Project assumes that the task started and finished on time. In addition, entering actual start and finish dates lets Project update the schedule to reflect actual timing. If you don't adjust a task's duration and you enter an actual finish date that is earlier than the planned finish date, Project assumes that the task started earlier than planned.

The Actual Start and Actual Finish fields appear on the Tracking table of any task-oriented view. If you prefer, you can record actual start or actual finish dates using the Update Tasks dialog box (see Figure 10-7). Select the task you want to update and click the Update Tasks button on the Tracking toolbar, or on the Tools menu, point to Tracking, and click Update Tasks.

Update Tasks				
Name:	Invitation list		Duration:	1d
% Complete:	0%	Actual dur: 0d	Remaining dur:	1d
Actual			**Current**	
Start:	NA		Start:	Fri 10/24/08
Finish:	NA		Finish:	Fri 10/24/08
Help		Notes...	OK	Cancel

FIGURE 10-7 You can use the Update Tasks dialog box to record actual start or finish dates for the selected task.

In the Actual area, click a list box arrow to display a calendar and select the task's start or finish date. When you enter an actual start date, Project changes the task's planned start date. When you enter an actual finish date, Project changes the planned finish date as well as the Percent Complete, the Actual Duration, the Remaining Duration, the Actual Work, and the Actual Cost fields. If you set only an actual finish date and not an actual start date, Project also fills in the actual start date.

Recording Actual and Remaining Durations

You can record progress by recording actual or remaining duration values. The Actual Duration field for a task shows the amount of time that you needed to complete the task. When you use this approach, Project updates the Actual Start, Actual Cost, Actual Work, and Percent Complete fields. In some cases, Project also updates the Actual Finish field, too. When you record an actual duration without a remaining duration, Project calculates and fills in the Remaining Duration value.

Suppose that you enter an actual duration that is equal to or less than the planned duration. In this case, Project assumes that the task is progressing on schedule. If you didn't enter an actual start date, Project sets the actual start date equal to the planned start date.

Suppose that you set an actual duration that is greater than the planned duration. In this case, Project assumes that the task is finished but that it took longer than expected to complete. Project fills in the Actual Finish field using the planned finish date and adjusts the planned duration to match the actual duration. Project also changes the Percent Complete field to 100% and the Remaining Duration field to 0%.

> **NOTE** If you set calculation options so that Project updates the status of resources when you update a task's status, Project updates the work and cost figures for resources when you supply an actual duration for a task.

The Remaining Duration field shows how much more time you need to complete a task. Suppose that you enter a value in the Remaining Duration field without entering a value in the Actual Duration field, and that the value you enter is higher or lower than the existing figure. In this case, Project assumes that you are changing the planned duration of the task instead of tracking actual progress for the task and adjusts the schedule based on the new planned duration.

But suppose that you enter a value in the Actual Duration field and follow that entry with a value in the Remaining Duration field. Project assumes that the work for the task will be completed based on the Remaining Duration value and sets the Percent Complete value based on a combination of the Remaining Duration value that you supplied and the original planned duration. Entering **0** in the Remaining Duration field is the same as entering **100%** in the Percent Complete column. Project assigns the planned finish date to the Actual Finish Date field. If this value is not correct, you can change the Actual Finish Date field.

Recording Actual Work

Updating the Actual Work field to record progress is the best approach to use when you schedule tasks based on the availability of certain resources. Typically, you use timesheet information to make your entries. Although you can enter actual work from either the Task Usage view or the Resource Usage view, the Resource Usage view will be easier to use if you're entering progress information from timesheets, because this view lists resources followed by the tasks assigned to them.

You can record total actual work for resources using these steps:

1. On the View menu, click Resource Usage to display the Resource Usage view.

2. Right-click the Select All button and, on the shortcut menu that appears, click Work. Project displays the Work table.

3. Drag the divider bar almost completely to the right edge of the screen to reveal the Actual column:

4. Under the appropriate resource, find the task for which you want to record progress.

5. Enter a value for the resource in the Actual column.

NOTE If you opt to work in the Task Usage view, use the Tracking table and enter values into the Actual Work column. You also might want to move the Actual Work column because it appears at the right edge of the Tracking table. Click the column heading to select it. Release the mouse button; once the column is selected, drag the column heading to the left until the vertical bar marking the column's proposed location appears where you want it. When you release the mouse button, Project moves the column. The Task Usage view and the Tracking table also work well when you want to record costs in the Actual Costs field on the days they occur.

You can also use this view to enter a resource's work on a task on the day the work occurred; when you use this approach, Project calculates the value in the Actual column for you. Display the Resource Usage view and the Work table using Steps 1 and 2 above. Then on the Format menu, point to Details, and click Actual Work (see Figure 10-8). Project adds a row for every task on the right side of the view.

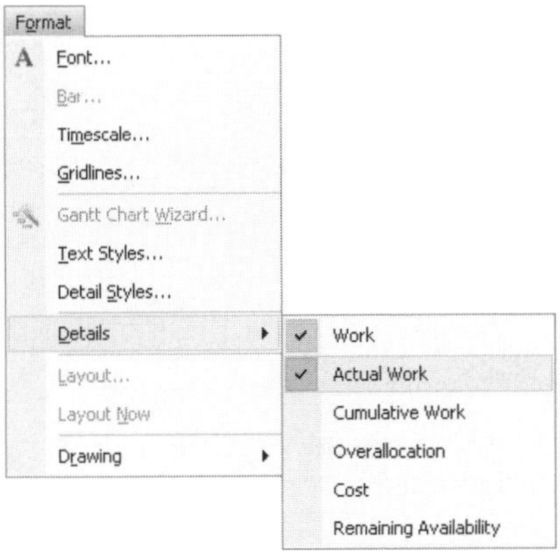

FIGURE 10-8 Adding the Actual Work row to the Details portion of the Resource Usage view.

In the Details portion of the view, enter the hours for the correct resource and task on the Actual Work row in the column of the day on which the work occurred (see Figure 10-9).

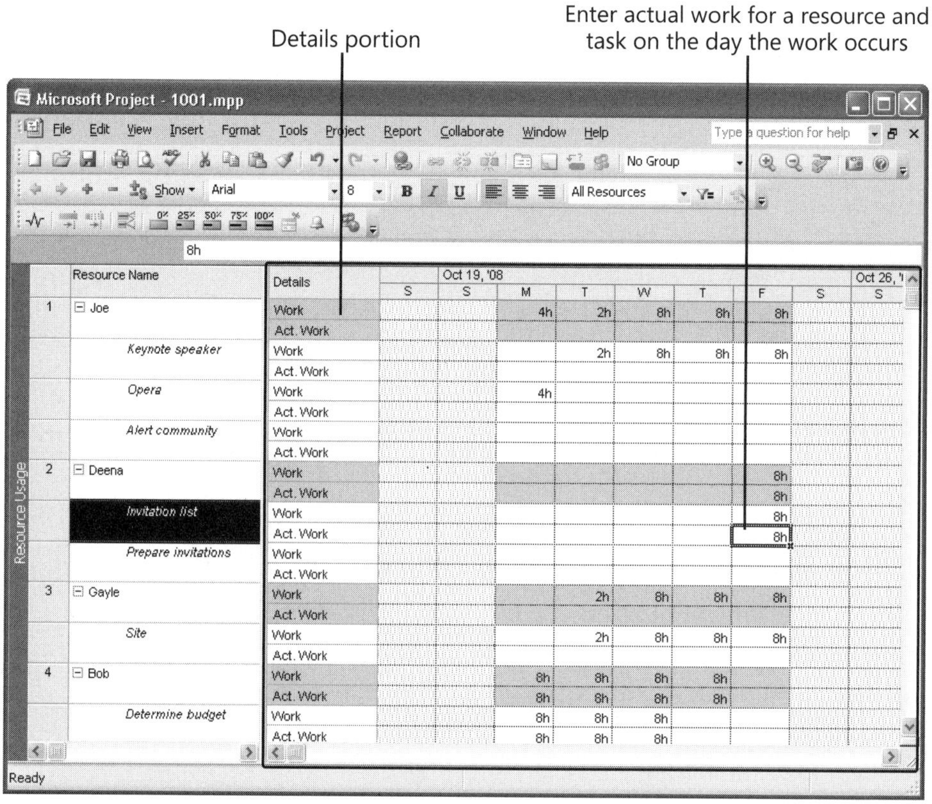

Details portion

Enter actual work for a resource and task on the day the work occurs

FIGURE 10-9 Recording actual work for a resource and task on a specific day.

If the timescale of the Details portion of the view doesn't display the time period for which you want to enter information, click the name of a task that you want to update, and then click the Scroll To Task button on the Standard toolbar.

TIP By the way, this handy tool works in all task-oriented views; if you can't see, for example, the Gantt bar for a particular task in the Gantt Chart view or the Tracking Gantt view, select the task's name, and then click the Scroll To Task button. In the Resource Usage view, click the name of the task under a particular resource.

ADJUSTING THE TIMESCALE

In the Details portion of both the Task Usage view and the Resource Usage view, the default timescale shows each day. If you want to record progress in some other increment—such as weekly—you can adjust the timescale to display weeks instead of days. On the Format menu, click Timescale. Project opens the Timescale dialog box. To change the timescale to, for example, weekly, click the Middle Tier tab, and in the Units list, click Weeks. Then hide the other tiers by clicking One Tier (Middle) in the Show list.

Tracking the Use of Materials

Although it may not seem important to track the use of Material resources, they do affect the cost of your project. You update actual work for Material resources the same way you update actual work for Work resources. To record progress for Material resources, you might find it easiest to work in the Resource Usage view and record total work for the Material resource in the Actual column on the Work table. Or if you want, use the Act. Work timephased field in the Details portion on the right side of the view. Make sure you display the Actual Work row: on the Format menu, point to Details, and click Actual Work. Then on the appropriate day, across from the resource under the appropriate task, record the amount of the Material resource that was used.

CHAPTER 11

Dealing with Management

EVEN THOUGH YOU'RE THE PROJECT MANAGER, chances are you answer to someone else in your company. To deal effectively with your own management, you need to keep your project's goal in your own mind and the mind of your management; it's easy but costly to lose focus of the original intent of the project. And of course, circumstances change—they always do during any project. Some of those changes will require support from your management, and you'll need to sell management on the need for these changes. You'll need to document why you want to make the changes, including providing budget information. In this chapter, we'll look at a collection of tools that you can use to help you prepare your case for management and for other project stakeholders.

Approaching the Change Discussion

When you plan to approach management to discuss changes to the project plan, you need to document why you're asking for the changes. Even when you present a strong case and management reviews your evidence explaining why you can't meet a particular schedule or budget and what you suggest as alternatives, management might ask you to do the impossible anyway. If you document your concerns, your documentation might have you looking like the smart employee instead of the one whose project failed.

Microsoft Office Project 2007 can help you identify alternatives. You can try out various "What happens if I try cutting costs by removing resources?" or "What happens to the project costs if I add resources to shorten the schedule?" scenarios, saving each as a different project file. You can then print reports of these files—both standard and visual—to show to management, and filter the files to help your bosses focus on areas such as the critical path.

> **SEE ALSO** See Chapter 9, "Determining How to Communicate with Your Team," for more information on the reports available in Project and using additional software.

You also can create a table, such as the following one, that shows the tradeoffs involved in saving time or money. You won't find a feature in Project that creates this table; it's simply a useful way that project managers have found to document change for their bosses and to help management compare the costs and duration associated with the original plan as compared to a proposed alternative.

TASK NAME	ORIGINAL DURATION	ORIGINAL COST	PROPOSED DURATION	PROPOSED COST	CHANGE IN COST
Task 1	1 month	$10,000	2 weeks	$20,000	$10,000
Task 2	2 weeks	$5,000	1 week	$7,500	$2,500
Task 3	3 weeks	$12,000	1.5 weeks	$25,000	$13,000

Baselines and interim plans are other tools you can use; these tools help you compare where you planned to be with where you are. Showing management a Tracking Gantt chart that shows you are so far off course that you won't recover without making some changes can be a persuasive argument to help you gain the support of management.

Explaining What a Network Diagram Says about Your Project

Consider using the Network Diagram to help you explain the flow of work to management. A Network Diagram presents your project much like a map for a road trip. Using the Network Diagram, you can determine how long the trip will take, identify potential bottlenecks, and find alternate ways to reach the destination.

The Network Diagram (see Figure 11-1) organizes the flow of project work using boxes that represent tasks. The lines and arrows that connect these boxes identify the sequence of tasks. To some degree, the lines and arrows also identify dependencies, because tasks on the left side of an arrow must occur before tasks on the right side of an arrow. That said, actual dependency relationships don't appear by default on the Network Diagram. There is no timescale on the Network Diagram because the focus of the view is workflow rather than timing. Tasks on the left side of the diagram happen earlier in the project than tasks on the right side of the diagram. The Network Diagram aligns vertically all tasks that happen in the same timeframe. Summary tasks appear in angled boxes while subtasks appear in square boxes and to the right of their summary task. Tasks on the critical path appear in red boxes with bold outlines while tasks not on the critical path appear in blue boxes. Each box also contains the task's projected start and finish dates. In-progress tasks have one half of an X through them, and completed tasks have a full X through them.

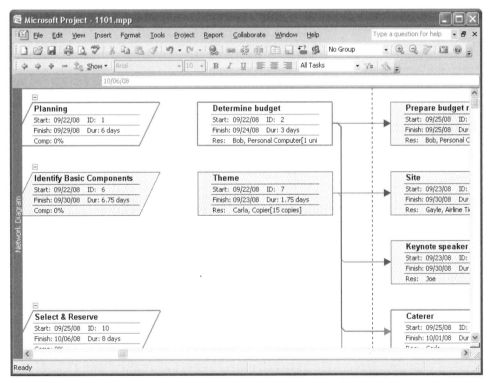

FIGURE 11-1 The Network Diagram can help you focus on the workflow of your project.

When using a Network Diagram, remember:

- After you complete a task, you can proceed to the next task indicated by the arrow leaving the task you completed.

- Before you can start a task, you must have completed all the tasks with arrows pointing to the task you want to start.

You need to put these two facts together to correctly interpret a Network Diagram. The first bullet says that you *can* proceed—it doesn't say you *must* proceed to the next task. So you can work on a different task. But the second bullet limits the tasks available for work, because you cannot work on a task that has uncompleted tasks pointing to it.

You can control much of the appearance of Project's Network Diagram to help you make your case. You can control the way Project lays out the Network Diagram and links boxes together. You also can control the shape, color, and line style of Network Diagram boxes, as well as the information that appears in the boxes.

You can use the Network Diagram toolbar to make many of these changes. To view this toolbar, right-click any toolbar and then click Network Diagram.

Changing the Network Diagram Layout

The facets of the Network Diagram layout that you can control include: whether Project lays out the diagram or you do, the arrangement of boxes on the diagram, the style and color of links, and some overall general options, like whether the background of the diagram is white or some other color you choose. To make changes to the way Project lays out the Network Diagram, on the Format menu, click Layout to open the Layout dialog box (see Figure 11-2).

From this dialog box, you can tell Project to let you manually position boxes on the diagram instead of having Project position them for you. You can also change the order in which Project displays the boxes. Using the check boxes at the bottom of the Box Layout area, you can hide or display summary tasks, keep tasks with their summaries, and tell Project to adjust the Network Diagram for page breaks. You also can change the row and column alignment and spacing along with row height and column width.

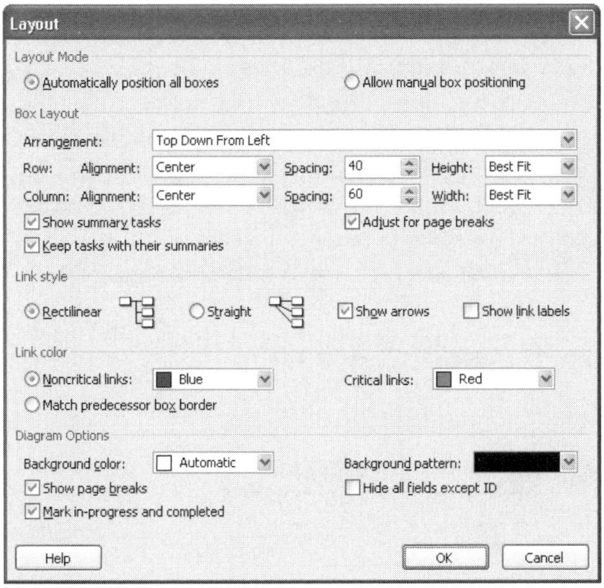

FIGURE 11-2 The Layout dialog box.

WARNING Be careful here; people who are familiar with Network Diagrams might get confused if yours uses a non-traditional layout.

In the Link Style area, you can control the style of the link lines, and you can choose to show arrows and link labels. When you display link labels, Project includes on the line connecting tasks the letters of the type of dependency that exists between the two tasks, such as FS to mark a finish-to-start dependency.

In the Link Color area, you can select colors other than red and blue for critical and non-critical links. If you select the Match Predecessor Box Border option, link lines assume the same color as the box of the predecessor task instead of using the colors of critical and non-critical tasks.

You can use the choices in the Diagram Options area to change the general appearance of the Network Diagram by, for example, setting a background color and pattern for the Network Diagram.

Changing the Style of Network Diagram Boxes

You can change the appearance of individual Network Diagram boxes or of a particular category of boxes. Project uses a set of templates that define the shape, color, and content of each box, based on the type of task the box represents. You can override the settings of these templates. Since formatting box styles one at a time can be lengthy, time-consuming, and confusing to the reader, I suggest that you format all of the boxes for a particular type of task, such as all critical tasks. In this way, you'll keep the appearance of each type of box consistent on your Network Diagram and make the diagram easier to understand.

To format all the boxes for a particular type of task, follow these steps:

1. On the Format menu, click Box Styles to see the Box Styles dialog box.

2. In the Style Settings For list on the left, click the type of task box that you want to format; its current format appears in the Preview window.

> **NOTE** You can select the Set Highlight Filter Style check box to choose formatting options for the selected box when it appears on a filtered Network Diagram. You can set all of the same options for the box in a filtered state as you do for its non-filtered state; just follow the steps in this section after you select the Set Highlight Filter Style check box.

3. In the Border area, click one of the 10 shapes for the box in the Shape list, click in the Color list the box's line colors, and click in the Width list a line width for the box's border.

> **NOTE** The Show Horizontal Gridlines and Show Vertical Gridlines check boxes control whether Project displays lines that separate each field on the box.

4. In the Background area, click in the Color list a background color for the box, and click in the Pattern list a background pattern for the box.

5. Click OK to save the changes.

Changing the Information Displayed in Network Diagram Boxes

In addition to controlling the appearance of the boxes on the Network Diagram, you can control the information that appears in each box. By default, Project displays in each box the task name, duration, ID, start and finish dates, percentage complete, and resource name, if assigned. You can display up to 16 fields of information in any box, but just because you can doesn't mean you should. If you display 16 fields, you'll overwhelm your audience. But you can select the type of information to display to help your audience focus on issues of concern. For example, you might want to display the Free Slack and Critical fields along with Early Finish and Late Finish fields if you want your audience to focus on scheduling issues.

When you change the information that appears in the boxes, you change template information. I prefer to make a copy of the template and change the copy instead of changing the template directly; that way, the original templates retain their settings in case I want to use those settings.

Follow these steps to change the information that appears in the boxes on a Network Diagram:

1. On the Format menu, click Box.

2. In the Format Box dialog box that appears, click the More Templates button to display the Data Templates dialog box:

3. Select the template that you want to change and click the Copy button to display the Data Template Definition dialog box. The Preview shows the current appearance of the box, and the Choose Cell(s) section lists the fields currently displayed in the box.

4. To change the contents of a cell of the box, click the corresponding cell in the Choose Cell(s) area of the dialog box. Using the list arrow that appears to the right of the cell, choose a field to display for the selected cell.

5. Use the Horizontal Alignment list and the Vertical Alignment list to align the text in the cell, and use the Limit Cell Text To list to select the number of lines for each cell; a cell can have as many as three lines.

6. Select the Show Label In Cell check box to include a label in the cell that identifies the field.

7. If you need more fields than are currently available or you want fewer cells in the box than currently exist, click the Cell Layout button to display the Cell Layout dialog box:

8. Specify the number of rows and columns—you can have up to four rows and four columns in a box—and click OK to redisplay the Data Template Definition dialog box.

9. Click OK, click Close, and then click OK once more.

Project redisplays the Network Diagram, but your changes won't appear if you made a copy of an existing template. You need to assign that template to the boxes in your Network Diagram that you want to display the information you set up. On the Format menu, click Box Styles to display the Box Styles dialog box (see Figure 11-3). In the Style Settings For list, select each of the types of boxes to which you want to apply the template by pressing and holding Ctrl as you click each type of box. If you want to select all box styles, click Critical, press and hold the Shift key, and click Project Summary. Then in the Data Template list, click the template you modified. Click OK, and Project assigns your template to the types of boxes you selected. Project changes only the information that appears in each box. Project doesn't change the box styles, so, for example, summary tasks still have slanted lines on their sides while subtasks appear as square boxes.

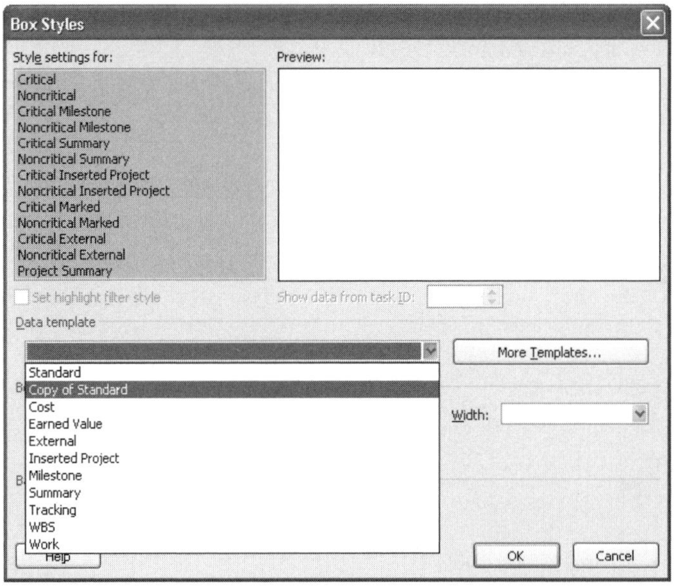

FIGURE 11-3 Use the Box Styles dialog box to assign your template to the boxes on your Network Diagram.

Reviewing Your Budget

Project costs and budget are always a consideration, but they take on a particularly impor-tant meaning when you discuss your project with management. Many project managers use *earned value management* as a technique to assess a project's schedule and cost status based on resource expenditures. Using earned value management, project managers can identify potential problems because it goes beyond comparing budget amounts to actual amounts. It helps you assess and predict your project's schedule and expenditures based on what has happened to date in your project.

For example, suppose that you find that you've spent $75,000 after four months of project work, but according to your project plan, you shouldn't have spent that much until completing six months of your plan. Although you appear to be over budget, you also need to consider where you are in your schedule before making the determina-tion. For example, it's possible that you might have performed more work than you scheduled in the first four months of the project. If you paid the amount you predicted for that work, you're actually on budget and ahead of schedule. It's also possible that you performed the amount of work you predicted for the first four months of the project, but you paid more than you estimated; in this case, you're on schedule but over budget.

Earned value management techniques aren't foolproof, but by using them you can make a fairly accurate assessment of your current status.

Understanding Earned Value Fields

Project automatically calculates values for a variety of earned value fields, eliminating the need for you to do the math. Three fields form the foundation of earned value management calculations:

- **Planned Value (PV)** Also known as Budgeted Cost of Work Scheduled (BCWS), this field reflects the budgeted cost of individual tasks based on the resources and fixed costs that you assign to the tasks when you schedule them.

- **Earned Value (EV)** Also known as Budgeted Cost of Work Performed (BCWP), this field indicates how much of a task's budget should have been spent up to the project status date or today given the actual duration of the task. For example, suppose that you have a task budgeted at $1,000 and work has been performed for one day. You find that after one day 25 percent of the work has been completed. The BCWP for the task at this point is $250.

- **Actual Cost (AC)** Also known as Actual Cost of Work Performed (ACWP), this field measures the actual cost incurred to complete a task. Before you complete the task, ACWP represents the actual costs for work performed on the task through the project's status date.

Table 11.1 describes the earned value fields Project calculates.

TABLE 11.1 Earned Value Fields in Project

FIELD	DESCRIPTION	MATHEMATICAL FORMULA THAT PROJECT USES	TYPES OF PROJECT FIELDS
SV	Schedule Variance represents the cost difference between current progress and the baseline plan	BCWP - BCWS	Task, resource, assignment, and timephased
CV	Cost Variance represents the cost difference between actual costs and planned costs at the current level of completion	BCWP - ACWP	Task, resource, assignment, and timephased
BAC	Budgeted At Completion represents the baseline cost	The sum of planned fixed costs + planned costs for all assigned resources	Task, resource, assignment, and timephased
EAC	Estimate At Completion shows the planned costs based on costs that are already incurred plus additional planned costs	ACWP + (BAC - BCWP) / CPI	Task
VAC	Variance At Completion represents the variance between the baseline cost and the combination of actual costs plus planned costs for a task	BAC - (ACWP + BCWP)	Task, resource, and assignment

FIELD	DESCRIPTION	MATHEMATICAL FORMULA THAT PROJECT USES	TYPES OF PROJECT FIELDS
CPI	Cost Performance Index	BCWP / ACWP	Timephased
SPI	Schedule Performance Index	BCWP / BCWS	Timephased
CV%	Cost Variance Percentage	(CV / BCWP) * 100	Timephased
SV%	Schedule Variance Percentage	(SV / BCWS) * 100	Timephased
TCPI	To Complete Performance Index. The TCPI value that is presented in Project reflects one of the two variations of the TCPI, TCPIBAC.	(BAC - BCWP) / (BAC - ACWP)	Task
Physical % Complete	Physical Percentage Complete represents your estimate of the progress of a task, regardless of actual work or time. Physical % Complete can be used as the basis for calculating earned value fields, effectively allowing the project manager to set the completion percentage rather than using the Project calculation based on actual work or duration. With typical settings, Project assumes that when 60% of the resources are used, 60% of the task is done.	Roll up BCWP on subtasks to BCWP on associated summary tasks	Task

Evaluating Variance

While all of the earned value fields have meaning, the ones that are probably of greatest interest to you are SV and CV, since they are the ones that tell you how far off target your project is. When you review your earned value fields, you can interpret the SV and CV values in the following way:

- A negative dollar amount in either field means you're behind schedule or over budget.

- A zero dollar amount in either field means you're on schedule or on budget.

- A positive dollar amount in either field means you're ahead of schedule or under budget.

Cost variances appear when your costs for resources turn out to be higher or lower than you planned. Schedule variances appear when the work on your schedule is running ahead of or behind schedule. Both cost and schedule variances can appear if the tasks in your project require more or less work than you planned or the people performing the work are working more or less efficiently than you planned.

Project contains four earned value tables that you can use to compare your expected costs with your actual costs and evaluate the relationship between work and costs.

You can compare the relationship between work and costs for tasks to estimate future budget needs using the Earned Value table for tasks (see Figure 11-4).

Task Name	Planned Value - PV (BCWS)	Earned Value - EV (BCWP)	AC (ACWP)	SV	CV	EAC	BAC	VAC
0 ⊟ **Earned Value**	**$4,209.00**	**$3,792.33**	**$4,145.67**	**($416.67)**	**($353.33)**	**$7,850.60**	**7,181.50**	**($669.10)**
1 ⊟ **Task 1**	**$2,005.00**	**$1,790.83**	**$2,044.17**	**($214.17)**	**($253.33)**	**$2,596.82**	**$2,275.00**	**($321.82)**
2 Subtask 1	$895.00	$895.00	$1,135.00	$0.00	($240.00)	$1,135.00	$895.00	($240.00)
3 Subtask 2	$467.50	$467.50	$467.50	$0.00	$0.00	$467.50	$467.50	$0.00
4 Subtask 3	$642.50	$428.33	$441.67	($214.17)	($13.33)	$662.50	$642.50	($20.00)
5 Subtask 4	$0.00	$0.00	$0.00	$0.00	$0.00	$510.00	$270.00	($240.00)
6 ⊟ **Task 2**	**$1,684.00**	**$1,481.50**	**$1,581.50**	**($202.50)**	**($100.00)**	**$3,081.34**	**$2,886.50**	**($194.84)**
7 Subtask 5	$351.50	$351.50	$351.50	$0.00	$0.00	$351.50	$351.50	$0.00
8 Subtask 6	$682.50	$630.00	$630.00	($52.50)	$0.00	$1,535.00	$1,535.00	$0.00
9 Subtask 7	$650.00	$500.00	$600.00	($150.00)	($100.00)	$1,200.00	$1,000.00	($200.00)
10 ⊟ **Task 3**	**$520.00**	**$520.00**	**$520.00**	**$0.00**	**$0.00**	**$2,020.00**	**$2,020.00**	**$0.00**
11 Subtask 8	$520.00	$520.00	$520.00	$0.00	$0.00	$1,300.00	$1,300.00	$0.00
12 Subtask 9	$0.00	$0.00	$0.00	$0.00	$0.00	$720.00	$720.00	$0.00

FIGURE 11-4 The Earned Value table for tasks.

Project calculates all of the fields on this sheet except BAC; you can type values into the BAC field to change information in the table.

The Earned Value table for resources (see Figure 11-5) displays the same fields as the Earned Value table for tasks; you can use this table to help you compare the relationship between planned and earned values for resources.

	Resource Name	Planned Value - PV (BCWS)	Earned Value - EV (BCWP)	AC (ACWP)	SV	CV	EAC	BAC	VAC
1	Joe	$650.00	$500.00	$600.00	($150.00)	($100.00)	$1,200.00	$1,000.00	($200.00)
2	Deena	$240.00	$120.00	$240.00	($120.00)	($120.00)	$960.00	$480.00	($480.00)
3	Gayle	$520.00	$480.00	$480.00	($40.00)	$0.00	$800.00	$800.00	$0.00
4	Bob	$960.00	$960.00	$1,200.00	$0.00	($240.00)	$1,920.00	$1,680.00	($420.00)
5	Carla	$750.00	$750.00	$750.00	$0.00	$0.00	$1,350.00	$1,350.00	$0.00
6	Intern	$0.00	$0.00	$0.00	$0.00	$0.00	$0.00	$0.00	$0.00
7	Long-distance calling	$0.00	$0.00	$0.00	$0.00	$0.00	$0.00	$0.00	$0.00
8	Personal Computer	$50.00	$50.00	$50.00	$0.00	$0.00	$50.00	$50.00	$0.00
9	Consultant	$0.00	$0.00	$0.00	$0.00	$0.00	$0.00	$0.00	$0.00
10	Copier	$4.00	$3.17	$3.17	($0.83)	$0.00	$4.00	$4.00	$0.00
11	Paper	$2.50	$2.50	$2.50	$0.00	$0.00	$32.50	$32.50	$0.00
12	Airline Tickets	$0.00	$0.00	$0.00	$0.00	$0.00	$400.00	$400.00	$0.00
13	Hotel Room	$0.00	$0.00	$0.00	$0.00	$0.00	$85.00	$85.00	$0.00
14	Budget-Labor/Materials								
15	Budget-Costs								
16	Rosie	$0.00	$0.00	$0.00	$0.00	$0.00	$0.00	$0.00	$0.00
17	Janet	$0.00	$0.00	$0.00	$0.00	$0.00	$0.00	$0.00	$0.00

FIGURE 11-5 The Earned Value table for resources.

The Earned Value Cost Indicators table displays only cost-related earned value fields so that you can compare the various cost factors related to tasks in your project (see Figure 11-6). To focus on the effects of scheduling variances on the cost of your project, use the Earned Value Schedule Indicators table for tasks (see Figure 11-7), which displays only schedule-related earned value fields.

Task Name	Planned Value - PV (BCWS)	Earned Value - EV (BCWP)	CV	CV%	CPI	BAC	EAC	VAC	TCPI
0	⊟ **Earned Value**	**$4,209.00**	**$3,792.33**	**$353.33)**	**-9%**	**0.91**	**$7,181.50**	**$7,850.60**	**($669.10)**	**1.12**
1	⊟ **Task 1**	**$2,005.00**	**$1,790.83**	**($253.33)**	**-14%**	**0.88**	**$2,275.00**	**$2,596.82**	**($321.82)**	**2.1**
2	Subtask 1	$895.00	$895.00	($240.00)	-27%	0.79	$895.00	$1,135.00	($240.00)	-0
3	Subtask 2	$467.50	$467.50	$0.00	0%	1	$467.50	$467.50	$0.00	1
4	Subtask 3	$642.50	$428.33	($13.33)	-3%	0.97	$642.50	$662.50	($20.00)	1.07
5	Subtask 4	$0.00	$0.00	$0.00	0%	0	$270.00	$510.00	($240.00)	1
6	⊟ **Task 2**	**$1,684.00**	**$1,481.50**	**($100.00)**	**-7%**	**0.94**	**$2,886.50**	**$3,081.34**	**($194.84)**	**1.08**
7	Subtask 5	$351.50	$351.50	$0.00	0%	1	$351.50	$351.50	$0.00	1
8	Subtask 6	$682.50	$630.00	$0.00	0%	1	$1,535.00	$1,535.00	$0.00	1
9	Subtask 7	$650.00	$500.00	($100.00)	-20%	0.83	$1,000.00	$1,200.00	($200.00)	1.25
10	⊟ **Task 3**	**$520.00**	**$520.00**	**$0.00**	**0%**	**1**	**$2,020.00**	**$2,020.00**	**$0.00**	**1**
11	Subtask 8	$520.00	$520.00	$0.00	0%	1	$1,300.00	$1,300.00	$0.00	1
12	Subtask 9	$0.00	$0.00	$0.00	0%	0	$720.00	$720.00	$0.00	1

FIGURE 11-6 The Earned Value Cost Indicators table.

To display the Earned Value table for tasks, the Earned Value Cost Indicators table, or the Earned Value Schedule Indicators table for tasks, first display any task-oriented view. Then right-click the Select All button, and click More Tables on the shortcut menu that appears. When Project displays the More Tables dialog box, click the appropriate table and click Apply.

To display the Earned Value table for resources, start in any resource-oriented view and follow the same procedures.

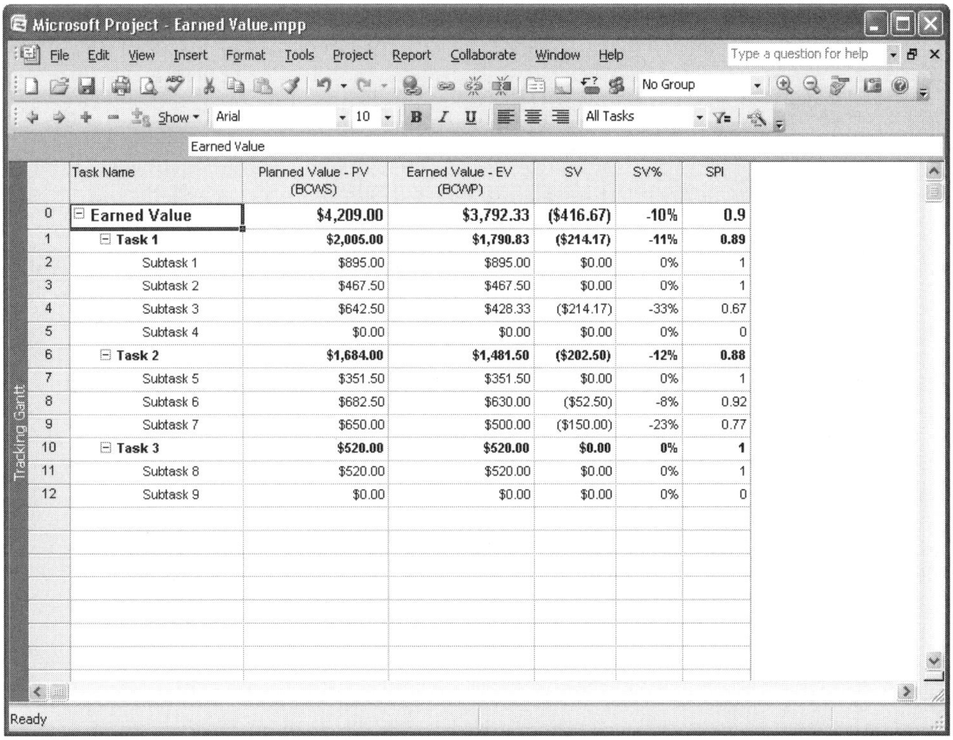

FIGURE 11-7 The Earned Value Schedule Indicators table for tasks.

TIP ✓ You also can use Microsoft Office Excel 2007 to analyze the data by printing the Earned Value Over Time visual report. On the Reports menu, click Visual Reports.

The Difference Between the % Complete and Physical % Complete Fields

Although their names are similar, % Complete and Physical % Complete aren't related fields. The information that appears in Project's % Complete field is the percentage of a task that is complete, just as you'd expect. If you don't enter a value in the % Complete field, Project calculates it for you by dividing actual task duration by total duration. Project uses the % Complete field to calculate the budgeted cost of work performed (BCWP).

Physical % Complete has no connection to duration information; instead, you use this field to enter your estimate of where a task stands. You can use the Physical % Complete field as an alternative way to calculate BCWP when the % Complete value does not accurately represent the real work performed on a task.

Calculating BCWP by Using Physical % Complete

You can set Physical % Complete as the default earned value calculation method for all new tasks in your project or you can calculate Physical % Complete for some but not all tasks.

You use the Calculation tab of the Options dialog box to select an earned value method. On the Tools menu, click Options, and click the Calculation tab. Then click the Earned Value button to display the Earned Value dialog box (see Figure 11-8).

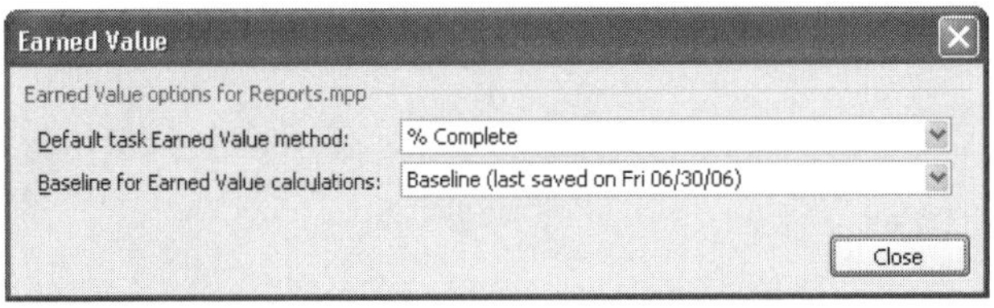

FIGURE 11-8 Use the Earned Value dialog box to choose an earned value calculation method.

In the Earned Value dialog box, in the Default Task Earned Value Method list, click Physical % Complete. Then in the Baseline For Earned Value Calculations list, click a baseline. Click Close and then click OK.

> **NOTE** You can clear baselines, but don't worry about losing Physical % Complete values. If you clear a baseline after entering Physical % Complete values for it, Project doesn't clear the Physical % Complete values.

To calculate BCWP for some but not all tasks, display a task-oriented view and select the task(s) for which you want to set the earned value calculation method to Physical % Complete. Click the Task Information button on the Standard toolbar to display the Task Information dialog box. Click the Advanced tab, and in the Earned Value Method list, click Physical % Complete (see Figure 11-9).

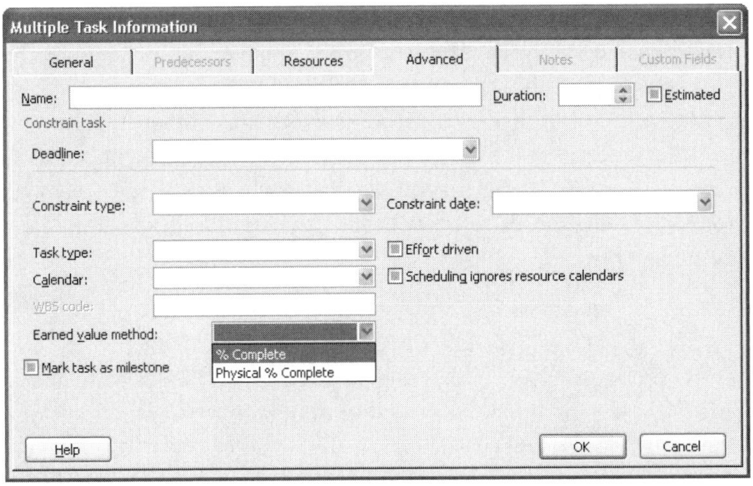

FIGURE 11-9 You can set the earned value method for one or more tasks from the Task Information dialog box.

> **TIP** ✓ To record Physical % Complete values, add the field as a column on a table in a task-oriented view. Then type appropriate amounts for tasks. You'll see other earned value fields update accordingly.

Managing Changes to the Plan 101

No matter how carefully you plan, things happen during your project that you didn't or couldn't anticipate. A task might turn out to be more involved than you expected. Or the client's needs and desires might change. Or a new technology might appear in the market that could make a portion of your plan obsolete. As a project manager, you need to respond to the new conditions that arise, being aware that a change early in your project may affect your project from beginning to end.

Most organizations that perform large projects put a formal change-control system in place that dictates how you assess and act on requests for changes. Even if your organization has such a system in place, make sure that you clarify exactly what the request is asking you to do and either request the change in writing or write it down yourself to confirm your understanding of the request.

When you assess a change request, look at how the change will affect all aspects of your project—what additional tasks and staff will be required, what tasks will potentially disappear, and how will the change affect the cost of your project. Also try to assess what may happen if you don't make the change. When deciding whether to implement the change, involve everyone affected by it in the decision process. If you decide not to make the change, tell the person who requested the change why you've chosen not to implement it. If you decide to implement the change, write down the steps needed to incorporate the change and update your project plan.

Be aware that some changes can result in *scope creep*—the gradual expansion of project work outside the scope you originally established for your project. Typically, scope creep occurs when your organization doesn't have a formal change-control policy in place that formally accepts changes and their associated costs and effects. Scope creep can also occur when the people who don't do the work associated with the changes decide whether to make changes. Finally, scope creep can occur if you have the feeling that you should never say "No" to a client or you believe you can do anything.

To avoid scope creep, make sure that you define your project's goals and objectives in sufficient detail so that everyone understands what your project will accomplish. Also, make sure that you assess all aspects of a change for the ways in which it will affect your project. Don't hesitate to be realistic and admit that you can't do everything. The world in general likes happy surprises and dislikes unhappy surprises; you'll do better if you under-promise and over-deliver rather than over-promise and under-deliver.

In response to change requests, you may ultimately decide that your current project plan no longer reflects what you actually need to do. The schedule, costs, and resources needed may be far from your original estimates. At this point, consider updating your project plan and then setting a new baseline.

> **TIP** ✓ Make sure that you keep a copy of your original plan and all subsequent modifications. Comparing the original plan to the new plan can help you become a better manager in the future and can support your performance assessment after you complete the project.

> **SEE ALSO** See Chapter 8, "Completing the Planning Phase in Project," for details on setting baselines.

Problem Solving in the Trenches

CHAPTER 12

You're Behind Schedule: Now What?

PLANS ARE, WELL, *PLANS*. After you record progress, you'll need to evaluate your plan to determine how closely it matches reality. In some cases, reality might be better—you might be ahead of schedule, under budget, or both. But in other cases, you might find that you're behind schedule, over budget, or both. So what do you do? In this chapter, we'll first explore ways for you to determine how reality compares to your plan. Then we'll look at approaches you can take to try to get back on track.

Comparing Estimates with Actual Progress

Once you start recording progress information using Microsoft Office Project 2007, you can review the progress of your project. The Tracking Gantt view, shown in Figure 12-1, provides the most effective picture showing where your project stands.

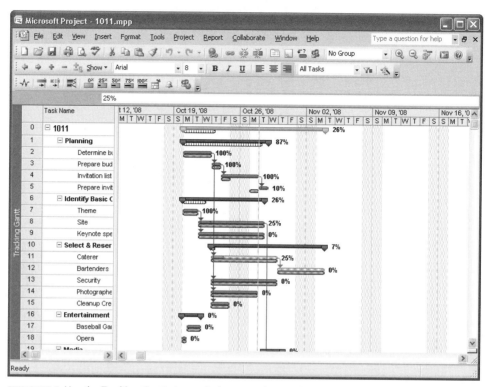

FIGURE 12-1 Use the Tracking Gantt view to help you understand where your project stands.

The bottom bar of each row on the chart portion of the view, which appears as black hatching on your screen, represents the baseline dates for each task. The top bar represents either the planned start and finish dates or, if a task has been completed, the actual start and finish dates for each task.

Understanding the Tracking Gantt View

The formatting of the top task bars in the Tracking Gantt view indicates each task's status. Interpret the formatting of the top task bars in the following ways:

- If the top bar of a task is blue, the task is not on the critical path; if the task is on the critical path, the top bar appears red. The percent complete appears on the right side of the top bar of every task.

- There appears to be no difference in the solid blue task bar appearing on top of a non-critical completed task and a non-critical task that hasn't yet started. If you look closely at a non-critical task that is partially complete, you'll notice that a small mark in the bar separates the completed portion from the uncompleted portion.

- For partially completed tasks on the critical path, the completed portion appears darker red than the uncompleted portion, and the distinction between the completed and uncompleted portion is easy to see. If the task is complete, the bar appears solid red.

While you're in the Tracking Gantt view, switch to the Work table (see Figure 12-2) by right-clicking the Select All button and clicking Work on the shortcut menu that appears. The Work table for tasks shows the total effort that is required from all resources to complete the task. And the Work table for tasks includes baseline information so that you can compare your progress to your original estimate.

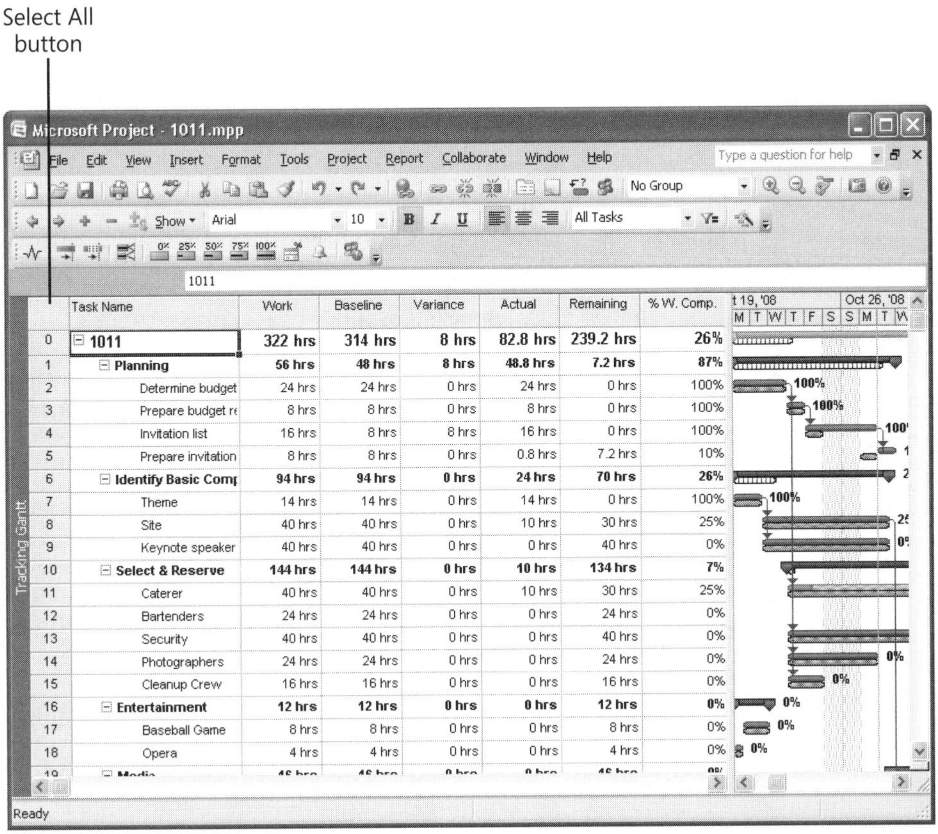

Select All button

FIGURE 12-2 Use the Work table to help you evaluate the progress of your project.

Work differs from task duration because work measures how many hours of effort are needed to complete a task, while task duration measures the amount of working time (for example, number of days) that is allotted to the task. Suppose that you've assigned two resources to a task that requires 48 hours of total work. Further suppose that the task duration is only two days. In this case, you need to extend the task's duration, or if the task is effort-driven, you can add two more resources to complete the task in the specified duration.

> **NOTE** You can view progress in any Gantt view; Project displays a thick black line in the middle of the Gantt bar to represent progress. If the thick black line extends the length of the Gantt bar, the task is complete.

Adding Progress Lines to a Gantt View

Assuming that you have saved a baseline for your project, you can add progress lines to any Gantt view of your project, such as the Gantt Chart view, the Tracking Gantt Chart view, and the Detail Gantt view. In Figure 12-3, I added a progress line to the Detail Gantt view. Project draws a line that connects tasks that are either in progress or should be in progress, and the lines indicate what the progress should be relative to either the current date or the status date. The lines pointing to the right of tasks represent work that is ahead of schedule as of the progress line date, and lines pointing to the left of tasks represent work that is behind schedule.

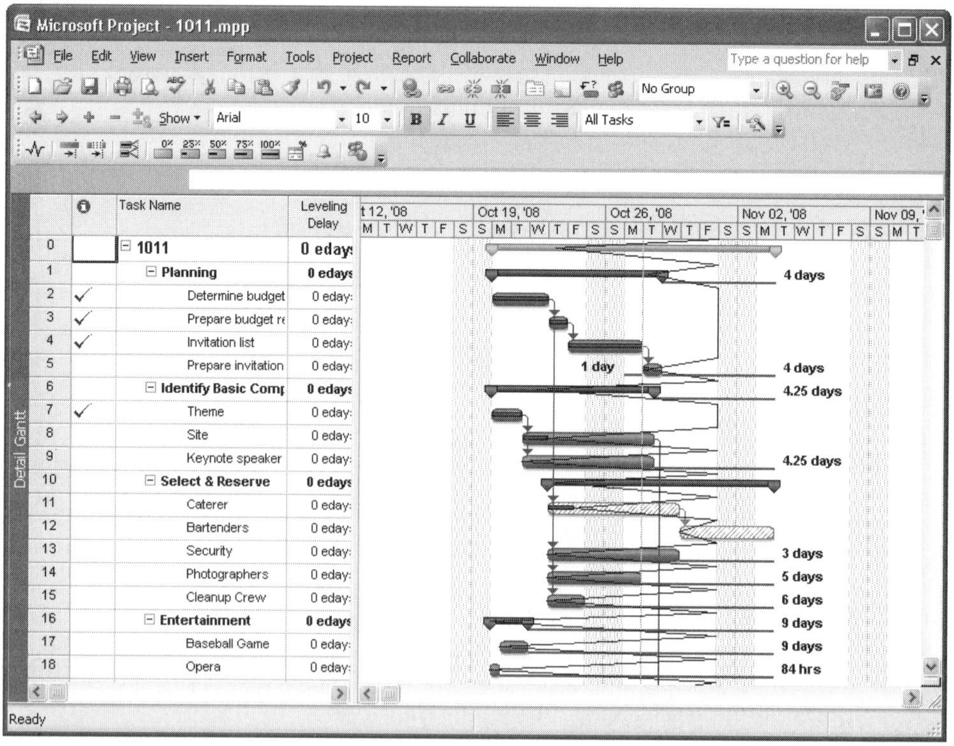

FIGURE 12-3 A Detail Gantt view that includes a progress line.

To add a progress line, display the Gantt view to which you want to add progress lines, and then follow these steps:

1. On the Tools menu, point to Tracking, and click Progress Lines to open the Progress Lines dialog box.

2. On the right side of the Dates And Intervals tab, select the Display Selected Progress Lines check box. Project makes the Progress Line Dates list available.

3. Click in the Progress Line Dates list to display a list box arrow.

4. Click the list box arrow to display a small calendar and select an "as of" date for the progress line.

5. At the bottom of the box, select either Actual Plan or Baseline Plan.

6. Click OK, and Project adds the progress line to the selected view.

As you can imagine, a progress line on a project with a large number of tasks can begin to look messy. But if you decide that you like progress lines, you can display them at varying intervals. You also can add specific dates to the Progress Line Dates list on the right side of the Progress Lines dialog box to display multiple progress lines on any Gantt view. If you decide to display more than one progress line, you might want to use the Line Styles tab of the Progress Lines dialog box to format the lines so that you can tell them apart. For example, you can set different colors for different lines.

> **NOTE** The options are limited; you can set one style for the Current progress line (the one identified in the Always Display Current Progress Line area of the Progress Lines dialog box), and one style for the other progress lines displayed.

To stop displaying progress lines, reopen the Progress Lines dialog box and clear any check boxes on the Dates And Intervals tab.

How Do You Get Back on Track?

There are *lots* of ways that your project can get off schedule:

- Your team might not be as experienced as you expected, so it is taking longer to do the work than you estimated. Also, you might not have allowed sufficient time for team members to become familiar with a task before starting to work on it.

- A task required more work effort than you estimated. For example, you might not have identified steps necessary to complete the activity.

- A team member might have spent less time on the task than he or she agreed to spend.

- Team members are inadvertently expanding the scope of a task.

- A particular team member might be more or less productive than you assumed when you developed the plan.

- Team members might be reporting the hours shown on the plan instead of actual hours worked because they think that's what you want to see.

- Team members might be recording 40 hours because they're supposed to work 40 hours—and they might be inflating or deflating the real work effort on your tasks.

Some of these problems are reporting problems, and you need to address them so that you get accurate reports going forward. Reporting problems mask other problems and can cause your plan to spiral out of control before you have a chance to fix it. Explain to your team that you're using the information they provide to help you determine when you may need to change aspects of the plan so that they understand your motives and can provide accurate information going forward. If your organization doesn't permit people to record more than 40 hours per week and members of your team work overtime, ask those team members to provide you with their overtime hours so that you have accurate information describing how long a task actually takes to complete. Explain to your team that you don't have a crystal ball and you can't make estimates concerning task durations with 100 percent accuracy. For this reason, you *expect* variations from planned values, but you need to minimize those variations for the project to be deemed successful.

Read on to find solutions for problems that don't revolve around reporting.

Sorting and Filtering

Sorting and filtering, discussed in Chapter 4 ("Finding the Information You Need") in the context of planning your project, can also be helpful when you're trying to focus on solving problems associated with a project being behind schedule or over budget.

For example, you can sort your schedule by task cost so that you can find the most expensive tasks and look for ways to trim them. If you've taken advantage of the Priority feature—discussed in Chapter 6, "Solving Resource Conflicts"—you can sort tasks by priority to try to find candidates to cut from your project. And you can sort your schedule by task duration to review the longest tasks, as they are the ones most likely to fall behind schedule due to their length. Tasks with long durations are riskier than those with shorter durations for the same reasons that bonds with longer maturity dates have higher yields. In the case of long-term bonds, you agree to loan money to a company. The longer the term of the bond, the greater the risk that something might happen to make the company unable to repay your loan; after all, predicting a company's health becomes more difficult—and more risky—50 years from now than five years from now. In the case of tasks with long durations, the longer a task takes, the greater the risk that something can go wrong to stop you from completing the task on time.

Filtering can help in the same way that sorting can—by helping you focus on certain types of tasks. Project contains a number of predefined filters that can help you when you're trying to identify and solve problems with your schedule:

- **The Critical filter** displays tasks on the critical path, which are the ones that must be completed according to schedule to make your final deadline.

- **The Cost Overbudget filter** displays the tasks that exceed budgeted expenditures.

- **The Incomplete Tasks filter** displays the tasks that haven't been marked as complete.

- **The Late/Overbudget Tasks Assigned To filter** displays, for a selected resource, the tasks that are running later than their baseline estimate or are over budget.

- **The Should Start By filter** displays the tasks that should have started by a date you specify.

- **The Slipped/Late Progress filter** displays the tasks that are running late.

- **The Update Needed filter** displays the tasks that should have had progress tracked by now.

- **The Slipping Assignments filter** displays the tasks that involve resource work that should have begun by now.

- **The Work Incomplete filter** displays the tasks that should have had all their work recorded by now.

- **The Work Overbudget filter** displays the tasks for which more work hours have been put in than you had estimated.

How Adding or Changing Resources Affects Timing

In the corporate environment, you'll often find the attitude that throwing money and people at problems can solve them. When tasks are effort-driven, that approach works.

On effort-driven tasks, the amount of effort put into the task drives how quickly the task gets completed. For example, an effort-driven task with a duration of four days and using a standard working day of eight hours requires 4 days times 8 hours per day to be completed—a total of 32 hours of effort. If you assign one resource to this task and the resource works full-time on the task, the resource will take four days to complete the task. However, because the task is effort-driven, if you place four resources working full-time on the task, they will complete it in one day—four resources each putting in eight hours of effort equals 32 hours of effort.

When you add resources to such a task, Project automatically shortens the task's duration and your schedule.

You also can take a look at modifying existing assignments to save some time. For example, if someone is working only 50 percent on a task, consider increasing the person's assignment units. Or if you have someone available who could perform a given task more quickly—perhaps because they have more experience—switch resources and then shorten the task's duration.

You might also consider having some people work overtime or be overbooked at various points during the project. Sometimes, there's no choice but to have the resource work that occasional 12-hour or 14-hour day; just make sure that management approves the decision.

Although adding resources to effort-driven tasks can reduce the amount of time needed to complete them, remember that depending on the resources' hourly rates, this approach may cost you more. And the resources need time to coordinate their efforts, so the time you save will not necessarily be the mathematical calculation that Project performs; you might consider adding a little time to the task to accommodate the inefficiencies of multiple resources. Finally, adding resources can cause additional resource conflicts if you use resources already assigned to other tasks in your project.

| **SEE ALSO** | For information on adding resources, see Chapter 3, "Pinning Down Your Budget." Chapter 6 contains information on swapping resources. |

Reviewing Dependencies

You can review and possibly adjust the dependencies in your project to help you save time. While reviewing dependencies, ask yourself questions like, "Couldn't the revision of the manual start a few days before we receive all of the feedback?" or "Can the electrician and the plumber work at the same time after the framer finishes?" If you've linked a task to another project and set dependencies for that linked task with tasks in your project, check with the other project manager to find out how the other project is progressing or if the other project manager has any tasks he or she can speed up.

SEE ALSO	For more information on linking projects, see Chapter 13, "Managing Cross-Project Conflicts."

NOTE	Don't forget to double-check any constraints you might have set. For example, you might have set a Start No Earlier Than constraint on a task to make sure it didn't start before the first of the year because you don't want to spend money on it in the current year's budget. To save time, you might be able to allow the task to start a week before the end of the year but bill the costs in January.

Using the Task Drivers button on the Standard toolbar, you can review dependencies or task constraints to understand what is causing tasks to fall in a certain timeframe. You simply select a task and then click the Task Drivers button, which displays a pane listing all factors that affect the timing of that task.

Using this feature, you can determine whether a task that you'd like to happen earlier could do so if you remove some dependency or constraint affecting it. For example, early in your planning, you may have thought that the training task couldn't start until all the equipment was delivered. But now that half the equipment is here, you realize you could start the training now and complete it later. By understanding what is driving the timing of the task, you can better search for a solution if that timing is causing problems.

You also can look at the Network Diagram view to review dependencies in relation to workflow. This view is particularly useful when reviewing dependencies if you add link labels to the dependency lines, as I did in Figure 12-4. To add link labels, on the Format menu, click Layout to display the Layout dialog box. Then select the Show Link Labels check box.

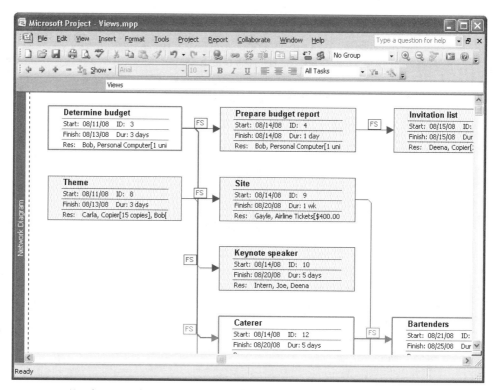

FIGURE 12-4 Use the Network Diagram view, with link labels displayed, to review dependencies.

The Relationship Diagram view, shown in Figure 12-5, can help you graphically review predecessor tasks and successor tasks. In this view, when you select a particular task, Project shows its predecessor tasks on the left side of the selected task and its successor tasks on the right side of the task. To display this view, on the View menu, click More Views to display the More Views window. Then click Relationship Diagram, and click the Apply button.

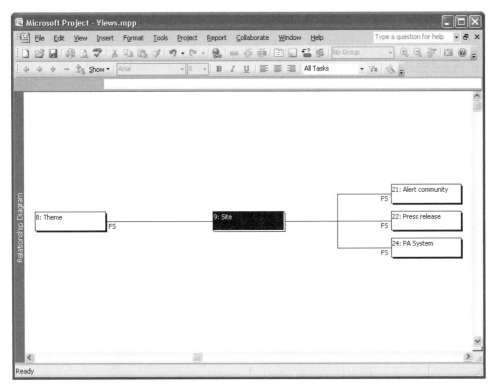

FIGURE 12-5 The Relationship Diagram view.

Or you can modify a sheet view, such as the Task Sheet view, to display both the Predecessors and Successors columns (see Figure 12-6). The Predecessors column appears by default in this view; you can drag its title to move the column closer to the Task Name column. To add the Successors column, click the heading of the column that should appear to the right of where you want to insert the Successors column. Then on the Insert menu, click Column. In the Column Definition dialog box, in the Field Name list, click Successors. Click OK, and Project adds the column to the view.

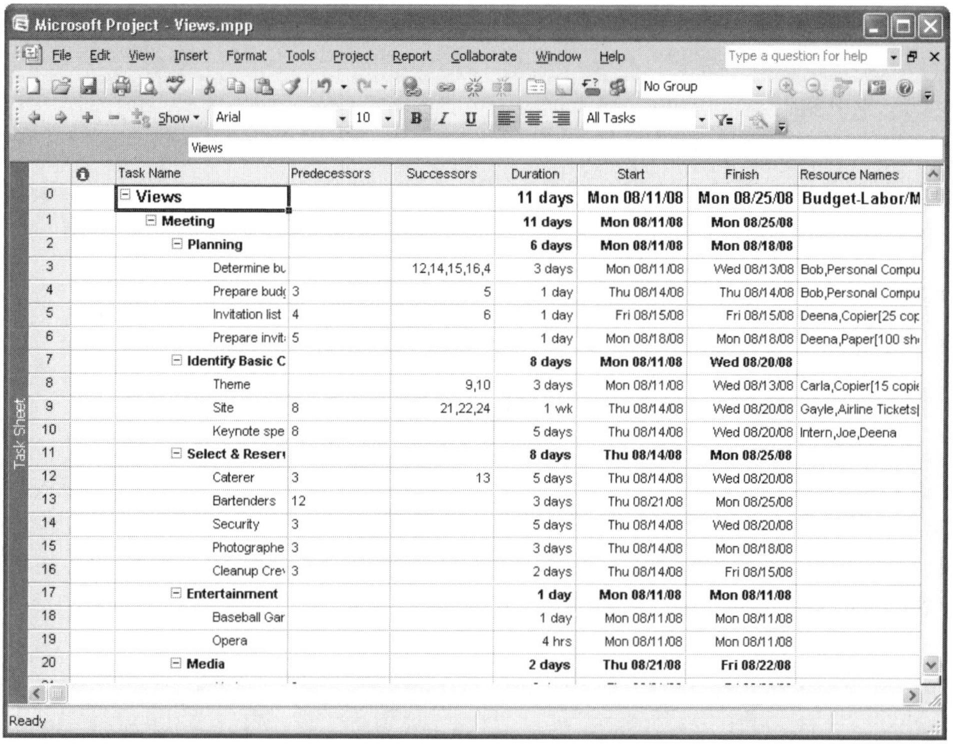

FIGURE 12-6 You also can examine predecessor and successor relationships in a modified version of the Task Sheet view.

Making Changes to Save Time

Saving time in Project means doing things faster, adjusting the timing of things to use up slack, or eliminating tasks. Taking any one of these actions can have a ripple effect, so you'll need to study the schedule after each change to make sure you don't fall victim to the "Law of Unintended Consequences."

To do things faster, you can assign more people to effort-driven tasks. For more information on this approach, read the section "How Adding or Changing Resources Affects Timing" earlier in this chapter.

In the preceding section, "Reviewing Dependencies," I described ways that you can review dependencies, looking for ways to change them to shorten your project.

You also can save time if you modify the scope of a task, but this approach can have an impact on quality. For example, if you inspect a product you're manufacturing twice instead of three times, you run the risk of producing an inferior product that presents problems down the road.

While you're examining your project, you might realize that a few things aren't necessary or have already been handled by someone else. You might find a task you can simply delete—and shorten your schedule. So select that task by clicking the task's ID number, and press the Delete key on your keyboard.

But suppose, after you've adjusted resource assignments and shifted task dependencies around to save time, and deleted tasks and assigned cheaper workers to save money, you still can't bring the project in on time and within budget. This is the scenario where you have to say to your boss, "You can have it on time and within budget, or you can have quality work."

If your boss chooses quality work, you'll be getting more time (and therefore more money to cover the costs of having existing resources work longer or having additional resources complete the work). In this case, update your project by pushing out the start dates or modifying the durations of tasks that are running late. You can use the Should Have Started Tasks report in the Current Activity Reports group to print a list of tasks on which you can focus.

> **TIP** If you have a Slack task, you also can add to its duration to provide other tasks with a little room to slip.

After you work in the extra time, make sure that the new timing of tasks doesn't cause new resource conflicts. You can use the techniques described in Chapter 6 to resolve any new resource conflicts that appear.

If your boss tells you to cut some corners and sacrifice quality, you have license to modify the scope of the project. You can cut out some tasks that might ensure higher quality, such as a final proofreading of the marketing literature. You can hire cheaper workers. You can use cheaper paper. In Project, here's how you can reflect these changes:

- If you want to delete tasks, click the ID of the task in any task-oriented sheet view and press the Delete key on your keyboard.

- If you want to use less expensive resources, replace one set of resources with another in the Assign Resources dialog box.

- If you want to use less expensive materials, on the Resource Sheet, change the unit price for materials or lower the price of a Cost resource.

Or you can take a broader approach and redefine the goal of the project. If your goal was to produce a new line of marketing materials, perhaps you can modify your goal to simply manage the design of the new materials and then leave the production to a later date or another project manager. To make such changes, you may have to shift or remove entire phases of your project.

When you take certain steps, your action may cause Project to alert you to a potential problem you might not have considered. For example, without realizing it, you might try to move a task so that it becomes scheduled to begin before the project's start date. In cases like this, Project shows you a Planning Wizard, like the one in Figure 12-7, that offers you options—typically to proceed, to cancel, or to proceed but with some modification. Read these alerts carefully and consider the pros and cons of what will happen if you proceed.

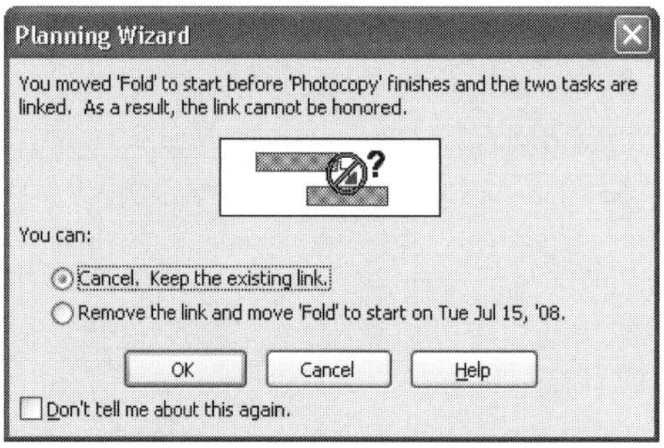

FIGURE 12-7 The Planning Wizard tries to steer you away from taking actions that might have unintended consequences.

Deciding When to Redefine Your Project

As you make changes to your schedule, you might want to consider rescheduling remaining work to start as of a particular date so that you can get things back on track in your schedule. You can quickly and easily reschedule any remaining work for partially completed or uncompleted tasks using the Update Project dialog box (see Figure 12-8). Start by displaying any task-oriented view. If you plan to update only selected tasks, select them by clicking their ID numbers. Then on the Tools menu, point to Tracking, and click Update Project.

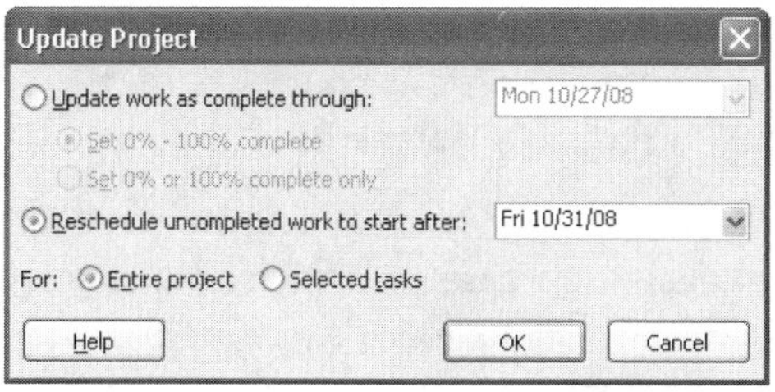

FIGURE 12-8 You can quickly and easily reschedule uncompleted work.

The Reschedule Uncompleted Work To Start After option reschedules the remaining portions of uncompleted tasks; Project uses the date that you select as the starting date for the remaining work. By selecting the day before you plan to resume work on uncompleted tasks, you ensure that Project doesn't schedule any remaining work for partially completed tasks for dates that have already passed.

Project reschedules partially completed tasks and tasks that have not yet started by setting a Start No Earlier Than constraint using the date you selected. When you reschedule a partially completed task, Project automatically splits the task between the completed portion and the remaining portion. If the completed portion of the task finished sometime before the remaining portion is scheduled to start, you see a split task on the chart portion of the Gantt Chart view.

> **NOTE** In the Update Project dialog box, you can choose to update your entire project or only selected tasks. When you update the entire project, Project sets the project status date to the date that you selected in the dialog box.

If your organization uses Microsoft Office Project Server 2007 and Project Professional, you can use the same technique to reschedule uncompleted work from a previous reporting period into the current reporting period after you process task updates from the Updates page in Microsoft Office Project Web Access into the project plan. As the project manager, start Project Professional and log into Project Server. Then in Project Professional, open the project containing work you want to reschedule. On the Tools menu, point to Tracking, and click Update Project to display the Update Project dialog box. Select the Reschedule Uncompleted Work To Start After option, select a starting date for the remaining work, and select either the Entire Project option or the Selected Tasks option. Click OK; after Project reschedules uncompleted work, on the File menu, click Publish to update the project stored in the Project Server database.

You also might want to consider setting a new baseline at this point so that you can later compare information from your original baseline, your new baseline, and actual progress information; the comparison process helps you learn from your experience. The baseline, as I described in Chapter 8, "Completing the Planning Phase in Project," stores a snapshot of your project at the time you save it. If you decide to set a new baseline, meet with your team and other project stakeholders and explain why you've decided to set a new baseline so that everyone involved is aware of the new baseline starting point.

To set a new baseline, on the Tools menu, point to Tracking, and click Save Baseline. In the Set Baseline dialog box that appears (see Figure 12-9), in the Set Baseline list, click one of the baselines you haven't yet set. That way, you can preserve the original baseline. Click OK to save the new baseline.

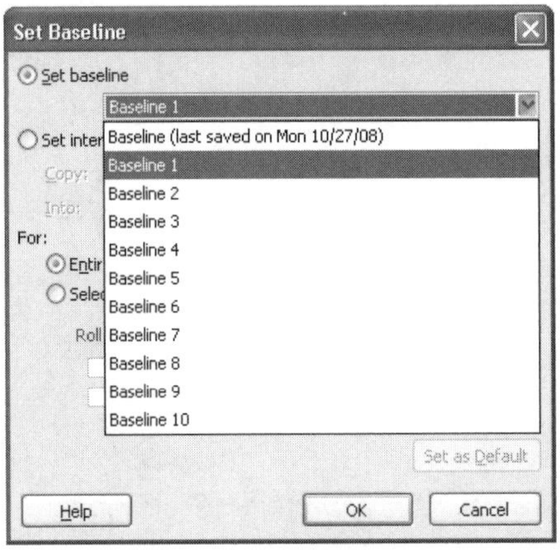

FIGURE 12-9 Select a baseline you haven't used to store new baseline information.

CHAPTER 13

Managing Cross-Project Conflicts

SOME PROJECTS ARE MORE COMPLEX than others—that's just a fact of life. Most project managers prefer to manage a complex project by finding ways to reduce its complexity. You can reduce complexity if, for example, you divide a complex project into phases and then establish each phase as a separate project. Microsoft Office Project 2007 refers to this process as *consolidation*, and you'll read about creating consolidated projects in this chapter. And to alleviate problems associated with sharing resources, you can set up and use a resource pool.

Examining Consolidated Projects

Most project managers say that large projects—projects with lots of tasks—are the most difficult to manage because they challenge even the best organizational skills. Project uses con-solidation to help you manage these types of projects. First you break large, complex projects into smaller projects (called *subprojects*) that aren't so complex; then you use consolidation to combine the subprojects and view the bigger picture of the large, complex project. For example, you might take the phases of a complex project and establish them as separate subprojects. A particular phase might be complex enough to be handled as a project on its own, with its own project manager and team. If you use consolidation techniques, you can still treat that project as a subproject in the consolidated project, retaining the dependencies.

> **NOTE** If you use the same resources for several projects, you can consolidate those projects so that you can level the resources to resolve overallocations. You also can use a resource pool to share the resources among the various projects that make up a consolidated project. See the section "Using a Resource Pool" later in this chapter for more information.

PROJECT SERVER AND CONSOLIDATION

Do you need to read this section if your company uses Microsoft Office Project Server 2007? You can get a lot of the same information from Project Server that you get when you use consolidation. But Project Server can't show you one critical path across a consolidated project. In the section "Examining the Critical Path of a Consolidated Project" later in this chapter, you'll see how consolidation affects the critical path. And in the section "Using Consolidation with Project Server 2007," you'll find out how to create a consolidated project when your organization uses Project Server 2007.

Setting Up Subprojects

You might decide when you begin a project that it is too large to handle in one Project file. Or you might start working before you realize that you need to use consolidation. You can take advantage of consolidation techniques in either situation.

If you decide to use consolidation right from the beginning of your planning process, create separate Project files for the various portions of the project that you'll treat as subprojects. Create tasks, assign durations, and create any necessary dependencies between tasks in each subproject file.

If you start the planning process and then decide to use consolidation, break the original project down into subprojects and create additional subprojects to accommodate the new tasks. Select all the tasks in the original project file that you want to save in your first subproject file, and click the Copy button on the Standard toolbar. Then click the New button; if prompted, select Blank Project to create a new blank project. Click the Paste button, and the tasks you copied from the original project appear in the new project.

In the new project, on the Project menu, click Project Information to display the Project Information dialog box, where you can establish basic information for the subproject, identifying its start date and scheduling method. Save the subproject and close it. Then repeat this process for each portion of the original project that you want to save as a subproject.

TIP   You can make Project display the Project Information dialog box by default each time you start a new project. On the Tools menu, click Options. On the General tab, select the Prompt For Project Info For New Projects check box.

You can close the original file and work in the subproject files to make them independent projects. When you're ready to connect the subprojects, read the next sections.

Consolidating Subprojects

When you're ready to create a consolidated project, you insert subprojects into another project file. Each subproject that you insert appears as a summary task in the consolidated project file, and Project calculates the schedules and costs of inserted projects like summary tasks. Project also displays an icon in the Indicator field to identify an inserted project (see Figure 13-1).

Inserted Project
icon

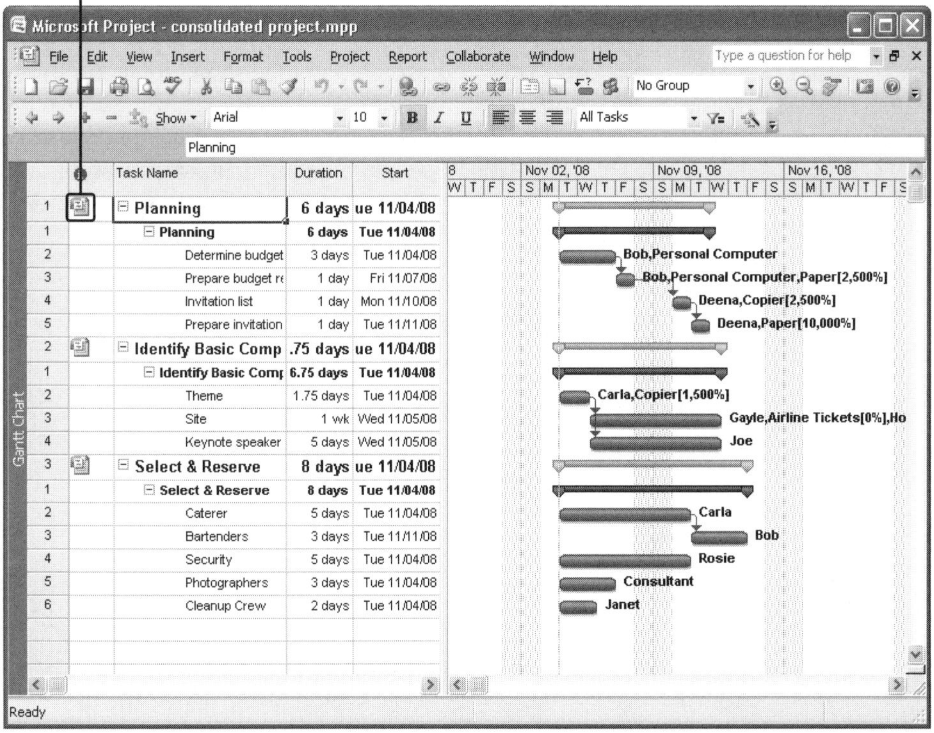

FIGURE 13-1 Project displays a special icon for inserted projects in the Indicator field.

To create a consolidated project, follow these steps:

1. Start a new project and switch to the Gantt Chart view.

2. Click in the row of the Task Name column where you want the inserted project to begin.

> **NOTE** Project places an inserted project immediately above the selected row.

3. On the Insert menu, click Project. Project displays the Insert Project dialog box, which looks and works like the Open dialog box.

4. Navigate to the folder that contains the project you want to insert.

5. Select the subproject file you want to insert.

6. Click Insert.

The inserted project file appears as a summary task, with its subtasks hidden (see Figure 13-2). If you move the mouse pointer over the icon in the Indicator field, Project displays information about the folder where the subproject file resides.

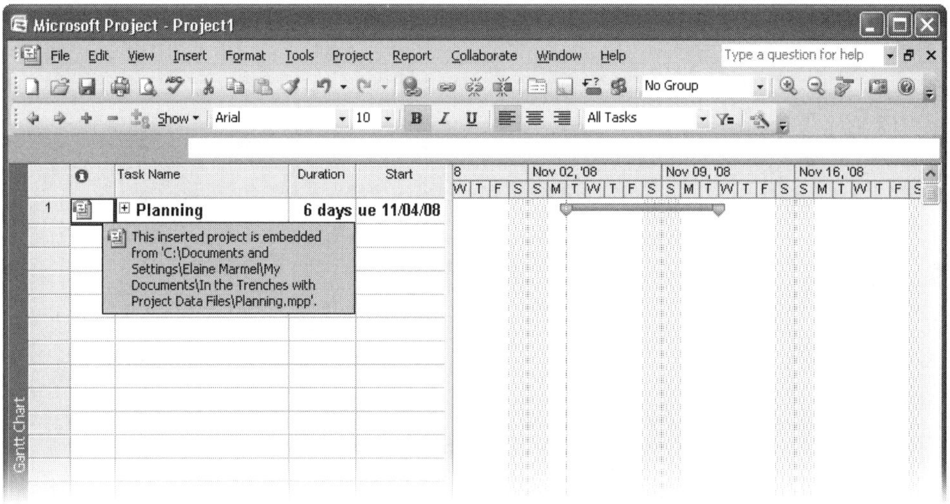

FIGURE 13-2 Inserted projects appear as summary tasks.

To view the tasks of an inserted project, click the plus sign in the Task Name column beside the name of the inserted project.

NOTE You can insert projects into a consolidated project at any level in the project outline. The outline level Project assigns to an inserted project depends on the level of the tasks above and below the inserted project. To line up inserted projects at the highest outline level in the consolidated project, collapse projects you've already inserted so that you can't see their tasks.

When you insert a project, the Link To Project check box is selected by default. Typically, you want this option selected because Project then connects the inserted project to its source file and retains and uses all of the information stored in the inserted file, including the information you provided in the subproject's Project Information dialog box concerning how to calculate the project schedule. If you clear the check box, you are simply copying tasks from one project to another. Project doesn't connect the inserted project to its source project; no icon will appear in the Indicator field and Project will ignore the information stored in the Project Information dialog box of the inserted project. If you make changes to the inserted project while working in the consolidated project file, Project won't prompt you to update the inserted project's source file.

When you link an inserted project to its source file, Windows treats that link the same way it treats any other link. For example, if you move the subproject file to a different folder, the link won't work anymore unless you update it. To update a link, double-click the inserted project in the Gantt Chart view of the consolidated project; Project displays the Inserted Project Information dialog box for the inserted project, which is the equivalent of the Task Information dialog box for any task (see Figure 13-3). Click the Advanced tab to view and update the path to the linked subproject file.

You can use the Browse button to navigate to the new location for an inserted project, and you also can unlink subprojects from their source files by clearing the Link To Project check box.

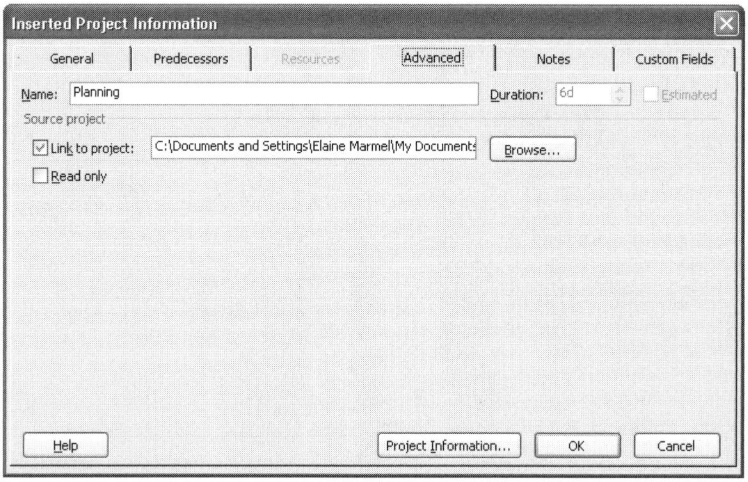

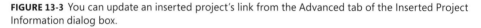

FIGURE 13-3 You can update an inserted project's link from the Advanced tab of the Inserted Project Information dialog box.

> **NOTE** If the link to an inserted project isn't valid and you attempt to expand the outline for an inserted project, Project automatically displays a dialog box that looks like the Open dialog box. Use this dialog box to navigate to the new location of the file, and click OK after you finish. This process also re-establishes the link between the files.

Linking Subprojects

The beauty of the concept of a consolidated project is that you can isolate pieces of a large, complex project into subprojects but at the same time maintain the subproject's role and position in the larger project. You establish a subproject's relationship to the larger project by creating dependencies.

You use the same four different types of dependencies between subprojects as those you use between tasks in any project: finish-to-start, start-to-start, finish-to-finish, and start-to-finish. And you can add lag or lead time to links between subprojects, just like you can to links between tasks.

> **SEE ALSO** For details on dependencies, see Chapter 2, "How Dependencies and Constraints Affect Your Project."

To link a task stored in one subproject to a task stored in another subproject, create a consolidated project and then follow these steps within the consolidated project:

1. On the View menu, click Gantt Chart.

2. Select the tasks you want to link:

A link between subprojects
looks just like any other link.

| | | TIP | To select noncontiguous tasks, press and hold down Ctrl as you click the name of each task. |

3. Click the Link Tasks button on the Standard toolbar. Project creates a finish-to-start link between the two tasks.

In the consolidated project, the link line between tasks across subprojects looks just like any other link line; no visual cue appears to make you aware that two subprojects are linked.

But if you look at either of the subproject files, you'll find an external task. The names and Gantt bars of external tasks are light gray. In Figure 13-4, Theme (the task that appears on Row 4) is an external task. If you point to the Gantt Chart bar, Project displays information about the task, including the fact that it is an external task.

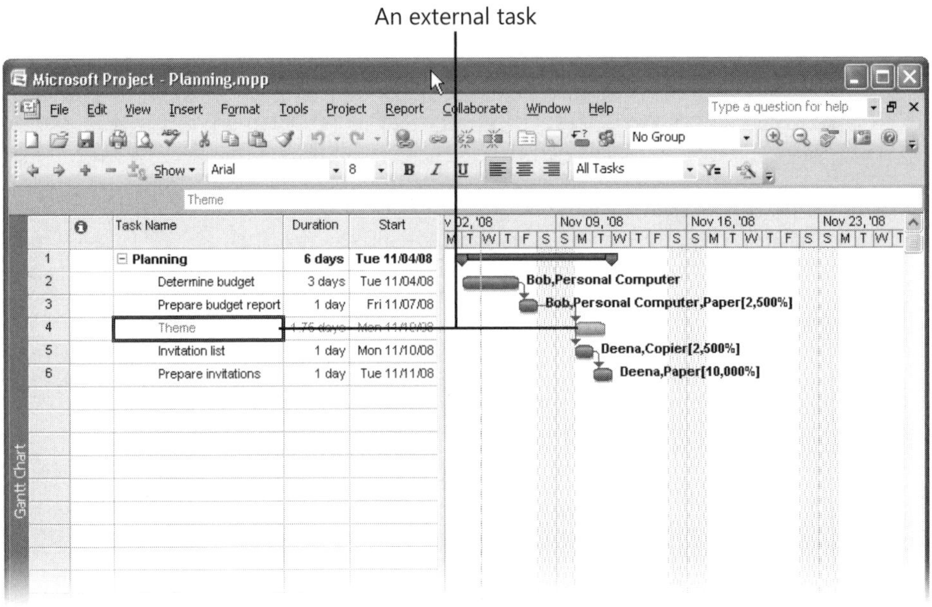

An external task

FIGURE 13-4 External task names and Gantt bars are gray in subproject files.

> **TIP** ✓ If you double-click the task name of an external task, Project opens the subproject to which the external task is linked.

You can make changes to a link between tasks in different subprojects using either the subproject file or the consolidated project file. You use pretty much the same technique regardless of the file in which you work.

If you choose to work in the consolidated project, double-click the line that links the two tasks. Alternatively, if you choose to work in the subproject, double-click the line that links an internal task to the external task. In both cases, Project displays the Task

Dependency dialog box. Figure 13-5 shows the version of the Task Dependency dialog box that appears when you open the dialog box from a subproject. The Task Dependency dialog box appears slightly different when you open the dialog box from the consolidated project; you cannot change the path of the link.

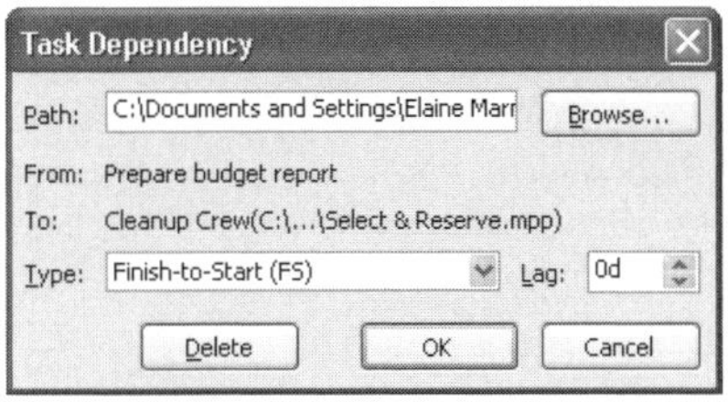

FIGURE 13-5 Use the Type list in the Task Dependency dialog box to change the type of link, and the Lag box to change the amount of lag time between the linked tasks.

> **NOTE**   As you would expect, when you close a consolidated project file, Project prompts you to save it. Because you're closing a consolidated project, Project responds a little differently than it does when you close a regular project. Regardless of whether you decide to save the consolidated project, Project will then ask if you want to save changes that you made to inserted projects. And here's a point of interest: If you save the subprojects—even if you don't save the consolidated project—Project saves any external tasks created when you linked subproject files.

Examining the Critical Path of a Consolidated Project

Project determines the critical path for a project scheduled from its start date by making calculations using the late finish date of the project. In consolidated projects, Project treats inserted projects like summary tasks by default and calculates the critical path using the finish date of the consolidated project to show you the overall critical path across all the subprojects. This behavior can hide the critical path of the subprojects. In Figure 13-6, each major phase is actually an inserted project. I set up the critical path for the consolidated project to display Gantt bars using a hatched pattern; notice that there are tasks in each inserted project that are not critical.

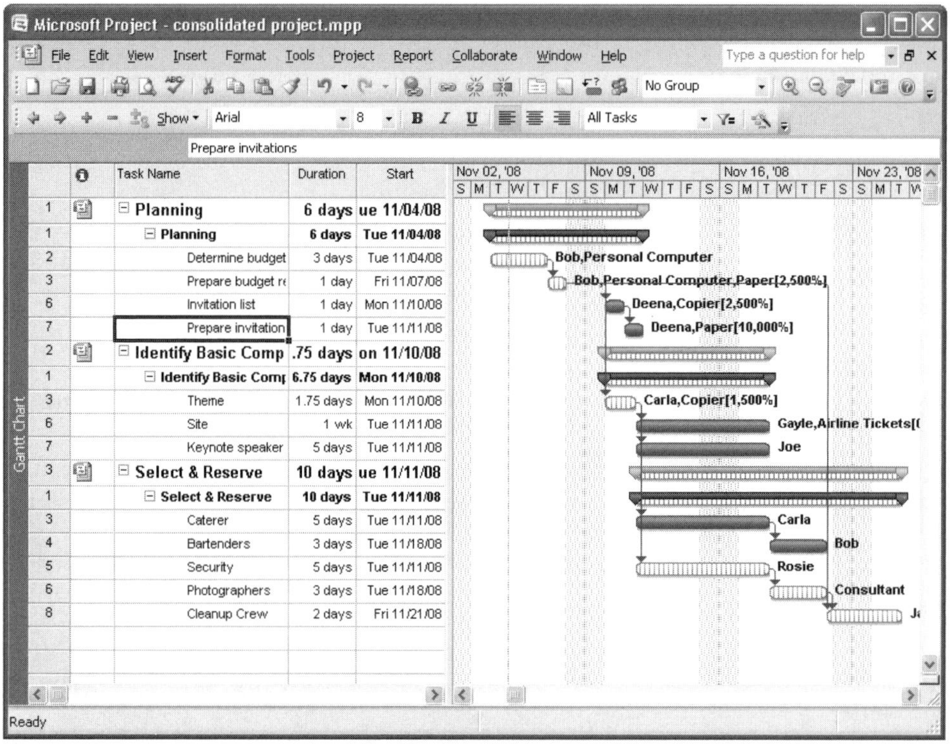

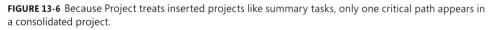

FIGURE 13-6 Because Project treats inserted projects like summary tasks, only one critical path appears in a consolidated project.

But you can view each subproject's critical path while viewing the consolidated project if you choose to not calculate subprojects as summary tasks. In this case, Project uses the late finish dates of tasks in the subprojects to determine the critical path; and while viewing the consolidated project, you can see critical paths as they appear in each subproject. In Figure 13-7, only one of the subprojects contains tasks that aren't critical.

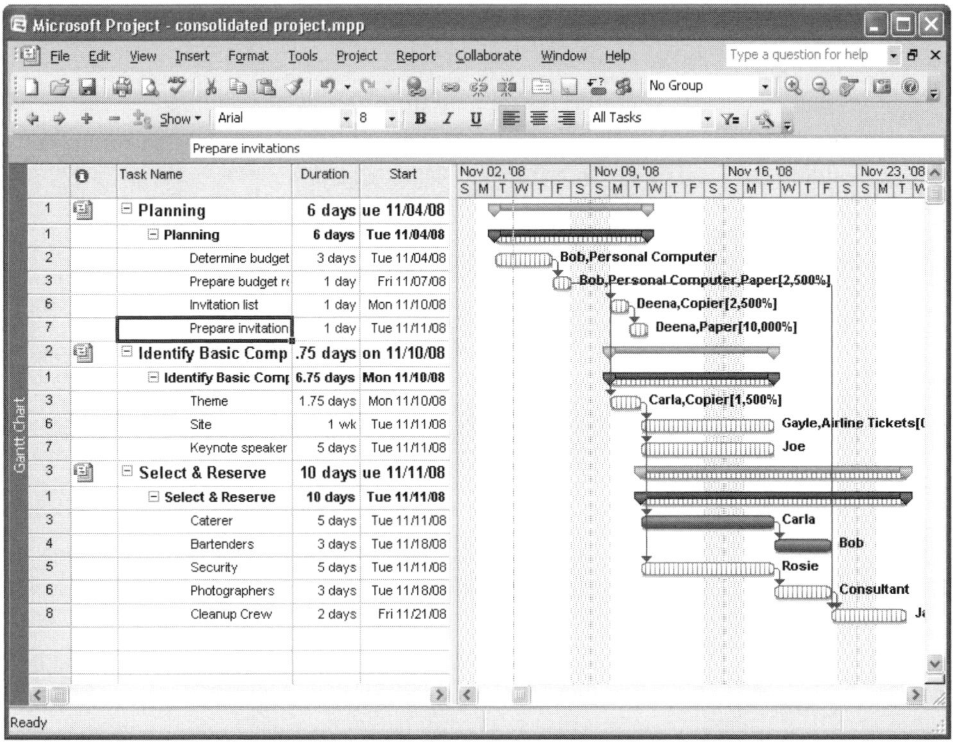

FIGURE 13-7 You can view critical paths for each subproject in a consolidated project.

To stop calculating inserted projects like summary tasks, follow these steps:

1. Display the consolidated project.

2. On the Tools menu, click Options to display the Options dialog box.

3. Click the Calculation tab.

4. Clear the Inserted Projects Are Calculated Like Summary Tasks check box.

5. Click OK.

Using Consolidation with Project Server 2007

If you use Project Server 2007, you'll need to use consolidation to view the critical path of several related projects. You create a consolidated project a little differently, but once you create it, you can create dependencies across subprojects the same way I described in the section "Linking Subprojects" earlier in this chapter. You can then view the critical path across the consolidated project, or you can view the critical path of each inserted project by using the steps in the preceding section, "Examining the Critical Path of a Consolidated Project."

To create cross-project dependencies in a consolidated project for projects residing in the Project Server database, follow these steps:

1. Log on to Microsoft Office Project Web Access.

2. Navigate to the Project Center page.

3. Press and hold the Ctrl key as you click the row for each project you want to insert into a consolidated project:

Click here to select
a project to insert.

4. Click the Edit button, which is indicated by the box in the graphic in the previous step. Project automatically creates a consolidated project like the one shown on the following page.

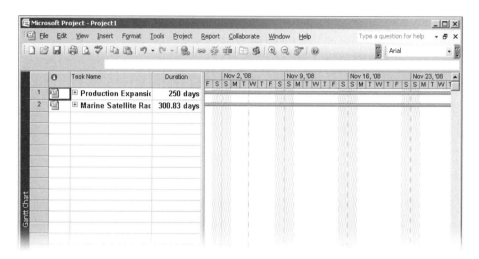

Use the techniques described in the section "Linking Subprojects" earlier in this chapter to set cross-project dependencies. You don't need to publish the consolidated project in the Project Server database, but if you save the inserted projects when prompted, Project saves your cross-project links in each subproject. The next time you open one of these subprojects, you will see the external tasks Project created.

Using a Resource Pool

Even if you don't use Project Server, working with a resource pool can be very helpful if your organization uses the same resources on multiple projects. A resource pool is nothing more than a set of resources that can be available to work on any project. Setting up a resource pool in Project can be particularly useful for project managers who need to share resources on different projects; a resource pool provides a good way to schedule shared resources and resolve resource conflicts. Even if you're the only manager and don't really share resources, setting up a resource pool can save you time when you create projects.

> **NOTE** One of the features of Project Server is the Enterprise Resource Pool, which is the server version of what I describe in this section. The method used to set up the Enterprise Resource Pool is actually similar to the method you use in Project to set up a resource pool.

When you connect a resource pool file to your projects, Project tracks the assignment of each resource across all projects that use the resource pool. So if a resource becomes overallocated, you see the same signals that you see if you simply overallocate a resource within your own project; overallocated resource names appear in bold red letters in various resource views in your project.

Setting Up a Resource Pool

Setting up a resource pool isn't difficult; you simply set up a Project file that contains only resource information. You can name it something clever like "Resource Pool." In Figure 13-8, you see the Resource Sheet of the Resource Pool project. This project contains no task information; it contains just resource information.

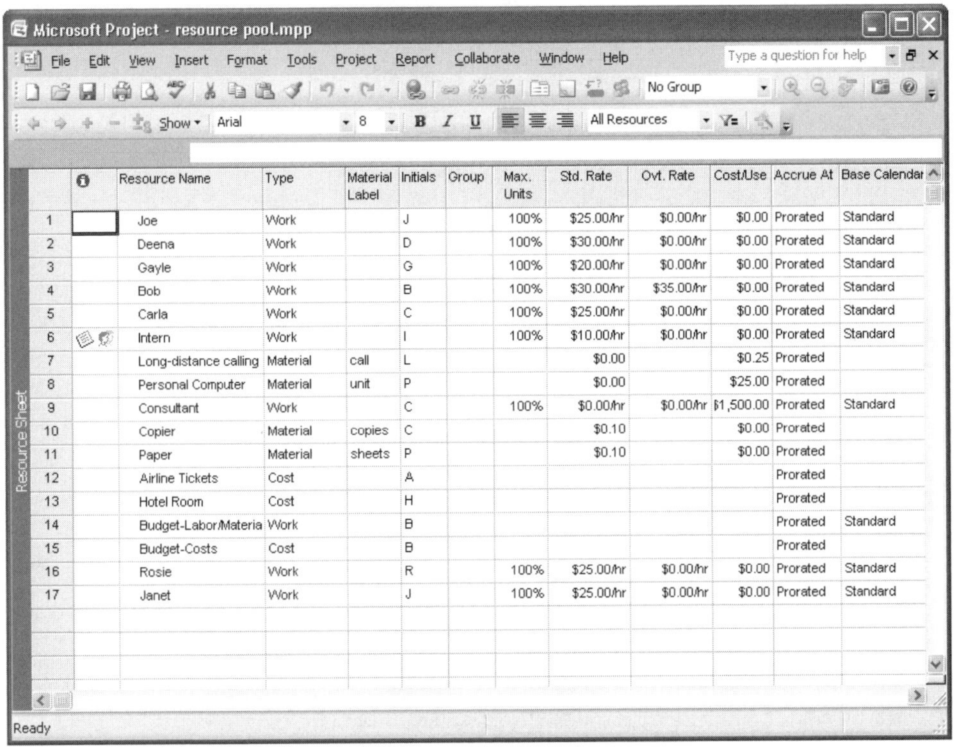

		Resource Name	Type	Material Label	Initials	Group	Max. Units	Std. Rate	Ovt. Rate	Cost/Use	Accrue At	Base Calendar
1		Joe	Work		J		100%	$25.00/hr	$0.00/hr	$0.00	Prorated	Standard
2		Deena	Work		D		100%	$30.00/hr	$0.00/hr	$0.00	Prorated	Standard
3		Gayle	Work		G		100%	$20.00/hr	$0.00/hr	$0.00	Prorated	Standard
4		Bob	Work		B		100%	$30.00/hr	$35.00/hr	$0.00	Prorated	Standard
5		Carla	Work		C		100%	$25.00/hr	$0.00/hr	$0.00	Prorated	Standard
6		Intern	Work		I		100%	$10.00/hr	$0.00/hr	$0.00	Prorated	Standard
7		Long-distance calling	Material	call	L			$0.00		$0.25	Prorated	
8		Personal Computer	Material	unit	P			$0.00		$25.00	Prorated	
9		Consultant	Work		C		100%	$0.00/hr	$0.00/hr	$1,500.00	Prorated	Standard
10		Copier	Material	copies	C			$0.10		$0.00	Prorated	
11		Paper	Material	sheets	P			$0.10		$0.00	Prorated	
12		Airline Tickets	Cost		A						Prorated	
13		Hotel Room	Cost		H						Prorated	
14		Budget-Labor/Materia	Work		B						Prorated	Standard
15		Budget-Costs	Cost		B						Prorated	
16		Rosie	Work		R		100%	$25.00/hr	$0.00/hr	$0.00	Prorated	Standard
17		Janet	Work		J		100%	$25.00/hr	$0.00/hr	$0.00	Prorated	Standard

FIGURE 13-8 A Project file containing only resource information.

> **NOTE** You can store task information in the file you intend to use as a resource pool, but that information would be available to anyone else who uses the resource pool. To keep things neat and easy to understand, I recommend that you store no tasks in the resource pool file.

In this "resource-only project," not only store resource names and costs, but also set up calendars to reflect available working time. Set up the working times your company uses by default on the Calendar tab of the Options dialog box. To set up your company's working times, on the Tools menu, click Options; then click the Calendar tab (see Figure 13-9).

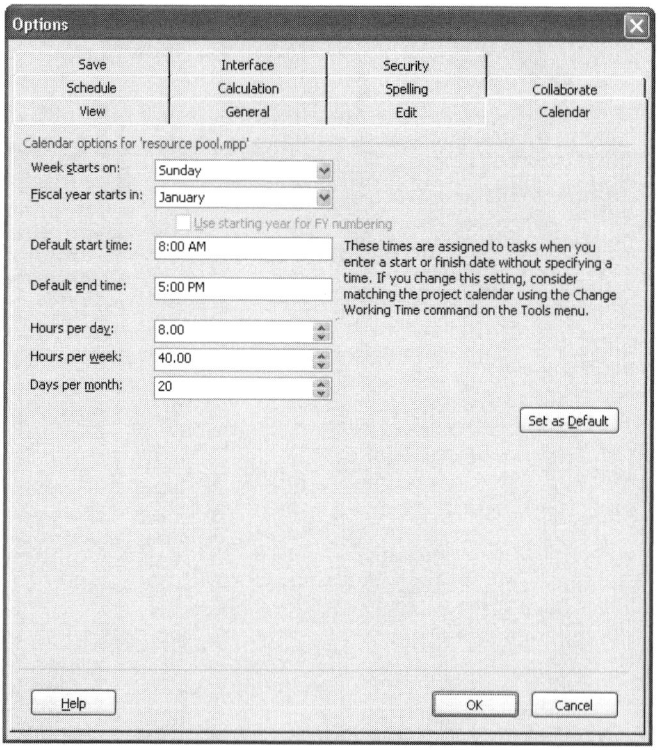

FIGURE 13-9 Establish your company's default working times using the Calendar tab of the Options dialog box.

Set up resource calendars by selecting a resource on the Resource Sheet (of any resource-oriented view) and clicking the Resource Information button. In the Resource Information dialog box that appears, click the Change Working Time button to display the Change

Working Time dialog box. Use this dialog box to establish any necessary calendar exceptions and specialized work weeks for the selected resource (see Figure 13-10).

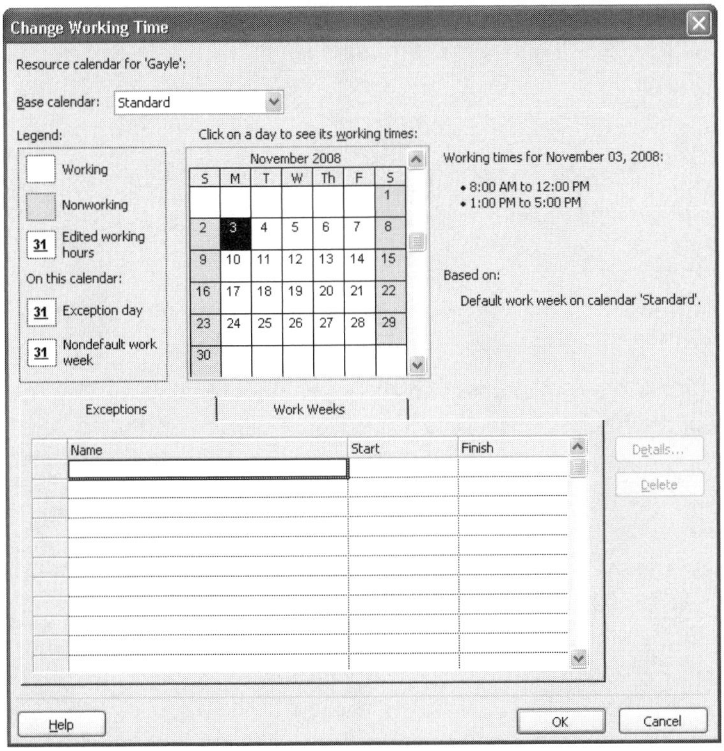

FIGURE 13-10 Establish working time exceptions and special work weeks in the Change Working Time dialog box.

SEE ALSO   For detailed information on setting up resources and resource calendars, see Chapter 3, "Pinning Down Your Budget."

After you create a Project file that contains resource information, use these steps to connect the resource pool project to a project in which you need to make resource assignments:

1. Open the project you set up containing resources—we'll call this project the "resource pool file" from this point forward.

2. Open a project containing tasks to which you want to assign resources—we'll call this project the "project schedule file" for purposes of this example.

3. While viewing the project schedule file, on the Tools menu, point to Resource Sharing, and click Share Resources. Project displays the Share Resources dialog box:

4. Select the Use Resources option and make sure that the resource pool project appears in the From list.

5. Select an option for handling calendar conflicts. If you select the Pool Takes Precedence option, the resource calendars in the resource pool file take precedence when conflicts arise.

> **NOTE** If you select the Sharer Takes Precedence option, the resource calendars in the file that contains your project schedule take precedence over the resource calendars in the resource pool file when conflicts arise. If you've followed my advice and not stored resources in your project schedule, your project schedule file contains no resource calendars. Once you connect your project to the resource pool, you can set up calendars in your project for resource pool resources, but nobody else using the resource pool would have access to the calendars you establish.

6. Click OK.

> **NOTE** You can store resources in a project that won't act as the resource pool, but you defeat the purpose of using a resource pool when you store resources in two places. So I recommend that you set up project schedules in Project files that don't contain any resources and then connect your files to the resource pool project when you want to assign resources.

If you switch to the Resource Sheet view of the project schedule file, Project displays all the resources that appear in the resource pool file. If you also stored resources in your project schedule file, those resources also appear, and you won't be able to distinguish between the resources in your project and the resources from the resource pool.

Save the project schedule file and the resource pool file.

Opening a Project Connected to a Resource Pool

When you come back at a later time to work on a project schedule file set up to share resources, you don't need to open the resource pool file; you can let Project open it for you. When you open the project schedule file, Project displays the Open Resource Pool Information dialog box (see Figure 13-11).

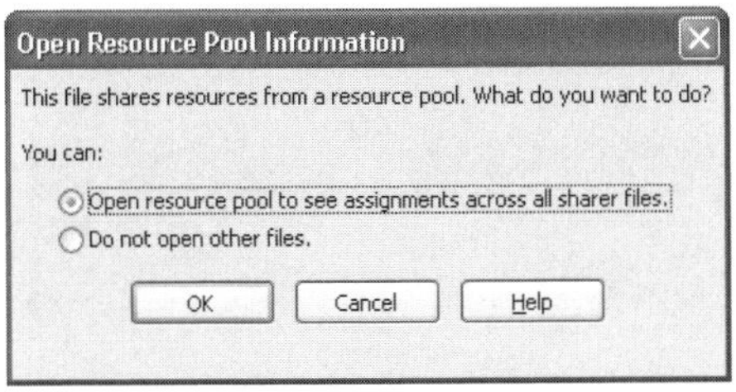

FIGURE 13-11 This dialog box appears when you open a project schedule file connected to a resource pool file.

> **NOTE**   You won't see this dialog box if someone else has already opened the resource pool file.

When you select the first option (Open Resource Pool To See Assignments Across All Sharer Files), Project opens the resource pool file for you. If you select the second option (Do Not Open Other Files), Project opens only your file. If you intend to make changes that will affect resources in your project schedule file, select the first option; otherwise, you won't see any resources in your project schedule file.

NOTE   For the technically inclined, when you opt to open the resource pool file along with your project schedule file, Project opens the resource pool file as a read-only file, which allows several people to use the resource pool file simultaneously.

How Project Handles Assignments from a Resource Pool

You'll find that working in a project schedule file that is connected to a resource pool file is no different from working in a project where you've stored resources in the project. You still assign resources to tasks using the Assign Resources window. In Figure 13-12, you can see three tasks in a project that starts on November 2; Bob is assigned to the first task for four days. In Figure 13-13, you can see four tasks in a project that starts on October 31; here Bob is assigned to the second task for three days.

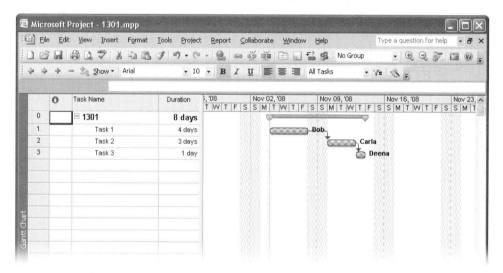

FIGURE 13-12 Bob is assigned to the first task for four days.

Both projects are connected to the resource pool file, and in this example, Bob is over-allocated. If you view the Resource Sheet in either project, you'll see that Bob's name appears in bold red letters (see Figure 13-14). You use the same techniques to resolve the overallocation that you'd use if the projects weren't connected to the resource pool project.

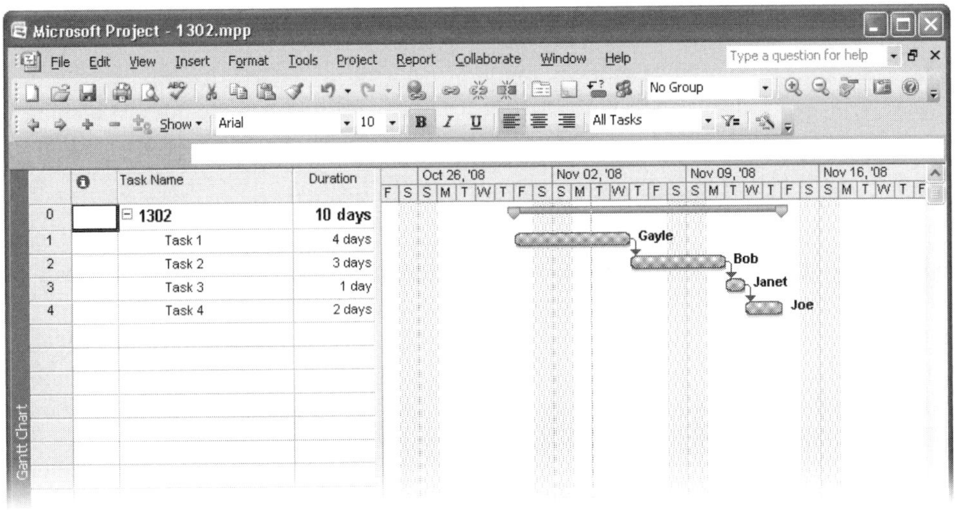

FIGURE 13-13 Bob is assigned to the second task for three days.

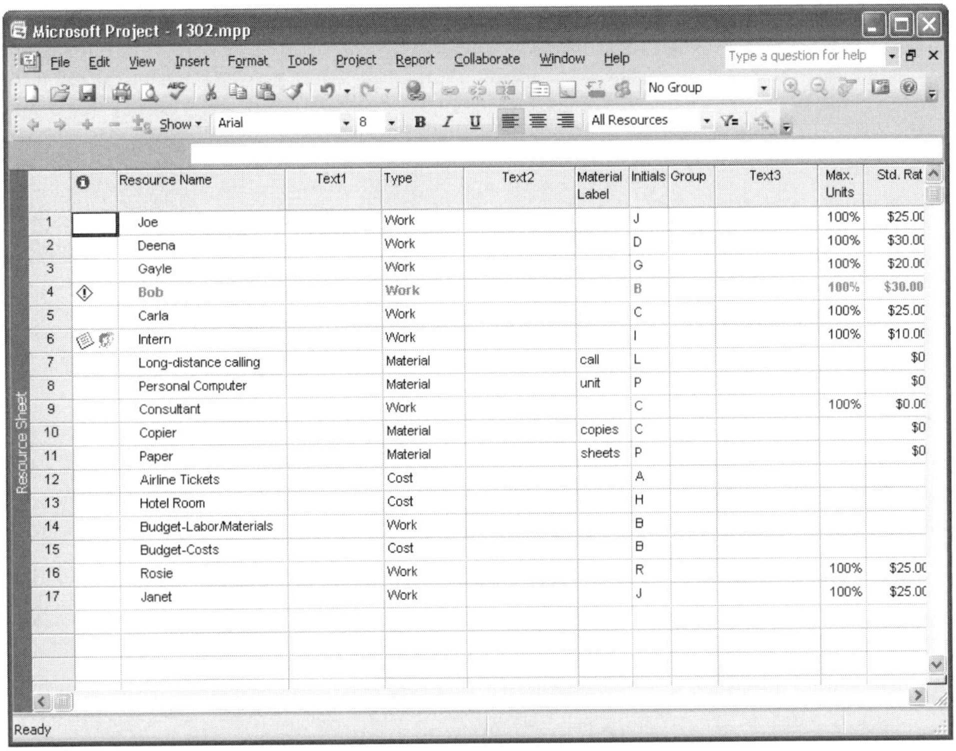

FIGURE 13-14 Bob's overallocated status is visible in any resource-oriented view in either project.

> **SEE ALSO** See Chapter 6, "Solving Resource Conflicts," for information on dealing with resource overallocations.

Updating the Resource Pool

If you make changes that affect resources to your project schedule file, you need to update the resource pool file so that others who are using the resource pool have the most up-to-date information. To update the resource pool, on the Tools menu, point to Resource Sharing, and click Update Resource Pool. This command is available only if you set up resource sharing and you make a change in your project while the resource pool file is open. You won't see any reaction from Project, but you'll have updated the resource pool file.

Suppose that you forget to update the resource pool and just click the Save button to save your project. In this case, Project displays a message, shown in Figure 13-15.

FIGURE 13-15 If you save your project without updating the resource pool, Project displays a dialog box offering to do it for you.

How to Quit Sharing Resources

You might decide that you no longer want to use the resource pool file. You can disconnect the resource pool for a specific project if you open that project, and then on the Tools menu, point to Resource Sharing, and click Share Resources. In the Share Resources dialog box that appears, select the Use Own Resources option.

You also can disable the resource pool for all files that are sharing the resources of one resource pool.

1. Click the Open button and navigate to and select the resource pool file. Project displays the Open Resource Pool dialog box.

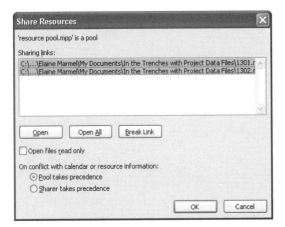

2. Select the middle option or the last option in this dialog box; either option lets you disable the pool.

3. Click the Open button and navigate to and select the Project schedule file that you want to disconnect from the resource pool. Repeat this step for each Project schedule file that you want to disconnect from the resource pool.

4. On the Window menu, click the resource pool file.

5. On the Tools menu, point to Resource Sharing, and click Share Resources. Project displays the Share Resources dialog box:

6. Select the project(s) that you want to disconnect from the resource pool.

> **TIP**
>
> You can select multiple noncontiguous projects by pressing and holding down Ctrl when you click the mouse, or you can select contiguous projects by pressing and holding down Shift when you click the mouse.

7. Click the Break Link button.

8. Click OK.

9. Save and close the resource pool file.

10. Save and close the project schedule file(s).

After you have disabled the resource pool, any assignments you made from the resource pool will remain in your project.

Index

A

accruing costs, 68–69
Actual Cost field, 274
actuals
    cost, calculating automatically, 250
    defined, 240
    recording, 240
    task duration, recording, 256–257
    work, recording, 257–258
additional software, 219, 220–221. *See also* Outlook
assigning resources, 55
    checking availability when, 75–78
    non-human, 56
    to tasks, 63–65
assignment data views, 104
assignment units, 15. *See also* tasks
assignments
    modifying, to save time, 292
    resource pools and, 300
    slipping, viewing, 291
audience, gauging, 215
AutoFilters, 99
availability, resource. *See* resource availability

B

Back Loaded contour, 163, 164–166
backwards scheduling, 130
base calendars, 124, 131
baselines, 206–207
    comparing to actual information, 209–210
    limiting, 207
    resetting, when rescheduling project, 300
    setting, 207–208
    viewing, 210, 286
beginning date. *See* start date
Bell contour, 163

blue highlighting. *See* change highlighting
booking type, setting for resources, 62
Budget report, 79–80
budget resources, 184
    assigning to categories, 186–189
    assigning to project summary task, 185
    creating, 185–186
    values, assigning, 189–192
budgeting. *See* costs
built-in filters, 99, 291–292

C

calculation options, 248–251
Calendar view, 85, 112
Calendar Wizard, 11
calendars, 9, 131–133. *See also* resource calendars;
        task calendars
    24 Hour, 9
    assigning to tasks, 125
    base, 124, 131
    copying, 12
    creating, 124
    exceptions, setting, 10–12, 73–75
    holidays, designating, 10–12
    Night Shift, 9
    scheduling projects and, 13
    Standard, 9
    work week, changing default, 10, 12
Cash Flow report, 79–80
categories, 186–189. *See also* grouping
central office organizational structure, 70
change management, 17, 281–282
charters, 4–5
circular reference errors, 18
clearing resource leveling, 173
codes, outline. *See* outline codes

codes, WBS. *See* WBS codes
collecting timesheets, 246
columns, table. *See* fields
combination views, 88–90
comments. *See* notes
communication, 213–214
conditional formatting of custom fields, 108–109
conflicts, resource. *See* resolving resource conflicts;
    resource conflicts
consolidation, 27, 285
    critical path for, 292
    linking projects, 246
    and Project Server, 286, 292–293
    and resource leveling, 286
    saving projects, 291
    setting up, 286–288
    of subprojects, 288–290
constraints, 45
    avoiding, 30, 47
    default, 45
    vs. dependencies, 47–48
    dependency conflicts, 47
    flexible vs. inflexible, 45
    inflexible, 126
    minimizing use of, 126–128
    modifying, 130
    precedence over dependencies, 47
    priority over dependencies, 126
    resource leveling and, 167
    reviewing, 293
    setting, 50
    on summary tasks, avoiding, 126
    task timing and, 126–128
    types of, 45–46
contours, 162–166
cost accrual methods, 68–69
Cost Overbudget filter, 291
cost rate tables, 180, 182–184
cost reports, printing, 79–80
Cost resources, 58
    assigning costs to, 178–180
    examples of, 177–178
    replacing expensive, 297
    when to use, 177
Cost table, reviewing project plan with, 198

cost variances, evaluating, 275–278
costs. *See also* budget resources
    actual, calculating automatically, 250
    assigning to cost resources, 178–180
    budgeted vs. planned, viewing, 192–194
    changes in over course of project, 180–184
    direct vs. indirect, 58
    distributing changes evenly, 250–251
    fixed, 66–67, 251
    over budget, troubleshooting, 200–201, 291–292.
        See also budget tasks
    per use, 66
    prorating, 68
    reducing, 194
    for resources, assigning, 65
    resources and, 292
    reviewing, 198, 273
    variances, 275–278
Critical filter, 291
critical path, 202–203, 292. *See also* critical tasks
critical tasks, 114, 133
    changing definition of, 138
    criteria for, 202
    in Detail Gantt view, 134
    displaying only, 204, 291
    grouping by, 204
    multiple, 205–206
Critical Tasks report, 233
cross-project dependencies, 290–291
current date, setting, 8
custom fields, 102–103. *See also* fields
    for budget categories, 186–189
    conditional formatting, 108–109
    creating, 104–106
    defining, 104
    displaying, 107
    vs. fields, 103
    formulas in, 108–109
    graphical indicators for, 108–109
    renaming, 105
    rules for, 104
    storing information in, 107–108
    types of, 104
cutting costs, 194, 291, 297–98

D

deadline dates, 48–50
Define Group Internals button, 102
delaying tasks, 168. *See also* resource leveling
dependencies, 29–30
    avoiding too many, 38–39
    changing type of, 35
    constraint priority over, 126
    vs. constraints, 47–48
    cross-project, 290–291
    deleting, 43
    to external projects, 44
    finish-to-finish, 32
    finish-to-start, 31
    lag/lead time, 36–38
    link labels, adding, 293
    predecessor/successor, 30, 115
    reviewing, 293–295
    setting, 34–35
    between subprojects, creating, 290–291
    types of, 30–33
    viewing, 40–42
Detail Gantt view, 134
    critical tasks in, 203
    progress lines, adding, 288
Detail Styles dialog box, 95
Details portion in views, 94–96
direct costs, 58
drop-down selection lists. *See* lookup tables

E

early finish and start dates, 136
earned value fields. 273–280
earned value management, 273
Earned Value table, 278
effort, assigning to resources, 119
effort-driven tasks, 15, 120
    calculations for, 120, 292
    fixed duration, creating, 122
employees. *See* resources
end date. *See* finish date
Enterprise Resource Pool, 61–63
equipment costs, lowering, 194
Excel reports, 221
exchanging overallocated resources, 150–153

F

fields, 93, 103. *See also* custom fields
    adding, 94–95
    hiding, 93, 96, 103
    types of, 104
    Text, 104, 187
    width, changing, 94
File Transfer Protocol (FTP) sites, 220
filtering, 98
    Apply vs. Highlight, 99
    with AutoFilters, 99
    with built-in filters, 99, 291–292
    by critical tasks, 204
    Enterprise Resource Pool, 63
    by resource availability, 76–77
    by resource overallocation, 148
finish date. *See also* constraints
    changing, to resolve resource overallocation, 159
    earliest possible, identifying, 136
    latest possible, identifying, 136
    recording, 256
    for resource availability, 72
    scheduling projects from, 129–130
    setting, 8
finish-to-finish dependencies, 32
finish-to-start dependencies, 31
fixed costs
    accrual method, setting, 251
    assigning to tasks, 66–67
fixed duration tasks, 15, 117
    duration adjustment when resources added, 144
    effort-driven, creating, 122
fixed units tasks, 15
    assigning resources to, 116
    duration adjustment when resources added, 144
fixed work tasks, 15, 118, 144
Flat contour, 162
float. *See* slack
form views, 86
forms for tracking reports, 243
formulas, creating, 108–109
free slack, 133
free time. *See* slack
Front Loaded contour, 163
FTP sites, 220

G

Gantt Chart view, 88–90, 111
    printing, 232
    for resource assignment, 64
    reviewing project plan with, 196
    timescale, changing, 89
generic resources, 25, 61
getting back on schedule, 290
    by adding resources, 292
    by adding time to schedule, 297
    by deleting tasks, 297
    by fixing slippage, 290
    by modifying task scope, 296–297
    problem identification, 290
    by redefining goal, 298
    by rescheduling tasks, 298–299
    reviewing dependencies and constraints, 293
goals, 4, 298
Graphical Indicators button, 109
graphical indicators in custom fields, 108–109
graphing resources, 77–78
grouping, 100
    by critical tasks, 204
    defining internals of, 102
    setting up, 101
    sorting in, 102

H

half-time, assigning resources to. *See* effort-driven
    tasks
hard constraints, 45, 126. *See also* constraints
highlighting changes. *See* change highlighting
holidays, designating on calendar, 10–12

I

incomplete tasks
    displaying, 291
    rescheduling, 299–300
Incomplete Tasks filter, 291
indirect costs, 58
inflexible constraints, 126
information flow, 215. *See also* actuals
interim plans, 206–208

L

lag time in task dependencies, 36–38
Late/Overbudget Tasks Assigned To filter, 291
lead time in task dependencies, 36–38
leveling resources. *See* resource leveling
lines of communication, 213–214.
    See also communication
link labels, adding to dependencies, 293
link style, changing, 267
Link Tasks button, 34
linking
    consolidated projects, 246
    subprojects, to source files, 290
    summary tasks, avoiding, 18, 39
lookup tables
    creating, 106
    default value, setting, 106
    editing, 187

M

manual start date calculation, switching from, 51
material resources, 58–61, 261
Microsoft Office Excel reports, 221
Microsoft Office Outlook. *See* Outlook
Microsoft Office Project 2007. *See* Project 2007
Microsoft Office Project Web Access. *See* Project
    Web Access
Microsoft Office Visio reports, 221
Microsoft Windows SharePoint Services.
    See SharePoint Services
Milestones Project Companion, 221
milestones, creating, 23
monitoring, 241–242. *See also* tracking
Multiple Baselines Gantt view, 210
Must Finish On constraint, 126
Must Start On constraint, 126

N

negative slack, 133
Network Diagram toolbar, 266
Network Diagram view, 41–42, 85, 114, 265
    box style, changing, 268–269
    boxes, modifying information in, 269–272

critical tasks in, 204
displaying changes, 272
layout, changing, 266–267
layout of, 266
link labels, adding, 293
link style, changing, 267
navigating in, 266
work flow organization in, 264–265
Night Shift calendar, 9
non-human resources, 56–58
nonworking time, setting, 12, 75
notes, printing/recording, 251–252
numbering schemes, 221. *See also* outline
numbering; WBS codes

O

organizational structure, 70–71
outline codes, 223–227
outline numbering, 222–224
Outlook, 219–220
overallocated resources. *See* resource conflicts
overtime, 153
avoiding, 78–79
resolving resource conflicts with, 153–154
shortening schedule time with, 292

P

part-time assignments, 156–158
part-time resources, 72
Peak column, 164
Percent Complete field, vs. Physical Percent
Complete field, 279–280
percentage complete
distributing evenly, 250
estimating, 252–254
updating quickly, 255
PERT Chart EXPERT, 220
phases, project. *See* project phases
picture views, 85
PivotTables, 235
placeholder resources, 25
Planned Value field, 273

planning projects, 4–5. *See also* monitoring; project
plan; tracking
finalizing, 195
reports, 221
task granularity, 14
tracking, 240–241. *See also* tracking
Planning Wizard, 298
pooled resources. *See* resource pools; sharing
resources
predecessor tasks, 294–295
presentations, tailoring to audience, 215
printing
cost reports, 79–80
Gantt Chart view, 232
notes, 252
reports, 232
priority
resource leveling and, 168–170
setting, 9, 170
sorting tasks by, 96–98, 170, 291
Priority field, adding, 169
problem solving, 214, 215
progress, viewing, 288. *See also* monitoring; tracking
progress lines, 288–290
Project 2007
cost calculation done by, 53
interoperability with Excel 2007 and Visio 2007, 221
resource allocation calculations, 144–145
Project Information dialog box, 7–8, 287–288
project management, 213
change management, 281–282
changing project plan, 263–264
communication and. *See* communication
distilling information, 215
organizational structure and, 71
time vs. money calculation, 264
project phases, 17. *See also* consolidation
project plan
change management, 281–282
changes to, discussing with management, 263–264
interim. *See* interim plans
Network Diagram view for, 264–265
reviewing, 196–199, 245

Project Server, 216
   consolidation and, 286, 292–293
   security considerations, 219
   status reports, 245
   Web access to. *See* Project Web Access
   when to use, 218
project statistics, 209–210
project summary task
   budget resources, assigning to, 186
   displaying, 186, 19–21
project templates. *See* templates
Project Web Access, 216
   reporting methods, 244
   reporting tracking information with, 244–245
project workspaces, 217. *See also* SharePoint Services
projects
   adding time to, 176
   baselines. *See* baselines
   calculation options, 248–251
   charters for, 4–5
   connecting with other projects, 26–27
   consolidated, saving, 291
   consolidation, 27. *See also* consolidation
   cost accrual methods, 68–69
   costs. *See* costs
   creating, 5–7
   critical path. *See* critical path
   deadline dates. *See* deadline dates
   finish date, setting, 8
   fixed costs, 67
   getting back on schedule, 290
   goals, redefining, 298
   goals, setting, 4
   inserting into other projects, 289. *See also* consolidation; subprojects
   managing simultaneously, 26–27
   numbering schemes, 221
   phases of. *See* project phases
   planning, 4–5
   priority, setting, 9
   reorganizing, 21
   reporting. *See* reports
   reusing information. *See* templates
   scaling down, 200–201
   scheduling, 8, 13
   scope, defining, 4
   scope, redefining, 200–201
   scope creep, 282
   start date, setting, 8
   starting from templates, 6
   status date, setting, 8
   summary task for. *See* project summary task
   tasks. *See* tasks
   as templates. *See* templates
   Web access to. *See* Project Web Access
prorating costs, 68

R

raises in pay, anticipating, 180–184
recording
   actual work, 257–258
   actuals, 240
   material resource progress, 261
   start dates, 256
   task durations, 256–257
   task notes, 251–252
recurring tasks, 24
redefining project scope, 200–201
reducing costs, 194
Relationship Diagram view, 114
   reviewing predecessor and successor tasks with, 294
   reviewing project plan with, 197
removing resources, 153
renaming
   custom fields, 105
   text fields, 187
renumbering
   outline codes, 224
   renumbering tasks, 98
   WBS codes, 232
replacing overallocated resources, 150–153
reporting problems, 290
reports, 220–221
   additional software for, 220–221
   Budget, 79–80
   Cash Flow, 79–80
   cost, printing, 79–80
   forms for, 243
   planning, 221
   printing, 232

Resource Usage, 56
   from resources, encouraging, 246
   from resources, on tracking information, 242
   reviewing, 232
   status, 245
   viewing by category, 233
   visual, 233–238
requesting additional time, 297
rescheduling. *See* getting back on schedule
resolving resource conflicts, 149–150
   by adding resources, 155
   with contours, 162–163
   with overtime, 153–154
   with part-time assignments, 156–158
   with shared resources, 155–156
   by staggering work time, 159–166
   by swapping out resources, 150–153
Resource Allocation view, 146–147
resource availability
   checking, when assigning resources, 75–78
   exceptions, setting, 73–75
   filtering by, 76–77
   managing, 72
   tracking, 72
resource calendars, 123, 132
   precedence, setting, 132–133
   setting up in resource pools, 297
   and task calendars, using together, 132–133
resource conflicts, 143
   avoiding, 78
   example of, 143
   filtering by, 148
   identifying, 145–148
   resolving. *See* resolving resource conflicts
Resource Form view, 86, 89, 198
Resource Graph view, 85
   identifying resource conflicts with, 145
   reviewing project plan with, 198
resource leveling, 167
   automatic, setting, 170
   clearing leveling values before, 171
   consolidation and, 286
   constraints and, 167
   criteria for, 167–168
   manually, 173–175
   order of, 167–172

priority and, 168–170
   range, setting, 171
   removing effects of, 173
   sensitivity of, setting, 171
   slack and, 167
   timeframe, setting, 171
resource pools, 27, 293–295. *See also* sharing resources
   assignments and, 300
   calendar conflicts, 297
   connecting with other projects, 297–298
   Enterprise Resource Pool. *See* Enterprise
      Resource Pool
   global, 54
   opening projects connected to, 299–300
   overallocated, 295
   setting up, 296–299
   tasks in, 296
Resource Sheet view, 59, 69, 87
Resource Substitution wizard, 65, 155–156
Resource Usage report, 56
Resource Usage view, 147–148
resources. *See also* cost resources; material
      resources; work resources
   actual work, recording, 257–258
   adding, to resolve overallocation, 155
   adding to effort-driven tasks, 292
   assigning, 55, 63–65, 75–78
   assigning to fixed units tasks, 116
   availability, 63. *See also* resource availability
   booking type, setting, 62
   budget. *See* budget resources
   calendars, setting exceptions in, 73–75
   categorizing, 58–59
   charts for, 56
   confirming expectations with, 245
   conflicts with. *See* resource conflicts
   contours for allocation of, 162–163
   cost accrual methods, 68–69
   cost analysis of, 292
   cost calculation for, 53
   cost per use, 66
   cost rate tables for, 180–184
   costs, assigning, 65
   costs, lowering, 194
   costs, viewing, 192
   creating, 60–61

resources *(continued)*
    editing, 61
    effect on tasks. *See* effort-driven tasks
    effort, assigning, 119
    from Enterprise Resource Pool, 61–63
    expensive, replacing, 297
    generic, as placeholders, 25, 61
    global resource pool, 54
    graphing, 77–78
    grouping. *See* grouping
    identifying necessary, 54
    leveling. *See* resource leveling
    non-human, 56–58
    overallocation, , 78. *See* resource conflicts
    overtime, avoiding, 78–79
    part-time assignments, 156–158
    removing, 153
    reporting, encouraging, 246
    reporting forms for, 243
    reporting tracking information from, 242, 244–245
    shared. *See* resource pools; sharing resources
    skills inventory, creating, 54
    spreading out workload. *See* contours; resource
        leveling
    staggering work time, 159–166
    summary tasks and, 18
    swapping out, 150–153
    timesheets, tracking progress with, 243–244
    types of, 58–59
    updating status when corresponding tasks
        update, 248
    work, vs. task duration, 287–288
    work calculation for, 118
reusing project information. *See* templates
reviewing
    budget, 273
    calculation options, 248–251
    constraints, 293
    dependencies, 293–295
    earned value fields, 275–278
    project plan, 196–199
    reports, 232
    task drivers, 293
    tasks, with resources, 245
    variance, 275–278
rows, table, 94

S

saving time. *See* getting back on schedule
scheduling overtime. *See* overtime
scheduling projects
    adding time to, 176
    backwards, 130
    calculation options for, 248–251
    calendar and, 13
    filtering and, 291–292
    getting back on track, 290
    from start, vs. from end, 8, 129–130
scope, 4, 297
scope creep, 282, 290, 296–297
security, 219
selection lists. *See* lookup tables
SharePoint Services, 217, 220. *See also* project
        workspaces
sharing files via FTP, 220
sharing resources, 155–156. *See also* resource pools
sheet views, 87. *See also* tables
shortcut menu, adding fields to, 95
Should Start By filter, 291
single costs. *See* fixed costs
skills inventory, 54–55
slack, 133
    building in, 137–141
    calculation of, 133, 202
    delaying tasks with, 133
    fields, adding to view, 134
    free, 133
    identifying, 134–136
    negative, 133
    resource leveling and, 167
    total, 133
slippage, fixing. *See* getting back on schedule
Slipped/Late Progress filter, 291
Slipping Assignments filter, 291
soft constraints, 45, 126. *See also* constraints
sorting tasks, 96–98
    cutting costs by, 291
    by duration, to fix scheduling problems, 291
    by priority, 170
Split command, 89
splitting tasks. *See also* resource leveling
splitting views, 89–90, 150–151

spreading out resource workload. *See* resource leveling

staggering work time, 159–166

Standard calendar, 9

Standard leveling order, 168

start date. *See also* constraints
- automatic calculation, switching to, 51
- changing, effect on tasks, 128
- changing, to resolve resource overallocation, 160–161
- earliest/latest possible, identifying, 136
- recording, 256
- for resource availability, 72
- setting, 8, 128
- for tasks, avoiding, 22, 30
- unexpected/incorrect, 50–52
- viewing tasks by, 291

start-to-finish dependencies, 33

start-to-start dependencies, 32

status date
- changes, updating tasks based on, 249–250
- default, 247
- setting, 8, 246–247

status reports in Project Server, 245

status updates, correlating for tasks and resources, 248

subprojects, 285. *See also* consolidation
- consolidating, 288–290
- critical path, 292
- dependencies, creating, 290–291
- linking to source files, 290
- location of, viewing, 290
- saving, 291
- setting up, 286–288
- as summary tasks, stopping, 292
- viewing tasks of, 290

substituting resources, 150–153. *See also* Resource Substitution wizard

subtasks. *See* tasks

successor tasks, 294–295

summary tasks
- constraints, avoiding, 126
- creating, 18
- deleting, 17
- for entire project. *See* project summary task

linking, avoiding, 18, 39

moving, 21

resources and, 18

subprojects as, stopping, 292

T

tables. *See also* sheet views
- column headings. *See* fields
- Cost, 198
- cost rate. *See* cost rate tables
- hiding columns, 93
- overview of, 91
- row height, changing, 94
- selecting, 92
- switching, 92

task calendars, 123, 132
- creating, 125
- precedence, setting, 132–133
- and resource calendars, using together, 132–133

Task Drivers pane, 115

task drivers, 40, 115, 293

task duration, 17
- assigning, 22–23
- effort-driven tasks and, 120
- part-time assignment effect on, 156–158
- recording, 256–257
- remaining, viewing, 257
- resource effort effect on, 119
- rule of thumb for, 23
- shortening, by adding resources, 292
- sorting by, to fix scheduling problems, 291
- vs. work, 287–288
- zero, 23

Task Form view, 86, 89

Task Information dialog box, 34–35

Task Sheet view, 87, 295

tasks
- actual information for. *See* actuals
- actual work, recording, 257–258
- adding to project phases, 17
- appearance of, in Tracking Gantt view, 286–287
- arrows between, 31
- assigning calendars to, 125
- assigning resources to, 63–65

tasks *(continued)*
automatic renumbering of, 223
automatic updating of, 246
boldface. *See* summary tasks
building in slack, 137–141
calendars for. *See* task calendars
changing type of, 16
confirming plan for, 245
constraints, 126–128. *See also* constraints
costs, displaying, 198
creating, 14
on critical path. *See* critical path; critical tasks
deleting, 17, 297
dependencies. *See* dependencies
duration. *See* task duration
Earned Value table, 278
effort-driven. *See* effort-driven tasks
finish date, recording, 256
fixed costs, 66–67
fixed duration, 117
fixed units, 15, 116, 118
fixed work, 15
granularity of, 14
incomplete, displaying, 291
indenting, 18
lag/lead time, 36–38
length of, and tracking frequency, 242
leveling, preventing, 168
link lines, 31
linking. *See* dependencies
milestones, 23
monitoring. *See* monitoring
moving, 21
notes, recording, 251–252
order of, setting. *See* dependencies
outline numbering, 221–227
over budget, displaying, 291–292
percent completion changes, distributing evenly, 250, 252–254
predecessor/successor, 115, 294
priority, sorting by, 291
recurring, 24
red. *See* critical tasks
removing resources from, 153
renumbering permanently, 98
rescheduling, 298–299

resource effort, effect on duration, 119
resource overallocation to. *See* resource conflicts
in resource pools, 296
resources, adding, 144
resources assigned to, displaying, 86
scrolling to, 260
slack, calculation of, 133
sorting, 96–98, 170
start date, avoiding, 22, 30
start date, changing to avoid resource overallocation, 159
start date, filtering by, 291
start date, recording, 256
start date, unexpected/incorrect, 50–52
start date calculation, manual vs. automatic, 51
status, viewing, 286–287
status bars, 286–287
summary. *See* summary tasks
timing of, 113
tracking. *See* tracking
types, and project schedule, 116–117
updating, based on status date change, 249
updating corresponding resource status, 248
updating quickly, 255
WBS codes for. *See* WBS codes
without slack. *See* critical tasks
team communication. *See* communication
team members. *See* resources
templates
creating, 5–7
for Network Diagram boxes, changing, 269–272
starting projects from, 6
storing resources in, 5
Text fields, 104, 187
tightening schedule. *See* getting back on schedule
timescales, changing, 89, 261
timesheets
actual hours, recording, 244
collecting, 246
effort deflation/inflation caused by, 290
tracking progress with, 243–244
timing
constraints and, 126–128
task type and, 116–117
of tasks, 113
views for, 111

to-do list. *See* tasks
Top Level Tasks report, 233
total slack, 133
tracking. *See also* monitoring; tracking
    frequency of, determining, 241–242
    material resources, 261
    planning, 240–241
    with Project Web Access, 244–245
    resource reporting, managing, 242
    tasks, automatic updating based on, 246
    with timesheets, 243–244
tracking changes. *See* change highlighting
Tracking Gantt Chart view, 288
Tracking Gantt view, 199
    baselines in, 286
    critical tasks in, 204
    task status in, 286–287
Tracking toolbar, 252–254
travel costs, lowering, 194
troubleshooting schedule problems, 290
24 Hour calendar, 9

U

uncompleted tasks. *See* incomplete tasks
Unlink Tasks button, 43
Update Needed filter, 291
updating projects, 298–299
usage views, changing timescale of, 89

V

vacations. *See* resource availability
variance, evaluating, 275–278
Variance table, 210
views, 83
    for assignment data, 104
    Calendar, 85, 112
    combination, 88–90
    creating custom, 84
    Detail Gantt, 134, 203
    Details portion, 94–96
    displaying, 84
    filters in. *See* filtering
    form, 86

    Gantt Chart, 64, 88–90, 111, 196
    groups and, 101
    Network Diagram, 41–42, 85, 114, 204
    Peak column, 164
    picture, 85
    primary focus of, 84
    Priority field, adding, 169
    Relationship Diagram, 114, 197
    removing split from, 90
    Resource Allocation, 146–147
    Resource Form, 86, 89, 198
    Resource Graph, 85, 145, 198
    Resource Sheet, 59, 69, 87
    Resource Usage, 147–148
    sheet, 87
    splitting, 89–90, 150–151
    Task Form, 86, 89
    Task Sheet, 87
    timing and, 111
    Tracking Gantt, 199, 204
Visio reports, 221
visual reports, 233–238

W

WBS Chart Pro, 220
WBS charts, 237
WBS codes, 228
    customizing, 230–231
    displaying, 229
    renumbering of, 232
Web Access. *See* Project Web Access
work
    over budget, viewing, 292
    vs. task duration, 287–288
work breakdown structure codes. *See* WBS codes
work flow, viewing in Network Diagram, 264–265
Work Incomplete filter, 292
Work Overbudget filter, 292
Work resources, 58–59, 61
Work table, 252–254
work week, changing default, 10, 12
workers. *See* resources
working days, setting, 73–75, 296

What do you think of this book?

We want to hear from you!

Your feedback will help us continually improve our books and learning resources for you. To participate in a brief online survey, please visit:

microsoft.com/learning/booksurvey

...and enter this book's ISBN-10 or ISBN-13 number (appears above barcode on back cover). As a thank-you to survey participants in the U.S. and Canada, each month we'll randomly select five respondents to win one of five $100 gift certificates from a leading online merchant. At the conclusion of the survey, you can enter the drawing by providing your e-mail address, which will be used for prize notification only.*

Thank you in advance for your input!

Where to find the ISBN on back cover

ISBN-13: 000-0-0000-0000-0
ISBN-10: 0-0000-0000-0

9 0 0 0 0

0 000000 000000

Example only. Each book has unique ISBN.

* No purchase necessary. Void where prohibited. Open only to residents of the 50 United States (includes District of Columbia) and Canada (void in Quebec). For official rules and entry dates see: **microsoft.com/learning/booksurvey**

Stay in touch!

To subscribe to the *Microsoft Press* *Book Connection Newsletter*—for news on upcoming books, events, and special offers—please visit:

microsoft.com/learning/books/newsletter